GENDERED COMMODITY CHAINS

GENDERED COMMODITY CHAINS

Seeing Women's Work and Households
in Global Production

Edited by Wilma A. Dunaway

STANFORD UNIVERSITY PRESS

STANFORD, CALIFORNIA

Stanford University Press
Stanford, California

Printed in the United States of America

Library of Congress Cataloging-in-Publication Data

Gendered commodity chains : seeing women's work and
households in global production / edited by Wilma
A. Dunaway.
     pages cm
  Includes bibliographical references and index.
  ISBN 978-0-8047-8794-9 (cloth : alk. paper)—ISBN
978-0-8047-8908-0 (pbk.   )
  1. Women—Employment. 2. Women—Economic
conditions. 3. Households—Economic aspects. 4. Sex
role—Economic aspects. 5. Globalization—Economic
aspects. I. Dunaway, Wilma A., editor of compilation.
  HD6053.G4633 2013
   331.4—dc23   2013026234

Typeset by Westchester Book Services in Sabon

CONTENTS

Immanuel Wallerstein

A mere fifty years ago, women were a marginalized and largely unobserved social group, both in social life and in the writings of social scientists. They were one of the principal forgotten peoples along with socially defined "minorities" and persons practicing socially repudiated sexualities. The subordination of women to men goes back a very long way, possibly to the inception of human collective life. It has no doubt taken different forms in different kinds of historical social systems. The advent of the modern world-system built around a capitalist world-economy continued this subordination in new ways. There was one important change. One of the major legacies of the French Revolution was to define the "people" as the locus of sovereignty and, therefore, of the formal equality of all "citizens" who constituted this "people."

Were not women people? The story ever since then has been to develop all kinds of rationales to deny women their status as part of the sovereign "people" and, therefore, to negate their claims to equal rights with men. A struggle over legitimacy ensued, and that struggle was grounded in conflict between theoretical equality and practical inequality.

The world-revolution of 1968 had as one of its major features the revolt of the forgotten peoples, both in social life and in the structures of knowledge. Feminist movements arose to pursue these demands in every sphere of life. Slowly, women were able to obtain rights to suffrage, which changed something but, as it turned out, not all that much. In the history of feminist movements, the world-revolution of 1968 gave a new and important impetus to their organizations. Most particularly, feminist movements raised the issue, previously not in the forefront of their consciousness, of women in the structures of knowledge.

A major part of this effort was to make the distinction between sex (an old category) and gender (a new one). Sex refers to a biological construct. Therefore, it had been considered a given in social contexts. One could not change one's sex, or so it was believed (at least before the advent of the technological advances of more recent years). Gender as a concept refers not to biology but to the social definition of social roles. And social definitions are clearly open to manipulation and transformation.

The concept of gender made possible a considerable advance in the social sciences. It permitted analysis of the ways in which the world-system has institutionalized sexism, legitimating thereby the practical subordination of women to men. It helped uncover the multiple ways in which children (starting from their earliest life) were socialized into expectations and practices that continued the unequal treatment. And, of course, it led to the creation of research and teaching structures that would continue such analyses within universities, in specialized literature, in national and international organizations, and even in governmental bureaucracies.

Slowly, the concept of gender opened up new arenas of social science work beyond the old ghetto of studies of family life. Yet, half a century later, it is astonishing how many arenas remain sheltered from these concerns. There is an incredible amount of foot-dragging and resistance to introducing gender in very many subject areas. One of these areas has been the now-blossoming arena of studies of commodity chains.

The realm of commodity chains is relatively new. It was created out of the concern of those involved in world-systems analysis to demonstrate that "transnational" economic transactions are not a recent phenomenon, a form of "globalization" of what had previously been intrastate economic behavior. Instead, it was argued that "commodity chains" crossing multiple state borders had been the basic and continuing reality of economic life in the modern world-system from its outset in the long sixteenth century.

Once this area of study was launched, more and more scholars realized how much could be learned about the ways in which the axial division of labor functioned and made possible the enormous transfer of surplus value from producers throughout the modern world-system to a small group that accumulated ever-expanding capital, the basic objective and normative pressure of capitalism as a historical system.

How was it possible not to notice that these commodity chains were gendered? Indeed, not only were they gendered, but gender was itself a principal constitutive feature of the commodity chains. Obviously, there has been political, economic, and scholarly resistance to incorporating gender into the structures of knowledge. That it was possible for this neglect to be challenged is a tribute to the continued pressure from the "forgotten people" not to tolerate such forgetting.

This volume may not be the first in which anyone has introduced gender into discussions about commodity chains, but to my knowledge it is the first that has made gendered commodity chains the issue under discussion. This book calls attention to "hidden women's work" in "laborer households." This is the point. The work is *hidden*. But by whom? Obviously, by all of us.

And here the social scientists bear the most guilt. For is it not the very point of the social sciences to uncover the hidden that lies under the surface of all social phenomena? Is it not the very point of the social sciences to uncover in whose interests and in what ways realities are hidden and then justified as normal, as inevitable, indeed, as rational?

This book opens the discussion. It does not close it. We have a very long way to go in uncovering the hidden, in elaborating the processes, in showing how they continue to reinforce and expand the inequalities, and in understanding the fact that rationality is in the eyes of the beholder.

But if we have a long way to go, we do not have a long time in which to do this work. The modern world-system is in its terminal crisis, in which the existing system cannot continue and is, therefore, in the midst of a bifurcation and transition into the system (or systems) that will replace it (Prigogine 1996: 157–62, Wallerstein 1995a: 155–63). The world is collectively choosing between two alternative possible futures: one that continues the worst features of the present system (perhaps in an even worse form) or one that shifts our civilizational orientation to that of a relatively democratic, relatively egalitarian world.

Part of this terminal crisis is a crisis in the structures of knowledge, in which the concept of gender is playing a key role. We shall either move toward a radically reconstructed epistemology in which reconstructed historical social sciences will play a key unifying role, overcoming the modern divide between the sciences and the humanities, or we shall not do so. The effort to overcome the antiquated structures of knowledge that have dominated the world-system for two centuries now is part and parcel of the effort to tilt the choice toward the civilizational option of a relatively democratic and relatively egalitarian world.

The work on gender is very difficult because of the resistance, but it is also very urgent. We have, as the saying goes, not a minute to lose, which is why this book constitutes an important contribution not merely to the social sciences but to the larger world political scene.

ACKNOWLEDGMENTS

This collection of essays is the result of a collaborative effort between the Fernand Braudel Center at Binghamton University and the School of Public and International Affairs at Virginia Tech. We gratefully acknowledge the funding support for this project received from the Fernand Braudel Center, Binghamton University; the School of Public and International Affairs, Virginia Tech; and the Institute for Society, Culture and Environment: Global Issues Initiative, Virginia Tech.

Six individuals were invaluable in project planning and final manuscript development. At Binghamton's Fernand Braudel Center, Richard Lee and Amy Keough went beyond the call of duty to demystify the process of decision making across two university campuses in states with very different fiscal policies. Jane Collins and Don Clelland provided extensive research assistance and advice about theoretical approaches in the development of early working lists of potential scholars to be invited to participate. Each of them undertook that extra work when they were overloaded with other obligations. I would also like to thank the two external reviewers, who contributed a great deal of time and effort to their assessments.

ABBREVIATIONS

BAS	Bureau of Agricultural Statistics
BFAR	Bureau of Fisheries and Aquaculture
CAWN	Central American Women's Network
ECLAC	Economic Commission for Latin America and the Caribbean
EPZ	export-processing zone
GCC	global commodity chain
GNCC	global nursing-care chain
GVC	global value chain
ILO	International Labour Organization
MEC	María Elena Cuadra Working and Unemployed Women's Movement
UNDP	United Nations Development Program
UNFPA	United Nations Population Fund
UNRISD	United Nations Research Institute for Social Development

Andrea Akers is a master's student in anthropology at Colorado State University, where she has participated in projects working with the Pine Ridge and Cheyenne River Indian Reservations. Her undergraduate honors thesis explores the gendered effects of capitalist incorporation on Pine Ridge households. Her master's thesis focuses on Lakota antisystemic resistance to tourism.

Carmen Bain is Assistant Professor of Sociology at Iowa State University. Her research interests include the political economy of global agrifood systems, the relationship among gender, social change, and development, and the gendered dimensions of international development aid for agriculture. Her work has appeared in several social science journals and edited collections.

Dave Broad is Professor of Sociology at the University of Regina, Saskatchewan. He analyzes work and the labor market, problems of world development and underdevelopment, the links between global economic restructuring and the casualization of labor, and the related issues of poverty and social welfare. He is the author or editor of four books and numerous articles about these subjects.

Donald A. Clelland is Professor Emeritus of Sociology at the University of Tennessee, where he taught graduate and undergraduate courses in international political economy and world-systems analysis for more than twenty years. He is the coauthor of one book and has published numerous articles in social science journals and edited collections.

Jane Collins is Professor of Community and Environmental Sociology and Gender and Women's Studies at the University of Wisconsin. Her research on gender and labor has focused on family farms in Peru, the commercial agricultural sector in Brazil, the apparel industry in the United States and Mexico, and the low-wage service sector in the United States. She has published three books and several articles that focus on commodity chains.

Saniye Dedeoglu is Associate Professor of Labor Economics and Industrial Relations at the University of Mugla, Turkey, and has been a Marie Curie Research Fellow at Warwick University, United Kingdom. She is the author or editor of two books. Her research interests are women's industrial work, international labor migration, and the Turkish ethnic economy in Europe.

Wilma A. Dunaway is Professor of Sociology in the School of Public and International Affairs at Virginia Tech. She specializes in world-systems analysis with emphases on the study of sexism, gendered work, households, enslaved families, indigenous peoples, and Appalachia within the modern world-system. She has authored or edited six books and numerous articles and book chapters.

Maria Cecilia Ferolin is associate professor of sociology at Iligan Institute of Technology, Mindanao State University, Philippines. She specializes in global political economy and women in development. She has published several articles in western journals about the state of Philippine fishing households.

Marina Prieto-Carrón is Senior Lecturer in geography at the University of Portsmouth, UK. Since 1997, she has collaborated with the Central American Women's Network, and she works with Latin American women's labor rights groups. Her research is interdisciplinary, encompassing human geography, development, international politics, and gender.

Priti Ramamurthy is Professor and Chair of the Department of Gender, Women, and Sexuality Studies at the University of Washington, Seattle. She is the coauthor of one book and has published numerous articles about feminist commodity chain analysis, the Indian middle class, gender, globalization and agrarian change in India, agricultural biotechnologies, and commodity cultures.

Robert J. S. Ross is Professor of Sociology and Director of the International Studies Stream at Clark University. He is past Chair of the Political Economy of the World-System Section of the American Sociological Association. He has published two books and numerous articles about the globalization of capital and labor. He is a member of the Board of Directors of the Sweatfree Purchasing Consortium.

Nadia Shapkina is Assistant Professor of Sociology at Kansas State University. Her research interests are related to gender, migration, and globalization. She examines sex trafficking of women from the post-Soviet region, as well as transnational antitrafficking campaigns. Her articles have appeared in American, European, and Russian journals.

Kathleen Pickering Sherman is Professor and Chair of the Department of Anthropology at Colorado State University. Her current research focuses on community-based development on several Lakota reservations in South Dakota. She is the author or coauthor of three books and numerous articles that focus on the impacts of capitalism and globalization on indigenous communities.

Nicola Yeates is Professor of Social Policy at the Open University in the United Kingdom. She is the author of two books that focus on global care chains and numerous articles about social policy and welfare from a global perspective. She is a former editor of *Global Social Policy* and is the Vice Chair of the United Kingdom Social Policy Association.

GENDERED COMMODITY CHAINS

Introduction

Wilma A. Dunaway

> *The specter of women's work haunts capitalism.*
> —Clough and Halley 2007: 107

Unpaid household labor is now the principal work activity of fewer than one of every four women worldwide (UNICEF 2007). Globally since the 1970s, "officially counted" female labor-force participation has been steadily rising except in a few societies, and the increase in women's visible inputs into global production has been the subject of considerable international scholarship. Between 1980 and 2000, women's economic activity rate expanded almost everywhere, narrowing the gender gap in labor-force participation. Thus females now account for one-third or more of the on-the-books personnel of export industries (UNICEF 2007), and export agriculture is now feminized (Deere 2005). Even more surprising, men's economic activity rate has declined everywhere except the Caribbean. Women now account for one-third of the manufacturing labor force in developing countries, and females hold more than one-half of the industrial jobs in Asia (Barrientos, Kabeer, and Hossain 2004). In much of the Global South, females account for a majority of the waged labor force in export agriculture, and they are more heavily concentrated than men in service jobs that provision the supply chains of global production. Because there are fewer opportunities for males, women are now less likely to withdraw from the labor force during their childbearing years. However, women are also economically active through informal-sector and unpaid contributions. In the twenty-first century, females account for a majority of the income earners in the informal sectors of a majority of Global South countries, generate a significant proportion of global commodities through subcontracted work they complete in their households, and provide most of the unpaid family labor needed to support household-based farms and businesses that are dominated by males (United Nations 2003).[1]

ASSESSING THE GENDER STATE OF THE FIELD

The numbers of females supplying labor to global production systems began to balloon in the late 1970s and early 1980s (UNRISD 2005). During the

1

same period, commodity chain analysis originated in the world-systems perspective. Terence Hopkins and Immanuel Wallerstein (1977: 127–28) envisioned a commodity chain as "a network of labor and production processes," as many chain analysts emphasize, but they also stressed that the chain map needs to reflect "the reproduction of the labor forces involved in these productive activities." They argued that the chained network is grounded in sexism, racism and drains of surplus from worker households. Their concept emphasized

1. intermingling of several forms of waged and nonwaged, free and unfree labor;
2. extraction of visible and hidden surpluses from households;
3. gendered and racial exploitation of workers; and
4. economic devaluation of household-based work, especially that of housewives (T. Hopkins and Wallerstein 1977, 1984, 1986, 1994; Wallerstein 1995a, 1995b).

Hopkins and Wallerstein (1994: 49) focused sharply on the pivotal question: "If one thinks of the entire chain as having a total amount of surplus value that has been appropriated, what is the division of this surplus value among the boxes of the chain?" It was obvious to them—in ways that subsequent scholars did not pursue—that worker households "routinely produce real surplus, which is in fact fed right into the world-economy" (T. Hopkins and Wallerstein 1977: 60). They argued that commodity chain analysis needs to take into account the surpluses that capitalists derive from two hidden inputs supplied by worker households: (1) the reproduction of labor forces and (2) the provisioning of low-paid waged workers. Consequently, they cautioned scholars to conceptualize a commodity chain in terms of multiple levels of surplus extraction from worker households at every spatial node of its lengthy network.[2]

Over the two decades that followed the formulation of these world-systems roots, commodity chain analysis developed along three divergent intellectual directions: the radical world-systems approach, the mainstream global commodity chains generated by Gereffi and his associates, and the industry-centric global value chains.[3] Although there are significant differences among these intellectual threads, what they have in common is that a majority of the accumulated research in each of these perspectives has "degendered" this approach in ways that early world-systems thinkers did not intend (Dunaway 2001). Throughout the 1980s, when commodity chain analysis was emerging as a field of study, feminists drew attention to the ways in which the widening of capitalism in the Global South was (re)segregating males and females between formal and informal labor sectors and between waged and nonwaged ways to earn income. Despite this growing body of gendered knowledge, the majority of commodity chain analysts continued to focus on the small numbers of waged workers within export-production networks or to ignore workers entirely to focus on firms. Even though feminists provided additional clues in the 1990s that neoliberalism was targeting and exacerbating nonwaged, casualized, and informal labor mechanisms, most commodity chain analysts did not heed those warnings and design investigations that would explore the production strategies that were widening Global South's feminization of poverty (United Nations 2003). Since 2000, feminist evidence of the significance of women's work in global production networks has continued to mount.[4] However, the growing accumulation of industry-centric studies of value chains during this decade pushed the field even further away from the gendered roots of commodity chain analysis.[5] In the second decade of the twenty-first century, feminists are still alarmed that "the gendered questions at the heart of international political economy continue to be neglected" (Bedford and Rai 2010: 2). Similarly, Salzinger (2003: 13) notes that considerations of gender "are strikingly absent in analyses of transnational production." Although numerous investigations of women's work in global production have been published since 1980, very few of these analyses use commodity or value chain analysis. As of December 2012, the published work of scholars who have "gendered" commodity or value chain analyses represents less than one percent of the total accumulated research in the three subfields of this approach.[6]

With respect to households, the track record of all three intellectual threads has gone even further astray from world-systems roots, for these important structures of the capitalist world-system almost never make an appearance in commodity or value chain analyses (Dunaway 2001; Salzinger 2003). When their ground-breaking book was published, Gereffi and Korzeniewicz (1994: 12) admitted that their researchers had failed to assess the linkages between households and commodity chains. As Nicola Yeates (2004b: 378) has observed, a majority of analysts "have neither positioned the household as a site of production within commodity chains nor theorized the relationship between household production and the transformation of commodity chains." In her seminal overview of the three scholarly threads of chain analysis, Bair (2005) assesses the state of the field by calling attention to three predominant debates that cut across all three approaches. Gendered labor strategies, gender inequality, and worker households are absent from those debates.[7] Subsequently, Bair (2010: 205, 224) called for feminist analyses of the gendered nature of globalized production, stating that a satisfactory approach will "look to how gender, as a set of context-specific meanings and practices, intersects the structure of global capitalism and its systemic logic of value extraction and capital accumulation."

The authors of the essays in this book argue that it is intellectually shortsighted to ignore gender, women, and households in this way. Indeed, it is not possible to examine current global trends accurately or to assess directions for activism realistically without attention to the scope of women's work and to widening gender inequalities. In light of the gendered gap in the scholarly literature about commodity and value chains, the Fernand Braudel Center at Binghamton University and the School of Public and International Affairs at Virginia Tech developed a collaborative research project involving an international group of interdisciplinary scholars. We sought out those scholars who have conducted gendered analyses of commodity or value chains, those who have developed research and conceptualization on the emerging significance of women in global production systems, and those who have been scholar-activists in the struggle for living wages and less gender-biased working conditions within global production networks. Although their theoretical underpinnings and research frameworks vary considerably, four themes resonate throughout the accumulated work of these scholars and throughout the essays that are offered here.

THE FALSE ANALYTIC DIVIDE BETWEEN PRODUCTION AND REPRODUCTION

The first theme that resonates across this group of scholars is the conviction that degendered commodity and value chain analyses are grounded in a false analytic divide between production and reproduction. More than three decades ago, Lourdes Beneria (1979: 216) pointed out that economic change needs to be "analyzed from the perspective of the different effects on the sexes, a dimension that has often been neglected." She argued that analyses should concentrate on two levels: (1) how the transformation alters the productive and reproductive functions and the gendered division of labor of households and (2) how economic restructuring affects communities and societies by imposing new conditions under which social reproduction must occur. In line with Beneria's thinking, scholars of commodity and value chains need to investigate three types of social reproduction: biological reproduction that occurs within households, the presence or absence of social safety nets to sustain the labor force during economic crises, and the social reproduction of worker households and communities (Dickinson and Russell 1986).[8] Among the most fundamental challenges to conventional economics and economic history posed by a gender perspective is the importance that one might attach to everyday life, argue Bettio and Verashchagina (2008: 32–34). Preoccupied with "productive" activities as represented by commodified labor and market exchanges, Western economists marginalize the reproductive sphere (Peterson 2003). In the same vein, most commodity and value chain analysts have treated market and household as discrete and disconnected spheres. By following that sexist approach, these scholars deny that capitalists benefit greatly from externalization of the costs of reproduction and maintenance of the labor force to households and communities (Wallerstein 1995b).

Mainstream economists recognize that capitalists are able to keep their prices competitive only because they do not have to pay for reproduction (Terleckyj 1975: 230–31). However, economists have dismissed the structural relationship between the production of commodities and the social reproduction of the labor force by treating reproduction artificially as though it is not a factor of production (Mies 1986). Because production and reproduction are far more intertwined than economic theory admits (Terleckyj 1975; Dickinson and Russell 1986), the authors of the essays in this book call for a more holistic understanding of socioeconomic activity that overcomes masculinist and productivist biases. We contend that there is a need for more compelling questions and deeper insights into the ways in which the productive and the reproductive spheres are inextricably linked and overlapping (Clough and Halley 2007). For help with rethinking, we can return to the intellectual roots of the world-systems conceptualization of commodity chains. Terence Hopkins and Immanuel Wallerstein (1977: 127–28) stress that chain mapping needs to reflect "the reproduction of the labor forces involved in these productive activities." In reality, "no production system operates without a reproductive system," and reproductive mechanisms are the "intimate Others" of globalized production systems (Truong 1996: 47). However, the term "reproductive" should be understood to mean far more than biological reproduction, maintenance of human workers, and historical community persistence because the capitalist system, its infrastructure and its processes must also be reproduced (Marx 1990: vol. 1).

There are five ways in which reproductive labor is a routine element of commodity chains. First, it is in the reproductive sphere that workers are socialized in the characteristics of a "good" worker. Learned skills, such as time management, work ethic, moral integrity, and interpersonal relationships are essential to efficiency, productivity, and profitability. Second, production and reproduction share the same material and social bases, even though theorists artificially separate them. In the neoliberal period, a disproportionate share of fiscal resources has been allocated to global productive systems, and historical public expenditures for social reproduction have been eliminated (Katz 2001). When production absorbs, pollutes, or destroys too much of a society's ecological and social resources, reproductive spheres are threatened. As a result, poverty and hunger have expanded at the same time at which global productive systems have created greater wealth than has ever existed in the world (Sehgal 2005). In similar fashion, ecological resources have been disproportionately allocated to (or polluted or wasted by) global productive systems and have been withdrawn from reproductive uses. In these two contexts, the reproductive needs of laborers and communities have been "unhinged from production" (Katz 2001: 710) to such an extent that much of the reproductive value of shared material resources is exported away from the people and communities that need them most for survival. Consequently, hunger and malnutrition are common in developing countries that export vast amounts of food through food commodity chains, and medicines are not applied where they are most needed because people "cannot afford them" (United Nations 2004: 114). In reaction, households develop extra-market survival strategies to overcome the shortfalls in basic needs caused by productive systems that are no longer synchronized with reproductive systems.

Third, much of the labor required to generate the commodities that fill chains crisscrossing the globe takes "nonwaged" forms that are closely tied to reproductive spheres. Many household activities have been incorporated into markets and commodity chains, including artisan crafts, agricultural crops, fishing, and aquaculture. Thus household members simultaneously complete household tasks and produce for the market, and a researcher cannot easily see where reproductive activity ends and productive activity begins. Much of this activity occurs in informal sectors where two-thirds of the people of the Global South earn livelihoods. Commodity chains routinely integrate informalized and casualized labor forms with factory production, and much of this work is household based. Family members, especially females, supply unpaid labor to capitalist enterprises that are based in households (e.g., farms, textile workshops), and these forms of women's work constitute a gray zone in which the females themselves do not demarcate boundaries between reproductive and market-oriented activities (United Nations 2003). In this context, a woman's reproductive labor is extended to the capitalist enterprise, as is the case with wives who provide cleaning, food preparation, and family networking functions for their husband's export textile shops or commercial fishing or aquaculture operations (see Chapters 6 and 8 in this book). When the female homeworker subcontracts commodity production, she further clouds the demarcation between reproduction and production, especially because she draws from her accumulated pantry of reproductive resources and child labor to complete the work for which she will earn income. All her work, both productive and reproductive, will be rendered invisible in commodity mapping and in public records.

Fourth, "the market" has broken down the analytic distinction by commodifying traditional reproductive functions. Monetarization of subsistence resources generates household reliance on wages to be used to purchase survival needs from markets. Thus reproductive resources must be secured from markets supplied by productive systems that generate commodities for exchange (Wallerstein 1995a). Households "move their unpaid reproductive labour into the commodity and services market, earning ways with which to purchase goods and services which replace unpaid domestic service" (Pearson 2000: 223). In addition, markets commodify reproductive functions to such an extent that all forms of domestic work and biological reproduction can be purchased. Hospitals and health-care personnel sell health and reproductive services, and women's bodies are controlled by commodities that regulate or prevent reproduction. Even the human conception and birthing process can be profitably replicated through market mechanisms that do not require women (Mies and Shiva 2001: 174–95). To complicate matters, the world-economy has structured an international division of reproductive labor in which domestic servants, nurses, and sex workers migrate from poorer countries to sell their services in richer countries (Chapters 10 and 11). In this global marketing of transnational laborers, the distant consumers shift their reproductive work to transnational migrants. In this way, the costs of social reproduction are externalized to the labor-exporting country, and expenses are kept low where most of the benefits accrue (Katz 2001). At this point, the reader should seriously question that there is any clear division between production and reproduction. If the analytic distinction were as great as economic theory suggests, reproductive labor would stay outside the market and not become an economically valuable commodity.

Fifth, the contradictory narrow space between the reproductive sphere and the workplace threatens the efficiency and profitability of productive systems. The burdens of unpaid household labor and child care deter the entry of females into waged labor and many forms of productive self-employment at exactly the time when commodity chains are targeting such females for low-paid production. When they do increase their labor-force participation and their income-earning activities, "women's increased role in the labour markets of the global economy has not been matched by an increased participation of men in unpaid domestic work" (Pearson 2000: 228). It should be of economic concern to capitalists seeking cheap female laborers that women spend more time than men on unpaid work. Indeed, women spend 50 to 70 percent as much time as men on paid work but almost twice as much time as men on unpaid work. On an average day, a Global South female allocates 2.5 more hours than men to reproductive basic needs (United Nations 2003). The murky space between reproductive labor and productive labor is further confounded by dangerous behaviors that females encounter when they enter the workplace. Who is responsible for the safety of women and girls who face harassment or physical threats on the way to

workplaces (Chapter 13), especially in societies where females are just beginning to enter the public labor force? Why do male workers inappropriately
harass female peers for "reproductive" services in workplaces if the division
between the two spheres is so clear (Chapters 6 and 13)?

In reality, the operations of commodity chains are not separate or shielded
from a mythological sphere to which "the reproductive" or "the "gendered"
is consigned, locked away so as not to contaminate "the economic." The real
world is far messier than many economic theories have claimed. In fact, "markets, with all their risks and variable performance, embody gender hierarchies as they are found in society and its institutions" (UNRISD 2005: 65).
Consequently, inequalities are structured by and within commodity chains,
including those grounded in patriarchy and gender. Indeed, every node of
every commodity chain is shaped by the gender and patriarchal relations
of its geographic and social space, and the sexual division of labor in
households is often replicated in productive nodes of commodity chains.
Jennifer Bair (2010: 209) observes that export-oriented production "depends on the intersection of social organization . . . and a set of patriarchal
ideologies and practices, which together create a particular opportunity structure for exploiting female labor." Consequently, capitalist labor strategies
(especially in the form of lowered remuneration for females) benefit from
the gender inequalities and patriarchal constraints that characterize the societies in which production and distribution occur (Werlhof 2007). Because the
labor market is segmented by gender, race, and ethnicity, women are concentrated in fewer, lower-paying occupations that are characterized by poor
working conditions and few prospects for advancement. In short, "there are
reasons for caution in equating women's paid work with empowerment"
(UNRISD 2005: 68).

WHY WE NEED TO BRING HOUSEHOLDS INTO COMMODITY CHAIN ANALYSIS

The second theme emphasized in this book is the notion that laborer households are central to the operations of commodity chains. Fernand Braudel
(1979: 28–29, 16) argues that we cannot understand the most complex layer
of history—the economy—unless we investigate how the ethnographic
details of people's everyday lives are intertwined with it. In similar fashion,
feminist economists contend that one of the "most fundamental challenges
to conventional economics and economic history posed by a gender perspective is the importance that one might attach to everyday life" that "encompasses the daily tasks of reproduction" situated within households and local
communities (Bettio and Verashchagina 2008: 32). However, the everyday
life of workers, their households, and their communities has been "the great

absentee" from much of economic history (Braudel 1979: 16), from measures of economic growth (Perelman 2011), and from a majority of commodity and value chain analyses (Raworth and Kidder 2009).

It is important to recognize that households "add value" to commodity chains. Indeed, households are centers of forms of both productive and reproductive labor that are essential to commodity chains. The linkages that women forge between households and commodity chains are hydralike, shooting out in multiple directions. It is a conceptual mistake to draw an analytic distinction between the household sphere and production because the household is just as much a capitalist unit of production and reproduction as are the farm, the factory, and the marketplace (Mies 1986). To detect the entire surplus that is generated by and extracted from the workers who produce and move goods within commodity chains, we must examine households where the labor forces of all commodity chains are created and sustained.

Thus scholars need to integrate households because they are now increasingly the sites of activities that feed into (or challenge the continuation of) production systems. Household laborers often produce supplies and provide services that provision the production process (Beneria 2001; United Nations 2003). Half the Global South population consists of peasants who ground their export agriculture, fishing, or aquaculture within households, and their reallocation of labor triggers conflicts between household subsistence needs and commodity marketing. Moreover, their debt bondage supports their production of crops for export while endangering their household reproduction (Brass 1999). Much of the production and processing of global commodities now occurs within households, not in factories. As feminist scholars have argued for three decades, much commodity output is structured through low-paid piecework within households that absorb many of the costs of production that core factories paid in the past (Elson and Pearson 1981; Prugl 1999; Carr, Chen, and Tate 2000). By the mid-1990s, half the workforce of the global garment industry consisted of home-based workers who "feed productive profit-making output from their homes into the more formal manufacturing companies or their intermediaries" (UN-RISD 2005: 82). At the turn of the twenty-first century, 70 to 80 percent of these homeworkers were females (United Nations 2003), whose economic inputs have been excluded from national GDPs and from scholarly commodity and value chain analyses.

Households provide a second significant service that "adds value" to commodity chains. Capitalists maximize profits by externalizing costs of production to households (e.g., costs assumed by workers who produce a commodity at home, impacts of ecological degradation) and to the ecosystems that provision them. In addition to shifting costs of laborer reproduction to households, capitalists externalize many of the real costs of commodity production to households, communities, and ecosystems (Chapter 3). These externalized costs are not unusual or extraordinary; rather, they are "part and parcel of normal capitalism, and they are to be found at every node/link of every commodity chain" (Wallerstein 1995b: 11). Within a commodity chain, externalities serve three purposes: (1) Employers are more competitive when they keep labor costs low by externalizing costs to households. (2) Capitalists maximize profit taking through externalized costs. (3) Because of externalities to production, hidden unpaid labor and inputs acquired at below global market value are embedded in commodities and passed on in the form of cheap consumer prices (Chapter 4). Increasingly, these externalized costs place social reproduction at risk in many Global South societies as ecological resources, food, and public funding are captured by export chains (Sehgal 2005).

There is a third way in which households are crucial to capitalism: they are the structural end points of commodity chains. Without households, consumer goods would have far fewer arenas for marketing and profit taking. Disproportionately, women collect and process the capitalist goods that are used by households (and dispose of the associated waste). "In the modern world-economy the organization and composition of households embodies the construction of consumption" (Gereffi and Korzeniewicz 1994: 12). However, consumption is no more gender neutral than the production end of a commodity chain. Key transnational corporations control the development and distribution of new consumer goods and define the spatialities and target groups that will be the markets for commodities. Consequently, consumption is structured around and reinforces gender inequalities, as well as the polarization between rich and poor countries. Men and women do not consume commodities equitably, and there are significant disparities in consumption by females of different national, racial, ethnic, and class positions. Global South workers do not just produce commodities for others to use; they actively seek to be consumers in ways that confound their past understandings of gendered institutions (Chapter 2). Increasingly, Global South poor households are targeted to be the "new markets" for imported consumer goods in the twenty-first century. Consumption of modern commodities leads to alteration of traditional labor strategies and cultural norms, and the impacts of these changes on households are gendered. Dialectically, consumption stimulates change in such a way that gendered inequalities can be minimally altered while patriarchy is reconsolidated (Werlhof 2007). Consumption of cheap goods can simultaneously "improve" the living conditions of worker households and threaten household survival labor strategies and resources. Metaphorically, then, consumer goods are simultaneously "the good, the bad, and the ugly" in their impacts on households.

However, households can also threaten productivity and profits within commodity chains because laborer activism and resistance are often nurtured there, especially in the Global South, where there are fewer meeting places. Especially during economic downturns, households are loci of antisystemic resistance. Workers resist the "lean" policies within production systems to try to ensure that waged employment "is remunerated minimally at the level of household reproduction" (Wallerstein 1995b: 1). In addition, house-holders challenge the commodification of their provisioning resources and of their informal-sector production. Historically, peasants and indigenous peoples have resisted when capitalist encroachment has threatened their ancestral lands. Peripheral social movements resist decline in livelihoods caused by capitalist expansion and press for land reform when natural resources become concentrated in the hands of agrarian capitalists. Women's activism is overwhelmingly based within households, where they often combine income earning with resistance and employ household resources to mobilize their movements (Wallerstein and Smith 1992). Even though such resistance confounds the flow of factors of production and lowers profit margins, the vast majority of analysts of commodity and value chains ignore these elements of household-based labor.

Is bringing in households and women an impossible task? No, it is not. The inputs of women and households into commodity chains are publicly visible (as case studies in this book demonstrate), and they are being increasingly documented by states and by international development agencies. Females now constitute a majority of the workforce in Global South areas of capitalist expansion, and those females typically suffer greater degrees of income inequality, poverty, malnutrition, and health problems than their male counterparts (Selwyn 2012: 108–26). In addition, a high proportion of commodity chains structure putting-out and subcontracting systems that require productive labor to be undertaken within households (Barrientos 2011). Moreover, it is not impossible to quantify unpaid, nonwaged, and informal-sector labor. Since the 1920s, some mainstream American economists, including Nobel laureate Simon Kuznets (1941: 1:10), have argued that several forms of unpaid household labor need to be taken into account in measures of economic growth and gross national product. Moreover, the contribution of household labor to economic growth is routinely covered in undergraduate textbooks (Perelman 2011: 200–212). For two decades, mainstream international organizations have been prioritizing research about these undocumented forms of labor and about the linkages among households, gender, and commodity production. In the 1990s, the United Nations and the World Bank began to fund national time-use surveys to quantify unpaid household labor (Clermont and Aligisakis 1995; African Centre for Women 2002).[9] As a result, twenty-three Global South countries and two Western nations now report an economic value for unpaid household labor within their GDP. The United Nations Statistics Division (2011) has published guidelines for integrating unpaid work into national accounting procedures. A current United Nations project focuses on the "political and social economy of care" in order to articulate this unpaid household labor "with the commodity economy" (Budlender 2007: 1–2). Similarly, the World Bank has encouraged Global South countries to develop methods to document the economic value of their informal sectors. Since 1995, the bank has fostered more than five thousand working papers about statistical approaches to measure the informal sector, and its databases include a wide array of statistical information for most Global South countries. A 2012 search of the bank's website calls up 486 projects that were funded between 2000 and 2011 to develop a model that can be used in the Global South to define and quantify the informal sector. In addition, other extensive private scholarly projects have developed strategies to measure time allocation in Global South households (e.g., Antonopoulos and Hirway 2010).

THE FALSE ANALYTIC DIVIDE BETWEEN INFORMAL SECTORS AND COMMODITY CHAINS

The third theme is a criticism of the tendency of commodity and value chain analysts to practice their art as though there is an artificial divide between formal, on-the-books expenditures and those that are hidden in informal sectors. In effect, these investigators do not make an analytic distinction at all because their chain mappings pinpoint only formal inputs and treat informal inputs as though they never occur. In reality, however, the twenty-first century world-economy is stimulating many more precarious forms of work than formal waged employment. Informal sectors absorb the vast majority of workers in the Global South, and women are more concentrated in these jobs than males. As a result, most of the workers in commodity chains are off the books and hidden, and capitalists prefer to keep them there because doing so allows them to keep production costs lean, consumer prices low, and profits higher.[10] Every commodity chain that originates in the Global South is supported by thousands of laborer households, but these workers and their families acquire only a minority of their survival needs from formal wages in capitalist sectors. On average, a single multinational corporation does not employ enough waged or salaried workers to account for more than 1 percent of the total available labor force in a Global South country (UNRISD 2005). To conceptualize the full role of reproductive labor and households in commodity chains, scholars must assess the extent to which capitalism exploits nonwaged workers (both unpaid and paid), especially women.

Rather than adapting a form of commodity and value chain analysis that describes only the easily discerned waged workers and a few managerial subcontractors, scholars need to assess the ingenuity of capitalists at using household-based informal-sector goods and services, subcontracting, and outsourcing, as well as informalized workers at their productive sites (e.g., the types of labor described in UNRISD 2005). Such informal labor is both a historical and a contemporary feature of capitalism that is much more common than waged labor (Tabak and Crichlow 2000). Consequently, such "non-waged labor is a condition of—and not coincidental to—the so-called productive economy" (Peterson 2003: 14). For that reason, commodity and value chain analysts who ignore such workers will describe only a small proportion of productive laborers and will misunderstand the degree to which the productive and the reproductive spheres are commingled. We cannot so cleanly separate women's reproductive labor from work that is aimed at the external economic arena. Much income-earning activity occurs in the home, and women contribute significant invisible labor to male-dominated economic activities. In order to capture much of the economically valuable work of women, we must pay attention to the conceptual importance of the informal sector, those nonwaged, undocumented economic activities that result in the sale of commodities or services. Historically and worldwide today, women earn most of their income and generate household resources outside waged occupations (United Nations 2003). Moreover, many females are trapped in households that are grounded in "unfree" agricultural, workshop, or subcontracting labor strategies that bind them as debtors within commodity chains (Brass 1999; Chapters 9 and 12).

WOMEN'S INEQUITABLE LABOR PORTFOLIO IN GLOBAL PRODUCTION

The fourth theme is the need for commodity and value chain analysts to incorporate the diverse portfolio of forms of female labor more fully. At the macrostructural level, a commodity chain is the global mechanism that ensures the inequitable division of surplus among the core, the semiperiphery, and the periphery. Long before those expropriations can occur, however, the commodity chain structures the maximal exploitation of underpaid and unpaid labor. If we are to make gender visible in the commodity chain, we must investigate how and where surplus is produced by women at every node of the network because females are the invisible workforce of global commodity networks. However, it is in the analysis of women's work that commodity and value chain mappings are probably weakest. Conceptually, we need to stop being blinded by oversimplified stereotypes about women being trapped in housebound labor outside the reach of market forces. If we search only for "manifestations of their private roles as housewives and mothers," we miss the real "dialectics of waged and unwaged labor" that characterize most women's resource accumulation (Collins and Gimenez 1988: 22–23). Zillah Eisenstein (1990: 139–40) admonishes us to employ a "multigridded conceptualization" of women's work, taking into account differences of race, class, ethnicity, marital status, age, and religion. Finally, we need to move away from the naive and outdated notion that all work done by women in households is without economic value and is outside the market. We need to investigate how women's work is embedded within a gendered division of labor that allocates different tasks and statuses to women and men. It is not enough, however, to search out "women's work" as a distinct category from "men's work." That can lead us only toward silencing and homogenization of much of women's work that is disguised behind class and racial divisions among women. An effective examination will pinpoint women's and men's differential access to and control over material resources alongside the structural inequalities that exist among females.

In short, we must take special care when we are analyzing the work done inside women's households because some of that work is almost always aimed at the marketplace (Dunaway 2001). To varying degrees, depending on their class and racial positions, Global South women engage in a complex portfolio of forms of agricultural and nonagricultural labor that include the following:

Unpaid labor to sustain the household, clan, or family
Unpaid labor associated with biological reproduction and child rearing
Unpaid labor that subsidizes male-dominated market farms and enterprises
Waged or salaried labor in formal documented contexts
Waged or salaried labor in informal sectors
Production or selling of goods or services in the informal sector
Business operation inside or outside the household
Income-earning homework that is subcontracted from exporters
Unpaid charitable or community work

Although contemporary commodity chains integrate females into numerous visible and concealed labor forms, their income earning has not eliminated gender inequality and patriarchy. Men are more likely to be concentrated in formal, more closely regulated occupations, while females are consigned to more precarious informal and casual jobs (Barrientos, Kabeer, and Hossain 2004). In comparison with men, women are still more likely to experience temporary jobs, lower pay, precarious subcontracting, excessive overtime, denial of rightful benefits, higher unemployment, and extreme levels of health risk (UNRISD 2005).

These disparities make it clear that commodity chains structure, preserve, and exploit gender inequalities. These chained networks are grounded in sexism, racism, and economic devaluation of household-based work, especially that of females (T. Hopkins and Wallerstein 1977, 1986). In addition to several visible but undervalued contributions by females, commodity and value chain analyses need to take into account the surpluses that capitalists derive from two hidden inputs: (1) the reproduction of labor forces and (2) household provisioning of low-paid waged workers. Cumulatively, the essays in this book call for visioning commodity chains as more than simplistic material boxes that exclude too many gendered processes. They emphasize that every node of the lengthy network of a global commodity chain encompasses (1) multiple levels of surplus extraction from worker households and from women, (2) patriarchal mechanisms that lead to public invisibility and economic devaluation of women's diverse portfolio of forms of labor, (3) several nonmaterial or cultural manifestations of the local impacts of globalized production and consumption systems, and (4) activism and resistance by households and by grassroots organizations.

ORGANIZATION AND FORMAT OF THIS BOOK

In addition to selecting a few junior scholars who are doing cutting-edge gendered research on commodity chains, project supervisors asked senior scholars to reflect on their accumulated research to develop an essay that offered key ideas from their conceptualizations of women's work and gender within commodity chains. Therefore, a majority of these essays are derived from assessment of ten to thirty years of research, and several of them are the culmination of intense intellectual revisiting and rethinking of nearly a lifetime of scholarship. All the authors were sensitive to presenting their essays in such a way that a novice could use the concepts and methods of inquiry to learn how to bring gender, women, and households into future analyses of global production. Some essays employ a conceptual framework that is drawn from two decades or more of case studies; others are grounded in rich ethnographic, archival, and feminist methodologies. All these scholars have kept women and gender inequality at the heart of their frameworks. In order to depict real-life circumstances more closely, they have decentered and broadened their conceptualizations to capture the diversity of unpaid and non-waged forms of labor that coexist inside households with formal waged work.

Each of the essays in this book is designed to stimulate readers to think about commodity chains in gendered ways they may not have previously considered. We seek to help readers think in innovative ways that will move them outside closed commodity boxes (Chapter 1) so they can see (1) the contributions of women and households that lie beyond formal-sector documentation and (2) the material and nonmaterial impacts of global integration on women and their households. For that reason, project supervisors invited essays from scholars who enrich commodity chain analysis by introducing feminist conceptualizations and methodologies that scholars might avoid because they think that these approaches are too difficult to integrate into their investigations. The book is organized into six parts that intersect multidimensionally with the intellectual themes discussed earlier in this introduction.

As indicated previously, feminist investigations of globalization and commodity and value chain analyses have overwhelmingly developed as separate threads of scholarship. Although ours is not the first call to bring gender into investigations of globalized production (e.g., Pearson 2000; Beneria 2001; Bair 2010; Bedford and Rai 2010), Part I breaks new ground in conceptualizing how commodity chain analysis can be feminized. These scholars pinpoint constructive feminist critiques of past approaches, but they also propose new directions that investigators can pursue to bring women and households into their research. In Chapter 1, Jane Collins queries whether commodity chain analysis has become so conflated with neoclassical economics and neoliberalism that it is no longer useful for more critical or feminist purposes. She responds by laying out a history of alternative approaches that are less mechanistic and less gender blind. She calls for a more critical version of commodity chain analysis that incorporates five feminist conceptual vantage points. First, she points out that feminists treat the commodity chain as a mnemonic device for organizing complex information and do not reify it as a "thing" that is either total or perfect in scope. Second, a critical feminist analysis makes the social reproduction of labor visible. Third, a feminist approach treats waged labor as a complex social relationship rather than a simple cost. Fourth, feminist commodity chain analysis opens up the black box of the commodity by revealing the subsidy from nature. Fifth, feminist commodity chain research does not accept that the logic of connection among sites is purely economic. She insists that feminist approaches offer richer elaborations by incorporating a "logic of connection among sites" that is more than economic because it brings in social reproduction of labor and ecological subsidies to production.

As Bair (2010: 224) points out, "The gendered global assembly line is a real abstraction," but it has nonmaterial effects on workers and communities. She insists that the material aspects of global commodity chains should not be the end point of feminist political economy, reasoning that "while certain commitments may encourage an emphasis on the local and specific, social reality remains multileveled and dialectical in its causal dynamics. Our inquiry into the relationship between difference and capital must grapple with this complexity in order to generate novel understandings of how and why difference matters for the globalization of production." Chapter 2 represents such a novel understanding.

In Chapter 2, Priti Ramamurthy draws upon two decades of ethnographic research in India to explore the material and nonmaterial contradictions of gendered work in global commodity chains. She offers gendered critiques of past realist approaches and lays out the elements of feminist commodity chain analysis. At the heart of her essay is the notion that feminist analysis conceptualizes commodities as things that work materially and semiotically in global capitalist circuits to accomplish the social reproduction of labor and of capital. Production generates more than material commodities, she insists, because it also generates the ambiguities and contradictions experienced by workers. She calls for an interpretive methodology that apprehends the perplexity that workers experience, often in surprising, unpredictable ways that exceed the logic of capital, over the ways in which their labor, their pasts and their presents become commodified. That perplexity is connected to the multiple temporalities in which production and social reproduction occur, so that past, present, and future labor forms, disparate work spatialities, and contradictory cultural norms are connected in complex dialectical ways. In her conclusion, she suggests several questions that might be pursued in feminist commodity chain analyses.

Drawing on ideas advanced by world-systems foundational thinkers and radical feminists, Part II demonstrates how investigators can bring semiproletarianized households and unpaid workers into their analyses of commodity chains. In Chapter 3, Wilma Dunaway conceptualizes the household as an important analytic tool that permits researchers to explore the wide range of women's work that is subsumed in exported goods. Her goal is to move scholars beyond the conceptual biases that have caused them to ignore the variety of forms of unpaid and paid household-based labor that are embedded in commodity chains. She contends that researchers cannot develop an accurate depiction of a commodity chain unless they investigate how the complicated, messy details of people's everyday lives are intertwined with it. To map a commodity chain fully, she insists, scholars must integrate unpaid and nonwaged work that capitalists make invisible in order to keep labor costs low. It is essential to investigate nonwaged labor because the vast majority of workers in commodity chains reside in semiproletarianized households that merge erratic wages with resources acquired from nonwaged efforts. These households are valuable to capitalists because they (1) provide concealed subsidies to commodity chains and (2) are the sites for externalization of production costs from them.

In Chapter 4, Don Clelland integrates three decades of scholarship about unpaid labor into his innovative focus on dark-value-extraction chains. Before surpluses are transferred between regions of the world, he contends, capitalists expropriate much of their aggregated surplus from peripheral households through hidden mechanisms that operate within commodity chains. Employing the example of the Brazilian coffee commodity chain, he demonstrates empirically that the transfer of dark value by means of degrees of monopoly and unequal exchange mechanisms lowers the price considerably. He brings gender into commodity chain analysis by delineating the origins of that dark value in forms of labor (i.e., unpaid household and reproductive work, informal-sector inputs, and low-paid labor) where women predominate and in externalized costs of that labor.

The three chapters of Part III explore the ways in which a variety of forms of female labor (paid and unpaid, formal and informal) are integrated into commodity chains. These scholars call attention to the ways in which commodity chains break down the boundaries between worker households and production sites while reconsolidating gender constraints on women. Moreover, the demarcations among informal, formal, and unpaid household labor can become quite blurred in many global production systems, especially textile commodity chains.[11] The authors also pinpoint the ways in which global production processes threaten the survival of workers and the social reproduction of households and communities. In Chapter 5, Robert Ross draws upon two decades of research to explore the extent to which global commodity chains rely on nonwaged informal-sector and sweatshop labor. He offers conceptual clarification of the terms "informal sector" and "sweatshop" and points out that both historically and in the contemporary period, the production stages of the textile industry have been structured around gender biases. As core manufacturing has shifted to the Global South, exporters have creatively married "off-the-books" labor strategies with formally documented workers. It is in sweatshops that the worst working conditions and the most severe exploitation of female workers exist. Pressure on those mobilizing production (e.g., middleman jobbers) will cause them to protect their margins by extracting greater value from workers and by externalizing costs of production to laborer households. Workers more vulnerable to these cost-lowering strategies are those who are favored for employment; this explains the concentration of female workers in textile production.

In Chapter 6, Saniye Dedeoglu breaks new ground through a decade of ethnographic research about three types of Muslim women's work in Turkey's garment commodity chains. In workshops controlled by men, wives provide unpaid labor as middlewomen who employ their family and community networks to recruit laborers. The division between female household duties and workshop duties is quite murky. These small workshops target the most impoverished women, so the commodity chain benefits from several forms of female unpaid labor. The second group consists of immigrants who are recruited to work in small workshops or as subcontracted homeworkers.

Employers take advantage of the illegal status of these females by paying them below-subsistence wages, withholding benefits, and working them overtime in violation of government standards. The third group consists of teenaged girls who enter factory work before marriage. In all these contexts, employers organize their workplaces to reconsolidate traditional patriarchal constraints on females.

In Chapter 7, Carmen Bain calls attention to the special vulnerabilities of temporary female peasant workers in globalized agriculture. Even though the governance strategies of lead firms play key roles in shaping relationships of power and inequality, the implications of such strategies for workers, women, and gender relations have received inadequate scholarly attention. Against the backdrop of the fresh-fruit export industry in peripheral countries, such as Chile, she points out that these casualized *temporeras* are invisible in employers' public accountability. In this way, gender inequalities are entrenched in corporate food and labor safety standards that claim to protect worker safety. Lead firms seek to control other actors within the chain by implementing practices that produce an inequitable gendered division of labor throughout the network. Bain contends that advocacy of greater participation by women in standards construction will not bring meaningful results as long as firms externalize from these codes the casualized labor forms in which females predominate.

The two chapters in Part IV explore the integration of indigenous and peasant households into global commodity chains. Despite the deep reach of global commodity chains into rural areas of the world, peasants still make up more than half of the world's population, and indigenous peoples still control some of the world's richest ecological areas. Through land-grabbing and public-dispossession policies (Harvey 2003), these groups are often defined by their own national governments as "unwanted peoples" who are an impediment to development (Bodley 2008), and more often than not they are tenuously integrated into global production systems through some of the most exploitative and racist labor strategies (Pearce 2012). In Chapter 8, Kathleen Sherman and Andrea Akers push the typical boundaries of commodity chain analysis by reflecting on nearly two decades of innovative ethnographic research on indigenous households and women. First, they demonstrate that nonwaged activities dialectically (1) lay the foundation for household survival, (2) make them vulnerable to exploitation by actors in export commodity chains, and (3) situate them in spatialities in which noncapitalist cultural forms can be preserved in ways that resist destruction by capitalism. Second, they explore the ways in which indigenous poverty and culture have been incorporated into specialized externally governed commodity chains made up of NGOs and profit-taking businesses. They introduce the notion of "informal provisioning chains" and argue that these local networks are more beneficial to indigenous households than the external commodity chains that reach into their community.

In Chapter 9, Maria Cecilia Ferolin takes us into a Philippine seafood-extractive enclave. To repay external debts since 1980, the national government has reallocated ecological resources and public funds to expand export fishing and aquaculture while marginalizing small peasant producers and deemphasizing food production for local consumption. She points out that export prices do not reflect the true costs of producing fishery commodities because hidden household subsidies and externalities are concealed in the commodity chain. As fishing households become integrated into global food chains, both as exporters and importers, and in the face of the loss of ecological resources that once supported their livelihoods, peasant fisher women have developed an uneasy and inequitable array of coping strategies that includes debt bondage, intensified self-exploitation through working longer hours, increased self-deprivation through eating less, purchasing fewer survival needs, and removing children from school.

The two chapters of Part V examine the feminization of transnational labor migration (Sassen 2000). Parrenas (2000: 577) observes that "production is not the sole means by which international divisions of labor operate in the global economy. Local economies are not solely linked by the manufacturing production of goods. In globalization, the transfer of reproductive labor moves beyond territorial borders to connect separate nation-states." Along with the feminization of labor strategies in production systems, females are now integrated through commodified transnational labor-migration chains into an international division of reproductive labor (Parrenas 2000) that has been formulated as part of the export agendas of several Global South countries that benefit economically from the remittance payments of domestic servants, caregivers, and sex workers who are sent abroad. As a result, households are increasingly globalized in material and nonmaterial ways as marriages become long distance and a significant proportion of youth in exporting countries are growing up separate from at least one parent (Bryceson and Vuorela 2002; Safri and Graham 2010).[12]

Reflecting two decades of research in Chapter 10, Nicola Yeates calls attention to the global care chains that consist of thousands of female domestic servants, caregivers, and sex workers who migrate from peripheral countries to supply reproductive labor previously provided by females in richer countries. She first explores the intellectual progression from commodity to care chain and then provides an overview of the global care-chain perspective. Using transnational migration of nurses as her in-depth example, Yeates pinpoints the determinants of labor flows, the roles of states, governance and credentialing, immigration regimes, and labor recruitment, brokerage, and management. Like other commodity chains, these care chains extract surplus value from poorer countries and transfer it to richer countries. For those countries that export nurses into these global labor chains, the trade constitutes a form of superexploitation because of its deleterious effects on public health and social reproduction.

In Chapter 11, Nadia Shapkina exposes a second type of global care chain through her cutting-edge research on the international sex trade. She contends that decreasing opportunities for household survival have resulted in a growing array of illegal transnational labor-migration strategies that are being structured by alternative global commodity chains. Export of women for the sex trade has been led by transnational organizations that have high capital to establish market strategies to sell sexual services. The transnationalization of production and consumption in the sex trade is grounded in the transnational migration of reproductive labor, and these workers are increasingly integrated into global commodity chains that merge illicit and legal capitalist enterprises and intermediaries. Sex tourism delivers customers to "exotic" destinations to consume sexual services, and sex trafficking is organized as an underground source of cheap laborers for places of sexual consumption.

Through two very different conceptual approaches of senior scholars with significant accumulated research, Part VI brings social reproduction and worker and household resistance to the center of commodity chain analysis in both the core and the Global South. Social reproduction encompasses "the material social practices through which people reproduce themselves on a daily and generational basis and through which the social relations and material bases of capitalism are renewed" (Katz 2001: 709). Marx (1990: vol. 1) conceptualized the value of labor power in terms of the means of subsistence that were necessary for the maintenance of the entire worker household. For social reproduction of households and communities to occur, "socially necessary wages" must accrue to workers that are sufficient to cover the current survival needs of households, as well as costs involved in generational reproduction of future workers. Even when wage rates provide for maintenance of a single worker in a capitalist enterprise situated in the contemporary Global South, this income is not sufficient to support the entire household. Furthermore, capitalists externalize to households and to public budgets the costs associated with generational labor reproduction and community recovery after ecological degradation, loss of natural resources needed for future subsistence, and the accumulation of hazards from export agriculture, fishing, aquaculture, mining, and manufacturing. As several case studies in this book demonstrate, modern capitalists are threatening Global South social reproduction through the labor and resource-extraction strategies they implement within their commodity chains.

However, global capitalism is structured around an artificial division between the economy and social reproduction. Consequently, "the arena of social reproduction is where much of the toll of globalized capitalist production can be witnessed" (Katz 2001: 710) because neoliberal states have gutted public and human services in national budgets to implement development strategies that prioritize economic growth over human well-being. Despite these crises in both the Global North and the Global South, commodity chain analyses ignore the arena of social reproduction, which becomes "the missing figure in current globalization debates" (Katz 2001: 710). Moreover, gender inequalities have characterized international advocacy of broader labor rights for Global South workers, so that activism has occurred to the exclusion of calls for action on the social reproductive threats that disproportionately affect women (Vosko 2004; F. Robinson 2006). According to Ruth Pearson (2004: 618), we need conceptually to "link international inequalities with the specific contributions of women to international trade while emphasizing how the sexual division of labour still gives women overwhelming responsibility for reproductive tasks at all levels of society."

In Chapter 12, Dave Broad revisits two decades of scholarship about how decomposition of industrial commodity chains in the neoliberal era has altered labor patterns and threatened social reproduction for working-class households at the center. He argues that the prediction of an inevitable proletarianization of labor has not proved historically correct and that twenty-first-century labor is being increasingly informalized at the core. He emphasizes that as capital frees itself from full-time proletarian labor and reasserts the historical norm of semiproletarian labor, worker households must absorb the uncertainties and identify nonwaged alternatives to proletarian livelihoods. At the same time, households are faced with elimination of labor rights and public social reproduction benefits. However, the capitalist push for cheaper labor and cuts in social safety nets will have an unexpected contradictory effect. He concludes that the informal sector is a breeding ground for resistance in both core and periphery and that such struggles are likely to become a labor hallmark of the twenty-first century.

In Chapter 13, Marina Prieto-Carrón re-examines fourteen years of research among Nicaraguan maquiladoras. She employs women's ethnographic accounts to demonstrate that the divisions between production and social reproduction are not clear cut. Moreover, she is convinced that the division between the productive and the reproductive arenas is no clearer in the labor rights struggle than it is in women's working lives. She calls for feminist commodity chain analysis that recognizes and rethinks the intersections among women's paid work in export-commodity production, their multiple forms of formal, informal and unpaid work, social reproduction, and worker rights. Violations of women's rights in the workplace are usually mirrored and reinforced in households. In addition, labor rights are shaped by gender-based societal norms. By exploring the holistic social reproductive approach of a grassroots women's organization, she argues that labor rights activism needs to be gendered in three ways.

FUTURE RESEARCH DIRECTIONS

This book offers a variety of conceptual guideposts and case studies that will aid novices and more senior scholars as they identity the kinds of research questions and methodologies that they can employ to bring gender, women and households into their commodity and value chain analyses. This introduction has been designed to direct the attention of researchers to (1) past oversights of the field that have left gaps in the scholarly literature that need to be addressed, (2) crucial conceptual issues that can stimulate research questions, and (3) scholars and previous studies that can serve as exemplars to be emulated. For both research and classroom use, we have made an extensive effort to develop a bibliography that encompasses the cumulative scholarship that incorporates gender into the fields of commodity and value chain analysis.

All told, the authors of the essays in this collection have conducted more than one hundred years of historical and contemporary research about in export-production systems, and their work spans every continent of the globe. Each of us is ready to respond to inquiries and to offer intellectual and methodological advice about research projects that will incorporate women and households. As our case studies demonstrate, one does not need to be an "expert" in feminist theory to bring women and households into commodity chain analyses. Because so few gendered commodity and value chain analyses have been developed to date, there is a great deal of room for attention to geographic areas and categories of women who have been overlooked. This is indeed an arena of scholarship that is open to cutting-edge contributions. However, researchers will need to push their thinking beyond a mechanistic search for economic value that can be easily found in corporate and public account books. As Jennifer Bair (2011: 196) observes, a majority of global value chain research "focuses on how actors within the chain can capture more value, but work within this tradition too rarely interrogates how that value is defined. . . . Ironically, then, for a framework that is ostensibly focused on the creative capture of value, value has been something of a black box within this approach. While value chain researchers may, like Pandora, have good reason to keep this box closed, it is by looking inside that we can begin to produce a better sociology of development."

We urge readers to think outside the "closed boxes" that make up so many diagrams of commodity chains and (1) to see undocumented waged and nonwaged women's work, (2) to seek out the ways in which nonwaged workers and households embed hidden value in commodities through unpaid and underpaid labor and inputs, (3) to reveal gendered production costs that are externalized to households and communities, and (4) to pinpoint the ways in which global production networks (as well as the decomposition of global commodity chains) threaten social reproduction of households and communities and often trigger resistance. Most of all, this collective of scholars hopes that readers will construct future projects in line with the call of Jane Collins to "recover some of what neoclassical economics makes us forget: living, breathing, gendered and raced bodies working under social relations that exploit them" (Chapter 1).

PART I FEMINIST CRITIQUES AND ADVANCES OF COMMODITY CHAIN ANALYSIS

CHAPTER ONE

A Feminist Approach to Overcoming the Closed Boxes of the Commodity Chain

Jane Collins

Several years ago, Leslie McCall (2005: 772) posed this question: "What happens when particular methods become conflated with particular philosophies of science [in ways that] prevent freer flow of knowledge?" She was writing about the faithful and nearly monogamous relationship between quantitative sociological methods and positivism. But it is possible to raise the same question about the way in which business frameworks steeped in marginalist economics have hijacked the study of commodity chains. Has the study of commodity chains become so conflated with the philosophies of science that underpin neoclassical economics that we can no longer use them for other, more subversive ends? What are the prospects and possible models for critical versions of commodity chain analysis?

THE "BLACK BOX" OF THE COMMODITY

A quote from cultural critic Susan Willis (1991: 52) sums up much that is fascinating about commodity chain research: "If, as Marx defined them, commodities are the containers of hidden relationships . . . those social relationships are all the more concealed by the movement of production to the Third World." Willis's statement points to the mystery that Marx argued was inherent in commodities—they are "containers of hidden social relations." Cracking them open—that is, examining the materiality of their production and circulation—allows us to recover some of what neoclassical economics makes us forget: living, breathing, gendered, and raced bodies working under social relations that exploit them; bodies living in households with persons who depend on them and on whom they depend; and bodies who enter into the work of making a living with liveliness, creativity, and skill.

Wilma Dunaway (2003b) maps this mystery beautifully. She argues that creative applications of commodity chain analysis can make visible not only the waged labor in fields or factories that gives a commodity its value, but also the unwaged labor in families and households that produced the laborers themselves. She also points to another mystery hidden in the commodity's black box that the method can help probe: the subsidy drawn from nature when capitalists and consumers destroy and deplete resources. Traditional economic analysis and those versions of commodity chain analysis that accept its premises consider both social reproductive labor and environmental costs "externalities." Dunaway (2003b: 196) suggests that commodity chain analysis, performed in other ways, can help make visible and begin to account for these "transfers of value that are embodied in commodities but do not show up in prices."

Willis's statement also points to the concealment of the social relationships that produce commodities when production and consumption are widely separated in space. Given that the larger context of the statement is a narrative that traces items in a grocery store to their origins, this is not a claim that distance makes the relationships unknowable, but rather an invitation to discern connection. Willis poses the challenge of tracking relationships across space and difference, of exploring our ties to people who may be unknown to us but who are linked to us across space and time by the goods that pass through our hands. The challenges of opening the black box of the commodity to reveal its hidden sources of value and of tracing these global connections can take us in a critical and liberatory direction that is distinct from the mechanistic approaches to commodity chain analysis that have gained popularity since the 1990s.

AN ALTERNATIVE HISTORY OF COMMODITY CHAIN APPROACHES

Most accounts of the origins of commodity chain analysis locate it within world-systems analysis and date its origins to articles published in the journal *Review of the Fernand Braudel Center* in 1977 and 1986 by Terence Hopkins and Immanuel Wallerstein. The influence of historian Fernand Braudel on world-systems theoreticians is well known, but Dunaway (2003b) has pointed to the study of commodities as a specific link between Braudel's history and Hopkins and Wallerstein's sociology. Braudel's (1982) historical work focused on the material organization of society. His first volume of *Civilization and Capitalism* is titled *The Structures of Everyday Life*, and each chapter focuses on a commodity, from daily bread, food and drink, houses, and clothes and fashion to technology and money. Dunaway (2003b: 189) argues that Braudel used commodities to highlight connections between daily life and the flow of history. She writes, "By examining commodity chains, we can do the type of research that Braudel . . . loved; we can simultaneously overlay the 'double register' of history: the global and the local."

Although Braudel's method of connecting local and global was un-doubtedly an influence, Wallerstein points to another reason for tracking the flow of commodities: "The whole commodity chain idea arose because Terry [Hopkins] and I wanted to show that what people were describing as very new in the late 20th century was part and parcel of the capitalist world-economy from the beginning. It was a way of spelling out our insis-tence that we were dealing with a world-economy and not with a series of autonomous states interacting."[1] In fact, the *Review* articles on commodity chains mapped the analytical strategy that Wallerstein (1974, 1980) had pursued in his series of books titled *The Modern World-System*, in which he detailed the role that flows of gold and silver, textiles, and lumber—as well as the availability of salt cod and herring—had played in successive waves of struggle for hegemony in the world-economy. This analytic focus on com-modities as a locus and a means of struggle for dominance was not unique to world-systems analysis but was shared by dependency theorists con-cerned with the Third World's entrapment in the export of primary prod-ucts and by Marxist theorists of unequal exchange (Love 1980).

Like most ideas, the commodity chain approach did not have a single point of origin. For anthropologists, the idea that one could understand how the global intersects with the local by tracing the flow of commodities derives from a very different body of work: the set of interlinked commod-ity studies carried out in the 1950s as part of Columbia University's People of Puerto Rico project. Headed by anthropologist Julian Steward, the proj-ect examined how Puerto Rican communities were connected to the global economy through the production and trade of specific commodities. Sidney Mintz began his research on sugar under the auspices of this project, as did Elena Padilla Seda. Eric Wolf studied coffee communities; Robert Manners, tobacco; and Raymond Scheele, the elite families of the island as a whole (Steward 1956). Jennifer Bair and Marion Werner (2011: 989, 993) have written that commodity chain analysis should begin to take into account "layered histories and uneven geographies of capitalist expansion, disin-vestment, and devaluation," as well as the "historically particular sets of social relations [that] secure commodity production."[2] If scholars broaden their view of antecedent work to include these earlier commodity studies, as well as subsequent anthropological research that has built on them, they gain a repository of historically grounded, sociologically rich models for conducting commodity chain analysis (e. g., Roseberry 1984; Mintz 1986; Striffler and Moberg 2004).

There are other traditions of commodity chain research as well. Jeffery Paige's *Agrarian Revolution* (1978) documents the impacts of different con-figurations of export agriculture on local class relations in postcolonial settings. His *Coffee and Power* (1998) shows how elite domination of a particular export crop structured the entire economic and political system of several Central American nations in the twentieth century. Paige says that the People of Puerto Rico project, especially the work of Wolf and Mintz (Steward 1956), "had a profound influence" on his work. He also notes the importance of Harold Innis's (1930, 1940) "staples thesis" of Canadian development and of Albert Hirschman's (1977, 1986) reinterpretation and extension of it in shaping his approach to the study of commodities.[3] All these authors emphasize social relations and power. Their work is steeped in history, and they actively interrogate the relationship between local and global. All of them incorporate economic, political, sociological, and even cultural aspects of life. What they do not account for very well are the multiple and intersecting dimensions of inequality that structure the flow of commodities.

Around 2000, a number of scholars studying commodity chains began to move in a very different direction. Projects like the Institute for Development Studies' Innovation and Value Chain Initiative and Duke University's Global Value Chains Initiative tried to standardize the method in ways that made it more consonant with traditional forms of economic and business analysis (Gereffi and Kaplinsky 2002). The mission statement of the Global Value Chains Initiative says that it "seeks to develop an industry-centric view of economic globalization" and "to test and develop the GVC framework with the aims of creating greater analytical precision, intellectual impact and policy relevance.[4]" One of the key essays (Gereffi, Humphrey, and Sturgeon 2005: 92) defining the Initiative's approach contains the following explanation.

> If a theory of value chain governance is to be useful to policy-makers, it should be parsimonious. It has to simplify and abstract from an extremely heterogeneous body of evidence. . . . Clearly history, institutions, geographic and social context . . . will influence how firms and groups of firms are linked in the global economy. . . . Our intention is to create the simplest framework that generates results relevant to real-world outcomes.

Focusing narrowly on competitiveness and industrial upgrading, these approaches have adopted the models and concepts of marginalist economics. In fact, Dunaway (2003b: 185) has suggested that they "have done the work of mainstream economists better than they do it themselves," with the end result that their analyses emphasize things rather than people. Jennifer Bair (2005) argues that this work represents a definitive break with the world-systems-inspired tradition, moving research on commodity chains away from historical and holistic analyses and toward a network-based, organizational approach. Given these projects to standardize commodity chain analysis and to render it "mainstream," what are the prospects for wresting back a version that is useful for exploring the gendered and raced mysteries of unaccounted value and global connection?

We do not have to start from scratch in this project because many feminist analysts of commodity chains have already paved the way. In a 2005 article, I argued that the burgeoning popularity of commodity chain approaches in the 1990s (before most of the aforementioned attempts to standardize and discipline the field) was a response to post-structuralism's critique of grand theories of development, which faulted the economism, determinism, and Western bias of Marxist and Weberian-influenced "theories of everything." As a result of taking to heart this critique, many scholars—particularly feminists—were left casting about for ways to do research that addressed social and economic change in what might be called "realist" ways, but that did not seek simple models of causation, did not define everything in terms of its economic value, and did not make Western hegemony seem inevitable. At this juncture, many people saw commodity chain analysis as a way to study what Lourdes Gouveia (1997: 309) called "relatively durable macro-institutional arrangements," but with more room for contingency, agency, discourse, and culture. Jane Dixon (2002) used commodity chain analysis in this way in her work on chicken; Melanie DuPuis (2002), on milk; Laura Raynolds (2001), on bananas; Harriet Friedmann (1988) on grain and food aid; Priti Ramamurthy (2004), on cotton; Deborah Barndt, (2002) on the tomato; Jane Wills and Angela Hale (2005), on global textiles; Brenda Chalfin (2007), on shea butter; and Nicola Yeates (2009a), on global care chains. I tried to do this in my own research (Collins 2000, 2003) on grapes from northeastern Brazil and on the global garment industry.

Anna Tsing (2009: 149) explains with more precision how the analysis of what she calls value chains permits us to study the local operations of global capital. She suggests that studying such chains allows us to imagine the "bigness" of global capital without losing sight of its heterogeneity because value chains offer a model for "thinking simultaneously about global integration, on the one hand, and the formation of diverse niches, on the other." Commodity and value chain analyses are valuable research tools in three ways. First, they help us think through how capitalist firms adapt their production and commerce to local conditions and how corporations make use of local inequalities to reduce the costs of labor. Second, they offer a model of global capitalist projects that takes into account their engagement with local economies and cultures. Third, they allow scholars to focus their attention on questions of diversity within structures of power—diversity that is critical not only for capital's accumulation strategies but also for modes of resistance to capital's projects.

FEMINIST COMMODITY CHAIN ANALYSIS

What does feminist commodity chain analysis look like? It is not simply tracing the gendered effects of commodity production. As useful as this may be for some purposes, tracking the gender segmentation of the labor force in production or processing nodes and providing gender breakdowns of costs and returns at various points in the chain are not all that a feminist analysis can offer. Rather, as suggested earlier, feminist commodity chain research has the potential to open up the black box of the commodity in several ways, as well as to trace unexpected patterns of global connection.

The first way in which a critical feminist analysis can demystify commodities is by treating waged work, wherever it occurs along the chain, as a complex social relationship rather than as a simple cost. This means documenting not only the labor intensity of the production process, the number of jobs created, and the gender and ethnic composition of the workforce but also the nature of the labor process, the forms of workplace control, and the ways in which the needs of firms for a particular kind of labor at a particular price intersect with local social relations of gender and ethnicity. Wherever a global commodity chain touches down, it intersects with local social relations. As Patricia Fernandez-Kelly (1983: 101) wrote decades ago, when multinational firms employ local workers, they can accentuate and deepen existing gender and ethnic inequalities by harnessing them and enhancing the illusion of their naturalness, or they can contradict prevailing local notions of social order by introducing new divisions of labor and new notions of skill. As Tsing (2009: 150) puts it, "Supply chains don't merely use preexisting diversity; they also revitalize and create niche segregation. . . . Diversity forms part of the structure of capital rather than an inessential appendage."

In research on the global apparel industry (Collins 2003), I found that treating labor as a complex social relationship required examining how managers deployed paradoxical discourses of "skill" to map the vulnerability of potential workforces. It entailed listening to workers' stories about how new waves of global competition affected the pace of their labor and their wage bargain, and it involved observation of new systems of workplace control that achieved world-class quality standards in contexts of sweated labor and high turnover. The ethnographic documentation of these relationships contains an implicit critique of accounts that measure wage cost per unit of production or the "labor efficiency" of operations. It uncovers the active work that global firms do to access pools of low-wage workers and to maximize surplus extraction through intensifying the speed and quality of production. And it reveals the active efforts of workers to gain control over the pace of their work and other labor conditions and over the wage bargains and other deals they strike with the firm.

This kind of analysis is not relevant only to factory work. Feminist commodity chain researchers have been among the few to recognize that services also travel in global circuits. Nicola Yeates (2005a) and Rhacel Parrenas (2001) have investigated the migrant nannies, nurses, and domestics who participate in an international division of social reproductive labor. The commodity of care operates in complex relationships to other commodity chains. As Saskia Sassen (1996) and Pellow and Park (2002) have shown, the intensification of labor in high-end services can generate demand for low-waged service professions. As commodified care work becomes a larger part of the economic pie, the firms that organize its provision seek new strategies to reduce wage costs. The interpersonal labor of care has long been considered place bound and not subject to outsourcing, but recruiting immigrant workers can achieve the same ends by constituting a "deportable" and thus vulnerable workforce. Even low-wage workers in jobs with nonstandard work hours and no sick leave need to purchase care and services that substitute for their labor at home. This creates paradoxes of interest in which both wealthy and poor women depend on keeping wages for care work low (but poor women more so because they receive those low wages themselves). Standard commodity chain analysis has paid little attention to service-sector work, care work, or the complex relationships between manufacturing and service-sector commodities.

The second way in which feminist analysis can open up the black box of the commodity is by making the social reproduction of labor visible. The concept of the social reproduction of labor can be traced to Friedrich Engels (1972: 71), who wrote that material life has a "twofold character: on the one side, the production of the means of existence, of food, clothing and shelter and the tools necessary for production; on the other side, the production of human beings themselves, the propagation of the species." Feminists have reworked and elaborated this concept in their attempts to make visible many forms of unmeasured and unpaid domestic work involved in "the propagation of the species." The concept of social reproductive labor encompasses the activities necessary to keep households and communities functioning and allow them to send productive members out into the world. It includes the activities that reproduce and support individuals from day to day, as well as from year to year and across generations. Although researchers often gloss social reproduction as child care, it also includes care for the ill and the elderly, the work of consumption, cooking, cleaning, paying bills, talking to teachers and doctors, and dealing with landlords, creditors, and banks. It can involve, especially in times of high unemployment and low wages, activities that supplement wages by generating income, such as market gardening or babysitting, or that reduce the cost of living by substituting for purchases, such as gardening for home consumption or making clothes.

Some theorists have emphasized the ways in which these kinds of labor support capital accumulation. In fact, this was one of the contentious claims in the domestic-labor debates of the 1980s. Many voices in that debate argued that households provided unwaged services vital to the reproduction of capitalist workers, allowing employers to lower wage costs by indirectly exploiting the labor of women in the home. They suggested that nuclear families, with their Ozzie and Harriet division of labor, were a structural component of capital (e.g., Fox 1980: 143). In the 1990s, many feminists took issue with this view and emphasized instead the liberatory potential of social reproductive work. For example, Julie Graham and Katherine Gibson (1996: 258) complained that "non-capitalist forms of production, such as commodity production by self-employed workers or the production of household goods and services, are seen as somehow taking place within capital. Household production becomes subsumed to capital as capitalist 'reproduction.' Our lives are dripping with Capital. We cannot get outside. Capital; it has no outside."

Graham and Gibson preferred to understand social reproduction as creating alternative economic spaces in the interstices of capital, that is, alternative systems of value that invert and contest dominant measures. For example, they argued, we prize use values produced within the home for having more time spent on them, not less, as in capitalist competition. As Barbara Bradby (1984: 126) wrote in the 1980s: "A three-course meal has much more 'value' in domestic terms than a quick snack, a carefully ironed shirt more than one pulled directly from a tumble dryer." In this view, social reproductive labor operates outside the discipline of capitalist institutions and implements its own definitions of quality and value, even, in Graham and Gibson's (1996: 264) words, "enacting a local and proximate" variety of socialism.

Between these two perspectives is one that sees the social reproduction of labor as connected to and shaped by capital accumulation in important ways but also as having some autonomy. During the 1980s, the Fernand Braudel Center at Binghamton University took this approach in the work of its long-term household study panel. This group of scholars defined households as income-pooling units where social reproduction is accomplished; they argued that a household's contributions wax and wane in connection with economic cycles. In eras of economic contraction, characterized by high unemployment and low wages, self-provisioning becomes more important as household members seek alternatives to the purchase of commodities. As employment tightens and wages rise, the space of autonomous production contracts, and more of a household's living is obtained through the market. This approach suggests that although social reproductive labor cannot be fully understood apart from knowledge of how it is connected to capitalist accumulation and social relations, it is not rigidly determined by these domains. As Joan Smith (1984) points out, nonwage work is not only invisible in capitalist accounting procedures but also immune to the direct domination of capital. In its specificity, it draws on home-made formulations of value and practices of self-provisioning that may be deeply local or cosmopolitan, liberatory or regressive.

Of course, the movement of activities back and forth between the realm of the market and the realm of private social reproduction is neither simple nor painless. This kind of strategic movement depends on the creativity and ingenuity of laboring classes. As Smith (1988: 140) demonstrates, the ability of households to respond to economic downturn by self-provisioning is conditioned by a host of factors that include women's labor-force participation rates, fertility rates, the quality and types of jobs available, consumer debt, the availability of state supports, and the existence of the knowledge and social networks needed for subsistence provisioning. Comparing the 1930s with the 1970s and 1980s, she argues that much of the fungibility of waged and unwaged labor "has been destroyed. . . . Unwaged household labor has ceased to be an alternative to waged work and instead has become its necessary companion."

Wallerstein and Smith (1992) revealed the contradictions that can arise when households in different parts of the world-economy seek to adjust their mix of waged labor and self-provisioning, that is, their market and non-market strategies for social reproduction. Although their research was conducted mainly in the 1980s, it still resonates. A *New York Times* report about the increase in the U.S. poverty rate included the observation that over one-quarter of young people twenty-five to thirty-four years old were living with parents in 2010 and that over half of them would be living in poverty if they lived on their own. This kind of income pooling, together with the reconfigurations of market and nonmarket work it entails, is an example of the social reproductive labor hidden in commodities as diverse as a McDonald's hamburger and a Wal-Mart T-shirt (Tavernise 2011; US Census Bureau 2011).

The third way feminist commodity chain analysis opens up the black box of the commodity is by revealing the subsidy from nature. We all know that traditional modes of economic analysis do not count pollution of rivers and streams, the clear-cutting of forests, the creation of urban brownfields, and the extinction of species as costs. Marilyn Waring (1989: 23) was one of the first to point to the paradoxes of this view: the more a country destroys its tropical forests, the more value it creates; clean air and water are not measured as assets in any national accounting framework; and things we think of as destructive of value, like warfare and cleaning up after an oil spill, contribute to GDP. Waring linked the failure to value social reproductive labor with the failure to value landscape, clean air and water, biological diversity, and leisure. This feminist critique gained some official traction in the Commission on the Measurement of Economic Performance and Social Progress, where feminist economists Nancy Folbre and Bina Agarwal brought social reproduction to the table (Stiglitz, Sen, and Fitoussi 2010). Agarwal's (1986) research on fuelwood, Vandana Shiva's (1992) research on the Green Revolution, and Nancy Peluso's (1996) research on forestry can all be seen as examples of feminist commodity chain research that opens up this aspect of the commodity's mystery.

Finally, feminist commodity chain research offers new possibilities for tracking global connections. Following the path of a commodity from start to finish seems straightforward only if we accept as a given that the logic of connection among sites is purely economic. Feminist researchers have explored a broader set of connections. They have paid greater attention to the consumption end of the chain, exploring how the Global North's preferences shape the Global South's production regimes and how concepts such as modernity and purity have influenced production and regulation of commodities like milk. Feminist analyses have emphasized, as Anna Tsing (2004: 32) puts it, that "knowledge moves" and theories travel. Their work has paid greater attention to the connecting power of ideas, such as how notions of skill or docility have shaped global sourcing decisions, or how legal doctrines of corporate responsibility shape an industry's contracting practices. They have been less likely than researchers who draw on mainstream economics to begin their stories in global power centers and more likely to start at the (imagined) edges and work toward hegemonic locales. This move not only enhances the visibility of actors in less power-laden parts of the chain but also shifts our assumptions about where agency happens.

Feminist analysis seems more aware that the commodity chain is a fiction, a mnemonic device, and a rubric for organizing complex information rather than a "thing." In my commodity chain analysis of the apparel industry, I was profoundly influenced by a passage written by art critic and essayist John Berger (1974: 40), which I read at a moment when I felt hopelessly lost in the complexity of my ethnographic data and paralyzed by the difficulty of imposing some kind of coherent narrative structure on the many things that mattered. Berger was writing about the problems of grappling with complexity in the late modern period, and especially the difficulty of telling a story sequentially as if it were simply unfolding in time. He observed, "This is because we are too aware of what is continually traversing the story laterally. That is to say, instead of being aware of a point as an infinitely small part of a straight line, we are aware of it as an infinitely small part of an infinite number of lines."

Scholars like Gary Gereffi value simplification in commodity chain analysis and subtract history and social context in order to create the most parsimonious framework possible, but feminists have remained more aware of this "star of lines"—the vectors of causality and meaning that traverse the story laterally. Pausing at the point of production to journey outside the factory gate and to explore the mysteries of social reproduction is to follow one of those lateral lines that is rich with significance for many commodity stories. Another line is tracking the circulation of gender ideologies and exploring the congruences and clashes between managers and laboring communities. These projects would be excised from an economist's version of commodity chain analysis, but they are part and parcel of a feminist version.

• • •

To paraphrase a statement of political philosopher Nancy Fraser (1989: 127), gender runs like pink and blue threads through every commodity chain, structuring production and consumption, invention and desire. Gender lies at the intersection of use value and exchange value—the place where social reproductive labor enters and leaves the market. I have argued that critical feminist versions of commodity chain analysis allow us to hold on to knowledge about global connection while delving deep into local processes that constitute and are constituted by them. Critical feminist analyses take us into the mysteries of value and the hidden social relations that sustain global capitalism. They have the potential to bring externalities to the center, to create new measures of value, and to critically engage global processes generating inequality. To answer Leslie McCall's (2005) question, they are too valuable and too politically powerful to leave to those who would use commodity chain analyses to improve business performance. The world's women need commodity chain analysts to map the global processes of capital accumulation that structure the inequalities they confront on a daily basis.

CHAPTER TWO

Feminist Commodity Chain Analysis

A FRAMEWORK TO CONCEPTUALIZE VALUE AND
INTERPRET PERPLEXITY

Priti Ramamurthy

Early one morning in the summer of 2010, I went to Railampadu village in southern India, eager to meet my perennially cheerful and spirited friend, Jamulamma, only to find her lying in a heap on the floor of her front porch. Something was very wrong. She arose crying. Sanjanna, her husband, had died just six days earlier. As he stood on the roadside waiting to take a bus to arrange his younger son's marriage, he had been killed by a speeding motorcyclist. As we grieved and shared stories of him over the next few hours, I could not help but notice that Jamulamma was wearing a polyester sari. The sari recalled a conversation Jamulamma and I had had in 1999. I asked her then why women like her who were formerly of untouchable caste, were working more often as landless, agricultural laborers in the expanding cotton fields surrounding the village but were wearing cotton saris less. She had replied, "How do I know? You tell me. Do the farmers tell us these things? Do the traders tell us these things? Do we have education to know these things?" Then, after a pause, she asked, "Who gains? Rehman [the village pesticide dealer] gains. [Textile] mill people gain. City people gain. That's who gains. I like cotton cloth. It breathes. Absorbs." After another and longer silence, she pointed to her polyester sari and continued, "This poonam, it heats up under the sun, it burns the body and boils up inside of me. It's not good for a person's health. It stinks with body sweat. It's like paper. It blows [showing how it slips from her breast, immodestly]. Why buy it? It's cheap."[1] Jamulamma had gone on to tell me, "Now only old women wear those coarse 'control' cotton saris [the low-cost, hand-loomed cotton saris that are subsidized by the state to keep handloom weavers fed]. Poonams are modern. They are brightly colored and do not fade. But they cling to the body." Still later she had added, "What else will we wear? We work in the field all day, in the sun, in the rain. Poonams don't tear. They don't fade. They don't crumple. Dirt and mud just wash away. They dry easily." Jamulamma's perplexity about her consumption of polyester saris—both desired and hated, both modern and of unhealthy and unknowable future —is an example of a more widespread phenomenon, a condition, I suggest, that is useful in thinking about commodities and their global peregrinations in capitalist circuits.

My own perplexity over Jamulamma's polyester poonam is related to one of my most cherished memories of fieldwork in 1999. Egged on by their sisters-in-law, two widows gaily dressed themselves in the polyester saris they were not supposed to wear because poonams are considered too bright, too colorful, too clingy, and, all in all, just too sexy for widows, who are desexualized in the normative gender order. I recall the interlude as a joyful moment of female sociality, a respite from grueling work routines, and a form of resistance to the normative gender order. Eleven years later, however, here was Jamulamma, a widow now, wearing a polyester sari. Had normative gender regimes shifted for the better, so that widows were no longer censured if they wore polyester saris? Were poonams no longer signifying sexualized objects? Had the Indian multinational company that made polyester succeeded in making poonams the only option for poor rural women? How do we make sense of our perplexity as feminist ethnographers when we are faced with sadness, small pleasures, big questions, and seemingly little resistance to the global production and consumption of commodities?

In this essay, I reflect on my conceptualization of feminist commodity chain analysis as a methodology to track how value is created in global capitalist circuits of production and consumption, and I seek to apprehend and to demystify the perplexity that the generation of surplus value produces, often in surprising ways and in excess of the logic of capital. Feminist commodity chain analysis enables scholars to account for why people desire modern things and find them pleasurable and why they consent to producing modern things in modern ways, even if they are troubled, unsure, and hesitant about these new social practices. The essay is organized in three sections. First, I define feminist commodity chain analysis and discuss my ethnographic approach. Second, I differentiate feminist commodity chain analysis from "realist" global commodity chain analysis. The third section lays out the main elements and theoretical genealogies of feminist commodity chain analyses. The perplexity of people as they produce and consume commodities is foregrounded throughout this section to suggest how we may approach questions of capitalist modernity and scholarly engagement as feminist researchers. I also provide examples from my research to illustrate the application of feminist commodity chain methodology.

DEFINITION AND METHODOLOGY

Feminist commodity chain analysis is a method for researchers (1) to pinpoint and investigate the different nodes of a global commodity chain in which women are key agents, (2) to understand how gender and sexual ideologies structure social relations and code value in the production and consumption of commodities, and (3) to track how value is created, extracted, and distributed in commodity circuits so as to accomplish the social reproduction of labor and of capital. My primary methodology for doing feminist commodity chain research has been ethnography. The ethnographer observes human cultural and material interactions slowly, over many years, from close enough but at a remove from immediacy to maintain adjacency. Its very "untimeliness" enables us to grasp the contingencies of the present and the ways in which the present comes to be through the past, at least the relatively recent historic past (Rees 2008: 8–11). Fernand Braudel (2012: 243, 271) clarifies these multiple temporalities.

> Whether we are dealing with the past or present, an awareness of the plurality of temporalities is indispensable to a common methodology of the sciences. . . . The temporalities that we differentiate are bound together. It is not so much duration that is the creation of our mind, but the splitting up of this duration. And yet these fragments come together again. . . Hence, to enter mutually into one of these temporalities is to be part of all of them.

Consequently, ethnography is always belated and derivative, relying as it does on discussions of other discussions and memories of discussions. At least initially, we can make sense of such discussions only through some sort of epistemic collaboration, as the opening account of my conversations with Jamulamma illustrates. An ethnographer's acceptance of fieldwork as being always unfinished and ongoing is what gives ethnography its sense of emergence and possibility. In the process of my fieldwork, I have been surprised, again and again, by the open-endedness of commodity chains and by the perplexity of people who are puzzled by the experiential contradictions of capitalism as it textures and complicates their everyday lives. When it calls attention to the perplexity that derives from living in multiple temporalities, feminist commodity chain analysis can be characterized as ethnography speaking back to empirical theorizations of global commodity chains.

In this essay, I reflect on more than two decades of ethnographic research in villages in the Raichur doab, the dry land strip between the Krishna and Tungabhadra Rivers in the southwestern Telengana region of the southern Indian state of Andhra Pradesh (Ramamurthy 2000, 2003, 2004, 2010, 2011). This research is part of a larger, long-term project about gender, technology, globalization, and agrarian change. Grounded in secondary sources and in close readings of the economic and cultural texts of advertisements, websites, and government and corporate reports, my historical research supplements the ethnography. I have focused on two commodity chains: (1) the cotton commodity chain, which consists of cotton textiles and garments (especially Madras shirts), cotton fiber, and cottonseeds (which are manually manufactured and marketed to cotton-fiber farmers each season) and (2) the polyester and poonam sari chain.[2]

A FEMINIST CRITIQUE OF "REALIST" COMMODITY CHAIN ANALYSIS

World-systems theorists Terence Hopkins and Immanuel Wallerstein (1986: 159) define a commodity chain as a "network of labor and production processes whose end result is a finished product," and they are interested in determining which actors control, appropriate, and distribute surplus value. Gereffi and Korzeniewicz (1994) usefully track "value added," the amount by which the value of an article is increased at each stage of its production.[3] Their approach delineates a process of production that transcends national boundaries, and they specify the networks that make the finished product possible. By identifying where and how value is added, they examine the spatial features of economic globalization and the new institutional relationships that enable it at different geographic and organizational scales. Their central focus is the reorganization of production salient to contemporary capitalism and, in particular, the shift from nation-based development agendas to strategies enacted by multinational corporations. They reveal the drivers or lead firms that control the process of integration across national boundaries and determine how upgrading takes place intra- and intersectorally.[4] Consequently, their approaches distinguish between commodity chains that are "producer-driven" and those that are "buyer-driven." These realist analysts underscore why historical deliberations on globalization are important, and they suggest methodologies that can be applied to recognize linkages and scales of analysis beyond specific places and nation-states. Moreover, their understanding of governance is defined in terms of the changing relationships among institutions, the state, and different kinds of transnational corporations (Gereffi 2001).

Despite their research innovations, most researchers who apply these approaches have excluded the gendered aspects of commodity chains (see the Introduction to this book). At a very basic level of analysis, there is a compelling case for the integration of female workers into any investigation of commodity chains. My critique begins with the absence of an accounting for labor, specifically women's labor, in the "new international division of labor" that has accompanied the "trade-led globalization" described by realist commodity chain analysts. I see four ways in which this absence manifests itself. First, the pattern of industrialization emphasized in many of these commodity chain constructs has been "light" manufacturing that is "female-led as much as export led" (Joekes 1987: 19). More women than men work in these labor-intensive, export-oriented sectors, such as the garment, electronics, and footwear industries that fueled the growth of the Asian newly industrializing countries (South Korea, Malaysia, Singapore, Taiwan, and Thailand) in the 1970s and 1980s and later Bangladesh, Brazil, China, Mauritius, Mexico, Sri Lanka, and South Africa.[5] Since the 1990s, there has also been significant feminization of agriculture. Export-oriented agriculture has triggered the cultivation of nontraditional crops (especially fruits, vegetables, horticultural products, and biofuel sources) that have displaced traditional colonial plantation commodities, such as tea, coffee, cacao, tobacco, rubber, and sugar. Women and girls are disproportionately represented among the workers who generate these agricultural exports. In addition, the feminization of agriculture is well documented in own-account cultivation, in contract farming, and in the growing numbers of female wage laborers.[6] Furthermore, the global service and care sectors (particularly domestic service and nursing) disproportionately employ females (Nakano-Glenn 1992; Hondagneu-Sotelo and Avila 1997; Parrenas 2001; Chapter 10 in this book).

Second, most realist commodity chain analyses ignore impacts of globalization on women's work, even though such changes have been documented by other scholars. Many scholars and international organizations now emphasize the extent to which women are economically active in all regions of the world (United Nations 2003). Equally important, the conditions of irregularity, casualization, and insecurity that once distinguished "women's work" from "men's work" now characterize many kinds of labor, whether female or not (Werlhof 1983, 1984; Standing 1989). In my research in rural India, for example, I have documented that the labor conditions of children and men are being feminized in smallholder agriculture (Ramamurthy 2010).

Third, there is a lack of attention in realist commodity chain analysis to how states and transnational corporations deploy racial and gender ideologies to facilitate their production and labor strategies. On the one hand, the widely diverse gender, racial, and cultural politics of states and corporations form ideological underpinnings for their economic agendas, and they shape the inequalities of global commodity flows (Enloe 1990). On the other hand, gender ideologies are integrated into (and often altered by) corporate and state export agendas. The classic research of Elson and Pearson (1981) demonstrates that gender is transformed in unpredictable ways by production processes in global assembly lines. Gender ideologies have been intensified or recomposed in some instances and decomposed in others (Pearson 1998). In my research on Japanese and Indian textile mills (Ramamurthy 2000), an Indian multinational (Ramamurthy 2003), a U.S. multinational (Ramamurthy 2004), and Indian and U.S. agricultural biotechnology companies (Ramamurthy 2011), I have examined how gender ideologies permeate their self-representations and are central to the reproduction of capital on an extended scale.

Fourth, women and gender are silenced because realist commodity chain analysts fail to recognize the importance of the household as an institution critical to global commodity production and circulation. States that promote export-oriented production and overseas migration have selectively adopted "familial" ideologies that prioritize national economic growth over household security and survival. In the process, the costs and burdens of global and national economic restructuring are passed on to women in their households. When national structural adjustment policies "liberalize" economies in favor of private capital, common ecological resources are redistributed away from households, and public social services (including government subsidies for food and health care) are cut. Women have borne the brunt of these negative impacts and have responded by increasing their unpaid and undercompensated work in the informal economy, expanding their reproductive labor to enable household survival, and migrating transnationally to secure new income sources (Beneria and Feldman 1992; Elson 1995a; Parrenas 2001).

To respond to these critiques, realist commodity chain analysis could quite easily incorporate gender by adding an analysis of women's labor and of gender ideologies at each node of the commodity chain and at institutional scales that include the household. Indeed, this is the approach I took in an early exposition of feminist commodity chain analysis (Ramamurthy 2000). Realist commodity chain analysis is deeply flawed by its failure to account quantitatively for women's work and for households, but it is also weakened by its lack of attention to the qualitative elements of the lives of actors in these vast networks. For that reason, I draw a sharp distinction between what I term "realist" commodity chain analysis and feminist commodity chain research. In addition to the conceptual shortcomings I have previously discussed, I choose the term "realist" to describe these forms of global commodity chain analysis because they ignore that which is imagined or dreamed. In contrast, feminist commodity chain research is concerned both with real lives and with how they are imagined. It questions forms of knowledge construction that assume that reality is completely knowable and can be explained by empirical analysis alone. Consequently, I now offer a more radical approach and propose "feminist" commodity chain analysis as an alternative rather than an additive to "realist" commodity chain analysis.

CONCEPTUAL ELEMENTS OF FEMINIST COMMODITY CHAIN ANALYSIS

My conceptualization of feminist commodity chains has six elements. The first element of feminist commodity chain analysis is a reflexivity that seeks to destabilize master narratives of globalization that naturalize gendered and racialized constructions of difference and reproduce binaries between the First World and the Third World. Feminist literature on gender and racial difference and postcolonial and Third World feminism (A. Davis 1981; hooks 1984, 1992; Mohanty, Russo, and Torres 1991; Grewal and Kaplan 1994; Alexander and Mohanty 1997) alert us to the masculinist undertones of realist commodity chain theorizations, like Gereffi's (2001) characterization of the "seminal" contributions of corporate "drivers." In contrast to such realist approaches, feminist commodity chain analysis does not assume a linear path to progress. Nor does a feminist analysis assume a unilinear flow of investments from the First World to the Third World or from cores to peripheries or a unidirectional flow of commodities from peripheries to cores. Instead, feminist commodity chain analysis starts from the assumption that global commodity chains, as connections across times and places, are neither linear nor unidirectional nor closed.

In my study of the polyester sari commodity chain, for example, I found that the Indian multinational Reliance Corporation manufactures the polyester in poonam saris from imported oil and with imported technology and capital. The company codes its workers as male, transnational "knowledge workers" and simultaneously claims to be nationalist in two spatialities. By asserting its presence as a new global Indian company, it announces India's arrival on the world stage as an emerging powerhouse. This corporate stance coincides with the story that the government of India tells the world as evidence of the success of the country's economic liberalization. By supplying good-quality, cheap polyester saris for mass consumption, Reliance Corporation can claim that it fulfills the promises of national development by providing more adequately for the poor than the old socialist Indian state ever managed to do. In my ethnographic research, I found that women wearers of polyester saris, like Jamulamma, are attracted by Reliance's development discourse about the affordability and durability of polyester saris, but they are also perplexed by their consumption, critical of it, and troubled by their alienation from the cotton they grow. Simultaneously, they continue to desire fine and exorbitantly priced cotton saris, but they disparage the huge quantities of pesticides sprayed on cotton and the high cost of poisoning to fieldworkers. (This was before the widespread adoption of Bt cotton in the first decade of the twenty-first century, which has, arguably, decreased pesticide use.)[7] Even as they ridicule the dumpy, outdated hand-loomed cotton saris that the socialist state once provided to the poor, Jamulamma and her peers reflect on the age, class, and caste borders that are constructed, policed, and transgressed through their polyester sari wear. Polyester saris are meaningful to them as markers of modernity. These garments are youthful, feminine, sensual, and sexy because they are colorful, bright, soft, and clingy. They follow the contour of the female body much better than thick cotton saris. However, older women, especially widows, are supposed to be asexual, so they are chastised for wearing polyester saris. At least, they used to be some years ago, but this gender constraint may be changing, as Jamulamma's story may reveal.

The second element of feminist commodity chain analysis is an exploration of how gendered individual and collective identities are constituted through the process of production. Simply put, production generates more than material commodities. The theoretical genealogies of this conceptualization can be found in the feminist literature about value and gender performativity (Spivak 1987; Butler 1990, 1993; Joseph 1998; Raynolds 2001). Feminist commodity chain analysis examines how gendering takes place within and through the process of production, as well as how gendering dynamically changes and is changed by the process. This approach also highlights how processes of gendering articulate with other social systems of differentiation, like age, ethnicity, race, caste, and class.

For example, cottonseed production in rural southern India depends on the symbolic gender order at two levels: (1) the sexualization of plants that are manually cross-pollinated and (2) the gendered division of labor that defines female and male as differentially suited to various kinds of agricultural work. The floral sex work of cotton cross-pollination is based on and enables heteronormative and unequal gender relations that are considered "normal" in other social domains. Until about 2000, this floral sex work was ideologically constructed to be fit only for children (especially girls) to do. Because of complex economic and historical transformations since 2000, Dalit or formerly untouchable-caste men in smallholder households have crossed that gender barrier and are now doing what was once considered female work. In the process, new ideologies of masculinity (linked to being "efficient workers" who are "technical" or technologically savvy) have emerged. At the same time, however, these men steadfastly refuse to take on "housework," which they obstinately continue to define as "women's work." Even though they have chosen to withdraw from wage labor, men and women are perplexed by the new work regimes of cottonseed production. Sanjamma, a woman in her fifties, was remarkably proud of her sons for their high cottonseed productivity levels, but she complained that the interminable work of cross-pollinating cotton flowers left her with no time at all to visit her sisters for celebrations. Indeed, she feared that she would "only see them at their funerals." On the one hand, Yeshepu, a Dalit man in his thirties, exultantly contrasted the dignity of own-account cultivation of cottonseed with many prior years as an indentured laborer for others. On the other hand, he was perplexed that he remained "a coolie" to the seed company. He is a contract farmer for a company that controls every aspect of his production of cottonseeds. For day-to-day household consumption, he takes credit advances from the seed company against his future production.

The third element of feminist commodity chain analysis is the importance of gender in theorizing class in nonessentialist terms. The genealogies of theorizing gender as a structure, an identity, and an "analytic of power" derive from post-structuralist feminists (e.g., Scott 1986). This contribution of feminist commodity chain analysis illuminates the tendency in the most political versions of realist commodity chain analysis for an essential identity, "the working class," to sneak back in as the basis of a common political ground for all laborers worldwide. In his celebrated study of sugar, Sidney Mintz (1986) acknowledges the importance of gender, but only as supplementary to his exploration of class.[8] Although he demonstrates how sugar was a time and money saver that made possible women's entry into the working classes in Britain, he ignores how the same processes produced "working-class woman" differently in the Caribbean than in Britain. Through a comparative study of Meiji Japan and colonial India in the late nineteenth and early twentieth centuries, I show that dependence on imperial Britain for milled cotton cloth drew on and produced very different conceptions of "woman" in the two countries, with very different consequences for females in the two settings. In Japan, young unmarried daughters who were sent to become mill workers broke gender conventions to join militant movements. In contrast, only married Indian women were allowed to work outside their households, but they were gradually eased out of factory work by "rationalization" that led to the banning of women from night shifts. In contemporary southern India, my ethnographic research has documented changes in the search for good daughters-in-law. Alongside old criteria for daughters-in-law who value familialism (i.e., devotion to the patrilineal, patrilocal, multigenerational joint family) are new criteria for strong and efficient floral sex workers. Indeed, mothers-in-law now demand to know "how much 'service' in cross-pollination" a prospective daughter-in-law has accumulated. But mothers-in-law in joint families are perplexed when sons leave the joint family to produce cottonseed for themselves, and they blame their daughters-in-law for their sons' newfound autonomy from patrilineal families. "Perplexity" is the term that best describes the shock they express when they recognize how their own labor has become so commodified in the new regime. As Maniamma, a female in her fifties, put it, "Thanks, god, for these strong arms. [As long as] I have strength in them, and can do this crossing work, my daughters-in-law will feed me." Despite her careful selection of her sons' spouses, Maniamma could not be sure that these "modern" daughters-in-law would take care of her in her old age.

The fourth element of feminist commodity chain analysis is a recognition of the constitutive link between production and consumption as "a unity of opposites," following Marx (1990: 2: 118–25). One of the main characteristics of the new regime of "flexible accumulation" is the ability of producers to cater to ever-changing consumer fads and to different classes of consumers worldwide (Harvey 1989). However, realist commodity chain analysts have not explored questions of household consumption or of the diverse relationships between consumption and production in different parts of the world (Gereffi and Korzeniewicz 1994: 12). Feminist commodity chain analysis directs attention to consumption as a necessary mapping of how commodities connect people in distant locations and enable them to imagine and perform their places in the world. The theoretical genealogies of this focus are the Frankfurt school of cultural theorists (Adorno 1991), recent theorizations of the link between consumerism and neoliberalism (Appadurai 1986; Comaroff and Comaroff 2000), and transnational feminist cultural studies (Kaplan 1995; Grewal 1999).

Through analysis of a 1995 Land's End brochure, I have demonstrated that "Madras" shirts are consumed in the United States not only for their intrinsic material qualities but also because they ideologically promise to bring global uplift to the poor Indian families who produce them (Ramamurthy 2004). In the villages of southern India where the cotton for Madras shirts is cultivated, employers and families distribute to workers modern consumer goods produced by multinational corporations (e.g., processed cookies and movies for children, poonams, skin lightening creams, face powder, and shampoo for daughters-in-law). These incentives are intended to motivate workers to meet the modern, unrelenting production schedule in the cotton fields and to tie their labor to production for the entire season. Nevertheless, these items of consumption and the social practices of giving them are imagined as tokens of "affection" for children and female laborers. For instance, Sarojamma was perplexed that her daughters-in-law were not willing to work as hard as she, even though she provided them modern poonams, shampoo, powders, and creams. On the one hand, she criticized her daughters-in-law for caring only about the balance in her bank account. On the other hand, she posited that her fulfillment of their consumer desires was a stark contrast to the patriarchal oppression she suffered at the hands of her own mother-in-law, a female she feared and obeyed to a much greater extent than her daughters-in-law "respected" her. Consequently, love, care, and desire are simultaneously joined to the exploitation of labor and the reformulation of patriarchy.

The fifth element of feminist commodity chain analysis is the recognition that poor, rural producers desire the products of their labor and imagine themselves as global, cosmopolitan citizens when they generate commodities for global markets. The empirical methodologies of realist commodity chain analysis ignore the unpredictable and generative loose-endedness of global commodity circuits and obscure the myriad ways in which people make meaning of and for themselves. In short, realist commodity chain analysts typically do not entertain the idea that producers may wish for the products they produce. For instance, Mintz (1986) ignores the desires of Caribbean sugar producers while providing a fascinating discussion of the creation of British working-class tastes for sugar. As I document in my research, marginal rural Indians are neither dupes nor creative appropriators of global commodities. Consumption materializes gendered identities and codes bodies through class and other social differentiations, but it is also a vehicle for uplifting and dignifying modes of social being. Consumer advertising can serve as a pedagogy of modernity (Modern Girl Research Group 2008). This theorization contrasts with those versions of "global feminism" that represent Third World women in universalist terms through First World consumption of their products.[9] For example, a 1995 Land's End brochure exhibits an image of a weaver and his wife who loom the "madras" cloth. The accompanying text suggests that consuming madras shirts will not just feel good but will also help this man and his family. Pity for the man is evoked by quoting him as saying he is too poor to wear the cloth he weaves, but in the accompanying image he is wearing "madras." Sounding more like a global citizen than a supplicant, he says, "Sometimes I think about the people in America who will wear it. I wish always a good relationship between India and America."

The sixth element of feminist commodity chain analysis is its focus on the household as an institution that produces and consumes global commodities while ensuring social reproduction of laborers. The genealogies of theorizing households through an institutional analysis derive from feminist development studies (Kabeer 1994). To make labor of various kinds available for commodity production and consumption, households diversify livelihoods, pool incomes, and spread risk in multiple ways (see Chapter 3). Feminist commodity chain analysis emphasizes the gendered spatial and temporal organization of households (e.g., how marriage and kinship patterns are changing, whether multiple generations are coresident, who migrates to earn wages). Feminist commodity chain analysis also theorizes the household as a discursively and materially contested space. The genealogies of theorizing the household as a contested space derive from feminist approaches to agrarian transitions (Friedmann 1978; Carney and Watts 1991; Hart 1992). Capitalism constantly needs labor that, unlike wage labor, is not free to move because it is spatially tied through relationships of debt, the threat of violence, or kinship. Unfree labor is not simply a phenomenon that can be relegated to "traditional" spaces that have not transitioned to advanced industrial capitalism. Nor is it a dying relic of the past. Rather, it is a predominant feature of contemporary global capitalism (Brass 1999). Feminist commodity chain analysis reads struggles over meanings and normative gender ideologies within households as situated within larger political and economic processes of change, specifically, at the interface of "free" and "unfree" labor.

In an essay (Ramamurthy 2011) about the hybrid-cottonseed chain, I use feminist commodity chain analysis to study the ways in which marriage and kinship relations in households are being commodified, reorganized, and contested. The households in question are smallholders who primarily rely on unpaid family labor to cultivate less than two acres of irrigated land to produce cottonseed. I characterize these households as "smallholder capitalists" because they (1) are deeply embedded in the market economy and (2) have recently become linked to the global chain of agricultural biotechnologies through contracts to produce seeds for Indian and foreign multinational companies. It is noteworthy that men in these households have stopped hiring out their labor for daily wages in order to take up own-account cottonseed cultivation. This labor reallocation is occurring even though cottonseed production is so risky that the returns are often minimal or negative. Many men, like Yeshepu, are perplexed by their desire to pursue this direction and even call it "ghasam," or indenture to the seed companies. However, their withdrawal from wage labor becomes understandable when it is set against the backdrop of longer histories of caste oppression and migration. Lower-caste men hope for improved quality of life through modern commodities and for better futures for their children, however uncertain achieving success may actually be in practice.

Cottonseed production is so labor intensive that it is difficult for smallholders to meet labor demands solely with unpaid family labor. Doing so requires a joint household that encompasses parents, multiple coresident sons, and their wives and children. Two, and sometimes three, generations of laborers in smallholder households are floral sex workers. In addition to the search for daughters-in-law who are skilled at floral sex work, there is a willingness to negotiate a lower dowry payment for a prospective daughter-in-law who is a good fieldworker.

Tensions are exacerbated between coresident sisters-in-law and mothers-in-law who provide unequal contributions to fieldwork and to household reproductive work. Sometimes these uneven labor allocations precipitate a rupture in the joint household. For example, Thimakka complained that her younger coresident sister-in-law had done less work than other females in their joint household. Once she was cultivating her own field, she "was working from sun up to sun down. If only she had shown this mindfulness then," Thimakka insisted, "it would have been good for us all. . . . We'd have none of this outstanding debt to clear." Thus smallholders not only must consent to labor in new and demanding ways but also must commit to govern themselves with greater degrees of self-discipline. Consequently, parents express uneasiness about arranging marriages of daughters and nieces with men who belong to cottonseed households. Maniamma, for instance, refused to acquiesce to her brother's request that his daughter marry her son, although such consanguineous marriage arrangements are common. She argued that she could not bear to see her niece suffer from such hard fieldwork. She was also wary of how the other coresident daughters-in-law would behave if the niece was permitted to do less fieldwork. Other parents told stories of paying higher dowries for their daughters in order to keep them out of households that would require them to do floral sex work. The burden of maintaining joint households falls on mothers-in-law, who employ labor incentives that range from cajoling daughters-in-law with modern consumer goods to sending them to their natal homes for respites. Nevertheless, mothers-in-law like Sarojamma are perplexed when daughters-in-law reduce familialism to monetary transactions. She philosophized,

> The world, mankind, society has become like that. They see cinemas and have learnt from them. Aren't those representations and this life? No one thinks about the difference. There's no thought [by daughters-in-law] to care for their in-laws. Even if they don't listen to us, we have some affection for them. However much we earn, we can't take it with us. Can neither eat it, nor take it. When someone dies, only the goodness and badness of their lives linger.

Feminist commodity chain analysis conceptualizes commodities as things that work materially and semiotically in global capitalist circuits to accomplish the social reproduction of labor and of capital. It is an interpretive method that apprehends the perplexity that people experience in thousands of nodes of commodity chains, often in surprising, unpredictable ways that exceed the logic of capital. Feminist commodity chain analysis calls for (1) an accounting for female labor at each node of a commodity chain; (2) the recognition that the conditions of all labor, not just women's work, can be feminized; and (3) openness to the unpredictability of the relationship between patriarchal gender ideologies and the workings of capitalism.

Feminist commodity chain analysis asks questions, such as the following, that are typically ignored by realist commodity chain analysis.

1. How does difference, especially gender difference in relation to other forms of difference (e.g., national or racial), inscribe the policies and governmental programs of states and corporations that create the infrastructure for global commodity circuits?
2. How do policies and programs both attract and perplex the workers involved in global commodity circuits?
3. How do global commodity circuits alter gendered individual and collective identities?
4. How does the performance of gender change dynamically when people are conscripted into new work regimes?
5. How do poor producers imagine, desire, and inhabit the modern products of their labor through gendered identities and codes?
6. How are production and consumption linked in people's lives and imaginaries?
7. Are modern consumption practices being deployed in the service of modern production practices? How do the pedagogies of modernity generate global cosmopolitanism and perplexity?
8. How are the experiential contradictions of capitalism being expressed as perplexity? For example, how are love, care, and desire being joined to the exploitation of labor and the reformulations of patriarchy?
9. How is gender as an identity and as a structure analytically useful in the exploration of power and class formation in nonessentialist terms?
10. What are the gendered aspects of commodity chains that fracture in unpredictable ways?
11. How is the household an institution for the production and consumption of labor and of global commodities?
12. How do the perplexing contestations of labor, meanings, and ideologies in households index and contest the contradictions of capitalist modernity?

Perplexity is an affect that is experienced personally, but it is also a more generalized subjective condition of contemporary capitalism. The epistemology and language to express the duality between the inherent contradictions of capitalism and the subjective experiences of it are drawn from the cultural field. Consequently, perplexity will be experienced diversely in different locations, depending on how histories, cultural production, and uneven political and economic geographies converge and diverge. Moreover, perplexity is what scholars feel when they are confronted with contradictions about their own participation in the production and consumption of feminist scholarship in global circuits, like this essay. Our scholarly perplexity offers an opening for us to engage the puzzlement of others alongside our own search for understanding. However, we will need to recognize that we will probably not build new conceptual alliances quickly. Nor will it be easy to facilitate epistemic collaboration around the difficult interpretive work of untangling relations of power and determining accountability within commodity chains.

PART II CONCEPTUALIZING SEMIPROLETARIANIZED HOUSEHOLDS AND WORKERS IN COMMODITY CHAINS

CHAPTER THREE

Through the Portal of the Household

CONCEPTUALIZING WOMEN'S SUBSIDIES
TO COMMODITY CHAINS

Wilma A. Dunaway

To begin, I would like to take a brief journey back in time. It is 1750 in a Cherokee village in the North Carolina colony on the Atlantic coast of North America. Over the past fifty years, deerskins have become the most valuable commodities exported to western Europe from this place (Dunaway 1994). For two months, Huntetsa and her clan sisters have knelt in the distant forest to rip the hides from forty slain deer. After each kill, the women have transported the raw skins on their backs, with their infants strapped in cradleboards across their breasts. For every deer that her husband kills, Huntetsa will labor thirty to fifty hours to process its skin for export to British leather manufacturers. Home from the hunting, she must join the other women to work village crops and to make a long trek to the British fort, where they will trade ginseng, baskets, and crafts for imported Scottish salt and Dutch hatchets.

Leaders of the matrilineal clans worry about the future. The deerskin trade has become a putting-out system that has trapped these indigenous Americans in debt bondage. Traders advance imported goods against future hunts, but deer are almost extinct. Every spring, the British governor at Charleston, South Carolina, instructs traders to demand Cherokee lands as payment for accumulated debts. British officials refuse to negotiate those transactions with matrilineal clans and thereby destroy the historical political rights of women. Clan leaders express mounting concern that women are so preoccupied with deerskin processing that they have little time to cultivate and store subsistence crops. As their villages become more deeply embedded in the global fur trade, Cherokee households suffer rising malnutrition, lose many traditional livelihoods, and become dependent on imported tools and foods.

Now, let us fast-forward 240 years. When contemporary analysts mapped this deerskin commodity chain, they drew boxes that identified male hunters, traders, commission merchants, industrialists, and European waged laborers. Absent from those boxes were the Cherokee women and households that provided a majority of the labor and hidden inputs and absorbed the economic, political, cultural, and ecological costs externalized by producers of this commodity. Indeed, scholars have ignored the centrality of households and women to export production in all the contexts I have explored over the past two decades. My accumulated household research encompasses different historical eras in Western and non-Western settings, including eighteenth-century indigenous Americans, eighteenth- and nineteenth-century Appalachians, enslaved African Americans, colonized African peasants, and contemporary Philippine peasant fishers (Dunaway 1994, 1995, 1996, 2003a, 2003b, 2008, 2010; Dunaway and Macabuac 2007). What all my research contexts have in common is that the non-waged and unpaid labor of households was sucked into the world-economy in ways that commodity chain analysts typically fail to see (see the Introduction). Despite these scholarly failures, the commodity chain concept is one of the most promising tools through which we can integrate households and women into research on globalized production processes.

GOAL OF THIS ESSAY

My goal is to offer conceptual guideposts that will help researchers see more clearly how they can investigate the variety of forms of household labor that are embedded in commodity chains. When scholars conduct research outside their own cultures, we cannot assume that structures and social positions hold the same meanings that they do in our own societies. Most especially, researchers will have a difficult time perceiving Global South households and housewives correctly if they do not put aside certain conceptual blinders derived from Western social science. To help with that process, I will offer some ideas that can help researchers unlearn, decenter, and rethink their Western notions about households and housewives. Then I will lay out a conceptual road map that researchers can employ to bring households and women into their commodity chain analyses.

What Is a Household?

All workers are reproduced and sustained within the many cultural variants of households. Every visible documented worker in a commodity chain resides in or is linked to a household that sustains him or her through non-waged livelihoods. But what is a household? Western scholarly literature that emphasizes the household as having its own economy outside capitalism provides little guidance in understanding this concept broadly enough to encompass the diversities that are evident over historical time or across cultures and ethnic groups.[1] Western feminism focuses on nuclear families in which the inequitable roles of wives and husbands are explored (e.g.,

Matthaei 1982), but a majority of the world's households differ sharply from these narrow vantage points. Scholars need to unlearn their tendency to see the world through the lens of Western peculiarities by moving their conceptualizations away from a singular search for waged laborers or for units that consist of parents and children (Werlhof 1983). On the basis of my diverse research, I think of a household as a unit in which members inequitably pool and redistribute labor, resources, and survival strategies that are grounded in both unpaid and paid (nonwaged and waged) income sources. Although many households worldwide are organized around marriages, a household does not always contain individuals who are related by kinship ties. Nor should we think of a household as necessarily having all its members located in the same space. On the one hand, members can be migratory laborers, either nationally or transnationally. On the other hand, households do not survive alone because they are linked to a support network. For example, a single Global South waged worker is provisioned by three to ten households (Dalla Costa and Dalla Costa 1999).

Although I cannot exhaust all the possible household composition patterns, I mention a few examples to help readers decenter their thinking. A household can be a polygamous African compound in which several wives and sets of children provide unpaid and paid labor to produce export crops, informal-sector goods, and survival needs (Rodney 1982; Dunaway 2010). Many households have far-reaching ties to clans, so their women do not function like the isolated housewives depicted so frequently in Western feminist theories (Dunaway 1994). Among Brazilian and Indian street children, there are composite, nonkin groups that behave like households to pool labor and resources within an inequitable hierarchy grounded in gender and age differences (Scheper-Hughes 1991). A household can be a commune of ostracized Indian widows (Mies 1981; Harriss-White 2003), or it can be a family that has restructured itself to accommodate the long-term transnational labor migration of a spouse (Matthei 1996; Parrenas 2000; Yeates 2004b). And we should not overlook the great numbers of nonwaged peasant sharecropping households that are tied to commodity chains through debt bondage to landlord-exporters (Deere 1990; Brass 1999; Bryceson, Kay, and Mooij 2000; Spieldoch 2007).

Who Is a Housewife?

We must also overcome the limitations of theories that conceptualize the housewife as a unidimensional female constrained inside her household, away from public work arenas. Grounded in class, racial, and cultural biases, the "separate-spheres" claims of Western feminist theory emphasize patriarchal gender conventions that limit powerless women to their households and reserve public income earning for males (e.g., Matthaei 1982).[2] In contrast, Maria Mies, Veronika Bennholdt-Thomsen, and Claudia von Werlhof (1988) argue that housewifization is the process that obscures the economic value of household contributions to capital accumulation (Werlhof 1983; Mies 1986). Invisible unpaid labor has been a structural necessity of capitalism to such an extent that household-based work, not waged labor, has been predominant in the modern world-system (Werlhof 1984: 140–41).

So who is the housewife, and how do we recognize this actor? Although a majority of housewives are females who are disadvantaged by structural sexism, a housewife does not have to be a woman. For example, we observe a housewife in the African male teenager who is a waged worker in export agriculture in order to raise his siblings after parental deaths from AIDS (Schlemmer 2000). The housewife is that individual who combines unpaid reproductive and provisioning work with an array of paid inputs into capitalist commodity production. To a much greater extent than other household members, this individual juggles a diverse portfolio of forms of productive and reproductive, paid and unpaid labor that cycle throughout the day, must be periodically altered, and must be expanded during crises. On a daily basis, the housewife must resolve time, resource, and cultural conflicts between reproductive unpaid work and productive income-earning labor. This individual stands out in the household because she or he works longer hours and self-exploits for the survival of the unit to a greater extent than other members. Even though this labor is necessary for human survival and capitalist cost cutting, much of this person's workload is economically devalued and socially invisible (Werlhof 1983).

More than anything else in the twenty-first century, what distinguishes the housewife is the role this individual plays to sustain the household and capitalism simultaneously. Maria Mies (2010: 166–67) explains that housewifization of work "is still the most profitable type of labour for capital accumulation, even today in our globalised economy. . . . Housework will become capital's most desired and optimal form of labour relations. . . . Men too will be forced to carry out 'housewifised' work." These housewives are not isolated at home and focusing on the invisible and economically devalued work of caregiving and provisioning of families; they are also employed at economically valuable work that remains invisible. Off the formal books and outside public accounting, these housewives combine invisible reproductive work with hidden production for export. Examples are the Indian lacemakers described by Mies (1981), the home-based subcontractors who work as outsourced labor for Asian firms (Carr, Chen, and Tate 2000), the women who supply unpaid labor to their husbands' contract farming throughout Asia (United Nations 2003), the contemporary Turkish wives who supply unpaid labor to make their husband's small textile shops profitable (see Chapter 6), and the Philippine peasant fishers whose households are trapped in debt bondage to the traders and exporters who control seafood commodity chains (see Chapter 9).

Conceptual Guideposts to Bring Households into Commodity Chain Analysis

Households represent millions of structural units that enable commodity chains to conceal the economic benefits they acquire from workers. If capitalists compensated households fully for production inputs, prices would be driven too high for most commodities to be economically competitive (see Chapter 4). For that reason, a commodity chain is more than a long string of spatial points at which scholars prioritize firms or distant buyers and sellers. Figure 3.1 encapsulates the model I have developed from my accumulated research. If we are to think outside the closed boxes of the typical commodity chain map, as Jane Collins urges in Chapter 1, we need to move beyond firms, buyers, or marketing corporations as our units of analysis. In the sections that follow, I will explore two questions that help us integrate households into commodity chain analysis: (1) What labor subsidies do households and women provide to commodity chains? (2) What invisible costs do commodity chains externalize to households and women?

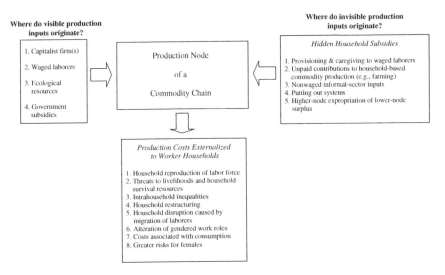

Figure 3.1. Surplus expropriation from households by the production node of a commodity chain

HIDDEN LABOR SUBSIDIES FROM SEMIPROLETARIANIZED
HOUSEHOLDS

More than anything else, a commodity chain is an interconnected network
of nodes at which households are directly and indirectly exploited to permit
surplus extraction through five types of hidden subsidies. The first level of
hidden subsidies occurs because the vast majority of the world's workers
have never been fully transformed into the wage laborers that both Marx
(1990: vol. 1) and mainstream development theories predicted (Werlhof
1984; United Nations 1999). In reality, there are so many nonwaged workers in the world because proletarianization reduces profit levels in the capitalist world-economy (Frobel 1982). Thus "partiality of wage labor" is a
historical hallmark of the modern world-system (Wallerstein 1995b: 1), and
capitalists have never generated "households whose incomes are based entirely upon remuneration through the wage mechanism" (Stauth 1983:
189). Most Global South households "derive the bulk of the means of subsistence for their families from outside the wage economy" (Arrighi and Saul
1968: 149). In the twenty-first century, the numbers of nonwaged laborers are
growing faster than workers are being integrated into waged jobs (Tabak and
Crichlow 2000). As a result, most households merge erratic wages with resources acquired from nonwaged efforts.

Nonwaged inputs into commodity chains are "the great 'Other' of the
market" because capitalism lays a "veil of invisibility" over household-based
work (Blumberg 1979: 448). However, "the secret of all capitalist life" is
that unwaged labor supplies much of the surplus that capitalists accumulate
(Dalla Costa and Dalla Costa 1999: 176). In short, women's unpaid labor
serves to lower the value of labor power and to cheapen wage rates (Dalla
Costa and James 1970) such that both men and capitalists benefit directly
from unpaid household labor (Delphy 1976). Indeed, capitalists promote
the continued existence of semiproletarianized households because they
make possible two types of surplus appropriation: (1) "the lowest possible
wage" (Wallerstein 1995a: 91) and (2) the exploitation of "producers who
work without wages" (Werlhof 1984: 15). In both instances, exploitation is
defined as "the expropriation of surplus value" in which the worker produces greater surplus than she or he consumes (Folbre 1982: 318). These
semiproletarianized households serve two essential functions for commodity chains. On the one hand, they reduce the wage bills of the capitalist, who
does not have to pay the full cost of provisioning the labor force (Wallerstein 1995b). On the other hand, they enable capitalists to appropriate
surpluses that are generated by noncommodified and nonwaged workers
(Werlhof 1983). Because this household-based labor provides significant hidden subsidies to commodity chains, it is deeply integrated into the process of

capital accumulation (Brass 1999). Indeed, the various forms of nonwaged household labor "are not outside of surplus value production, but constitute the very foundation upon which this process can get started" (Mies 1986: 31). In short, households have been "pillars of accumulation" throughout the history of capitalism (Werlhof 1984: 19).

Unpaid Contributions to Capitalist Commodities

In reality, the semiproletarian household is a locus of production in which members simultaneously provision themselves and produce for the market (Wallerstein 1984). Consequently, the second category of hidden subsidies consists of unpaid labor contributions to capitalist commodity production that is based within households, for example, peasant fishing (see Chapter 9) or home-based textile production (see Chapter 6). Women and girls are more likely to be the unpaid workers in such family-based enterprises (United Nations 2003). Virtually every wife and most children are expected to provide labor to the market-oriented production of the husband, but that "family labor" is neither valued economically nor publicly documented (Boydston 1986). In agricultural and fishing households, for example, women's labor remains hidden behind that of adult males (Mies, Bennholdt-Thomsen, and Werlhof 1988; Dunaway and Macabuac 2007). A Philippine couple's recollection of a fishing trip provides an example of this type of invisible labor. While the wife was hauling up their net, sudden high winds and waves capsized the boat. She held on to floating paddles and worried about drowning, but she still instructed her husband to save their catch. While she flailed desperately in the water, he threw his body over their net filled with crabs, thinking that they might finally have a valuable export commodity that would bring them enough income to get out of debt (Illo and Polo 1990: 48–50). Despite such risks, this type of unpaid female worker is excluded from official accounts of inputs into export seafood production. Most policy makers and scholars claim that Philippine fishing is a male arena and that, more specifically, women do not fish in boats (MSU Naawan Foundation 2006).

Low-Paid Nonwaged Inputs into Capitalist Commodities

The third category of hidden subsidies occurs when households provide low-paid nonwaged inputs into commodity production. There can be direct and indirect flows into the production process from household provision pools and from the informal sector (Portes 1983). Women's crafts, ecological resources, and recycled garbage receive low prices when they are integrated into commodity production. Nonwaged household workers also supply foodstuffs, raw materials, and services that are absorbed into the commodity-production process. For example, nineteenth-century West Virginia households built barrels in which salt manufacturers exported their valuable commodity down the Ohio River to Cincinnati and New Orleans to support meatpacking factories and Lower South cotton plantations (Dunaway 1996). Early twentieth-century African housewives sold foods and clothing at cheap prices to company stores that, in turn, provisioned low-waged gold miners at exorbitant cost (Dunaway 2010). Contemporary Philippine fisher wives collect small wild fish and construct fishing gears that support fishponds and commercial fishing (Dunaway and Macabuac 2007).

Putting-Out Systems

The fourth category of hidden subsidies occurs when workers contract to undertake home-based production for commodity chains. Beneria and Floro (2002: 13) point out that "an increasing number of global firms and domestic enterprises have become involved with workers outside the 'traditional workplace' through the process of decentralization, outsourcing, and subcontracting, that extend the link between the formal and informal sectors. They have also tapped further into the seemingly abundant female supply of labor by creating new forms of 'putting out systems' whereby workers produce goods or perform tasks in their homes." For instance, much of early twenty-first-century Asian manufacturing integrates such low-paid household piecework, and many large core retailers acquire their cheap consumer goods through subcontracted homework (United Nations 2003). Such putting-out systems have been an enduring historical feature of capitalism (Littlefield and Reynolds 1990), and these labor arrangements are disproportionately feminized (Dangler 2000). Capitalists routinely integrate these nonwaged workers directly into their commodity chains by employing a wide array of labor mechanisms that range from home-based piecework (Chapter 6), contract farming, and sharecropping to debt-bondage systems that are controlled by capitalists, landlords, traders, or wholesalers who provide credit to households (Chapter 9). By employing putting-out mechanisms, capitalists can benefit from cheap nonwaged labor and inexpensive material inputs from households (Portes 1983; Beneria and Roldan 1987). Households assume many production costs, including the use of unpaid family laborers and the provision of unpaid inputs, such as equipment and electricity. Despite the significance of their labor inputs into commodity chains, most of these homeworkers are not counted either in national statistics or as part of the waged labor force (Carr, Chen, and Tate 2000; United Nations 2003).

Higher-Node Expropriation of Lower-Node Surplus

The fifth category of hidden subsidies occurs when households at lower nodes of a commodity chain subsidize capitalists or consumers at higher nodes. In effect, the commodity chain structures a network in which consumer and laborer households at higher nodes benefit from exploitation of households at lower nodes. For instance, half the nineteenth-century Appalachian population was malnourished and died younger than the national average. Still, those workers produced cheap exports that fed factory workers in England and the northeastern United States (Dunaway 1996). Colonized Africa's forced laborers died by the thousands while they were extracting the raw materials for rubber, gold, palm-oil, and mineral commodity chains that fueled industrial expansion in the United States and western Europe (Dunaway 2010). In the contemporary Philippine shrimp commodity chain, women provide cheap nonwaged inputs into seafoods that are exported to provision low-paid Chinese industrial workers. In this context, the threats to survival and livelihood experienced by peasant fishing households keep the global prices of shrimp low and permit working-class consumers to avoid the real costs of production (Dunaway and Macabuac 2007).

INVISIBLE COSTS EXTERNALIZED BY COMMODITY CHAINS TO HOUSEHOLDS

In addition to these hidden semiproletarian subsidies, capitalists maximize profits by externalizing production costs to households and to the ecosystems that provision them. In reality, capitalists externalize most of the real costs of commodity production. "Externalized costs are unseen and unpaid bills that . . . are part and parcel of normal capitalism, and they are to be found at every node/link of every commodity chain" (Wallerstein 1995b: 11). It is crucial to understand that capitalists do not stumble accidentally into or rarely use externalization strategies. Capitalists adopt these mechanisms purposely (Laffont 2008) because they comprehend that such strategies determine their degree of monopoly in obtaining cheap production inputs. Prices do not reflect the full costs of producing a commodity because the benefits of cost externalization are received free by capitalists and by consumers (Clelland 2012). While surpluses flow up commodity chains from the Global South, there is a downward transfer from the core of social risks and ecological entropy (Biel 2006) in the form of eight mechanisms of externalization.

Household Reproduction of Current and Future Labor Forces
Reproduction of the labor force may be the most significant category of costs that are absorbed by households. Let me stress that capitalists are just as aware as feminists of the economic value of having households pay for rearing, educating, and socializing their workers. Mainstream economists

recognize that capitalists keep their prices competitive because "human capital is self-productive," allowing employers to evade paying for these benefits (Terleckyj 1975: 230–31).[3] Moreover, university business schools routinely use textbooks that teach the next generation of capitalists to employ externalization of labor-force production as a cost-cutting mechanism. At the most fundamental level, capitalism transforms women into "the last link in a chain of exploitation, permitting by their unpaid labour the reproduction" of the work force (Mies, Bennholdt-Thomsen, and Werlhof 1988: 29). Despite their dependency on women's reproductive labor, capitalists externalize child rearing outside the realm of the economic in order to extract the hidden value of unpaid household labor (Folbre 1991; J. Nelson 1998). Labor that earns money in the capitalist workplace or marketplace is defined as "productive." Concomitantly, labor inside the household is devalued by the myth that it generates no surplus that can be appropriated (Wallerstein 1995a).

Consequently, the parasitic relationship between waged labor and household reproduction constitutes "the basis of all capitalist relations of production" (Bennholdt-Thomsen 1984: 266). Even though it is not priced in the marketplace, housework produces economic value, and its unwaged character makes it highly profitable.[4] The housewife's unpaid work is "embodied in the waged labor, and it is a direct input into production." Thus the housewife generates economic surpluses without selling her work time to capitalists. When she reproduces or cares for a waged household member, she makes available to the commodity chain free of charge her invisible, devalued mothering and caregiving (Boydston 1986: 21–22). In this way, "the extremely different conditions of work of the free wage laborer and the housewife constitute the two poles of a continuum of capitalist conditions of work relations and of production" (Werlhof 1984: 140). Through her reproductive labor, the housewife produces commodified labor power that a household member sells to a capitalist situated in a node of a commodity chain. In this sense, the obscured biological (re)productivity of the housewife is a prerequisite for the productivity of the waged laborer who is a visible part of a commodity chain (Mies 1986). By externalizing outside the range of production costs that labor that women and households undertake to reproduce, care for, and socialize waged workers, capitalists eliminate high costs from their operating budgets in order to be market competitive (Terleckyj 1975).

Capitalist Threats to Livelihoods and Household Survival

Even though it cannot grow without the hidden subsidies that accrue from households, capitalism threatens household survival and livelihoods by generating chronic scarcity of income and resources (Goldfrank, Goodman, and Szasz 1999).[5] In all the contexts I have studied, export commodity chains have concentrated control of land and ecological resources into the hands of a few large enterprises and have degraded ecosystems so extensively that food resources and livelihoods have been threatened for a majority of the households (Dunaway 1996, 2010; Dunaway and Macabuac 2007). In addition, capitalist enterprises employ a minority of Global South workers while "preventing the majority from entering the occupational niches that export-oriented economic policies foster." As a result, "workers are leaving waged employment and self-employment *at earlier moments* in their lives, and they are becoming disposable earlier and younger than in the past" (Gonzalez de la Rocha 2001: 92).

Through deep exploitation of households, commodity chains appropriate so much of workers' provisioning resources that workers cannot sustain themselves. As agricultural production has been increasingly integrated into world commodity chains, food self-sufficiency has declined sharply throughout the Global South. Capitalism "has always been unsustainable since it has assumed, from the start and continues to assume, extermination and hunger for an increasingly large part of humanity" (Dalla Costa and Dalla Costa 1999: 17). Peripheral countries now import two-thirds or more of the food needed for local consumption, and this importing raises the prices of basic survival needs above levels that most households can afford (Spieldoch 2007). Since 1990, the numbers of malnourished people in the world have risen, and per capita calorie intake has steadily declined in the Global South (Patnaik 2008).

Household Restructuring

The third category of externalized costs results when households are forced to restructure after they are integrated into commodity chains. Such household restructuring occurs in reaction to capitalist incorporation of a geographic area (Dunaway 1994), to offset the effects of the widening and deepening of the reach of commodity chains (UNRISD 2005; Dunaway and Macabuac 2007), or to survive the growth and crisis cycles of the world-economy (Wallerstein and Smith 1992; Gonzalez de la Rocha 2001). In reaction to cycles of the world-economy, Global South households repeatedly alter their composition (McGuire, Smith, and Martin 1986). In reaction to resource shortfalls, households engage in fosterage arrangements through which they relocate children to neighbors or kin to work for their subsistence (Rosas 2002; Dunaway and Macabuac 2007). Some households absorb ill or elderly extended kin to expand the pool of available income and resources (Dunaway and Macabuac 2007), or households may take in nonkin members to earn income from boarders or to acquire additional workers for home-based enterprises (Rosas 2002; Dunaway 2008). In the face of severe poverty or mounting debts, households may indenture their children (Dunaway 1996, 2010; Schlemmer 2000).

Household Disruption Caused by Labor Migration

In every historical era, commodity chains have destabilized households by removing members for labor migrations. In order to centralize capitalist labor forces in cities, capitalists depopulate rural areas, decompose households, and weaken their provisioning capacity (Goldfrank, Goodman, and Szasz 1999). Thus externalized costs result from the household disruption associated with labor migration (UNRISD 2005: 106). In colonial Africa, for instance, one-quarter of the population of every village was forced to migrate annually, and women in these households were left without adequate workers to produce subsistence or to meet local colonial tax quotas. To overcome these labor shortfalls, households sought credit from landlords, employers, and merchants and became entrapped in long-term debt bondage (Dunaway 2010). In the twenty-first century, two patterns of labor migration are fragmenting households over great distances. First, migration for income earning is increasing within most Global South countries. Second, women's reproductive work is being restructured internationally to shift the "care" work of affluent housewives onto peripheral women. Since 1980, the transnational migration of Global South women has led to significant alteration of motherhood through an international division of reproductive labor (Chapter 10). Through the international transfer of caregiving, reproductive labor of migrant domestic workers and nurses is removed from peripheral children to support more affluent women in other countries. In turn, the migrant women must transfer their child care and unpaid household labor to poorer females in their home countries (Parrenas 2000).

Alteration of Gendered Work Roles

The fifth externalized cost is the alteration of gendered work roles when households are integrated into commodity chains. Capitalists maximize profits through housewifization of workers without respect to gender (Werlhof 1984). During economic downturns, women take on more men's work in order to replace lost resources normally generated by husbands (Dunaway and Macabuac 2007). As capitalists target the cheap labor of Global South females, men are increasingly pushed out of income-earning opportunities (United Nations 2003). Of necessity, women's work is shifted to others, and this shift leads to the partial housewifization of husbands or children (Pearson 2000; Gonzalez de la Rocha 2001). However, the substitutes never assume the full housewife workload, and this causes longer work hours for women and resource shortfalls for households (Dunaway and Macabuac 2007).

Intrahousehold Inequalities

In order to manage resource scarcities caused by export production, households engage in two inequitable strategies. First, they practice "risk spreading" (Baker 1995: 126) through diversification of livelihoods into an ever-widening labor portfolio in which work is inequitably allocated (Haddad and Kanbur 1990). Because households reflect market values, waged laborers and male export producers contribute less total work toward household survival than their nonwaged peers (United Nations 2003).

> If at least one worker is engaged in wage labour, and surplus value is being expropriated from him, the total number of hours worked by family members will necessarily be greater than the total hours embodied in their total consumption bundle, because the wage worker is bringing home a contribution which embodies less hours than his work. Exploitation, in other words, comes home. But the burden of exploitation is not necessarily shared equally. (Folbre 1982: 322)

Even when wives provide significant income to their households, their contributions do not afford them enough leverage to persuade males to assist with housewifely work. When total paid and unpaid work hours are calculated, it is clear that women work longer hours and are active in a greater variety of forms of labor than males (Beneria and Roldan 1987). Especially during crises, households manage labor time through self-exploitation that is reflected in an intensified workload for females. Housewives take on the burden of double or triple work days, but males typically do not match the level of female contributions through the same degree of self-exploitation (Moser 1996; Rosas 2002).

The second household strategy is the inequitable pooling and distribution of resources. Even though males are overrepresented in income-earning jobs, women routinely contribute more of the total resource pool. Furthermore, women and men budget income differently. In many Global South households, husbands withhold part of their earnings and leave women to make up shortfalls (Dwyer and Bruce 1988). Women are expected to assume responsibility for the medical and educational expenditures of children, and crises do not necessarily cause husbands to lower their leisure expenditures. Indeed, "husbands and wives differ in the definition of the basic necessities of the family complex, their consumption priorities, the way in which income should be distributed, and the proportion to be allocated for the common fund" (Beneria and Roldan 1987: 123). When resources are scarce, women prioritize the nutrition of family members to a greater extent than husbands. Thus income-earning women spend three-quarters of their funds on family food, compared with one-quarter of male income. Moreover, increased female income leads to additional household spending on food, but an increase in male income does not necessarily expand survival resources (UNICEF 2007).

In addition, females receive an inequitable share of the total pool, especially food. The hierarchical order for resource allocation is especially marked in differential access to protein. Capitalism externalizes to mothers the nutritional battering of children associated with resource scarcities in about one-third of peripheral countries (Scheper-Hughes 1991). Wage- or income-earning males (followed by wage-earning older offspring) take precedence over nonproductive children, but the mother almost always receives the lowest allocation. During food shortages, nonproductive children do not receive an equitable share in comparison with adult or teen males, and girls receive the lowest allocations. In addition, income-earning males are more likely to receive health care than pregnant women or sick children (Scheper-Hughes 1991). When resources are limited, households are more likely to invest in the education of boys. Households are more likely to terminate schooling of girls when additional workers are needed (UNICEF 2007). As a result, women account for 70 percent of the world's illiterate adults (United Nations 2004: 37). When resources are scarce, female fetuses are more frequently aborted, and infanticide and selective neglect are most often directed toward girls (Wadley 1993). Household power struggles over allocation of labor and resources are evidenced by the rising incidence of domestic violence. Worldwide, male violence toward women and children is highest during (1) economic downturns and (2) when women become pregnant. In addition, domestic violence increases in contexts in which women contribute more household income than males (UNRISD 2005: 106).

In short, the household is a unit of human capital accumulation, but it is also a space in which the housewives who sustain that life receive an inequitable share of resources because their work is devalued. Why do we see such ruthless behaviors in this unit of human nurture? In reality, the household is a capitalist structure in which conflicting interests lead to power struggles over scarce labor time and resources. Because market relations intervene in their internal processes, households exhibit patterns of exploitation and competition (Ulshofer 1983: 191). Much like the marketplace, households do not democratically allocate resources or labor time. Instead, decision making is manipulated by the most powerful (Wilk 1987). Because they reflect the capitalist valorization of income-earning labor, households allocate an inequitable share of their resources to waged workers (Wilk 1987). Parallel to class and racial divisions in capitalist societies, households determine work assignments and resource access using a hierarchical order based on income-earning capacity, gender, and age, with the male wage earners at the top and mothers falling last (Hoodfar 1984).

Greater Risks for Females

The greater risks that females suffer represent a significant category of externalized costs because gender differences constitute many of the starkest inequalities within commodity chains. A majority of women control very little wealth, and there is a worldwide trend toward feminization of poverty (United Nations 1999). Females are disproportionately endangered by the ecological degradation that accompanies capitalist development, and they are the household members who provide the labor needed to care for those made ill by environmental risks or resource depletion (Shiva 1988; Thomas 1990).

Integration into commodity chains brings destructive economic results for women. In the face of capitalist expansion, Global South women lose artisan jobs and local markets to imports (Mies, Bennholdt-Thomsen, and Werlhof 1988). To keep production costs low, capitalists are breaking the bodies of peripheral girls and young women at an alarming rate. By eliminating safety equipment and sanitary working conditions, corporations externalize to females the health costs of industrial injuries and disabilities, work-related diseases, and the higher incidence of birth defects and mother mortality due to exposure to chemicals and industrial waste (Chapter 7). Most of these women live in countries with grossly inadequate health-care services (United Nations 1999). To complicate matters, domestic violence increases when capitalist enterprises target female workers and exclude males (Mies 1986).

Costs Associated with Consumption of Capitalist Commodities

The final category consists of externalized costs associated with consumption. Capitalists "maintain households of a shape and form that will create an optimal market for wage-goods" (Wallerstein and Dickinson 1982: 441). Through the work she does to locate and purchase, assemble, and use commodities, the consumer-housewife does unpaid labor that lowers the prices of capitalist goods (Mies 1986). As poor countries become increasingly dependent on food imports, women must work every day to locate scarce goods at affordable prices, transport them home, and prepare them for consumption. At the same time, the household faces rising prices for foods that were previously obtained through household provisioning or informal-sector activities (Werlhof 2007). In addition, households and communities absorb any health risks triggered by consumption, as well as the ecological degradation caused by waste disposal. Moreover, reallocation of household labor time toward the pursuit of capitalist goods leads to the decline of subsistence and handicraft production and causes loss of survival resources and livelihoods (Arrighi and Saul 1968; Dunaway 2010).

• • •

Because of the parasitic relationship between waged labor and housewifization, the vast majority of the world's workers are situated in semiproletarian households. On the one hand, these households are the loci of human capital accumulation because they reproduce and invest their limited resources in the future labor supply. On the other hand, they represent millions of structural units that enable capitalists to conceal their systematic extraction of surpluses from workers and from women. In spite of the immiseration capitalism causes, these units persist through their management of scarce labor time and resources, their restructuring of household boundaries, and their alteration of gendered labor roles. In their internal dynamics, these households mirror the structural contradictions of capitalism. Consequently, they are characterized by inequities and by power struggles that result in females working longer hours for which they are allocated fewer resources than males.

Full mapping of a commodity chain cannot occur until scholars bring in unpaid and nonwaged work that capitalists make invisible in order to keep consumer prices cheap (Chapter 4). To construct a more accurate depiction of those hidden benefits, scholars must enter through the doorway of the household. It is beyond this portal that we find the forgotten housewife, working long hours to contribute surpluses that do not appear in the account books of the capitalist enterprise or in the government's tally of the gross national product. Capitalists keep production costs low and prices cheap through two types of hidden structural mechanisms. First, households provide to commodity chains a wealthfare system derived from concealed subsidies that accrue from five structural levels of labor and surplus extraction. Second, capitalists externalize production costs to worker households through eight mechanisms.

Formal history obliterates the everyday hardships that poor people suffer. To paraphrase Anton Chekhov, the happy capitalist feels at ease only when the semiproletarians bear their burdens in silence. Unless the capitalist can exploit them with little public scrutiny, the level of surplus extraction will be endangered.[6] In the early twenty-first century, the semiproletarian household in poor countries is at greater risk of extinction than ever before. We have reached the point, warns a United Nations study, at which households are no longer able to reproduce themselves because the current situation is unfavorable for the operation of household survival mechanisms (Gonzalez de la Rocha 2001: 89). If that is true, we must ask ourselves: How, then, can capitalism survive? The invisible labor of the household and the housewife are structural necessities of capitalism. Indeed, the secret of all capitalist life is that unpaid labor supplies much of the surplus "dark value" that capitalists accumulate and that consumers enjoy through cheap goods (Chapter 4).

CHAPTER FOUR

Unpaid Labor as Dark Value in Global Commodity Chains

Donald A. Clelland

I ask you to redirect your thinking away from claims of "value added" at various nodes of a global production network. Contrary to that view, commodity chains are surplus-extraction chains that are grounded in massive transfers of what I term "dark value." The drain of dark value, which includes vast hidden extractions of unpaid household and informal-sector labor, is a necessary and intrinsic component of commodity chains. Exploitation is "the expropriation of surplus value" from a worker or household that produces greater surplus than she, he, or it consumes (Folbre 1982: 318). This exploitation is the dark value I seek to conceptualize and measure. At every node of a commodity chain, dark value is embedded as a hidden surplus that is externalized from prices. Consequently, commodity chains are dark-value-extraction chains. These value drains benefit not only the capitalists who have constructed the world-system but also core consumers of all classes and thus legitimize the structure of the system. In the first three sections of this essay, I will conceptualize (1) surplus and surplus drain in the modern world-system, (2) extraction of dark value through commodity chains, and (3) mechanisms of dark-value extraction from households. By exploring the Brazilian coffee commodity chain in the final section, I explain how both capitalists and consumers extract dark value.

WHAT ARE SURPLUSES IN THE MODERN WORLD-SYSTEM?

Let me begin by returning to the roots of the foundational question: what is meant by the concept "modern world-system"? The history of modern capitalism is the history of the appropriations of surpluses by elites who replaced political mechanisms with the extraction of surpluses by means of commodities. Such transfers occur both within and across political boundaries. In other words, surplus drain is a driving force in the explanation of the origins and reproduction of the world-system as we know it. These surplus drains occur through control over the means of monopoly power that allows the capitalist to exploit labor, ecological resources, knowledge, and technology (Clelland 2012). Through the process of commodification, the modern world-system transfers a large portion of the global surplus from the periphery to the core. However, capitalists first expropriate much of that aggregated surplus from peripheral households through hidden mechanisms that operate within commodity chains. In order to lay the basis for my argument about the linkages among uncosted household labor, dark value, and commodity chains, I need to revisit a few foundational concepts.

What Is Surplus?

The first question that needs a brief review is what is meant by "surplus." Baran and Sweezy (1966: 29) define economic surplus as "the difference between what a society produces and the costs of producing it." In simplest terms, the surplus is the value of goods, services, and money that remains after the reproduction needs of any system have been met.[1] I am convinced that the groundbreaking work of Baran and Sweezy did not go far enough in its conceptual challenge and that scholars must push their ideas in five additional directions. First, the economic surplus should be viewed as a foundational component, not just of societies, but of firms, households, and the capitalist world-system as a whole. Each of these systems is driven toward continuous expansion of its surplus. Second, we need to pinpoint the origins of surpluses. On the one hand, surplus is extracted from any of the factors of production, not just from labor power (as in classical Marxism), but also from land, resources, energy, knowledge, technology, and capital. On the other hand, we must recognize that the bulk of surplus extraction is realized through degrees of monopoly (Kalecki 1954), not through the competitive markets emphasized by mainstream economists and classical Marxists. By degree of monopoly, I mean the control of any mechanism that reduces the costs of production or increases sales prices in variance from a fully competitive market. The capitalist world-economy is a degree-of-monopoly system because capitalists seek to avoid market competition through "competitive advantage." Third, we must rethink how we calculate surplus to reflect the points of origins of the hidden surpluses that capitalists expropriate to sustain their degrees of monopoly. In actuality, the total world surplus is far greater that the cumulative GDPs. To arrive at a realistic estimate of surplus, we must take into account the value of all reproductive costs. We should think of the modern world-system as an iceberg economy (Mies, Bennholdt-Thomsen, and Werlhof 1988) in which uncosted labor and resources make up the thicker submerged ice layers that are blocked from view beneath a thin top stratum that is counted as the visible official economy.

Fourth, we need to determine who collects the surplus, how it is expropriated, and how it is used. Because everyone wants a share, struggles to obtain the surplus are at the heart of real-world economics and politics. The capitalist world-system is structured to ensure the concentration of surplus into the hands of capitalists and state elites (in the form of profit, rents, interest, and taxes). On the one hand, these groups are motivated to expand the surplus in order to broaden their consumption of luxury goods. On the other hand, the key to the continuation of the world-system is reinvestment of surplus into expanded reproduction of the system, that is, accumulation. In addition, capitalists share part of the surplus with members of the managerial-professional class who perform the functions of capital and with segments of the working class (Wallerstein 1995a). Fifth, capitalists may surrender opportunities for surplus by passing on hidden surplus in the form of lower prices to commodity buyers. I will return to this key point later.

What Is Surplus Drain?

The second concept that needs to be revisited is "surplus drain."[2] Without surplus drains, there is no core, no periphery, no world-system as we know it (Clelland 2012). However, neither mainstream economists nor most Marxists have integrated surplus drain into their theories. The concept of international "economic drain" was central to parliamentary debates about the East India Company in the late eighteenth century and to the Indian independence movement beginning in the late nineteenth century (Karmakar 2001). However, these theories are generally rejected or ignored by orthodox Marxists and by mainstream economists and social scientists who employ the nation-state as their basic unit of analysis. Both classical and neoclassical economists make "free trade" and "equal trade" basic assumptions of their models and thus deny the importance of unequal exchange and asset seizure. In its focus on the industrial proletariat, the Marxist theory of revolution also ignores the importance of surplus drain for understanding capitalism. One is reminded of the thought of Upton Sinclair (1934: 107) from a century ago: "It is difficult to get a man to understand something when his salary depends on his not understanding it." Sinclair's notion is directly applicable to mainstream economists and can be applied to those Marxists whose revolution depends on their not understanding it. Before Baran (1957), forty years of Marxist and heterodox thought about development, imperialism, and dependency largely produced blockage theories whose underlying assumptions were not that different from those of modernization theories. Classical Marxist theories of imperialism did not lead to the discovery of surplus drain.[3] These were largely theories of emerging national corporate and financial monopolies gaining control of states that then violently competed for the control of colonies that supplied access to markets, resources, and cheap labor (Fieldhouse 1961). In other words, these were theories about the core. In the 1940s, heterodox Latin American economists argued that the world was structured as an industrial core and an agricultural periphery, and the terms of trade between the sectors deteriorated for the periphery. Surplus drain, however, was viewed as a consequence of differing levels of productivity gains rather than as a long-term project of the core. Economic Commission for Latin America and the more radical *dependistas* viewed peripheries as dependent on the core and emphasized the numerous ways in which the core blocked peripheral development, still with little clear conceptualization of surplus drain (Love 1980; Chilcote 1982; Prebisch 1984).

Surplus-drain theories are neo-Marxist extrapolations from Marx's (1990: vol. 3) theory of surplus value. Paul Baran (1957) introduced the concept of economic surplus (as distinct from surplus value) as key to Marxist analysis of economic growth, and he contended that loss of portions of the economic surplus is an important cause of underdevelopment. Andre Gunder Frank (1969) expanded on this idea with his thesis that the satellite/metropole nexus is an intentionally structured development of underdevelopment for the purpose of ensuring the transfer of surplus to the core. In focusing on surplus transfer, Baran (1957) and Frank (1979) ignored the linkages between cheap labor and surplus drain and chose instead to prioritize commodity sales and repatriation from investment and taxation as sources of surplus transfer. In making this conceptual choice, they moved away from the orthodox Marxist emphasis on the linkage between labor exploitation and surplus creation. It was not until Emmanuel's (1972) theory of unequal exchange that international wage differentials were recognized as major sources of surplus drain. Subsequently, Amin (1974) incorporated this notion into his analysis of "accumulation on a world scale." Concurrently, Wallerstein (1974) introduced world-systems analysis, a perspective in which a unitary multistate capitalist system is driven by surplus drain, particularly the value extracted from underpaid labor throughout the system. At the birth of world-systems analysis, Terence Hopkins and Immanuel Wallerstein (1977: 49) identified the most significant question that needs to be answered through commodity chain analysis: "If one thinks of the entire chain as having a total amount of surplus value that has been appropriated, what is the division of this surplus value among the boxes of the chain?"

Historically, all world-systems have been driven by relations of surplus transfer. Precapitalist systems structured mechanisms of surplus drain between regions, primarily through plunder and tribute. What, then, distinguishes the capitalist world-system as a structure of surplus drain? In contrast to earlier systems, the capitalist world-system is characterized by the highly rationalized extraction of surplus by means of commodities. World polarization into rich and poor zones is a consequence of routine forms of quasi-monopolistic commodity production and distribution across regions. Foundational thinkers (A. Frank 1969, 1979; Amin 1974; Wallerstein 1974) emphasize surplus drain as the driving force that causes impoverishment and dependency of the periphery in order to accumulate wealth and dominance at the core. Capitalists and core states structure the world-economy to ensure the continuous flow of economic surplus from peripheral zones, including internal peripheries. Semiperipheral zones are drained by the core and, in turn, extract surpluses from peripheries.

A second distinguishing feature of capitalist surplus drain is the need to widen the reach of the system in order to ensure its growth and survival. Commodified production requires territorial expansion. Thus capitalism was borne of colonialism and incorporation of noncapitalist arenas. Capitalism is a system both of cheap factors of production and of near-monopoly capital markets. For that reason, the zones of the trimodal structure of the modern world-system are defined by exploitative relationships. The system is based on minimizing costs of production in order to maximize profits. Capitalists are driven to identify and integrate locations where they can take advantage of the lowest costs of production to generate commodities for marketing in areas where prices are highest. Thus transnational capitalists want to buy or produce cheap in the periphery and sell dear in the core.

In contrast to other scholars, world-systems foundational thinkers envision core and periphery as relationships of surplus transfer, not as geographic or national categories. Andre Gunder Frank (1969: 23) conceives the modern world-system as a "hierarchy of core-periphery *complexes*, in which surplus is being transferred." Wallerstein (1995a: 31–32) defines core and periphery in terms of the "transfer of part of the total profit (or surplus)" from one zone to another. "Such a relationship is that of coreness-peripherality. . . . We call the losing zone a 'periphery' and the gaining zone a 'core.' " He insists that we should define "core" as "those who are living off the surplus value produced by others" and "periphery" as "those who are not retaining all of the surplus value they are producing." Wallerstein (2000a: 4) is convinced that core growth derived from these surplus drains: "The shift of surplus towards the core concentrated capital there and made available disproportionate funds for further mechanization, both allowing producers in core zones to gain additional competitive advantages in existing products and permitting them to create ever new rare products with which to renew the process."

What Is a Commodity Chain?

A commodity chain is the most important mechanism for the extraction of surplus across zones, particularly over the past two centuries.[4] In contrast to most scholars, I do not view a commodity chain as a network of corporate spaces of production and distribution. On the one hand, the commodity chain is devised to ensure capital accumulation in the core. On the other hand, it is a surplus-extraction chain that is designed to subsidize the endpoint purchases of consumers. In its entirety, a commodity chain encompasses resource extraction, construction of components, assembly, transport, wholesaling, retailing, and service. Within each node, one finds "relations of production," including the extraction of surplus labor that is not covered by wages. In addition, each point of linkage is a relationship of upward surplus drain, typically through transactions among capitalist firms. As a commodity moves up the chain, each capitalist usually has a greater degree of monopoly than those below. That degree of monopoly is reflected in the capitalist's ability to constrain the transmission of costs of production from below. By degree of monopoly, I mean the ability to lower costs or raise prices beyond what would be possible in a purely competitive economy. Technically, this is a "degree of oligopsony" in which a few buyers control prices. The large wholesaler or retailer at the end of the chain may hold a true degree of monopoly through control of sales markets. As a result, the commodity chain operates to extract surpluses at all levels of the structure of the world-economy. In other words, the relationship that exists between nodes in the commodity chain has the same form as the core/periphery relationship and, in turn, the same form as the relations of production within each node of the chain. This abstract model assumes that all these relationships are typically not between equals (as in the abstract model of neoclassical economics) but between unequals, actors with differing degrees of market power. At all three levels, then, the relationship is one of surplus extraction.

As a general rule, labor costs, resource prices, profit rates, and rents increase with movement up the chain, and a portion of the surplus (potential profit) collected at each node is passed to the node above.[5] At each node, capitalists buy cheap and sell "semidear"; that is, full control of realization of the potential surplus is constrained by the relative monopsony power of the buyer. In order to buy cheap, the capitalist lowers costs by externalizing part of the costs of the production process to cheaper producers. Mainstream economists are quite aware that the best strategy that a firm can follow to outperform other competitive firms is "overall cost leadership," that is, cutting costs of production deeper than the competition (Porter 1980: 35–36). Thus the firm that is higher in the chain cuts costs by outsourcing part of its internal production. Capitalists lower in the chain sells semidear by passing on part of their potential surplus in the form of a reduced price, allowing the capitalist with a degree of monopoly to buy cheap. In this way, commodity chains are surplus-transfer chains that permit accumulation at multiple levels and ultimately concentrate accumulation in the core.

EXTRACTION OF DARK VALUE THROUGH COMMODITY CHAINS

Although there are various forms of surplus drain from periphery to core, I will focus on only one mechanism: the extraction of surpluses through dark value in commodity chains.[6] Capitalism is a system of surplus drain that requires an enormous base of extraction of dark value. Dark value emerges at the lowest beginning points of a commodity chain, occurs at every node, and is encapsulated within the commodity when it is sold at the end of the chain. At every node of the chain, dark value arises from "dark energy," that is, the intrinsic value of cheap and unpaid labor that becomes embedded in commodities. Once dark value is incorporated into a commodity, it never disappears, and it grows as it advances through the chain. By the time a commodity has gone through numerous nodes of a global chain to arrive at the doorstep of the consumer, it has incorporated not only the embedded inputs of Marx's (1990: vol. 1) paid labor power but also massive amounts of underpaid and unpaid labor. The value of this labor is what I term "dark value." The term is inspired by the recognition of physicists that imperceptible "dark matter" and "dark energy" account for 95 percent of the universe. Just as invisible and unexplained dark energy provides most of the energy in the cosmos and drives the continuing expansion of the universe, dark, uncosted, and underpaid energy drives the expansion of the capitalist world-system.

What Is Dark Value?

Because dark value is found in all factors of production (capital, labor, land, natural resources, energy, knowledge), hidden transfer occurs any time a capitalist obtains a component of production at less than the average world-market price. Thus dark value is embodied in four types of hidden subsidies to commodity chains: (1) undercompensated formal labor, (2) underremunerated or unpaid inputs from households or the informal sector, (3) cheap natural resources, and (4) ecological and human externalities that are "economically free" to capitalists. Because these transfers are externalized from economic accounting, a full calculation of dark value would require analysis of millions of surplus drains that are derived from unpaid household labor, underpaid labor, undervalued resources, and savings through uncosted human and environmental externalities.

Dark value is deeply embedded in every economic transaction or commodity and thus is the silenced partner that renders every visible documented surplus drain more beneficial. Dark value is distinctive in three ways. First, these surplus drains are "free" inputs to capitalists; that is, they are externalized from calculation of the costs of production. In this way, commodity chains are "efficient" because they minimize production costs by extracting hidden surpluses for the direct profit of capitalists higher in the chain. Second, dark-value drains occur as uncosted contributions to recorded surplus. That is, they represent "opportunity surpluses" that exceed the visible profits that are recorded in company account books. If there is a degree of monopoly, the hidden value may be retained by the capitalist as "extra surplus value" (Marx 1990: 3: 114–117). Alternatively, the dark value may be passed on to the consumer in the form of cheaper commodity prices. It is advantageous to the capitalist to expand the degree of monopoly by underpricing competitors and thereby to increase sales volume and long-term profits. Such a degree of monopoly is most often found near the beginning or the end of a commodity chain. Dark value can be differentiated in a third way. Because dark value is dependent on the existence of mass consumption, its relative economic significance intensifies over time. Logically, the transfer of dark value to the core expands over time as the volume of trade increases. Thus rising consumption in the core triggers deeper extraction of hidden peripheral surpluses by capitalists. More dark value is produced for the benefit of core inhabitants today than ever in the history of the modern world-system.

Dark Value and Unpaid Labor

The commodity chain not only extracts surpluses from workers and resources for which capitalists pay but also is a chain for the extraction of value from unpaid and underpaid labor and resources. According to Marx (1990: vol. 1), capitalism constructed a proletariat for the purpose of extracting surplus value and, thus, profit. World-systems analysis derives from this conceptualization but stands in dialectical opposition to it. In world-systems analysis, the capitalist system is driven by the search for, and the incorporation of, unpaid and underpaid inputs, especially labor (Wallerstein 1995b). Such thinking is not alien to mainstream economists. Indeed, they recognize many of these unpaid costs as "externalities" to production costs (Stewart 2001) but do not integrate these externalized costs into their basic models. In contrast, unpaid costs are not recognized in most Marxist analyses. However, the capitalist system is driven not toward the production of wage labor, but toward the production of unpaid and underpaid labor, that is, toward a semiproletariat that realizes over its lifetime only part of its total livelihood from wages (Mies, Bennholdt-Thomsen, and Werlhof 1988). In short, my argument is that capitalism is dependent on, even driven by, microstructures of "dark energy" in the form of unpaid and underpaid labor that never appears in the accounting of production costs.

How, then, is dark value produced? The full contribution of labor to a commodity consists of the total work hours—costed and unpaid—that are embedded in production and reproduction of labor power. Peripheral workers survive in households that are the provisioning units in the underlying substratum of the capitalist world-economy. Household labor and resources subsidize the below-subsistence wages that are paid to peripheral workers (Dunaway 2012). Capitalists are able to drain hidden surpluses from households because a majority of the world's workers earn only a portion of their livelihoods from waged labor. Indeed, these semiproletarianized households derive the greater proportion of their resources from nonwaged activities and thus inadvertently encourage capitalists to pay below-subsistence wages (Wallerstein 1995a).

MECHANISMS OF DARK-VALUE EXTRACTION
FROM HOUSEHOLDS

Because the world-systems concept "semiproletariat" assigns economic significance to unpaid labor, its perspective stands in opposition to Marxism. Perhaps the greatest mistake in Marxist political economy, and its greatest shame, was the decision to take the standpoint of those who drive the system and their apologists, the classical economists (and subsequently the neoclassical theorists). Thus, for Marx (1990: vol. 3), one must understand the "value form" (*Wertgestalt*) from the vantage point of those who construct and control capitalism. This is the system driven by productive capitalists, those who produce commodities. Success in this system depends on quantifying the source of value, obtaining it, and expanding it. Paying attention to these factors requires the keeping of books. The value form is transformed into the money form and is then entered into the books as costs of production, prices of commodities, and distribution of the ensuing surplus. At an abstract level of analysis, the only source of the surplus is the underpayment of waged labor, which appears on the books as split between the costs of labor ("variable capital") and "surplus value." The tendency of Marx(ism) is to treat the incorporation of unpaid costs, such as seized land, resources, and slaves, as foundational components of "primitive accumulation," so Marx and Marxists are in accord with their enemies, mainstream economists, in assuming that unpaid costs are not sufficiently important to be included in their model of how the system works. Instead, both abstract models assume that the costs of reproduction of labor within households are fully recompensed by the wages paid by capitalists. It is as if a sign was posted above the door of every household stating, "You are now entering the realm of the production of labor power, the source of all value. No Marxists are admitted beyond this point."

Semiproletarian households, not wage-earning males, are the foundational units of the capitalist world-system. Capitalists prefer such households exactly because they do not require complete payment for their reproduction. Members of households, typically women and children, provide unpaid labor and alternative income sources that support the (re)production of waged labor (Werlhof 1983, 1984). Drawing on ideas from radical feminists (Mies, Bennholdt-Thomsen, and Werlhof 1988), I argue that women's work provides most of the dark energy that drives the whole system. This position is brilliantly captured in a single sentence offered by Claudia von Werlhof (1984: 131): "The proletariat is dead; long live the housewife." Feeding into every node in a commodity chain are chains of households that (re)produce the labor power embedded in the commodity production occurring at that node. These chains include the work of women (and children) in provisioning, caring for, and maintaining the households. In addition to unpaid work, women and children often contribute value obtained from petty commodity production and trade. Even households that are seemingly isolated from capitalist commodity production in the "marginal" economy of the informal sector produce services that contribute to the reproduction of labor power in the formal commodity chain. Consequently, there is nothing outside the chain(s).[7] Almost all labor—paid or unpaid—contributes to chains of value that improve the core quality of life, but these are invisible gifts to commodity chains that increase household misery in the periphery.

Unpaid Household Labor

For these reasons, researchers need to extend their typical commodity chain mapping to integrate the hidden household chains that encompass the reproduction of labor, two-thirds of which is in the hands of housewives. Capitalism as a system is intrinsically based on the extraction of surplus from unpaid labor from worker households. The starting point of a commodity chain is the extraction of surplus from unpaid household work, and that unpaid labor contributes to the "expanded value" of a commodity at every production step in the chain. The household reproduces and partially provisions itself, and thus generates waged labor for the capitalist below its paid costs. In other words, the household provides vast benefits for each employer within a commodity chain. Thus all the capitalists that exist within the full span of a commodity chain extract from thousands of households the production of this unpaid value, but they conceal its embodiment in the finished product.

Unpaid household labor takes four forms. First, capitalists do not pay for women's biological reproduction and raising of the future generation of workers. Second, households engage in an array of forms of unpaid labor through which they scramble to provision themselves. A housewife spends much of her work life indirectly providing free, unpaid labor power to capitalists who do not pay the full cost of survival needs for labor power. Thus household collection of unpaid resources (e.g., water, fuelwood, ecological gathering) represents extraction of unpaid costs because this unpaid household work subsidizes the below-subsistence wages of household members. The third form of unpaid household labor occurs when housewives and girls provide unremunerated work to support male commodity production (e.g., agriculture or home-based subcontracting) that is household based. Fourth, housewives provide unpaid labor to locate and use capitalist commodities.

According to three decades of accumulated research, household members allocate far more time to these types of unpaid household work than to paid work, and females account for a majority of this unpaid work.[8] Because females inequitably bear the brunt of these dark-value transfers to millions of commodity chains, women's unpaid work is more crucial to capitalism than waged labor (Mies, Bennholdt-Thomsen, and Werlhof 1988). Peripheral households provide direct subsidies to capitalist commodity chains through allocation of unpaid labor and resources to sustain underpaid waged workers. In addition, peripheral households provide indirect subsidies to capitalist commodity chains when they absorb the costs of reproducing, maintaining, educating, and socializing the labor force from which capitalists benefit (Chapter 3).

From the standpoint of capital, the household produces a commodity to be sold, labor power. This is most directly evidenced in transnational labor commodity chains that are partially structured by states, as in the Philippines. Various forms of labor are educated, trained, recruited, transported, and sold as commodified labor. These exported workers include male ship and construction workers and female domestic servants, nurses, and sex workers.[9] At many points in these labor commodity chains, a surplus is extracted as the commodity moves up the chain. Thus the commodified labor that was created through the dark energy of the household is transformed into the visible value of the labor-market price. This price is a bargain for the receiving country. The dark value from distant households keeps the price low because the cost of production is borne elsewhere, as in the case of transnational migrant laborers (Chapter 10).

The Indirect Contributions of Informal-Sector Households

In addition to dark value extracted from the various forms of unpaid labor, capitalists drain hidden surpluses from semiproletarianized households that earn much of their livelihood from informal-sector activities. Indeed, commodity chains incorporate horizontal chains of simple commodity production and the informal sector in which nonwaged producers provide cheap labor to generate goods and services that provision underpaid waged laborers in semiproletarian households. In this way, cheap waged labor extracted by capitalists is dependent for its reproduction on even cheaper labor in the informal sector. In other words, these workers provide dark value to low-paid waged workers who, in turn, provide dark value to global commodity chains. For that reason, the overlapping simple commodity production and informal sectors are not outside capitalism (Portes 1983) but are intrinsic components of global commodity chains. Indeed, these sectors are "invisible" only because capitalists and consumers seek to deny that they are the beneficiaries of the surpluses extracted from the vast majority of the world's workers who are concentrated in the informal sector and the peasantry, where they cannot obtain adequate livelihoods (United Nations 2003).

A long dark-value chain of food producers and informal-sector activities is needed to generate the productive capacity and the survival maintenance of every waged laborer. By supplying low-cost survival needs to the waged worker, poorly remunerated informal laborers subsidize low capitalist wages. The daily life of the undercompensated peripheral wage earner entails the unequal exchange of one work hour for greater labor time from even cheaper nonwaged producers. For example, a waged laborer drains dark value from a lower-paid child caregiver who makes it possible for her to work outside her household. This flow of dark value cheapens the reproduction costs of peripheral labor and, thus, the wage level that capitalists pay. In addition to these kinds of indirect subsidies to capitalist production, there are several more direct informal mechanisms through which dark value is expropriated. Through contract farming and labor subcontracting, capitalists externalize costs of production to peripheral households whose bare subsistence level lowers prices for exports. Capitalists also drain dark value from export-commodity producers when they generate debt bondage through exploitative informal credit or financing mechanisms (Chapter 9).

EXTRACTION OF DARK VALUE BY CONSUMERS

Because this dark-value form of surplus drain is more extreme today than it ever has been in the history of the modern world-system, it is crucial that scholars remove the cloak of invisibility they usually cast over these uncosted production inputs. What happens to a commodity when it is put on the market? Many commodities are worth more than the price core consumers pay because cheap prices are grounded in distant unpaid and underpaid labor. Had these commodities been produced in the core, the labor costs would increase the purchase price by a factor of two or more. Consequently, all core consumers benefit from the extraction of surplus value from peripheral worker households.

Capitalists who have the advantage of such dark energy can expand sales by applying a portion of their unpaid production costs to lower prices. In this case, the full value of the embodied costs does not appear in the standardized commodity price and thus in profits. It is a hidden component of the recognized value of the commodity that is not reflected in the price. This concealed surplus is the dark value that makes low-priced commodities possible. Because employers have a high degree of monopoly over peripheral labor markets, the wage level often falls near or below the level necessary to maintain household subsistence. It is these highly feminized unpaid hours of reproductive labor that are embedded in low core consumer prices and concealed in profit accumulation. Workers who do the same tasks with similar skills and equipment earn hourly wages that differ by as much as a ratio of thirty to one between zones of the world-system. Core workers become unwitting beneficiaries of this exploitative system when they use one waged hour to purchase a product that embodies many more lower-waged hours of peripheral labor (Emmanuel 1972). Thus the core working class becomes a consumerist aristocracy of labor (Communist Working Group 1986).

Table 4.1 presents an example of the sources and benefits of dark value in a single commodity chain of Brazilian plantation-grown arabica coffee, which can be purchased at any U.S. supermarket. Put simply, the table demonstrates the drain of surplus at different nodes of a commodity chain.[10] It presents a simplified version of the coffee commodity chain, eliding two links at the peripheral end of the chain and three links at the core end. I am convinced that the flow of dark value found in this commodity chain represents the basic tendency found in all such chains throughout history. Observe the division of the final price along the chain. Nearly two-thirds ($4.55 of $7) of the final price in Column 1 is retained in the core. This fact should raise doubts about the validity of the concept "value added." Almost 90 percent of the visible surplus in Column 2 ends up in the hands of core corporations. Even though more than three-quarters of the paid labor is done in the periphery, 57 percent of the paid labor cost is incurred in the core. Indeed, a paid Brazilian coffee worker must labor nearly 8.5 hours to earn as much as a low-paid U.S. farmworker earns in one hour.

TABLE 4.1

Dark value embedded in a pound of Brazilian arabica coffee

1. Prices in official account systems	2. Visible inputs into retail price			3. Dark value added from cheap waged labor		4. Dark value added from unpaid household labor — Reproductive		4. Unpaid family farm labor	5. Total dark value added	
	Price components		Labor hours							
Primary producer	Paid labor	$0.84	.63	Labor	$6.03	Labor	$6.87	$6.87	Labor	$19.77
	Other production costs	$0.82	.05	OPC	$0.68	OPC	$0.54		OPC	$1.22
	Profit retained	$0.09	—	Total	$6.71	Total	$7.41	$6.87	Total	$20.99
Total price received $1.75										
Middlemen	Paid labor	$0.21	.04	Labor	$1.12	Labor	$0.44		Labor	$1.56
	Other production costs	$0.11	.01	OPC	$0.24	OPC	$0.11		OPC	$0.35
	Profit retained	$0.03	—	Total	$1.36	Total	$0.55		Total	$1.91
Value added $0.35										
Transporters	Paid labor	$0.10	.01	Labor	$0.20	Labor	$0.11		Labor	$0.31
	Other production costs	$0.21	.01	OPC	$0.20	OPC	$0.11		OPC	$0.31
	Profit retained	$0.04	—	Total	$0.40	Total	$0.22		Total	$0.62
Value added $0.35										
Core roasters and retailers	Paid labor	$1.55	.10							
	Other production costs	$2.00	.02							
	Profit retained	$1.00	—							
Value added $4.55										
Retail price $7.00										
Total visible inputs		$5.84	.87							
Total profit retained		$1.16								
Total dark value added					$8.47		$8.18	$6.87		$23.52

SOURCES AND EXPLANATORY NOTES: Estimates for Columns 1 through 3 were derived from Talbot (1997, 2004), Sarris and Hallam (2006: 356–75), and McArthur (2011) and standardized into 2011 dollars. For Column 2, the Brazilian farmworker wage rate is estimated at $1.33 per hour (McArthur 2011), the U.S. farmworker wage rate at $10.90 per hour (U.S. Department of Agriculture website). For columns 2 through 4, labor inputs are assumed to be one-third of the total expense for other production costs (OPC). For Column 2, the cost for the labor inputs to OPC for the primary producer is estimated at $6 per hour (the average wage of Brazilian manufacturing workers), at $10 per hour for transporters, and at $30 per hour for core workers ("Industry Report" 2006; U.S. Bureau of Labor Statistics 2009). Column 3 represents the estimated value of unpaid labor in cheap wage rates, that is, the difference between the wages that would be paid a U.S. farmworker for the work time and the actual Brazilian wage. Column 4 represents the unpaid household reproductive and provisioning labor to support wage earners and the unpaid household farm laborers. A conservative estimate of one unpaid farmworker was assumed. I conservatively estimated that household reproductive and provisioning work was equivalent in time to the paid labor in Column 2.

The real point of this table is to answer the question: who obtains most of the dark value that results from the production and sale of this commodity?[11] Column 3 estimates the unpaid labor in cheap wage rates. For coffee workers, this estimate is the difference between the wages that would be paid to a U.S. farmworker for the work time ($10.90 per hour) and the actual Brazilian wage ($1.33 per hour).[12] In similar manner, I have estimated the dark-value contributions of other workers, including those involved in producing supplies and equipment, termed "other production costs" in the table. Even though these estimates are conservative, the results are astounding. The dark value embedded in a pound of coffee exceeds the price. If the coffee were produced in the core, the price would more than double.

Dark-value analysis allows one to see that the system is structured to provide significant benefit not only to capitalists but also to core consumers. In this case, the dark value added from cheap labor in the various nodes of the chain is seven times greater than the profit extracted along the chain. This table reflects my previous theoretical discussion of the two options that capitalists enjoy with respect to dark value. By increasing prices, they can widen profits, or they can pay higher wages to core laborers and managers or finance advertising (accounted as "costs"). But it is hard to imagine that capitalists would use more than about 15 percent of the dark value in Column 3 in this way. The second option is for them to pass on price savings to consumers, in this case a benefit of $8.47. As Column 4 shows, the dark value is even greater because we also need to take into account the unpaid household reproductive and provisioning labor to support wage earners and the unpaid household farm laborers. As much as $15 worth of that unpaid labor is embodied in every pound of coffee consumed in the core. As Column 5 indicates, the full dark value added is more than three times the actual price paid.

Clearly, the overwhelming source of low coffee prices for U.S. consumers is the contribution of cheap and unpaid labor in the periphery. Table 4.1 also demonstrates that most of the dark value from cheap and unpaid labor is not extracted by core capitalists but, instead, is passed on to consumers. Capitalists retain only about $1.16 in profits (Column 2), but they pass on more than $23 in embedded dark value to consumers (Column 5). In the eyes of mainstream economists, these coffee businessmen are doing a fabulous job of reducing prices in order to provide competitive consumer goods. However, that low price conceals that (1) real people live in households that face threats to their survival caused by this system of commodity chains for export production; (2) the drain of potential surplus, mostly from labor but also from capitalists who are lower in the chain, is a loss of potential expanded reproduction (economic growth) to the peripheral producing country; and (3) core consumers have significant political and economic interest in maintaining this commodity chain system of production and surplus drain. Extrapolating from this example, we can clearly understand that capitalism is not only a world-system of accumulation in the core but also a system of "delivering the goods" to a majority of core workers by means of the expropriation of dark value from peripheral workers.[13]

• • •

In contrast to Milton Friedman (1977), who argued that "there's no such thing as a free lunch," I contend that the world-economy is structured to ensure free lunches for capitalists. From the origins of the modern world-system, one of the free lunches provided to capitalists is the extraction of dark value in the forms of unpaid and underpaid labor. The capitalist productive system is inescapably based on capture of the dark value embedded in unpaid and nonwaged household labor. The capitalist world-system is not grounded in anything approaching competition; rather, it is grounded in the acquisition of degrees of monopoly by capitalists. Thus capitalists construct long degree-of-monopoly commodity chains that extract hidden surpluses by controlling factors of production tightly enough to reduce production costs. As a result, the capitalist world-system is structured to benefit the core working and middle classes through dark value to an even greater extent than it benefits its instigators, the transnational capitalist class (W. Robinson 2004). This dark energy is partially captured by capitalists as profits and partially passed on as benefits to core consumers.

What is to be learned from this argument? The origins of dark value can be made visible through more accurate mapping of commodity chains. Because dark energy is disproportionally provided by households and by the females in them, analysts arrive at an underestimation of the labor required for production when they conceal the unpaid contributions of households. Through commodity chains, the capitalist "masters of the universe" accumulate on a world scale by draining pennies from the unpaid labor of those at the very bottom. It is this dark energy that drives the expansion and growth of the modern world-system. To recognize this fact is to view the world-system from the bottom up, where a majority of the world's worker households struggle to survive. Revealing the daily misery that derives from dark-value extractions from those households is the central rationale for undertaking commodity chain analysis. Indeed, that is the project to which world-system originators intended this concept to be applied. Other approaches to commodity chain analysis have the effect of teaching capitalists how to widen and deepen surplus drains from households and of assisting them to conceal their dark-value drains from the world's expanded working classes.

PART III WOMEN'S LABOR AND THREATS TO SOCIAL REPRODUCTION IN GLOBAL COMMODITY CHAINS

CHAPTER FIVE

In Chains at the Bottom of the Pyramid

GENDER, THE INFORMAL ECONOMY, AND SWEATED LABOR IN GLOBAL APPAREL PRODUCTION

Robert J. S. Ross

Civilizations built on class hierarchies, that is, all previous and extant modes of complex social organization, are pyramids of appropriation. At the top, the exquisite luxuries enjoyed by "masters of the universe" are the distilled and refined products of sweat handed up through layers of sub-chieftains who control stages in the production and consumption process, each raking off a piece of the action.[1] Always at the bottom of the pyramid are the direct producers—the "one-percenters" who are lucky if they hold on to a hundredth of the value of what they contribute to the world's wealth. They are the stitchers and the grain reapers, "those who," said Peter Mc-Guire (Carpenters Union general secretary, 1881–1902) "from rude nature have delved and carved all the grandeur we behold" (U.S. Department of Labor 2012: 1).[2]

From the perspective of the bottom of the pyramid, holding on to as much produced value as possible is the essence of class interest. The strategies of the parties to this contest are molded by the opportunities and dangers of changing industrial structures. But some of the formal properties of the strategies of extraction endure or reappear over time. Among these are sub-contracting stages of the production process as a means of avoiding organized resistance to extraction or exploitation. This strategy often entails the exploitation of gender norms, cultural practices, and household structures to facilitate the upward movement of value from the direct producers to the appropriators of luxury. In this essay, I examine one such pyramid of extraction by exploring the interaction of gender with the decisive moments in the apparel commodity chain: cutting and sewing where actual production takes place, as distinct from design and marketing and brokering.

GENDER BIASES IN THE APPAREL COMMODITY CHAIN

I begin with a finished textile commodity and deconstruct the production process. The first step is the design stage. Garment design is usually a process initiated from a brand name or a retail chain (for its proprietary or store brand). Alternatively, a producer may contract with a brand and be licensed to manufacture a garment of a given design using that label. On a global scale, design and marketing are controlled by Global North brand corporate headquarters. The design function is typically carried out in the headquarters of a brand or retail chain, although design is now starting to take place in Global South countries that specialize in textiles exporting.

In the next stage of production, a garment design is broken down to a pattern, often in the form of cardboard or paper layouts to be placed on a worktable with many hundred plies of material, ready to be cut with round or vertical mechanical blades or, more rarely, overhead lasers. Cutters in a traditional garment shop may also be responsible for the skilled process of expanding or contracting the basic pattern pieces for different sizes. This craft, marking and grading, can be replaced with computer-aided-design (CAD) technology, which is far more expensive than human labor. CAD and laser techniques are only employed in the production of expensive items or in specialized industrial niches.

Although designers are often female, pattern makers who lead the production process are usually men, and cutters (and markers and graders) almost always are. Among other responsibilities, they move large rolls of fabric over cutting tables, and the material is often stacked quite thickly. For whatever traditional or technical reasons, cutter pay is usually much higher than the pay of sewing-machine operators. Most of the hourly or piece-rate employees in garment production are sewing-machine operators, and females are concentrated in these types of jobs. Lest we fall prey to the myths of female "nimble fingers" in textile commodity chains, it is important to emphasize that males account for the vast majority of precision-instrument operators and repairers (Online Clothing Study 2012).

Although design is almost always carried out in destination markets, the cutting and sewing of more than 90 percent of finished commodities that will be consumed in core countries occur in semiperipheral and peripheral areas (American Apparel and Footwear Association 2008: 4). In the past decade, there has been a strong regional rotation in the source of U.S. imports from the Western Hemisphere to South and East Asia. Most garment production takes place in cutting and sewing factories or shops. It is an indicator of a region's rise in the global hierarchy of apparel production that its factories become "full-package" producers; that is, they move from textile cutting and sewing to full production of ready-to-wear clothing that is "hang-ready" for Global North stores.

INTERMEDIARIES IN THE APPAREL COMMODITY CHAIN

It is important to note the role of intermediaries in this industry and, as a matter of principle, in modern contract manufacturing in general. For example, the Li and Fung enterprise has $15 billion in revenues and supplies 40 to 50 percent of name-brand shopping-mall clothing. According to *Forbes*, Li and Fung

> spins [a] gossamer web: The company works with large, mostly Western apparel manufacturers and retailers—Wal-Mart and Target are among its largest clients—to develop the specifications for a particular garment, including the fabric weight, dye shade, and the finish and style of trim. Then [the company] . . . plug[s] those coordinates into a computer database of 15,000 suppliers, and then once the pool of potential manufacturers is narrowed sufficiently, send[s] an army of managers— known internally as "Little John Waynes"—into the field to personally negotiate prices and inspect quality. (Denning 2009: 2)

Allegedly controlling output from 14,000 factories, Li and Fung owns none (Kapsen 2009).

Reliance on such intermediaries has numerous advantages to the brands, but it broadens the layers of profit takers that are positioned in commodity chains between the direct producers and the final retail customers. Such agents relieve the headquarters staff, say, in Bentonville, Arkansas (Wal-Mart), from the burdens of language, culture, or detailed local knowledge. In addition, the use of these intermediaries adds a level of protection from direct responsibility and accountability for the management of labor that is akin to the political notion of plausible deniability.[3] Lying at the bottom of this pyramid are the sewing-machine operators and trimmers and, to an extent, the cutters and pressers. It is in the workshops that cut and sew that one encounters the shifting border of the formal and informal economies because these are the sites in commodity chains where gender norms of exploitation and the phenomenon of sweated labor most frequently operate.

THE SWEATED TRADES

From its outset in Paris, London, and New York in the 1870s and 1880s, production of ready-to-wear apparel, that is, mass-production cutting and sewing, was absorbed into modern industry as a hybrid with the older sweated trades of home workshops. The usage arose in the mid-nineteenth century when a number of manufacturing processes were based in home or tenement workshops. The organization of production depended on middlemen, the "sweaters," who commissioned the work of the producers, the "sweated," and sold the finished products to retailers or to later-stage manufacturers. As the ready-to-wear industry emerged in these three production contexts, immigrant home workshops became known as "sweatshops."

As captured in the iconic 1890 photographs of Jacob Riis, a tenement workshop in New York's Lower East Side was organized by a tenant who recruited female homeworkers or used female family members to produce for manufacturers. The tenement workshop sheltered the manufacturer from overhead costs, and often the manufacturer or the sweater rented the machines to the operators. However, the demands of quality and of efficiency in true mass production made factories better production sites, and the bulk of work was restructured in these large, centralized settings.

Export-oriented production was as significant in the clothing factories of Manhattan at the turn of the twentieth century as it is today in Global South cities, such as those in Bangladesh, Vietnam, and China. Then, as now, competitive realities of the industry kept wages and working conditions at fairly miserable levels. These competitive realities include ease of entry. Relative to the volume of sales they can produce, cutting machines, tables, and sewing machines are quite inexpensive. Even when the cost of pressing machines is added, it is still relatively easy to obtain the production equipment necessary to commence production. Thus the supply of apparel contractors is usually abundant in relation to demand.

Like the ferocious combat of scorpions in a bottle, factory and shop owners squeeze costs out of the most malleable part of the chain: the operators. Note that cloth is the largest single cost of apparel production (Online Clothing Study 2013).The implication is that cutting and sewing facilities have little leverage over these costs. The apparel assemblers are price takers for textiles. They are squeezed between concentrated buyers (chain stores, big brands, or globally scaled intermediaries like Li and Fung) and even more concentrated sellers (textile-mill operators).

Even though there was partial movement away from home workshops associated with physical squalor during the twentieth century, the term "sweatshop" broadened to include workplaces with low pay, long hours, and oppressive, that is, physically unhealthy or personally degrading, conditions. As early as the 1909 Shirtwaist workers strike, union activists called the largest factories in New York sweatshops. Despite the concentration of production in factories and the emergence of a sizable clothing-manufacturing industry, a home and microworkshop sector remained because these sites provided continuing advantage to actors in the industry.

WHY HOME AND SMALL WORKSHOPS PERSIST

For manufacturers, homes and microshops are places for overflow work. When deadlines approach or contracts are offered that are larger than a factory's current capacity, home workshops or very small shops can be mobilized to take the overflow (Chapter 6). In addition, very small or home shops provide protection from industrial conflict. During the great strike of 1909, the Triangle Shirtwaist Company and Leiserson, the two largest producers of this form of apparel, subcontracted the work to smaller shops and to agents, further decentralizing production into the tenements. This was the reason that the women who had started at the largest factories called a general strike in the industry. This reserve-capacity function is similar to the parallel production capacities within larger multiplant corporations. A contemporary example is Boeing's attempt to move production from its union Seattle facility to its non-union facility in South Carolina (Trottman 2011). From the point of view of larger manufacturers, these reserve-capacity functions have a more general and desirable effect. By maintaining a reserve production capacity in small shops and homes, they can keep wages low because of the competition for the work. The microshop and the tenement are the runaway shops, the outsourcing, the "race to the bottom" of a region's clothing industry (R. Ross and Chan 2003).

From the point of view of upwardly striving immigrants or migrants to a city, tiny shops or home workshops offer the chance to be owners. On the one hand, they capture only small fractions of the value they produce (under 10 percent). On the other hand, they are positioned a step above the sewing-machine operators, so they have a chance to accumulate a bit of savings, to expand if they are fortunate, and to be among the petit bourgeoisie. Involved here is a key structural element of apparel production: it has low barriers to entry. An industrial sewing machine can be purchased for $350 to $2,500, a cutting machine for $350, and tables for less. By raising capital from extended family or immigrant ethnic (or kinship migrant) networks, these individuals can fulfill ambitions to be rising members of the business class (Online Clothing Study 2013). For the women who sew in such settings, there are some perceived advantages. However, these are the contexts in which the norms of patriarchy, gender norms of the wider society, and the brutal realities of poverty converge to limit the options open to females (Chapter 6).

PATRIARCHY AND GENDER ROLES AT THE BOTTOM
OF THE PYRAMID

Most women who take jobs in sweatshops usually do so voluntarily in the sense that there is rarely physical coercion or a threat of violence that recruits them to or keeps them on the job. Of course, this is the great defense of neoclassical apologists for exploitation, that these jobs are better than the alternatives. However, this proposition overlooks poverty and patriarchal oppression as forms of coercion (R. Ross 2004). It is also true that actual coerced labor is a frequent, if not common, occurrence among migrant workers. For example, contract workers recruited from Sri Lanka and Bangladesh to work in Jordanian garment factories have their passports taken, are kept under restrictive physical conditions, and are sometimes subject to sexual harassment and rape (Kernaghan 2011). Chinese employers hold the first month's pay of migrant workers as security to ensure that they will fulfill their yearlong contracts and thus make it too costly for most of these laborers to escape from bad jobs. In a notorious case, Chinese owners created clones of migrant worker dorms in the U.S. Commonwealth of the Marianas (Guam) and were eventually found guilty of holding indentured labor, all in aid of exporting garments with a "made in America" label (R. Ross 2004). A sensational moment in the American media came in 1995 when seventy-two Thai workers were held as slaves, the longest for seven years, in El Monte, California, and were rescued only when a heroic escapee told her story to a brilliant young lawyer (R. Ross 2004; Su 1997).

In more formally regulated labor markets, traditional cultural and status norms constrain women's options to such an extent that they yield their labor power for less than they might otherwise obtain as more nearly free agents. For example, fathers or husbands, from motives both of protection and of control, may instruct Chinese women in New York's Chinatown to accept work only within the neighborhood (Chow 1992). In a market economy, these kinds of restricted options for income-earning work inevitably restrict earning power.

Shops with substandard labor conditions are usually chronic violators of health and safety regulations. These places are "more informal" in the sense that they are less careful about compliance with public laws. Because of the triple burden of child care, homemaking, and paid work, such shops may permit practices that facilitate women's roles as caretakers. Young children may be allowed to stay with them; hours of work may be suspended at mealtimes and resumed at night (Chow 1992). Another norm among migrants and immigrants that is linked to gender is the practice or requirement of seeking jobs with kin. This is related to the broader practice of seeking jobs with coethnics or employers from the workers' hometown or province. For instance, I visited a particularly miserable shop on the outskirts of Beijing, posing as a potential buyer of shirts. The shop's owner assured me that if I had larger volume needs than the shop had labor to produce, she could easily send "home" to Fuji to recruit more workers. The literature on such ethnic entrepreneurs sometimes lionizes such employers, pointing to their competitive advantage in so-called ethnic niche markets. These entrepreneurs are more exploitative from the point of view of those at the bottom of the pyramid. They are able to exploit vulnerable and partially immobile labor as a means of lowering costs in relation to potential competitors. When the potential workers do not speak the language or dialect of the host city or country, the advantage of the coethnic employer is clear, but the disadvantage of the worker in seeking more nearly advantageous employment is also clear.

Given restricted labor-market options, new opportunities for young and unmarried women to earn cash outside unpaid household work may seem to be a relatively liberating experience. When they are expected to labor for fathers or older brothers at home, even low-paying cash jobs may be quite appealing (Chapter 6). This is a rich paradox, but it is no more so than the birth of capitalism itself. To become a wage worker—a "wage slave," as the Industrial Workers of the World once termed it—is a step up from serfdom and legally coerced labor. Miserable wages are not a step up from unpaid household labor because women simply add a second shift to women's reproductive work. Despite the perceived benefits for females, working conditions in such facilities pose particular safety risks, especially for females, who account for a majority of the textile labor forces in the Global South.

FIRE TO FIRE

It is telling to compare the worst industrial disaster in U.S. history with contemporary working conditions in the Global South. The 1911 Triangle Factory fire in New York City resulted in the deaths of 146 immigrant females aged sixteen to twenty-five; locked doors caused those workers to die from smoke inhalation and toxic fumes. Examples from the Bangladeshi textile industry show that these twenty-first-century factories ground their labor practices in that same 1911 philosophy of the callous expendability of women laborers. The clothing industry has become Bangladesh's dominant export earner, and it grosses $20 billion annually from 5,000 factories that market to nearly all of the world's top brands and retailers. Since the end of the Multi-fiber Arrangement's national import quotas in 2005 and the increases in Chinese manufacturing wages, Bangladesh's share of U.S. clothing imports has risen to about 6 percent and has been increasing by about 25 to 30 percent annually. Housed in high-rise urban factories where the majority of workers are female, the industry suffers chronic factory fires (Clean Clothes Campaign 2013). During the night of November 25, 2000, in Dhaka, 45 workers, including 10 children, burned to death in a fire at Sagar Chowdury Garment Factory. In grotesque symmetry with the Triangle catastrophe, witnesses told newspapers that "workers were trapped because the only exit door on the ground floor was locked for security reasons and had to be broken open by firefighters." On April 11, 2005, 60 died and hundreds of workers were trapped when the Spectrum garment factory collapsed on them. On February 25, 2010, fire broke out on the first floor of the Garib and Garib sweater factory in Bangladesh. The thick acrylic smoke rose up to the eighth floor, impenetrably dark and toxic. Because the door was shut and windows were locked, 21 workers died. In December 2010, fire broke out on the ninth floor of a factory building of the Hareem group. Because exits were blocked, women jumped to their deaths to escape the flames. This deathly pattern was repeated on March 25, 2011, when 28 Dhaka workers died and 100 were injured (Clean Clothing Campaign 2010, 2013).

According to the Clean Clothes Campaign (2013: 5), there are "systemic hazardous conditions" in the garment industry throughout Asia, especially Bangladesh where 345 factory fires killed 1,170 workers between 2006 and 2012. Bangladeshi textile factories have been plagued with the same kinds of factory fires as New York City's Triangle Factory fire a century ago. In 2005, there were 110 deaths in 13 factory fires. Between 2006 and 2009, 213 factory fires caused 414 deaths. In 2010, 20 fires caused 191 deaths (Clean Clothes Campaign 2013). The vast majority of these textile and apparel factory fires are caused by electrical safety violations. For example, the Bangladeshi electrical system is overburdened and highly regulated. Factories are allowed permits for a designated electrical load for a set number of sewing machines and other equipment. The factory wiring is then installed at the level that is appropriate to the permit. When the factory subsequently operates double or triple the number of machines illegally, a fire often results.[4]

In addition to fires, a high proportion of Asian textile factories are housed in dangerously unsafe buildings that have caused many worker deaths and injuries, especially in Bangladesh and Pakistan (Clean Clothes Campaign 2013). Despite the great numbers of textile industry fires over the last decade, workers are also placed at risk in dangerous factories, especially in Asian countries. In Bangladesh alone, worker deaths from dangerous factory conditions have repeatedly occurred in numerous incidents since 2000 (Clean Clothes Campaign 2010). Bangladesh's garment industry grosses $20 billion or more annually from 5,000 factories that market to nearly all of the world's top brands and retailers. It has become an export powerhouse largely by delivering lower costs, in part by having the lowest wages in the world for garment workers (Yardley 2013). However, textiles contractors also cut costs by failing to repair buildings that are structurally unsound, by adding new floors to weak underpinning, and by sealing safety exits to make room for additional machinery (Clean Clothes Campaign 2010; Global Labour Rights 2010). In April, 2013, the deadliest disaster in garment industry history occurred when a Bangladeshi factory collapsed, killing 1,127 people and injuring more than 2,500 (Yardley 2013). Since a majority of Bangladeshi textile workers are females, it is highly likely that a majority of the dead and injured were women. However, media and government reports have failed to analyze the human costs in gender terms, thereby engaging in the kind of silencing of women in global commodity chains that the contributors to this book criticize.

MOVING TOWARD CONCEPTUAL CLARITY

There is a great deal of conceptual confusion about whether sweated workplaces are part of the informal sector, and rigid use of this notion leads to faulty conclusions and can lead scholars in the wrong directions. Low-wage factories, small workshops, microshops, and home-based production are often distinguished as falling categorically between formal and informal economic locations. The idea of an informal sector suggests economic activity that is unrecorded or even criminal. The "informal economy" is too often mistakenly taken to be the opposite of mainstream production and of global commodity chains. However, there is no theoretical reason to exclude from the informal economy the unrecorded practices of large corporations, particularly because they have close linkages with the growth of other informal activities. The idea of an informal economy does not require total invisibility. Furthermore, there is no strong or clear boundary distinction between an illegal or criminal informal economy and a formalized capitalist economy. In apparel-cutting and sewing shops, for example, workers may be asked to start work before they punch in on the legally required time clock. Portes, Castells, and Benton (1989: 12, 13) note "the systematic linkage between formal and informal sectors, following the requirements of profitability." The informal sector, they argue, "is unregulated by the institutions of society in a legal and social environment in which similar activities are regulated."

Methodological Dead Ends and Conceptual Black Holes

In the apparel industry, the subcontracting system allows for an elaborate and complex texture in which the formal and informal and the recorded and unrecorded are woven among closely related but fictively distinct entities. Some contractor practices are closely inspected; that is, they must meet strict quality controls. Others "escape" the notice of the commissioning principals and allow contractors and their subcontractors maneuvering room to record some legal activities while concealing illicit cash-only practices.[5] The conceptual clustering of formal and lawfully regulated practices as distinct from informal and often illegal practices is challenged by the realities of the global rag trade. Apparel production is unusual among manufacturing industries in that it appears to be a systematic lawbreaker in many countries. National or local minimum-wage and overtime laws are almost always more rigorous on paper than in practice, and health and safety rules are weakly enforced.

Defining hyperexploitation or sweatshop labor as unrecorded, off-the-books activity can lead to a methodological black hole. In an important article, Waldinger and Lapp (1993) applied an indirect but ingenious method of "input-output" analysis to contend that there was little sweatshop labor in the New York apparel industry. A discussion of their method and findings illustrates the ambiguity of the term "informal economy" and the dangers inherent in literally interpreting the notion that it is always "off the books." Waldinger and Lapp pointed out that in the 1980s, a series of scholars (including myself) generated estimates by citing each other's guesses. They then proceeded to examine whether indirect measures of sweatshops indicate a marked increase in "covert" workers. They argued that the consensus estimating technique that suggested as many as fifty thousand sweatshop workers in New York in the 1980s was based on erroneous guesses.

Waldinger and Lapp narrowly defined a sweatshop as one that is "covert" or in the "unregulated informal sector." They argued that a marked decrease in manufacturing wages as a proportion of value added in manufacturing would indicate an increase in covert production workers.[6] The proportion of production workers to all workers should also decrease if a substantial fraction of production workers are working off the books and are paid in unreported cash. They demonstrated that wages as a proportion of value added in the 1970s and 1980s declined by about 10 percent nationally and in New York. This decline indicates productivity gains, but there were no differences between the nation as a whole and the areas likely to have been affected by sweatshops. Further, they found no reduction in the number of production workers as a proportion of all workers in the garment industry. They concluded that there was a low wage immigrant garment industry, but that estimates of large increases in covert sweatshop employment were overstated.

Although there is reason for skepticism about estimates based on anecdote and even on informed opinion, there were severe methodological problems with Waldinger and Lapp's approach. The most important problem is embedded in their definition of "sweatshops" as those that are "off the books" and in the "informal sector." The "informal sector" in their frame of reference means economic activity that is not officially recorded and remains untaxed. In developing countries, examples are home workers and street vendors. In developed countries, it includes "off-the-books" activity. Therefore, the informal sector would include many illegal enterprises, such as prostitution or illegal drug sales, but also activity that intends to evade some laws in otherwise legal activity. Waldinger and Lapp assumed that the bulk of sweatshop workers would not show up as workers in tax or other official payrolls. However, government investigators demonstrate that shops that violate labor or health and safety regulations are frequently documented in official records.[7]

Evidence that the majority of sweatshops may be visible in some official records appears in the U.S. Government Accounting Office (GAO) (1994) study of tax compliance of sweatshops in New York and California. By analyzing violators known to the Departments of Labor of the two states, the GAO found that fifteen of twenty-one New York City sweatshops had filed state taxes at least once between 1990 and 1994; in California, thirty-eight of forty-four had done so. Of the ninety-four places in the two states, only eight had not filed unemployment payroll taxes. Such information challenges the statistical underpinnings of Waldinger and Lapp's method. Indeed, their conclusion results, in large part, from their definition of sweatshops as referring only to firms that are totally covert. They write, "While Chinatown's garment contractors may include many firms that cheat on hours and wage laws . . . they are clearly not underground." Violations among New York's Chinatown contractors are difficult to find, but Zhou (1992) surveyed over four hundred of Chinatown's women workers and found that their average wage was below the legal minimum. In its baseline survey of firms, the U.S. Department of Labor (1997) found that 90 percent of New York City's Chinatown shops were violators of labor laws. Yet, according to Waldinger and Lapp, these are not sweatshops because they are not "underground."

Waldinger and Lapp (1993) used a highly advanced statistical technique and found no evidence for a completely "off-the-books" apparel sector. When the U.S. Department of Labor found that about 60 percent of New York cutting and sewing shops violated wages and hours and other laws, the estimate of fifty thousand sweatshop workers turned out to be precisely correct—depending on definitions. Waldinger and Lapp's conclusion should have been that the concept "informal sector" is relative, not absolute, not that there was no significant sweatshop sector in the apparel industry.

Informal, Contingent

When one is looking outward from a North American context, it is important to note the variety of meanings of "formal," "casual," "contingent," and "informal" work. The United States is unusual, if not unique, in that all hourly employees except salaried personnel and those with union contracts (i.e., more than 75 percent of the workforce) are "employees-at-will" who may be released at the discretion of their employers. In China, such employees might be termed "informal" even though they are in firms that are registered and legal. In some countries, employees without term contracts may be considered "casual" because they do not have employment contracts. In other countries, informal activity is only that which is not visible in official record keeping and licensing.

The importance of this hairsplitting to commodity chain analysis is that globalization appears to break down formal, contract labor conditions into informal or contingent conditions. As core manufacturing has shifted to the Global South, exporters have creatively married off-the-books strategies with formally documented workers. The United Nations (2003) reports large increases in the informal sector worldwide and emphasizes that a majority of Global South workers are categorized in the informal sector and that the greatest job growth worldwide is occurring in sectors classified as informal. In most of these countries, women are concentrated in the informal sectors, where wages and working conditions are worse than those experienced by males, who are concentrated in higher-paying formal sectors. Shifting work from brand-owned factories to contractor and then subcontractor workplaces pushes employment-contract stability inward (both in the core-nation sense and in the corporate-headquarters sense) and pushes risk and contingency outward. This is the broader meaning of just-in-time inventory control and flexibility in labor markets, that is, that employers can legally fire at will.

GENDERED CONTROVERSIES ABOUT REGULATION

In this final section, I will examine two debates about how NGOs and governments can move forward to improve income and working conditions for female textile workers. The first controversy centers on the question of whether home-based production should be prohibited. Advocates for working women disagree about strategic initiatives to regulate the informal sector and women's working conditions. Again, apparel is an outstanding example. In the first half of the twentieth century, the U.S. labor movement saw the tenement sweatshop as an unmitigated evil. Various state-level schemes cloaked in justifications of public health attempted to regulate or abolish industrial homework. Not until the Fair Labor Standards Act of 1938 did the secretary of labor gain the authority to prohibit production of certain items of apparel in home settings. This authority was contingent on the secretary's showing that the minimum-wage and hours legislation could not be enforced under conditions of home production. By 1942, industrial home-work was largely abolished. This regulation was central to the success of clothing labor in gaining increased wages and greater safety for a period of about forty years. The prohibition of homework was based on an elemen-tary administrative and statistical reality: the more dispersed the point sources of a phenomenon, the more difficult it is to detect, inspect, and regulate.

There is an argument about whether textile homework should be le-gally abolished. Opponents argue that much of the livelihood of women and their families depends on industrial homework, so prohibition would harm women and should be resisted. There are historical parallels in this argument. The prohibition of child labor faced (and does face) similar claims that abolition of child labor will eliminate household survival re-sources of poor families that depend on the income contributed by off-spring. In both cases, one may acknowledge the difficulties of transition. In the short run, income losses would be harsh for families that depend on homework (or child labor). In the long run, however, higher wages and im-proved working conditions will redound to the benefit of this class of labor-ers because they will be able to capture more of the value they produce. The gender issue is clear. Moving work to factories and out of households may temporarily disemploy women but may increase the earning power of men. In the long run, in regard to child labor universally and homework in the United States, these family-intrusive regulations have worked to the ad-vantage of men, women, and children because they have broadened the capacity of the working classes to leverage bargaining power to household advantage.

The second controversy centers on whether private self-help organiza-tions and their partner NGOs can better address problems of informal-sector workers than public regulations. Workers in France, Canada, and Australia, all considered to have more influential labor movements than the United States, did not secure passage of laws prohibiting garment-sewing homework. Canada and Australia now have active apparel homework sec-tors, as well as NGO advocates trying to boost conditions for those workers. It is curious that U.S. formal regulation (whatever the enforcement) is more rigorous than in jurisdictions where the labor movement is more powerful. If, however, the Fair Labor Standards Act were to be rewritten today, it might have a different result.

Microshop and home employment is quite common in apparel work in India, and a large organization has arisen that receives global accolades for interventions on the part of informal-sector female workers. Attempt-ing to represent 1.3 million "self-employed," homeworking women, Self-Employed Women's Association is a much desired partner by Western

NGOs that are interested in improving labor conditions in garment and other production systems. I have found no evidence that SEWA or NGO attempts to monitor Indian homeworker labor conditions have achieved worker pay levels that approximate the wage levels of formal workshop employees. Nor has NGO advocacy produced major increases in the proportion of the value of commodities that is retained by workers rather than being concentrated in the hands of employers, traders, retailers, and buyers higher in the global chain. Moreover, Indian labor law excludes homeworkers from its purview, and many other countries exclude from legal regulation any workplace that employs a number of workers below a set threshold.

• • •

The lessons of the ancient apparel industry are highly applicable both analytically and in policy terms to contemporary analyses of commodity chains and gender.. Whether facilitated by low barriers to entry or to small-unit production or both, highly price-competitive links in a commodity chain will put working conditions at risk. Stages in the commodity chain that are more concentrated—in this case, textile retailing—will have price power over those that are more dispersed. Pressure on those who mobilize production (e.g., contractor factory owners, middle-sector jobbers) will cause them to protect their margins by extracting greater value from workers and by externalizing costs of production to laborer households (Chapter 3). Workers more vulnerable to these pressures are those who are favored for employment; hence the concentration of female workers in textile production.

Gender norms and cultural practices facilitate these forms of exploitation. These include all those practices of coethnicity and extended family ties that restrict employment options for females. The contrast between the availability of cash and unpaid household labor may dampen the pain of low pay and long hours. However, employers recruit women for the largest but lowest-paid number of positions and reserve the smaller number of higher-skilled, higher-waged jobs for males. It has become culturally chic to repeat the phrase popularized by Mao Zedong: "Women hold up half the sky." Even notorious sweatshop defenders like Nicholas Kristof and Sheryl WuDunn use the phrase. Perhaps we need this new version: "Women carry half the pyramid of power and exploitation on their backs. Maybe more."

CHAPTER SIX

Patriarchy Reconsolidated

WOMEN'S WORK IN THREE GLOBAL COMMODITY
CHAINS OF TURKEY'S GARMENT INDUSTRY

Saniye Dedeoglu

Since economic liberalization policies took effect in 1980, the garment industry has been the driving force of Turkish economic growth. Nearly 15 percent of national income derives from apparel exports.[1] The ready-made-clothing industry ranks as the country's second most important export earner after the automotive industry.[2] A classic example of a buyer-driven industry (Gereffi and Korseniewicz 1994), the textile and clothing sector became one of Turkey's most important exporters after the neoliberal turn in economic policies in the early 1980s (Table 6.1). Between 1980 and 2000, Turkey's share of world ready-made-clothing exports increased tenfold, making it the fourth-largest exporter of garments after China, the European Union, and Hong Kong (World Trade Organization 2008). By 2007, Turkey's textile exports reached US$14 billion. Expansion of the industry is attributed to government support and to the speed with which the textile industry shifted into ready-to-wear garment production (Senses 1994; Ansal 1995; Eraydin and Erendil 1999). Forty thousand firms operate in the country's textile and clothing sector. The main centers of clothing and apparel manufacturing are the Marmara and Aegean regions and cities such as Istanbul, Bursa, Tekirdag, and Corlu. Auxiliary inputs and raw materials are primarily produced in Istanbul, Izmir, Denizli, Bursa, Kahramanmaras, and Gaziantep.

Even though the country's industrial growth has been acknowledged worldwide, the Turkish economy has not been successful in generating employment for women. Averaging about 25 percent, Turkish female employment ranks lowest among Organisation for Economic Co-operation and Development countries. In 2008, more than 12 million housewives were not actively employed. It is this large pool of unemployed females that the garment industry seeks to exploit. The exporting success of the Turkish garment industry derives from (1) its ability to integrate those who are excluded from the formal labor force and (2) its capacity to capture those female labor reserves without providing job security or good working conditions. In

TABLE 6.1
Percentage export share of selected manufacturing sectors in Turkey

Sector	2011 (January– July)	2010	2009	2008	2007	2006	2005
Ready-made clothing	13.61	12.66	12.95	13.89	13.88	16.28	17.11
Automotive industry	11.90	14.83	18.44	15.04	21.61	18.74	18.35
Electricity and electronics	8.71	8.33	9.58	9.07	8.79	9.65	10.79
Machinery and parts	6.72	5.96	5.65	6.46	5.43	5.32	3.80

SOURCE: Calculated using data from Turkish Exporters'Assembly, http://www.tim.org.tr/tr/ihracat -ihracat-rakamlari-tablolar.html.

2010, there were 687,000 registered workers in textile industries and another 1.8 million hidden informal workers, a total of about 2.5 million in the sector. In the official employment statistics, women account for 37 percent of textile laborers, but there are 2.6 informal-sector workers (most of them females) for every formal waged worker. Consequently, women's employment in the textile industry is much higher than their average national employment rate (25 percent). Moreover, women make up an even higher share of ready-made-clothing workers, and they account for more than 40 percent of all clothing workers. In short, Turkish textile-exporting success has hinged on the industry's capacity to recruit different types of females to provide low-cost labor. In this way, females provide a majority of the hidden casualized inputs into this commodity chain (Chapter 3). Indeed, Turkey is a society in which women's economically productive labor is hidden and invisible because their contributions to the industry's export success are excluded from official employment statistics. For that reason, this study investigates how the garment industry integrates women into its export commodity chains.

CAPITALIST TARGETING OF GLOBAL SOUTH FEMALE WORKERS

Numerous case studies point to a rise in women's share of employment, especially in low-skilled, low-paying production occupations, as countries broaden their export orientation (Elson and Pearson 1981; Joekes 1987; Standing 1989; Cagatay and Ozler 1995). Many scholars have focused on the ways in which export-oriented production alters labor-force composition, kinds of labor-recruitment strategies, and the gender division of labor. Exporting industries have taken advantage of and reinforced women's structurally subordinated positions within the labor force and the family by adopting discriminatory hiring practices, paying women lower wages, and placing them in repetitive, monotonous tasks with no job security or advancement opportunities. As a consequence of women's low-ranking positions in factories, many of the tasks they perform are not covered by health and safety regulations. Nor are women provided with insurance and retirement benefits (Grossman 1979; Elson and Pearson 1981; Salaff 1981; Nash and Fernandez-Kelly 1983).

Scholars point to lower wage rates as being key to the growing proportion of females in export-oriented manufacturing. Writers also emphasize employer stereotypes about women's docility, subservience, and manual dexterity (Elson and Pearson 1981). Several scholars argue that young single women account for most of the rising employment (Salaff 1981; Nash and Fernandez-Kelly 1983; Heyzer 1986; L. Lim 1990; Wolf 1992). Many employers associate lower production costs with female workers because they claim that males are more unstable and less flexible (Elson and Person 1981; Nash and Fernandez-Kelly 1983; Afshar 1985). Feminists disagree about whether these new forms of female employment are experiences of liberation or of exploitation. A majority conclude that Global South women are exploited by global industries that pay below-subsistence wages (e.g., Chapkis and Enloe 1983; United Nations 2003), but a few (e.g., Nash and Fernandez-Kelly 1983) conclude that women benefit from employment. This study seeks to refine, challenge, and extend this earlier scholarship.

METHODS OF INQUIRY

This investigation is grounded in three phases of field research over more than ten years. In the first phase, I focused on how small family-based workshops integrated females into garment production. In the second phase, I explored how undocumented migrant women were absorbed into garment production. In the third phase, I examined how large factories based in the southeastern cities of Turkey use unmarried girls.

I undertook the first field study in Istanbul's garment industry over a fifteen-month period between early 1999 and mid-2000. In this phase of field research, I explored the role of women in the generation of this globally competitive industry, the ways in which females became the main providers of labor for Istanbul's garment firms, and the implications for gender relations of this integration into new waged employment opportunities. I interviewed women workers, owners of garment workshops and their families, factory managers, and those engaged in informal work and other forms of invisible work in the garment industry. I conducted fifty interviews with female workers in different segments of the garment industry and twenty-five interviews with factory managers and workshop owners. In the second phase of field research in Istanbul in 2007–8, I focused on the recruitment of immigrant workers by interviewing forty-five Azerbaijani females who had been integrated into textile production. I conducted the third phase of field research between June and August 2011 in southeastern cities of Turkey, where the expanding garment industry is generating more rapid job growth than any other economic sector. I interviewed thirty-five female workers in order to investigate how Turkey's textile industries are targeting unmarried girls in order to keep export costs low.

ORGANIZATION AND STRUCTURE OF THE GARMENT INDUSTRY

The primary markets for Turkish textile and clothing products are European countries (Bulgaria, England, France, Germany, Italy, Poland, Romania, Spain) and the Middle East (especially Iran and Egypt), followed by lesser marketing in Russia and the United States. Thus the production strategies of the Turkish garment industry are driven by consumer demands in these disparate foreign markets. Turkey's garment industry has attained its global success because it strategically employs lower-cost subcontracting linkages between factory production and small-workshop and home-based production. Because the production of the garment sector is organized around different market niches, sectors require different types of labor and subcontracting links. As the most globalized sector of the Turkish economy, Istanbul's garment industry produces for several types of international and domestic markets. The markets for which Turkish garments are destined determine the status of the country's industry in the global value chains. Istanbul's garment industry produces for three distinct sets of consumers: domestic consumers, European countries, and central Asian countries that were part of the former Soviet Union. Istanbul's garment industry has structured an undocumented but massive commodity circuit of informal international trade and labor migration between Turkey and former Soviet countries. There are now alternative markets in which international commodity trade is taking place at an informal but global level. Because the global commodity chain approach emphasizes commodity production that is usually for the markets of advanced countries, it neglects the diversity of formal and informal markets that shape international trade and garment production within Turkey. Still, this approach enables us to analyze the interconnectedness of all these differentiated aspects of production and consumption markets at the global level. Even garment production for domestic consumption is not free from the global competition of external companies.

In order to reduce infrastructure and labor costs, manufacturers establish subcontracting networks among different firms, but they also capture home-based workers. These networks provide industrial access to female and child workers who are untapped resources of cheap labor. Subcontracting between large and small firms enables exporters to be more competitive and flexible than companies that do not employ subcontracting. For instance, two types of subcontracting networks operate among Denizli's towel weavers: one between small family-owned enterprises and large-scale firms and one among large-scale firms (Ayata 1990). In this way, firms specialize in a certain part of the decentralized process. In the clothing industry, firms usually subcontract sewing and embroidery, while cutting, modeling, and quality control are done internally. On average, small- to medium-scale firms use twenty-three subcontractors, while large-scale firms work with only seven (Eraydin and Erendil 1999).

WOMEN WORKERS IN ISTANBUL'S GARMENT WORKSHOPS

In addition to extensive reliance on subcontracting relations between firms, the Turkish textile industry is characterized by a high degree of informalization of production (Dedeoglu 2008). Within the structure of the garment industry in Istanbul, the workshops in my study were small firms that employed ten to forty-nine workers. According to Istanbul's Textile and Apparel Exporters' Association, such small firms accounted for 64 percent of the four thousand firms in this city in 2000. My field research in Istanbul involved twenty-five garment establishments: five large-scale garment factories, one national representative for international brand names, and nineteen garment workshops. Three large corporate textile and garment factories produced goods for domestic markets, and two were mass producers of ready-made garments for export. The firm that represented international brands subcontracted production to workshops after receiving orders from foreign buyers. This firm's large warehouse is a massive storage facility for packaged finished products, a structure that is quite different from a majority of the sites where garment production takes place.

Through the large factories, I identified eight workshop subcontractors for close investigation. All but one were subcontractors for garment-exporting firms that produce orders for European and American brand-name fashion companies. Eight of the garment workshops specialize in orders from designers and brand-name companies, and eight produce garments such as T-shirts and sweatshirts. The remaining three target the Laleli Market, which is the heart of the "suitcase/shuttle" trade to the former Soviet countries. Accounting for 20 percent of total Turkish textile exports,

Istanbul's Laleli Market is an international trade center from which 10,000 firms and contractors market clothing, footwear, and other products for export. Aimed at export to former Soviet countries, Laleli is termed "Little Moscow" at tourism websites because the trade center caters to Russian-speaking wholesalers. Road signs and billboards are in Russian, area restaurants advertise foods preferred by these international buyers, and hotel employees and taxi drivers speak Russian.

Most Laleli-oriented workshops specialize in the sewing and trimming of parts of standardized products, such as T-shirts and sweatshirts. However, a few produce brand-name commodities that require highly skilled labor with expertise in a certain aspect of production, such as embroidery, lace making, needlework, or stitching. The workshops are male-owned family businesses that recruit workers from immediate family, extended kin, and neighbors. Thus women make up about 60 percent of all workers in the workshops, but they account for nearly 85 percent in garment sections of factories.

In family-owned establishments, labor is pooled within families. Because of the fluid and fluctuating nature of incoming orders, shifting production deadlines, and constantly changing order specifications, workshops depend on a reserve pool of family members and relatives. This core force provides flexibility that allows workshops to draw laborers into and out of production in reaction to the deadlines and required skills levels for orders. A reliable and loyal labor force willing to work long and unstable hours is vital to the operation of such businesses. The core female labor force consists of wives, mothers, daughters, and close family members of workshop owners. Female workers are crucial to the success of garment workshops because of their easy integration into garment production. The industry is able to tap into an abundant, hidden reserve of home-based pieceworkers and unpaid women for whom "helping" their family's enterprises is an extension of their domestic and marital obligations. In this regard, these Turkish women are similar to females globally. Worldwide, females represent a disproportionate share of the family members who provide unpaid labor to male-dominated farms and enterprises (United Nations 2003).

A core group of close family members and relatives works for fathers, husbands, or uncles who own these workshops, and the mothers or wives of workshop owners are the invisible hearts of this core force.[3] Female roles in these family businesses are quite diverse, ranging from direct contributions to production to cooking for workers and cleaning the workplace. These women not only are burdened with trimming and cleaning garments at home but also must organize their neighbors and relatives when extra labor is needed. Although they remain housewives, these women extend their domestic tasks beyond meeting the physical needs of household members to provide and maintain ties with relatives, neighbors, and friends who constitute a source of reserve labor. Their involvement creates an environment in which the workshop is viewed as a family setting for women's work that attracts more females into production. Although members of this group of women do not usually get paid for their activities, their contributions to garment production consist of a shifting blend of market-oriented, networking, and household and reproductive labor. In short, these workshops are heavily dependent on the unpaid labor of wives and daughters, as Dunaway describes in Chapter 3.

One workshop producing for the Laleli Market is run by a family whose members pool their labor to operate the workshop. The owner opened his workshop in the early 1990s with the support of his two brothers. Three brothers, one brother's wife, and the owner's daughters work together in the workshop, and all are skilled workers. The owner's wife (and the eldest bride of the family) contributes to production by doing decorative trim work from home and by organizing family members to work when extra laborers are needed to fill orders.[4] Even though she is not a skilled workshop worker, she oversees every detail of production, recruits new workers, cleans the workshop, and prepares lunches for family members and workers. While the wives work in the shop, the owner's mother cares for their young children. The survival of this family business and many others depends on the hidden unpaid inputs of these women. They sustain kinship networks in order to recruit cheap laborers from the reserve army of labor embedded in their families, but they also attract the financial resources of the community into the business when needed. Relying on community financial resources is a distinctive feature of these family-run workshops because bank loans are almost always out of their reach. To overcome the lack of formal credit mechanisms, females play a significant role in collecting start-up capital from extended family.

It is important to note that the roles of this core group of women vary over the course of their lives. Once young girls acquire garment-making skills and establish networks of contacts, they may find better working conditions and may even move into formal factory employment if their families consent. For married women, workshop jobs offer a different trajectory because their labor is more closely tied to household needs and family business cycles. If a family business closes, wives return to their household duties. If the business expands through partnerships with other workshops and increases the number of nonfamily employees, married women are excluded from the worker pool. For example, Seda began to work at a young age in her father's garment workshop. After graduating from primary school at the age of twelve, she began to work full-time and gradually acquired skills in garment making and sewing-machine operation. Her father was proud of her textile-production skills and of her diligent work ethic. After the family business closed, she began to work in a large-scale factory to which her father's workshop had subcontracted. Although Seda's mother had greatly contributed to production in the family's workshop, she could not consider such a new job.

Family-run workshops are highly dependent on immediate family and other kinship relations. These social ties enable firms to survive by providing flexibility in the production process under volatile and uncertain market conditions. By manipulating patriarchal gender relations and networks based on mutuality, solidarity, and trust, firm owners exploit their families' labor and financial resources. Women's roles in the maintenance and nurturing of these networks enable family-run businesses to tap into the financial and labor resources of their communities. By recruiting and mobilizing a physically immobile group, these employers transfer gender inequalities and patriarchal gender relations into their production processes. By structuring women's employment within the constraints of existing gendered work domains and the traditional expectations of housewives, these workshops preserve gendered spheres and inequalities. Through kinship relations and the gender ideology that wives should be helpmates to husbands, employers and workshop owners institutionalize gender inequalities in garment production. These forms of patriarchy allow them to tap into a low-wage and flexible female labor supply that is cheaper, easier to terminate, and less likely to resist inequitable work arrangements. In addition, workshop owners simultaneously exploit the unpaid services of housewives and daughters and the low-wage labor of paid females. The workshop itself is grounded in the structured gender inequalities of the household because it merges women's unpaid housewifely duties with the market orientation of the workplace. Through their "housewifized labor" (Chapter 3), these women make their husbands' export production profitable while their efforts remain hidden and economically devalued.[5]

Another group of female workshop workers is a more flexible workforce consisting of nonrelatives who lack the necessary family ties and community respectability that lead to permanent and secure jobs. Because these workers have weaker connections with the workshop than those in the core group, they are the first to be made redundant in times of crisis. Workshops outsource production to home-based females who are usually considered the poorest women in the community, but these females are paid monthly earnings that fall below the country's legal minimum wage. The women involved in home-based work are divorcées or widows, those whose husbands are not providing financial support for their households, or those who need extra cash for unusual expenses. Even though contract homework is a very profitable labor strategy, workshop owners—with the complicity of middlewomen wives—publicly entrench the cultural ideology that this piecework is "charity" to these vulnerable women. In turn, this ideology is employed by wives of workshop owners to shape the ways in which these low-status women receive assistance from other females in the community. Because these women are the neediest in the community, other females may aid them in their subcontracting work by getting together for tea gatherings or work parties. If there is a need to finish the work quickly, all the women get together and help the pieceworker women in their neighborhoods. The women of the community volunteer their labor in order to maintain the relations of cooperation based on such mutual help in anticipation of receiving the same kind of help from others in case they should ever be in similar need. As a result, workshop owners benefit from the hidden unpaid labor of many women who are not family members, but who are not formally linked to the production process.

The relationship between middlewomen and pieceworkers is constructed on the basis of "fictive kinship." Most women learn about home-based opportunities by word of mouth and through informal communication networks in the community. The relationships take on kinship overtones because middlewomen provide access to a regular supply of work. Thus daily survival requires maintaining membership in these social relations and community networks, so women continuously nourish this web of reciprocal arrangements (White 1994: 87, 133). A form of mutual indebtedness is maintained among females, and middlewomen manipulate these social relations in order to ensure a steady supply of work. The irregular nature of piecework and the strict rules of work completion have resulted in the composition of a complex alliance among women pieceworkers and middlewomen. In this way, workshop owners benefit from the extraeconomic (and patriarchal) relations underlying the organization of piecework in Istanbul's garment industry. This irregular structure of work has created a network of females in which a pieceworker subcontracts with a factory but shares her quota with other women in her household or neighborhood. In cases of surplus work or short production time periods, a pieceworker recruits the labor of her neighbors and pays them later. This practice of collaboration among women generates further flexibility in the organization of piecework and shifts the responsibility of middlewomen to find new subcontractors to pieceworkers.

IMMIGRANT WOMEN IN TEXTILE PRODUCTION

Because of fierce competition from China since 1995, Turkey's garment industries needed to slash production costs. For that reason, Azerbaijani immigrants were targeted as a strategic cheap labor supply. The open-border policy between Turkey and Azerbaijan led to a steady influx of migrants in search of work in its large informal sector. The garment industry absorbs many of these cheap workers because Azeri women and children are the main providers of cheap labor for the workshops that produce for the Laleli Market. These Muslim and ethnically Turk migrant women are usually from a rural background in the Nakhchivan region of Azerbaijan. Although males are more transnationally mobile and may circulate between Turkey and Nakhchivan every month, most of the women stay in Turkey after their one-month visas expire. Some of these families have remained in Istanbul for more than five years by following two survival strategies. First, they share a flat with another Azerbaijani migrant family to reduce living costs. Second, they get as many family members as possible into waged employment. For most of these Azeri women, garment work was their first experience of income earning. Because the garment industry targets women and children, the husbands are unable to earn income, so many stay in Azerbaijan. Because Turkish markets do not provide stable jobs for Azeri men, these women become the main providers for their families.

The most readily available form of income earning for Azeri migrants is in garment workshops that hire them to do the most manual and unskilled jobs. Women usually trim the sewed pieces, carry them between sewing machines, and clean the workshop. Only very young females are permitted to learn sewing skills and to upgrade to higher-paying jobs. In garment workshops, there is always a high demand for workers who do these kinds of manual jobs, but they are paid very low wages. Typically, Azeri women work twelve hours a day, six days a week, but they earn less than the minimum wage. Although overtime work is common, there is almost no pay for that additional work time. Employers interviewed for this project know that Azeri women experience the worst forms of abuse and exploitation in Turkey and that they are paid less than a Turkish citizen for similar work. Taking advantage of the illegal status of Azeri women, some employers fire them without paying wages they have earned.

Garment production in Istanbul relies heavily on three categories of women's flexible and cheap labor that allow this international industry to keep consumer prices low. Through their unpaid labor, manipulation of social and familial networks to recruit workers, and exploitation of family financial networks, female members of family-run workshops embed what Clelland terms "dark value" (Chapter 4) into the commodities they produce. The second category of women consists of subcontracted home-based workers who engage in this low-paid casualized labor to provide income for their impoverished households. The third category of women consists of Azeri immigrants who do not have legal residential status. Employers take advantage of their vulnerability and pay them lower wages than Turkish citizens receive. In addition, employers physically abuse them, force them to work longer hours, assign them to the worst jobs in the workshops, and terminate them without advance warning. Thus Azeri immigrant females supply the cheapest and most deeply exploited form of labor for Turkey's garment production.

WOMEN WORKERS IN SOUTHEAST TURKEY'S FACTORIES

Concentrated in the regions of Gaziantep, Kahramanmaras, Malatya, and Adiyaman, Southeast Turkey's textile industries increased their share of exports after 2008. The Turkish Clothing Manufacturers Association predicted the growth of this region's textile industry in 2007, and the 2009 National Strategy for the Textile, Clothing, and Leather Sector subsequently targeted it for expansion. National government investment incentives, tax abatements, and direct subsidies have been central to rapid development of this region's textile exporting. The effects of the incentives are visible in the subsectors that have emerged in different areas of southeast Turkey. For example, clothing production is subsidized in Adiyaman and is more dominant in this city, while Gaziantep receives subsidies for textile technology development and carpentry. The underlying reason for the success of the textile industry in the region is the investment incentives offered by the government to new factories. These incentives allocate free land or tax reductions to textile producers who generate formal employment. In most cases, the companies evade financial liabilities for social security and taxes. Most of these firms are formal, visible enterprises, but they rely heavily on informal employment strategies. Almost 20 percent of the workers are off the books and hidden in the shadows (Kunt and Zobu 2011).

Firms evade rules and regulations and generate informal labor strategies through several strategies. The most common violations are workdays of ten to twelve hours. Even in a formal garment factory, workers usually start around 7:00 a.m. and finish at 6 p.m. without earning overtime. Informal laborers work even longer hours, six days a week. These extended hours impede women's access to paid work in the region because they interfere with female household duties and generate hostility from husbands. Because textile work requires illegal overtime hours, most married women cannot participate in this type of income earning very long.

Another element of informalization in the region's textile sector is the payment of wages that fall below nationally mandated minimal levels. Many workers, especially those in small sweatshops, work for an amount that is about half the minimum wage. Firms evade the minimum-wage rule through three undocumented, illegal strategies. Firms do not fully pay workers for overtime, and they employ underage workers. Girls between twelve and fifteen earn about one-third of the wage paid by factories lo-cated in Adiyaman. Employers also require workers to return a portion of their income. Every month the firm deposits earnings to worker bank ac-counts set up by the employer; then employees return about half their wages to employers. The reduction is usually justified as the share of social security contributions to be paid by the worker, but employers acquire a hidden sub-sidy from workers by retaining part of these funds.

Most of the female textile workers are between seventeen and twenty-five years old, have a high-school education, and stay in the industry only two or three years. These females conceptualize their waged labor as short-term income earning before marriage. Despite the high turnover rate among these workers, the industry finds it advantageous to employ these young females. Employers stereotype them as having a "natural" proclivity toward garment making that is associated with household work and view them as more docile and submissive workers who will accept lower wages than males. Almost every clothing firm I visited was recruiting new female workers. To enhance their chances of attracting workers, forms employ subtle prestige-building strategies in the communities. First, it is easier for women to gain family consent for their employment when other relatives work for a firm. Second, families are more likely to permit their daughters to work in factories that are well known in the community. Thus factory representatives construct the community perception that work in some of these more highly respected establishments should be viewed as "public ser-vice." Factories gain community respectability through reliable and consis-tent employer payments of salaries and of taxes and by building visibility and good relations with the community. Foremen play a key role in this process. For example, foremen usually attend wedding ceremonies of their workers and bring presents.

Despite such employer attempts in the community, long working hours pose an obstacle to women's long-term employment in the textile and cloth-ing industry. Families find it unreasonable and unsafe for females to arrive home late at night or early in the morning. They are mainly concerned that working females will lose respectability in their communities and among extended kin. One interviewee explained that the organization of work into three shifts creates problems for working girls. When there is a problem in the factory," she said, "we have to work sometimes until 3 a.m. It creates tension at home for someone to drop me off so late. It is also a disturbing experience for my parents and relatives to see someone picking me up for factory work very early in the morning." Interviewees emphasized that com-munity evaluations have significant impacts on family decisions about per-mitting daughters to work, and women play key roles in setting commu-nity standards of gender respectability. Community discourse often defines working girls as trying to escape parental and patriarchal controls that are exerted on them at home. Such females are categorized as "not nice" because of fears that they will flirt with and date the males they encounter at work. In these traditional societies, marriages are arranged among close kin, so contacts between unrelated females and males are socially unacceptable. Communities punish those who cross this line by stigmatizing them as unrespectable and by excluding them from important supports and networks. In this context, women's paid work is seen as "unruliness" because they are challenging the gendered constraints on behavior that are entrenched in the patriarchal order. Women's attempts to earn livelihoods that support families receive little positive acclaim in the face of the community's fears of female rebellion against patriarchal standards. When women's work is conceptualized in this way, it is not socially acceptable and is only partially tolerated until females marry.

In some cases, however, married women must continue to work to support their households, and these females experience some of the worst stigmatization. They are closely scrutinized by their families, by their communities, and even by the males who work alongside them in the same factories. Male workers often ask them why their husbands allow them to work. One informant explained that women face accusations that they cannot fulfill their wifely duties toward their husbands because they are so preoccupied with paid work away from home. Male workers often demean their female peers by claiming that they would never permit their own wives to work in this fashion. Local cultural and patriarchal values dictate that women should be in their homes before evening prayer calls. For that reason, occupations such as teacher or civil servant are more respectable for females. These working females can be in their homes within established gender constraints, but waged women must be in factories at night.

• • •

The Turkish garment industry has maintained its world export rank by exploiting the unpaid and low-paid work of several categories of female workers. The industry integrates females who are excluded from the formal labor force, but it does not provide them documented waged employment, income security, or social reproduction benefits. Moreover, long work hours, unpaid overtime, and unhealthy working conditions generate an untenable context for women's long-term employment. Women are least likely to be employed long-term in small workshops because of the long working hours, low and irregular wages, and subcontracting of home-based production.

Employment in the textile industry has not stimulated the dismantling of traditional patriarchal controls over Turkish women that scholars like

Elson and Pearson (1981) predicted. In fact, new forms of subordination have emerged to ensure both private and public policing of women's behavior. The promise of strict behavior surveillance and protection of the virginity of girls in the workshops is the means through which employers secure agreement from families to permit young girls to work in their facilities. Before permitting daughters to work, families demand that they will be strictly supervised, and the families negotiate permission to engage in surprise visits to the workshops and factories. In this way, the familial "private gaze" over women's behavior is extended into the factory, where employers and foremen take on responsibility to watch and control women in the public sphere. Although some Western feminists have been optimistic about the degrees of female independence that will follow such waged employment, those degrees of liberation are not yet evident for women employed in the Turkish textile industries. Young girls may briefly enjoy a degree of independence, but that independence ends with marriage. In many ways, waged employment is accompanied by intensification of existing forms of gender subordination, especially in the consolidation of women's roles as housewives or mothers. Women's dedication and work are socially recognized and rewarded in Turkey by approving them as "good wives" and "good mothers," not as paid workers.

Indeed, these women are in structurally and socially contradictory positions. Although they are essential to and targeted for employment in the country's textile-exporting industry, their contributions are not documented in public statistics, and their employment is often publicly stigmatized. Communities and families simultaneously push wives and daughters toward new forms of waged labor and toward traditional patriarchal female roles. Females often need to work to expand household pools of income, but they are ridiculed for that work and categorized as "unrespectable." Despite their significant economic contributions to country and to families, these women are still primarily assessed by patriarchal standards of respectability and marriageability and by gendered definitions of appropriate behavior for housewives. Rather than attacking those gender biases, employers and factories exploit women in ways that are designed to entrench and reinforce gendered patriarchal barriers.

Chilean *Temporeras* and Corporate Construction of Gender Inequalities in Global Food Standards

Carmen Bain

Until recently, the state in the Global North was primarily responsible for developing and enforcing laws to regulate agriculture and food production, including food safety, environmental protection, and labor standards. However, the liberalization of international trade, the expansion of global commodity chains, and the intensification of neoliberal economic reforms have constrained the role of the state in this process. Instead, these changes have facilitated the proliferation of actors from the private sector and civil society who are increasingly participating in governing public goods. Of particular significance is the role of major food retailers, who have developed their own governance tools, including standards, audits, labels, and codes of conduct (Busch and Bain 2004; Henson and Reardon 2005). As a result, private standards now pervade the contemporary global agrofood system.

STANDARDS IN THE GLOBAL AGROFOOD SYSTEM

Food retailers use standards to differentiate markets for high-value products and to provide safety and quality assurances to consumers. Moreover, standards have become critical for image-conscious retailers who seek to manage risk by demonstrating corporate social responsibility. Executives of these companies want to limit the risks of liability or public embarrassment that derive from activist organizations and the media that push for greater corporate social responsibility by exposing their labor abuses and environmental degradation (Tallontire 2007). Standards, then, are powerful governance mechanisms that allow retailers to "act at a distance" to coordinate activities, define boundaries of quality, and shape the use of human and ecological resources across commodity networks (Busch 2000; Higgins and Larner 2010). Scholars operating within a global value chain framework have been at the forefront of analyzing how lead firms, such as retailers, seek to control other actors within the chain by implementing practices that produce an inequitable division of labor throughout the network.[1]

Commodity and value chains are mapped in terms of lead firms that exercise degrees of control over chain actors and subordinate firms. Lead firms play a significant role in specifying what is to be produced, how, and by whom. Predominantly located in richer countries, lead firms are usually multinational manufacturers, large retailers and brand-name firms. The power of lead firms stems from their market share and their positioning in chain segments in where they can appropriate high profits. A lead firm can "influence or determine the activities of other firms in the chain. This influence can extend to defining the products to be produced by suppliers . . . and specifying processes and standards to be used. This power is exercised through the lead firms' control over key resources needed in the chain, decisions about entry to and exit from the chain and monitoring of suppliers" (Gereffi, Humphrey, Kaplinsky, and Sturgeon 2001: 4–5).

Although the governance strategies of lead firms play key roles in shaping relationships of power and inequality, scholars who analyze global value chains have largely ignored the implications of such strategies for workers, women, and gender relations (see the Introduction and Chapter 1). Instead, their analytic focus is on firm-to-firm or firm-to-producer relations, and labor and gender relations are marginalized in their studies (Raworth and Kidder 2009). As part of a broader feminist effort to demonstrate the importance and necessity of bringing women and households into global value chain analysis, this essay investigates the gendered implications of private-sector standards for labor. To accomplish this, I examine the retailer-established standards known as GLOBALGAP within the Chilean export fresh-fruit sector.[2] Worldwide, GLOBALGAP is the most widely implemented farm-certification protocol for monitoring agricultural practices. One subsection of the protocol focuses on standards for worker health, safety, and welfare. Health and safety issues remain a major concern to agricultural workers around the globe, especially the acute and chronic illnesses associated with exposure to pesticides and other agrochemicals. Chile is a world leader in the implementation of GLOBALGAP and, therefore, a valuable site for assessing the implications of GLOBALGAP's standards for women and households. The bodies of Chilean peasants, especially *temporeras* (female temporary farmworkers), have become "spaces of sacrifice" (Harrison 2008: 1197) because they confront both the risks of being poisoned in the workplace and the gendered responsibilities of dealing with the costs and risks associated with pesticide poisoning in their homes and communities.

Standard setters "do not simply intervene in, and govern, pre-existing social problems or domains" but rather seek to construct a certain "'field of visibility'" (Miller and O'Leary 1987: 239). I will argue that GLOBALGAP standards construct a field of visibility that excludes and marginalizes women, households, and communities. From the perspective of major food retailers, this silencing is strategic. Labor is fundamental to the creation of value, and gender inequality is central to the success of lean production strategies within agroexport markets (Raworth and Kidder 2009). For retailers to maintain profit levels, however, labor standards must continue to reproduce inequitable gender relations within the workplace, the household, and society more generally (Werlhof 1984). Moreover, enterprises maximize profits by externalizing the social, economic, and environmental costs and risks of production to women, workers, and households (Harrison 2004; Pearson 2007; see Chapter 3).

GOVERNING THE GLOBAL AGROFOOD CHAIN:
A FEMINIST PERSPECTIVE

Governance is a key analytic concept within global value chain analysis. Raynolds (2004: 728) explains that governance should not be understood as some "pre-existing structural feature of commodity chains" because it is the process "through which key actors create, maintain, and potentially transform" activities throughout the commodity network. Focusing on governance strategies, such as standards, makes it possible to reveal the social relations inherent in the production of commodities (Guthman 2009). Until recently, states relied on uniform public standards to ensure that food is safe and to reassure consumers of a product's quality and consistency. In the past, standards were largely viewed as simple mechanisms to facilitate markets and trade or as technoscientific tools employed by specialists. However, social scientists have begun to explore how such governance mechanisms structure asymmetrical power relations and shape inequalities within commodity networks (Bowker and Star 1999). Moreover, researchers seek to deconstruct how developers of private standards employ them to privilege some socioeconomic and political interests over others (Bingen and Siyengo 2002).

In their analyses of governance, global value chain scholars have prioritized investigation of the impacts of standards on firms within the chain while largely ignoring labor and gender relations. However, the work of a small but important group of feminist scholars demonstrates the importance of integrating a gender perspective into global value chain analysis. Their work reveals that the integration of women as a source of low-cost, flexible labor has been central to the development of high-value commodity chains, such as fresh fruit (Dolan and Sorby 2003). Rather than simply "adding women" to their analysis, they have sought to develop an approach that combines global value chain analysis with Elson's (1999) concept of the gendered economy. A gendered value chain approach recognizes that value chains and their laborers are embedded within broader social and economic institutions that are not gender neutral. Moreover, these scholars contend that the reproductive household sphere cannot be separated from the productive market sphere (Barrientos, Dolan, and Tallontire 2003; Tallontire et al. 2005). Thus employment strategies within the value chain "reflect socially constructed gender divisions of labor" in both the labor market and the household (Barrientos, Dolan, and Tallontire 2003: 1515).

From this perspective, private standards, codes of conduct, and audits are central to shaping labor and gender relations (Barrientos, Dolan, and Tallontire 2003; Barrientos and Dolan 2006; Pearson 2007; Bain 2010b; Higgins and Larner 2010). These mechanisms are constructed and established within the value chain to regulate labor. For that reason, these governance tools reflect, transmit, and reproduce gendered patterns and inequalities that exist within labor markets and economic activity (Bain 2010a). A gendered value chain approach allows us to assess the extent to which standards could potentially address gender inequalities and the conditions of the marginalized (Tallontire et al. 2005). For example, Barrientos, Dolan, and Tallontire (2003) use a gender pyramid that shows three interlinked levels to understand the effectiveness of codes. They claim that many codes have been reasonably effective in dealing with the forms of intervention at the top of the pyramid that are related to conditions of formal employment. However, these codes typically ignore the bottom, broadest level of the pyramid that is grounded in more general social reproduction issues and entitlements (Higgins and Larner 2010). In earlier research (Bain 2010b), I have challenged their oversimplified view because I have found that private standards for worker health and safety at the top of the pyramid are also structured to exclude women in important ways. In short, these codes act at all levels to reproduce, reinforce, and exacerbate structural gender inequalities.

How do firms use standards to construct exclusion and marginalization of women? Retailers use their structural and market dominance to shape relationships of power and inequality (Dolan and Humphrey 2004; Raworth 2004). On the other hand, retailers employ significant nontransparent power, especially their discursive ability to shape ideas and frame the debate in contexts in which there is no public accountability (Clapp and Fuchs 2009; Tallontire et al. 2011). All technoscientific practices, especially in the workplace, are inherently political because they are imbued with power, ideology, and "normative determinations of the distribution of risks" (Harrison 2004: 195). Thus Tallontire (2007) questions the legitimacy, transparency, and lack of public accountability of private standards. To establish their credibility and legitimacy, retailers appeal to technoscientific norms and values (e.g., notions of objectivity, expert knowledge, value freedom) to shape the discourse surrounding standards and to frame the criteria for a "good" standard. Feminist science scholars argue that technoscientific language and practice are tools used by those in positions of power to "privilege some actors and forms of knowing while marginalizing others" (Konefal and Hatanaka 2011: 125). Through control over agenda setting, they determine who participates and whose voices are considered valid (Dolan and Opondo 2005), and they silence those who would question the politics and ethics of the process (Feenberg and Hannay 1995).

PESTICIDES AND WORKER HEALTH AND SAFETY

As a result of the globalization of green-revolution agriculture, there has been a dramatic increase in the use of agrochemicals. Pesticides, fungicides, and synthetic fertilizers are used to maximize yields, kill insects and eliminate plant diseases, and extend the storage life of crops. The expansion of global value chains in fresh fruit and vegetables has deepened the reliance of farmers and states on pesticides. In a global market, exporters are required to meet tough phytosanitary standards to ensure that they do not export plant pests or diseases into importing countries (Altieri and Rojas 1999). Pesticides are also integral to meeting retailer standards for product quality. For example, retailer demand for pineapples that are golden in color and ripen quickly led to the overuse of chemical inputs on pineapple farms in Ghana (Blowfield 1999).

Although pesticides became the solution for many of the challenges faced by retailers, exporters, and consumers, they became a major problem for the "less visible people" (Harrison 2004: 296). Exposure to pesticides is a significant but largely invisible health concern for agricultural workers, households, and communities around the globe. According to the World Health Organization, approximately 1 million serious cases of pesticide poisoning are reported each year (Zhang et al. 2010). Exposure can adversely affect the endocrine, immune, nervous, and reproductive systems and cause acute and chronic illnesses and birth defects, as well as death (Simoniello et al. 2008: 957). In addition, these chemicals can enter water sources and soils and pollute the air, so households and communities can be widely exposed to them (Petit et al. 2010).

When Chile emerged as a major world exporter of fresh fruits and wine in the 1980s, its agricultural sector became increasingly dependent on pesticides. Between 1984 and 2008, imports of pesticides increased 483 percent, from 5,577 tons a year to 32,545 tons a year. The Department of Epidemiology (DOE) within the Chilean Ministry of Health reports that the agricultural workforce lacks information about the risks of these potentially deadly chemicals and has not been adequately trained to handle them safely. Because government regulators rarely inspect farms, noncompliance

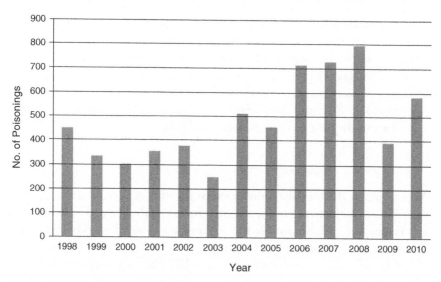

Figure 7.1.   Incidents of reported pesticide poisonings among Chilean workers, 1998–2010

SOURCE: Analysis of Chilean Department of Epidemiology data.

with public health and safety regulations is widespread (Vallebuona-Stagno 2003, 2005). The result is that exposed agricultural workers face a multitude of acute and chronic health risks that range from headaches and nausea to miscarriages, genetically deformed offspring, cancers, and death (Bain 2010a).

In 1993, the Chilean Ministry of Health began to monitor the problem by requiring that health centers report all incidents (confirmed or not) that appear to be related to pesticide poisoning. According to Chilean DOE data, there were 6,228 reports of acute pesticide poisonings of workers between 1998 and 2010 (primarily farm laborers), an average of 479 annually (Figure 7.1). However, the DOE cautions that these numbers underestimate the problem. Doctors often misdiagnose patients because it is difficult to confirm that pesticides are the cause of chronic health problems. Moreover, employers and doctors are reluctant to report incidents, and most exposed workers do not seek medical care (Bain 2010a).

Because of their economic marginalization, social vulnerability, and lack of workplace organization, peasant temporeras are at greater risk of pesticide poisoning (Raworth 2004; Bain 2010b). In Chile, approximately half of the four hundred thousand temporary agricultural workers are women. Although most temporeras want to work full-time, they are hired almost exclusively on a short-term basis. The integration of women as a source of low-cost, flexible labor was central to the development of a globally competitive export fresh-fruit sector in Chile. Small numbers of workers, largely men, are hired on a permanent basis, but even larger numbers of workers, largely women, are hired on a temporary basis to complete tasks, such as pruning, harvesting, or packing (Jarvis and Vera-Toscano 2004). A majority of temporeras do not have employment contracts. Instead, they are paid at piece rates, and most fall below the minimum wage (Jarvis and Vera-Toscano 2004; Raworth and Kidder 2009). Because the majority of temporeras are not enrolled in any social security system (for health insurance and retirement benefits), they are forced to access public health-care services as indigents, except for those few who are covered by their husbands' insurance programs. Despite the legal right to do so, less than 2 percent of temporary agricultural workers are organized into unions.[3] There are few incentives for workers to join because the rights of agricultural unions are highly constrained. For example, they cannot engage in collective bargaining. Furthermore, the temporary nature of employment is an obstacle to union organizing because workers who repeatedly exit and reenter the labor market fear being blacklisted. Within this nonunionized context, private-sector standards offer the potential to address the problems of pesticide poisoning for temporeras in a significant manner. In Chile, the principal certification system that includes labor standards is GLOBALGAP. As of April 2010, Chile had approximately 2,300 certified producers and was ranked among the top ten certified countries globally.

VIEWING LABOR STANDARDS THROUGH
A TECHNOSCIENTIFIC LENS

During the 1990s, food retailers confronted a number of high-profile crises that damaged their reputations, such as mad cow disease, widespread opposition to genetically modified organisms, and public exposés of the use of child laborers by their suppliers in the Global South. Concerned about the safety of the food supply, the British government and the European Union instituted new food safety laws and rules regarding maximum residue levels for pesticides. Development of standards was identified as an approach that retailers could follow to minimize reputational and economic risks. Consequently, a handful of leading British and European food retailers collaborated to set standards for agricultural practices in 1997. In an attempt to demonstrate to the public that they were practicing social and ethical responsibility, retailers launched GLOBALGAP in 2001.

Using the rhetoric of "good agricultural practices," GLOBALGAP claims that it "has become one of the leading drivers for implementing changes in farming practices towards sustainability" (GLOBALGAP 2007: 3). The protocol centers on requirements that fresh-produce suppliers meet standards for food safety and quality, but it also includes labor and environmental standards. To demonstrate compliance, producers must be independently audited by a third-party certifier. According to GLOBALGAP's website in 2011, its standards are "primarily designed to reassure consumers about how food is produced on the farm by minimizing detrimental environmental impacts of farming operations, reducing the use of chemical inputs and ensuring a responsible approach to worker health and safety as well as animal welfare." By 2011, GLOBALGAP was the most widely implemented farm-certification scheme for agricultural practices in the world and certified more than one hundred thousand producers from over one hundred countries.

GLOBALGAP (2007) employs the rhetorical claim that it has formed "an equal partnership of agricultural producers and retailers." Membership is open to retailers and food-service organizations, producers, exporters, and importers. In addition, certification bodies, consulting companies, and agrochemical companies may join GLOBALGAP, but they cannot join its governing board or the sector committees that set the standards. The Fruit and Vegetable Sector Committee is made of up seven retailer and seven supplier members who are elected every three years by their peers. Membership in this committee is extremely important because its main role is to review, evaluate, and approve GLOBALGAP benchmarks on fresh produce. Every three years, committee members assess emerging issues, gather input from stakeholders, conduct risk assessments, and revise the protocol (Bain 2010a).

GLOBALGAP (2007) argues that the agricultural mass market cannot afford rigorous, broad-based labor standards accompanied by full social audits. Within niche markets, such as Fair Trade or the Ethical Trading Initiative, full social audits are possible because of market demand. From this perspective, labor standards should be stratified on the basis of consumer willingness to pay for assessments of risk. For example, GLOBALGAP developed a module to deal with worker health and safety known as "Good, Risk-Based Agricultural Social Practice" (GRASP). Separate from GLOBALGAP certification, the GRASP module targets "risk-regions or risk sectors/branches" where the "risk of social misbehavior" is higher and is not adequately addressed by public controls. Compliance with these standards is monitored through document checks by third-party auditors, but GLOBALGAP admits that "complete social audits with in-depth investigations and worker interviews are NOT in the scope of GRASP."

GLOBALGAP draws on a combination of specialized discourse, appeals to expert knowledge and practice, and technoscientific norms and values to achieve credibility and legitimacy for its protocol (Higgins and Larner 2010). GLOBALGAP standards are celebrated because they have

TABLE 7.1
Excerpt of GLOBALGAP standards for workers' health, safety, and welfare

No.	Control point	Compliance criteria	Level
AF. 3.2	**Workers' health, safety, and welfare**		
AF 3.2.2	**Training** Do all workers handling and/ or administering . . . chemicals . . . plant protection products, biocides or other hazardous substances and all workers operating dangerous or complex equipment . . . have certificates of competence, and/or details of other such qualifications?	Records must identify workers who carry out such tasks, and show certificates of training or proof of competence. No N/A.	Major must
AF 3.4	**Protective clothing/equipment** Are workers (including subcontractors) equipped with suitable protective clothing in accordance with legal requirements and/or label instructions or as authorised by a competent authority?	Complete sets of protective clothing, (e.g., rubber boots, waterproof clothing, protective overalls, rubber gloves, face masks, etc.) which enable label instructions and/or legal requirements and/or requirements as authorised by a competent authority to be complied with are available, used and in a good state of repair. This includes appropriate respiratory, ear and eye protection devices and life-jackets, where necessary.	Major must
AF 3.4.2	Is protective clothing cleaned after use and stored so as to prevent contamination of the clothing or equipment?	Protective clothing is regularly cleaned, according to a schedule adapted to the type of use and degree of soiling. Cleaning the protective clothing and equipment includes the separate washing from private clothing and glove washing before removal. Dirty, torn and damaged protective clothing and equipment and expired filter cartridges should be disposed of. Single-use items (e.g., gloves, overalls, etc.) have to be disposed of after one use. All the protective clothing and equipment including replacements filters, etc., are stored apart and physically separate from the plant protection products/any other chemicals which might cause contamination of the clothing or equipment in a well-ventilated area. No N/A.	Major must

been developed by "independent experts" on the basis of "best practices," "risk assessment," and "independent" audits that ensure transparency. For instance, GLOBALGAP (2007: 3) insists that "the protocol has been developed by experts and is heavily risk assessed. By adhering to good agricultural practice we reduce the risk . . . with respect to worker safety and welfare." The organization also claims that "workers' health, safety and welfare have been an integral part of the GLOBALGAP technical standards" from the beginning. However, GLOBALGAP does not set rigorous labor standards or monitor agricultural practices through full social audits.

Growers are expected to maintain documentation that details how they comply with each of GLOBALGAP's standards, or what GLOBALGAP calls "control points." Third-party certifiers review this documentation to verify compliance with three types of "control points" that are tied to differing degrees of enforcement. "Major musts" require 100 percent compliance. "Minor musts" require 95 percent compliance. "Recommendations" are inspected by auditors, and compliance may be voluntary. However, no minimum percentage of compliance is set, and compliance is not a prerequisite for gaining certification. There are eighteen control points that deal with worker health, safety, and welfare. These standards specify written risk assessments of hazards to worker health and safety, worker training about hazards, protective clothing and equipment, and first-aid techniques. The standards also address worker welfare related to on-site facilities, for example, habitable living quarters and access to clean water. A core component of these standards applies to workers who handle or apply hazardous substances, such as pesticides (which GLOBALGAP calls "plant protection products") and biocides. Three of the four "major musts" are related to this area. Growers are required to train workers who handle or apply agrochemicals and to provide them protective clothing and equipment (Table 7.1).

CONSTRUCTING GENDERED FIELDS OF INVISIBILITY

By framing its labor standards through the use of technoscientific discourse and practice, GLOBALGAP (2007) maintains gender inequities by prioritizing standards for certain workplace practices while ignoring others. A key objective of retailers is to manage the risk of public criticism in relation to labor practices in cost-effective ways. On the basis of its risk assessments, GLOBALGAP has targeted its standards for worker health, safety, and welfare at reducing some of the most visible infringements of worker safety, such as the poisoning of pesticide appliers. From a worker-welfare perspective, these standards are enormously important. Pesticide applicators are the group of agricultural workers most directly exposed to agrochemicals on a regular basis (Simoniello et al. 2008). Consequently, GLO-BALGAP sets standards that specify that applicators must be provided with protective clothing and safety equipment and must be trained how to perform the task safely. According to the Chilean Ministry of Health, appliers who work on GLOBALGAP-certified farms benefit from these standards. However, these standards target only male appliers who are part of the more "privileged" layer of the workforce, that is, those hired on a full-time, permanent basis. However, workers dressed in street clothing routinely mix chemicals or apply them from a backpack or tractor without any protective gear (Simoniello et al. 2008).

Images of unprotected pesticide applicators raise the specter of a public relations scandal that could damage the reputations and profits of growers and retailers. With the extension of global value chains, social movement organizations often "name and shame" corporations into modifying their social and environmental practices (Raworth and Kidder 2009). The objective of these campaigns is to expose a corporation's undesirable or destructive behavior publicly with the intent of pressuring it to act in a more socially responsible manner. In reaction to public demands for corporate social responsibility, such forms of risk management allow retailers, large-scale growers, and exporters to modify some of their conventional agricultural practices in a manner that will protect their economic interests (Bain 2010a). Although GLOBALGAP standards pose some initial costs for growers, ODEPA (2005) suggests that it is economically beneficial for producers to increase the health, education, and skills of their full-time workforce.

A majority of GLOBALGAP standards are directed at applicators, so these standards do little to prevent the pesticide poisoning of women. Because of the gendered division of labor, temporeras do not typically work as pesticide applicators. From a risk perspective, there is little incentive for retailers to develop health and safety standards to protect temporeras. Campaigns for corporate social responsibility focus on issues that have the power to provoke a visceral and immediate response from the public in the Global North, such as the use of child labor or economic practices that destroy or pollute the ecosystem. Because the pesticide poisoning of women is largely invisible, it poses few direct risks for retailers. In addition, there are few economic incentives for growers to invest in providing safety equipment, training, or health care to their temporary workers (Standing 1999).

However, pesticide poisoning of agricultural workers occurs in gender-specific ways that put women at considerable risk. Women are typically present during all fieldwork, including pesticide applications. Consequently, the levels of exposure may be higher for females because male applicators are more likely to wear protective gear (Simoniello et al. 2008), even though the poisoning of women is less directly observable (Zhang et al. 2010). For example, in agriculture the skin is a major conduit for absorbing pesticides (Simoniello et al. 2008). Temporeras are hired to weed, prune, pick, and pack the fruit, and these activities expose them to direct dermal contact with pesticide-contaminated surfaces. In addition, women are frequently present during pesticide application and are exposed to significant risk from airborne pesticide drift (Simoniello et al. 2008; Dalvie et al. 2011). Unaware of the risks and the subtle ways in which they are being poisoned or fearful of losing their jobs if they complain, most women do not report nonacute incidents of pesticide exposure. According to the president of a temporera advocacy organization, women reported that

> the airplane goes by fumigating or tractor fumigators go by, and [women] have to move a little to the side so that the tractor can go by, but [they are] all wet from the liquids. Can you imagine that with these tremendous gusts women are having pesticides sprayed all over their bodies? Can you imagine the quantity of diseases that those women accumulate in their bodies? Can you imagine how we felt knowing that these women were viewed simply as tools for work, as disposable women?

Despite these risks, there is no GLOBALGAP requirement for protective clothing or special training for nonapplicators. The only direct standard that addresses them is the minor must that requires a warning sign for reentry intervals (typically forty-eight hours) after pesticides have been sprayed. In addition, there is a minor must requiring that "relevant instructions are in a visible place where all visitors or subcontractors can read them" (GLO-BALGAP 2007). In view of the seriousness of pesticide poisoning, this standard is strikingly passive, and it naively assumes that all these individuals can read. Most labor subcontractors are unregulated, operate illegally, and are notorious for not respecting labor laws or standards. However, growers hire them because of these kinds of cost-cutting measures. Some of the most egregious incidents of acute pesticide poisoning in Chile have occurred because subcontractors violated the forty-eight-hour reentry period. Temporeras are brought in by subcontractors to work in the fields without waiting for the required time between spraying and reentry (interview of DOE manager).

Although formal risk assessments can be valuable for addressing the acute exposure of workers to pesticides, their value for assessing chronic exposure is limited. Indeed, it is difficult to determine "the synergistic impacts of exposure to low levels of multiple toxins over long periods of time," (Harrison 2004: 295), and there is insufficient information about the effects of "chemical mixtures, so-called 'inert' ingredients, or a given pesticide's breakdown ingredients." Public health research shows that "cumulative exposures to low levels of multiple environmental toxins" are responsible for some of the most damaging effects on the human body (Harrison 2004: 295). Analysis of pesticide drift in California shows that "non-crisis" and "low-level exposures" of workers and communities have become so "naturalized" that nobody notices or reports them (Harrison 2008: 1203). Indeed, such risks are viewed as a routine part of the business of doing agriculture. Because GLOBALGAP does not directly confront these issues, its standards similarly naturalize and silence the chronic poisoning of women, workers, and communities (Harrison 2004).

The poisoning of workers has gendered outcomes because of female social reproductive responsibilities that include biological and generational reproduction, child rearing, provision of household basic needs, and care for sick, disabled, or elderly dependents (Pearson 2007). Exposure to agrochemicals can affect women's reproductive health and maternity outcomes in ways that include delayed fertility, spontaneous miscarriages, and birth defects (Naidoo et. al. 2011). Fetuses exposed in utero and young infants are particularly vulnerable (Eskenazi et al. 2007; Petit et al. 2010). For example, a woman exposed to agrochemicals is six times more likely to have a baby born with a birth defect than a female who is not exposed (Naidoo et al. 2011: 228). In addition, hazards posed by agrochemicals extend beyond the workplace and reach into the households of farmworkers. Pollutants accumulate in the home, carried on workers' bodies, clothes, and shoes and traveling from surrounding fields through water, soils, and air. Schoolchildren and the residents of agricultural communities are also exposed through pesticide drift (Simoniello et al. 2008; Zhang et al. 2010; Dalvie et al. 2011).

In short, the gendered social, political, and economic context in which women live and work is excluded from consideration in developing or enforcing GLOBALGAP standards. To keep production costs low, retailers and producers seek to externalize the costs and risks of agricultural production to workers' bodies, their families, rural communities, and their environment (Pearson 2007; Dunaway 2012). Lacking affordable access to health care, women bear the brunt of responsibility for providing the necessary care to children and other family members who are sickened, injured, or disabled through their exposure to pesticides in the workplace, schools, and the home. GLOBALGAP focuses on risk assessment and technological fixes that entrench gendered health and safety standards. In reality, women's bodies are subject to the negative health impacts of agrochemicals largely because of their marginalized status in the labor market. A gendered value chain analysis helps us understand that the buying practices of retailers are determinants of this economic marginalization and social vulnerability (Raworth and Kidder 2009). For example, retailer demands for rigid quality specifications, just-in-time delivery, and low prices have pressured growers to reduce their labor costs by increasing their use of temporary and subcontracted labor.

By wrapping standards in scientific rhetoric, GLOBALGAP ensures that it seats at the decision-making table only those stakeholders who possess "technical expertise" and imposes negative consequences on those "who do not have a voice" (Tallontire et al. 2011: 433). Through representation on GLOBALGAP committees, Chilean growers successfully oppose standards that they view as not allowing them enough latitude to constrain labor costs. The 2001 GLOBALGAP protocol required auditors to verify that growers were complying with fourteen standards related to government employment regulations, including ones on wages, child labor, hours of work, and labor contracts. As part of the process of "continuous improvement," the 2004 GLOBALGAP protocol reduced the monitoring to the appointment of "a member of management" to be responsible "for ensuring compliance with . . . national and local regulations on worker health, safety and welfare issues" (EUREPGAP 2004: 21). The certification procedure no longer takes into account whether a grower complies with public labor laws (Higgins and Larner 2010). Because labor accounts for about 70 percent of grower production costs, widespread noncompliance with minimum-wage and worker safety regulations allows growers to cut labor costs sharply (Bain 2010b). Obviously, the reduced monitoring represents a significant victory for growers.

Finally, it is important to mention the limitations of third-party certification for making worker concerns visible. GLOBALGAP standards are verified through a process of third-party certification that is couched in claims of scientific practice, transparency, objectivity, replicability, and validity (Higgins and Larner 2010; Konefal and Hatanaka 2011). Growers are shielded from public criticism through independent corroboration that they are complying with labor and environmental standards (O'Rourke 2006). However, this review process is inherently political because it is imbued with power, ideology, and normative determinations of how risks should be distributed (Harrison 2004; S. Brown and Getz 2008; Guthman 2009; Higgins and Larner 2010). Although the standards and the audit process are ostensibly "independent," they are established by GLOBALGAP to protect retailer interests. In monitoring pesticide use by growers, GLOBALGAP privileges the concerns of retailers and their customers over those of workers. GLOBALGAP standards for worker health, safety, and welfare are verified through a review of grower documentation of compliance. Few, if any, interviews with workers or observations of workplace practices take place. As a GLOBALGAP trainer in one of Chile's largest exporting companies explained, the certifiers "focus on going through all the paperwork.

They can verify different aspects of the paperwork but they don't. They might just ask for an explanation but they don't normally doubt anything that's in the paperwork." This kind of perfunctory paper pushing creates structural space for noncompliance with public labor laws (Bain 2010a). In contrast to its laxity about monitoring of worker safety, GLOBALGAP is much stricter about its standards for pesticide residues on fruit, requiring that growers have independent laboratories conduct tests for residues. This dichotomization of standards and monitoring grows out of GLOBALGAP's own cost analysis. Because pesticide residues are a major concern among consumers, the European Union has established standards for maximum residue levels that retailers are expected to meet. To enhance accountability and transparency, the British government has a website devoted to publicly naming and shaming those retailers and products that fail to meet European Union standards. From a risk perspective, retailers face considerable economic and reputational risk if growers fail to meet residue standards that protect consumers, but they face few risks or costs if growers fail to meet standards that ensure worker health, safety, and welfare.

• • •

Through standards grounded in claims of scientism, GLOBALGAP provides Chilean fruit growers and retailers a lofty platform from which to advertise to buyers that they are socially responsible. Feminist global value chain analysis that integrates labor and households is a powerful tool for revealing the gendered shortcomings of GLOBALGAP standards and for pinpointing the inequitable distribution of risks that derive from weak policing of these standards (Guthman 2009). In reality, GLOBALGAP standards do little to advance the well-being of a majority of Chilean peasant workers, more than half of whom are women. Instead, they are framed and advanced in such a way that they reproduce labor-market and household inequities based on gender. GLOBALGAP procedures to prevent incidents of pesticide poisoning are relevant only to that relatively small segment of full-time male workers who directly apply or handle pesticides. By excluding indirect forms of pesticide poisoning in the workplace, the home, and the community, GLOBALGAP standards render largely invisible the acute and chronic poisoning of temporeras, their families, and residents of agricultural communities.

GLOBALGAP standards are constructed to permit employers to externalize much of the risk of poisoning to women and to adjacent worker households and thereby to deny exporter responsibility for threats to social reproduction (Chapter 13). Framing pesticide poisoning as a technical problem devoid of social context legitimates the exclusion of workers, especially women, from defining the problem and advocating for solutions. By wrapping its rhetoric in technoscientism, GLOBALGAP assigns such matters to disembodied "experts" whose knowledge is treated as though it is more perfect than that held by affected workers and communities (Feenberg and Hannay 1995). However, decisions about who has the authority to establish such standards are situated, partial, and interested (Feenberg and Hannay 1995; Longino 1996). Standards aimed exclusively at male workers structure new gender inequalities and risks. Because females are excluded from the boundaries of risk assessment, standards like those generated by GLOBALGAP provide growers and retailers "stamps of approval" for limited labor safety that begins and ends at the farm gate. As Prieto-Carrón (Chapter 13) explains, such standards are developed in ways that emulate labor rights as articulated by unions, but they ignore potential negative impacts on social reproduction of households and communities.

Moreover, it is simplistic and impractical to advocate greater female participation in standards construction without addressing the question of power. A feminist global value chain framework illuminates the power inequalities that allow retailers and growers to prevent the development of effective safety standards. Retailers demand that growers bear more of the costs and risks associated with food safety, product quality, and just-in-time deliveries. In turn, growers seek to reduce their labor costs and responsibilities by subcontracting their labor requirements and by intensifying the exploitation and vulnerability of workers (Bain 2010b). Without the active engagement of Chilean women and workers, standards will continue to privilege the concerns of Northern retailers and consumers over Chilean workers, and the poisoning of temporeras will remain invisible. Unfortunately, the ability of temporeras to engage in determining the nature of their workplace conditions is highly constrained because farmworkers, especially temporary, subcontracted workers, are typically not organized (Raworth and Kidder 2009). But there is reason for optimism. Peasant women's activist organizations, especially Chile's National Association of Rural and Indigenous Women, which has eight thousand members, are fighting to address the pesticide poisoning of temporeras and to advance their social and economic rights. This activist group challenges the business view that worker health and safety and pesticide poisoning are technical problems that can be addressed by technocratic fixes. They work to publicize incidents of pesticide poisoning, to organize street protests and public forums, and to highlight the social, political, and ethical dimensions of labor conditions in the export fresh-fruit sector.[4]

PART IV INTEGRATION OF INDIGENOUS AND PEASANT HOUSEHOLDS INTO GLOBAL COMMODITY CHAINS

CHAPTER EIGHT

Informal Provisioning Chains versus Commodity Chains

MARKETING OF INDIGENOUS POVERTY AND CULTURE AS THREATS TO HOUSEHOLDS AND WOMEN

Kathleen Pickering Sherman and Andrea Akers

Indigenous peoples were the colonized involuntary contributors of the land, natural resources, and labor that fueled the emergence of the capitalist world-system in the sixteenth century (Wallerstein 1974).[1] The penetration of capitalism into new frontiers resulted in the subjugation of indigenous populations by European resettlers who exploited their labor and ecological resources (Fenelon 1998; Hall and Fenelon 2004, 2009; Bodley 2008) to resolve cyclical crises of accumulation (Amin 1974). Historical assessments of commodity chains feature indigenous people as producers of "commodities in the primitive sense" (Foley 1983: 87). For instance, the international fur trade incorporated indigenous communities to capture their labor and raw materials for export to world markets (Pickering 1995; Dunaway 1996; Carlson 2002; Kardulias 2007). Indigenous peoples have been treated as premodern obstacles to development, but their lands have been repeatedly grabbed for the agricultural, mineral, and other ecological resources that lie within their territories (Bodley 2008). These land grabs have either dispossessed them or forced them into commodity chains that absorb them erratically as low-paid contract or informal producers or as unfree workers (Harvey 2003; Pearce 2012). In addition to those forms of resource extraction, Western scholars, pharmaceuticals, and the Human Genome Project have mined indigenous communities for medical knowledge and genetic DNA that can be patented and used to produce health commodities that are distributed through vast global commodity chains that rarely benefit the indigenous source communities (Pareake 1996). Moreover, indigenous artifacts, religions, and cultural peculiarities are increasingly being integrated into cultural production chains for export (A. Pratt 2008) through "heritage tourism" in which "cultural brokers" represent indigenous peoples as tourist souvenirs (Blundell 1994, 269; Bair 2011: 177) and through the marketing of their artifacts, music, dancing, religious rituals and totems, fabrics, cosmetics, jewelry, cuisine, and myths (Gibson and Connell 2004; Pilcher

2008; Turner 2008). We will argue in this essay that the indigenous group we study in the United States is integrated into two types of specialized commodity chains that threaten household survival and cultural persistence. We will also contend that the households in this indigenous community benefit more from their informal provisioning chains than from externally controlled commodity chains.

TARGET AREA, METHODS OF INQUIRY, AND RESEARCH QUESTIONS

Our target population is the Lakota people of the Pine Ridge Indian Reservation in South Dakota. We used the indigenous household (as bounded by the Lakota people) as the unit of analysis for our research in order (1) to move away from the static and atomistic picture of individuals engaged in fixed relationships and activities and (2) to capture a more accurate depiction of how household membership and economic resources are dynamic and contested strategies that change, in some cases radically, over time (Pickering 2000a, 2004; Knack 2001). To accomplish these objectives, we collected longitudinal economic data from three hundred Lakota households on the Pine Ridge Indian Reservation between 2001 and 2010. We designed our questions to gather information on time allocation by household members, household consumption patterns, and social networks that shape household economic opportunities, decision making, and survival strategies.[2]

This essay will explore three questions about indigenous communities that have not previously been investigated by commodity chain analysts:

1. What is conceptually significant about the semiproletarian structure of indigenous households and their informal provisioning chains?
2. How and why is indigenous poverty integrated into external "buyer-driven commodity chains" (Gereffi and Korzeniewicz 1994: 7; Bair 2009: 19–21)?
3. Who benefits from the integration of indigenous culture into global tourism commodity chains?

CONCEPTUAL COMPLEXITIES OF SEMIPROLETARIANIZED LAKOTA HOUSEHOLDS

Capitalists benefit from employing workers who are located in semiproletarian households in which a decisive share of income is located outside the wage relation (Wallerstein 1995a). Fundamental processes of capital accumulation and unequal exchange are taking place within semiproletarian households around the world (Chapter 3), and such households predominate on Pine Ridge (Pickering 2000b). However, their economic significance remains obscured because these households are not embodied in the sexist forms that the imagination of "modernity" has constructed for the social sciences. The vantage points and practices of semiproletarian households have been obliterated from the hegemonic perspectives of (1) wage-based labor that can be measured by limited Western accounting methods, (2) labor and ecological resources that have value only after they are commodified, and (3) markets that are philosophically (but wrongly) defined to be "actors" with the capacity to resolve all "development" shortfalls and to meet all human needs (Wallerstein 2001). Rather than being touted for its worldwide expansion of modernity, the capitalist world-economy should be viewed as a small collection of well-endowed, feudal-like manor houses that are surrounded by multiple seas of poverty (Burns 1999: 125). As scholars, we need to try looking up from those seas where the majority of the world's population resides rather than down from the few manor houses. Only then will we be able to understand the need to document historically embedded economic and ecological practices, women's diverse forms of labor, and household reproduction strategies that are rarely acknowledged in commodity chain analyses. In our research, we have also emphasized the need for scholars to stop essentializing indigenous women and households as uncomplicated, passive victims. Dialectically, Lakota women employ household strategies to increase their returns from participating in commodity chains even when they are constrained by the unequal power relations in these systems (Pickering 2003).

Pine Ridge is situated on a far edge of the economic periphery of the core country in which it is located, and its people exist outside the boundaries of consciousness of a majority of Americans. Historically, U.S. government policies relentlessly pushed the Lakota people's transformation into individualistic, cash-based market participants. As part of numerous attempts to force Lakota household assimilation into the market economy, the Bureau of Indian Affairs implemented policies of individual allotment of tribal lands, mandatory vocational education, boss farmers instructing Lakota landowners in commodity agriculture, and relocation of Lakota workers to urban areas (Pickering 2000b: 64–66, 93–96). In the 1960s, capitalist production was concentrated in a series of failed experiments with factory work on the reservation. Like searchlights in the darkness that approached without warning, these short-term development strategies blazed for a moment and then moved on. Despite all the government interventions, formal economic markets have been slow to form on Pine Ridge, which has been the poorest U.S. county since 1980 (Pickering et al. 2006). There is virtually no thriving commerce because there are fewer than fifty Lakota-owned small businesses. With one or two exceptions, no local business employs more than twenty people, and most rely on two or three employees other than immediate family members. Even though Pine Ridge is the size of the state of Connecticut, it has no permanent banking services.

Overall, Pine Ridge people are redundant laborers in the world-economy, so they have not been incorporated into the kinds of agricultural, industrial, or service commodity chains that have expanded throughout the Global South. Despite the apparent economic isolation of the reservation, however, Lakota households are integrated into complex webs of commodity production and exchange that link them to global and national markets and to distant consumers. Households on Pine Ridge are predominantly semiproletarian units (Wallerstein 2004: 32–34) that rely most heavily on nonwaged sources of income and household resources (Dunaway 2012). Because their waged income is sporadic, part-time, temporary, or located off the reservation, household members must pool five other types of nonwaged income in a frequently shifting mix: (1) subsistence production for direct consumption (e.g., hunting, gathering), (2) informal-sector marketing (petty commodity production or microenterprise for cash sales), (3) intracommunity gifts across households, (4) barter of goods and services, and (5) public and private transfer payments. Intermittently, some Lakota laborers earn wages from production-driven commodity chains. However, most waged and microenterprise activities are undertaken to meet specific cash needs and therefore tend to be short term and episodic. Interhousehold networks redistribute goods, food, and cash through ceremonial and community events. These forms of household income are supplemented by transfer payments, including private retirement pensions, Social Security and Supplemental Security Income benefits, U.S. Department of Agriculture (USDA) food stamps or commodities, and welfare remittances from Temporary Assistance to Needy Families (TANF) (Sherman 1988; Pickering 2000a, 2000b, 2004; Pickering et al. 2006).

The Diverse Portfolio of Income-Earning Activities

One result of the lack of formal economic markets is that Lakota people engage in a broad mixture of economic activities in the short term and over the course of their lives. Waged opportunities are limited, and many of the waged jobs are short term, temporary, or part-time, so it is unlikely that any individual will have real job security. The Pine Ridge unemployment rate is 34.3 percent, but this figure is deceptive because 49 percent of the working-age population is not counted in the active labor force. Only 48 percent of the households have at least one full-time wage worker, and another 9 percent have at least one part-time wage worker. Consequently, households must simultaneously engage in a broad mixture of activities that allow them access to resources and support outside formal wage-labor markets, including informal exchanges of services, home-based informal-sector enterprises, subsistence practices, and retirement and welfare benefits. Nearly three-quarters of the households engage in subsistence activities, relying on wild food resources that require time either to hunt and gather or to network socially with those who do (Pickering and Jewell 2008:153).

Tiyospaye and Informal Provisioning Chains

Lakota economic practices are deeply embedded in historical social relationships that cut across households. The *tiyospaye* (extended family) is the defining feature of social, political, and cultural organization. Household composition is dynamic and fluid, and the concept of family embraces many different relationships and individuals. The boundaries between extended and immediate families is obscured by the fluidity and size of household composition, as well as the close interaction of family members on a daily basis. Coresident families are often multigenerational and can encompass distant and fictive kin, and households may raise offspring of extended kin. As individuals fluidly enter and exit households, they bring with them different skill sets and abilities that support repeated diversifications of livelihood strategies. Because of the significance of nonwaged household resources, the identity of Lakota individuals is not defined by their jobs. In initial conversations, Lakota people inquire about relationships through birth, marriage, or friendship that might establish common network links, unlike Westerners, who focus on the occupation or place of employment of new acquaintances.

Because these interhousehold linkages determine access to resources and economic information, it is risky for individuals to fail to prioritize them. According to one woman, Lakota life is grounded in an ethic of interhousehold sharing and caring.

> If we have food and if somebody doesn't have food, or they're hungry, you feed that person, you give them food. Because you know as long as you do that, you'll never be hungry yourself. . . . [People who fail to participate in these sharing practices] would sort of be like outcasts, basically. . . . They have separated themselves. Because in order to be involved in something, you have to be involved. You have to take time enough to ask, "Do you need help?" or "Is there anything I can do?"

Thus *tiyospaye* forms the basis for interhousehold exchanges of resources and labor because family relationships are the most significant networks through which resources are distributed and redistributed across the reservation. We think of these networks as informal provisioning chains. The laborers, households, and other actors within these networks do not engage in their "trading" to acquire competitive advantage or profit in the capitalist sense. Instead, they "deposit" or "withdraw" from the communal pool of services, knowledge, contacts, and goods in relation to their degree of current shortage or surplus. Thus "value" is determined in terms of contribution to the survival essentials of households and of the community, unlike commodity and value chains, in which value is expressed in prices of consumer goods and degree of profit taking. The extended family is central to the operation of these nonmarket and informal-sector linkages, and information about economic opportunities flows through networks of relatives and friends. In the same fashion in which capitalists move production inputs or partially assembled goods across nodes of a commodity chain that subsequently distributes a commodity to buyers, Lakota women use family networks to organize and manage rummage sales or secondhand-goods donations, and they use the same networks to redistribute goods they obtain.[3] Similarly, social and spiritual events are announced by word of mouth through kin-based networks. The location of ripe wild plants, labor needed to host ceremonial events, potential buyers for the products of home-based enterprises, and information about special programs or tribal opportunities are all accessed through family networks.

These informal provisioning chains are also sources of credit. In response to an open-ended question about what a household would do if it did not have money to pay a late bill, 26.4 percent of interviewees responded that they would approach family and friends for the money. Similar results were obtained from a series of open-ended questions about the people who provided various forms of support to the household, with 76.5 percent of the responses indicating an immediate or extended family member as the source of support. Tribal politics is a proxy for kinship relationships, and the lion's share of external resources flows through tribal governmental structures. For example, 58 percent of the available jobs are with either the federal or the tribal government. People commonly observe that tribal politicians and government workers prioritize their own family and friends, but they interpret this as nepotism only when they are outside that network. For that reason, 36.8 percent responded that they would approach a tribal government program to try to access the funds to pay a late household bill. As in the Turkish family textile workshops and the export-commodity-producing Philippine peasant fishing households described in Chapters 6 and 9, gender is a critical factor in Lakota interhousehold exchanges. The economic strategies of Lakota women are more diversified than those of men, and females infuse more of their cultural values, such as generosity and respect, into their economic activities (Akers 2011). Consequently, 69 percent of respondents who borrowed funds from relatives networked with women; this demonstrates the greater importance of females in maintaining these informal provisioning chains.

Cultural Exchange Traditions

Traditional nonmarket cultural and religious ceremonies are additional nodes of these provisioning chains that provide part of the material support of households. A majority of Lakota households participate in ceremonies, powwows, funerals, or other community events. These gatherings involve distributions of food and household goods, reinforcement of extended and fictive kinship relationships, and critical exchanges of information about scarce resources and opportunities. The average level of household participation in these events was twenty-six events per year, and each may run continuously for twenty-four hours a day over two to four days. Some households participate in more than two hundred per year. Viewed in light of the typical wage workweek of forty hours, the economic predominance of these nonwaged activities becomes apparent.

Unreliable Welfare Payments

Public welfare benefits have taken two inconsistent forms on U.S. Indian reservations, so indigenous households cannot treat them as resources on which they can rely as strongly as they do on informal provisioning chains that are grounded in interhousehold sharing, subsistence production, or informal-sector marketing. Direct public transfers to impoverished households are the first welfare strategy that is reflected in some reservation household budgets. In 1996, the U.S. government enacted reform legislation to require that welfare recipients (who are overwhelmingly women with young children) engage in wage work. Before welfare reform, families with children were eligible for Aid to Families with Dependent Children (AFDC) on the basis of degree of impoverishment and need. The government strategy behind welfare reform was to end "dependency" by encouraging welfare recipients to find wage-labor positions. The rationale for this reform was the questionable assumption that "full employment" is possible if the unemployed train themselves and seek out work hard enough. Reform conditioned welfare on pursuit of jobs, hence the inclusion of the term "temporary" in the new program's title. The ideology of full employment rings particularly hollow in rural Pine Ridge, which has experienced poverty for more than a century. Because welfare payments are never sufficient to support Lakota households, they are less significant sources of economic resources than informal provisioning chains. Less than two-fifths of Lakota households have participated in either TANF or AFDC, and only 15 percent received TANF payments between 2001 and 2010. Among 2010 TANF recipients, none had a job in the private sector, but 55 percent were temporary workers in government offices that were not planning to hire them permanently. The remaining 45 percent had not been able to find waged employment. In every instance, kin-based networks and nonwaged economic activities and resources made it possible for these households to withdraw from the TANF program.

Pine Ridge can rely even less on the second category of public provisions, health care and retirement. Like the larger American Indian population, the Lakota people of Pine Ridge are faced with some of the worst health disparities in the United States, including inadequate health-care services that contribute to extremely low life expectancies. On the one hand, higher mortality rates culminate in hidden wealth accumulation for capitalism in the form of labor subsidy of Social Security because the contributions Lakota people make to this public retirement program are never collected by the many workers who die prematurely. On the other hand, Pine Ridge residents are outside the reach of the kind of mixed public/private health-service commodity chains that operate in the mainstream United States, and they lack access to state-funded indigent health-care programs. Consequently, the prohibitive cost associated with institutional forms of private health care force Lakota households to assume responsibility for family-based caregiving, which falls inequitably to women. When a family member becomes ill, typically one of that person's female relatives will reduce her responsibilities and obligations to become a caregiver (Pickering and Mizushima 2008).

COMMODITY CHAINS OF FOOD AND POVERTY REDUCTION ON U.S. INDIAN RESERVATIONS

In the sections that follow, we will explore two specialized, externally governed commodity chains that operate exclusively on U.S. Indian reservations. First, we explore how U.S. treaty obligations to supply food rations are precariously embedded in commodity chains of the global agroindustrial food system. Second, externally controlled NGOs produce and distribute services that claim to reduce indigenous poverty. Ironically, these providers cannot benefit in the long term if they actually solve the problems their services are marketed to ameliorate, so these NGOs have vested interests in maintaining the very inequalities they claim to be seeking to end.

Federal Treaty Obligations and Agribusiness Commodity Chains

In exchange for massive Lakota land cessions, the U.S. government agreed in the 1868 treaty negotiated at Fort Laramie to create the Pine Ridge reservation and to provide "annual annuity payments" and "food rations" to its

Lakota residents. Most indigenous Americans interpret several forms of public fund transfers as U.S. government obligations under eighteenth- and nineteenth-century treaties negotiated in exchange for massive indigenous land cessions. Over time, the United States tied those treaty obligations to other economic agendas. Consequently, promised indigenous provisions have been embedded in commodity chains that are grounded in profit-making markets that are not designed to prioritize serving such human needs. In the 1950s, the U.S. Bureau of Indian Affairs commingled treaty food-ration obligations to Indian reservations with federal strategies for promoting increased global marketing of U.S. agricultural commodities. As a mechanism to stabilize agricultural export prices at fictitiously high levels, the U.S. government began to purchase agricultural surpluses through the USDA's Surplus Commodities Program (SCP). Subsequently, the SCP redistributed food surpluses as part of its national and global "aid to the poor" (McMichael 1994: 8). As a result, demands of indigenous peoples that the U.S. government meets its food-ration treaty obligations became intertwined with the emergent agroindustrial food system and its far-reaching array of commodity chains. Although indigenous Americans view the SCP as the continuation of rations promised under treaty rights, each of the foods provided is part of an externally controlled global commodity chain that makes only an erratic and inconsistent side trip to reservations like Pine Ridge. In other words, this program was designed to stimulate economic growth in U.S. agriculture sectors, subsidize export of agricultural exports, and alleviate the impacts of economic downturns on U.S. agriculture. Because meeting food-ration treaty obligations is not a function of the global commodity chains that export food surpluses to the rest of the world, the U.S. government purchases and distributes fewer reserves when there is strong global demand for these commodities. When food rations for Indian reservations, like Pine Ridge, constrain profit accumulation from export commodity chains, U.S. treaty obligations are not met (Jewell 2008). Because this program consistently prioritizes economic growth and stability of the country's agribusinesses, the needs of impoverished recipients on Indian reservations are decommodified in favor of consumers elsewhere whose purchases will generate greater wealth accumulation for U.S. agribusinesses.

The NGO Commodity Chain of Indigenous Poverty Reduction

Freire (1970) and Fox-Piven and Cloward (1971) argue that global elites criminalize, regulate, oppress, and disempower the poor under the guise of programs that "help." Many of the services nation-states once provided to the poor have been deemed government waste by neoliberal development agendas, so public funding for them has been eliminated, and those funds have often been shifted to economic-growth strategies and hidden subsidies to economic elites (Petras 1999). Pressures to privatize former public services have triggered an explosion of new NGOs that provide short-term, limited services and broker the needs of the poor, the environment, women, and children (Schutz 2012). The World Bank defines NGOs as organizations that are "characterized primarily by humanitarian or cooperative, rather than commercial objectives." However, this is not an accurate representation of the origins or economic motivations of many neoliberal-era NGOs (Korten 2001: 21). In his analysis of the role of Western NGOs in the Global South, Petras (1999: 434–35) describes them as a "new petit bourgeoisie" that promulgates neoliberal development agendas.

> The NGOs and their professional staff directly compete with the socio-political movements for influence among the poor, women and racially-excluded. Their ideology and practice diverts attention from the sources and solutions of poverty (looking downward and inward instead of upward and outward). . . . NGO "aid" affects small sectors of the population, setting up competition between communities for scarce resources and generating insidious distinctions and inter and intra community rivalries. . . . The net effect is a proliferation of NGOs that fragment poor communities into sectoral and sub-sectoral groupings unable to see the larger social picture that afflicts them and even less able to unite in struggle against the system.

Thus NGOs function as agents of social control over the poor by neutralizing and fragmenting discontent over the structural inequalities of neoliberal capitalism. In effect, NGOs further disempower the groups they claim to be helping when they position themselves as officially recognized "expert representatives" who have greater influence within governmental and economic settings than the communities for whom they claim to speak (Ferguson 1990). Moreover, they engage in "ideological mystification" to push the policy that poverty is best solved through individual initiative. While people lose jobs and poverty spreads, NGOs advocate "survival strategies" and "alternative livelihoods" that do not address the structural causes of impoverishment.

In the same period in which NGOs have proliferated all over the Global South, they have embedded themselves in U.S. Indian reservations. NGOs serve as a "a safety net" (Petras 1999: 432) for the burgeoning pool of middle-class (mostly Caucasian) professionals who have been negatively affected by job shortages in mainstream America. These professionals advocate the "civil society–free market–alternative development line," and their organizations "sell Indian poverty" to the wealthy foundations that fund development and poverty-reduction programs. The experience of indige-nous poverty is appropriated by these NGOs and sold in the form of "ex-pert research reports" and "innovative poverty-reduction strategies" to ex-ternally controlled, buyer-driven chains of funding organizations. Even though the collected knowledge is derived (and often distorted) from indigenous households, these NGO workers ensure their own access to accumulation and consumption in the current economy by producing commodities in the form of "policy recommendations" that earn them compensation (A. Ross et al. 2011). NGOs take advantage of Western scientific biases that privilege educated experts over indigenous knowledge keepers and producers. By re-stating in "scientific terms" the ideas extracted from indigenous people, NGOs produce knowledge commodities that become more valuable when they are marketed under the label of an NGO or an academic institution. In this way, NGOs position themselves as intermediary voices for indigenous communities and forestall any outward flow of critique or resistance to dis-tant funding sources (Mies and Shiva 2001).

Moreover, NGOs collect the information for their "expert knowledge commodities" by exploiting the unpaid labor of indigenous people, primar-ily females. On the Pine Ridge reservation, NGOs are subsidized by Lakota people, predominantly women, who provide uncompensated work to "teach" these external professionals about the local context, to contact and recruit relevant community members, and to assist with implementation of funded proposals. Even though NGO professionals are paid, they operate on the assumption that Lakota people will work for "free" because the projects are for the "good" of the community. Because women traditionally provide more of these kinds of community service than men, their contributions to this particular form of exploitation are disproportionate. Just as capitalists externalize costs of production to worker households and communities (Chapter 3), NGOs externalize much of the knowledge-production work-load to reservation households by expropriating the unpaid and invisible labor of Lakota women. Because they embrace the work ideologies of the market economy, NGO professionals assume that "unemployed" Lakota women are "inactive" and "able to volunteer" unused labor time. This prac-tice represents a fundamental contradiction of "poverty-reduction" goals be-cause it threatens the survival strategies of these semiproletarian households. In effect, the NGOs drain labor time from Lakota households and women who need to be applying those hours toward their own income and resource accumulation and toward informal provisioning chains.

As Petras (1999) has argued, NGOs often become agents of imperial-ism, both intentionally and unwittingly. Many of the organizations now operating on U.S. Indian reservations are rooted in the colonial history of imperialism toward indigenous Americans. Many of these charitable and educational foundations derive their operational funds from the capital accumulation of agroindustry, transportation, and communication systems that have expropriated indigenous resources from the seventeenth through the twenty-first centuries. Now, those derivative NGOs determine strategies for ending the indigenous poverty that those industries created. The true exploitative nature of the relationship between the donors and the recipients is concealed behind the benign guise of a "gift," and what is "good" for Lakota communities and households is constructed as a knowledge commodity that is defined and circumscribed by external interests. Moreover, those external NGOs accumulate a disproportionate share of the total pool of poverty-reduction funds for their "administrative services" and allocate less of the resources directly to impoverished households and communities (Fox-Piven and Cloward 1971). On the one hand, the commodity chain is really designed to generate employment for off-reservation middle-class professionals, not for the indigenous poor. On the other hand, this knowledge-construction process is designed to blame victims for their lack of livelihoods. Thus these NGOs do not pinpoint the structural linkages between indigenous poverty and commodification of reservation lands by the Bureau of Indian Affairs, which leases prime reservation lands to non-Indians (Pickering 2000b: 131–33). Because the funding sources themselves are historic products of successful capitalist accumulation, NGOs must develop approaches to Lakota poverty alleviation that do not challenge the structural inequalities of capitalism that made their donors rich. As a result, decisions about proposals submitted for funding competitions are devoid of antisystemic challenges. Because capitalist foundations, governmental agencies, and complicit NGOs control agendas of development and poverty alleviation, the crucial work of Lakota community healing and rebuilding will never be on the table.

Fundamentally, administrative procedures of NGOs and distant foundations (e.g., formal board structures, single-year projects, external evaluation, and repeatedly changing grant guidelines) deter communities from defining their own visions for the future. Furthermore, energy is diverted away from informal provisioning chains and toward winning the ever-elusive foundation support that will foster the kinds of short-term "development" and "modernization" projects that have repeatedly failed to reduce poverty throughout U.S. Indian reservations and the Global South. Funding sources also marginalize Lakota organizations, so they cannot compete with external NGO commodity chains (Pickering 2000b: 30–35). To complicate matters, Lakota communities are further disrupted because the economic positions of global capitalists shape and determine the buyer-driven NGO commodity chains. Like corporate enterprises, charitable commodity chains ebb and flow with the upturns and downturns in the wealth accumulation of individual capitalists and of the world-economy (Bergesen 1983). In times of economic expansion, there is increased need for capitalists to silence those who are being marginalized (Fox-Piven and Cloward 1971), so capitalists make larger donations, intending to obligate the recipients to the logic and purposes of capitalism and to circumvent resistance to exploiters who are offering to "help." In times of economic downturn, external aid declines as the wealth accumulation of capitalist donors contracts.

COMMODIFICATION OF TRADITIONAL LAKOTA RESOURCES AND CULTURE

Externally controlled NGOs have followed two broad practices in their "poverty-reduction" work on U.S. Indian reservations. First, they have marketed Lakota poverty reduction by reformulating indigenous knowledge into "expert" reports within commodity chains that limit public policy formation to approaches that will cut least deeply into the profits of capitalists. Second, NGOs seek, in their role as a new petit bourgeoisie acting in behalf of distant capitalists, to control the impoverished by implementing "entrepreneurship" strategies that resituate the causes of poverty in individual faults and shortcomings. In addition to these externally controlled NGO chains, Lakota labor and resources are being integrated into buyer-driven commodity chains that fetishize indigenous cultural traditions for marketing to distant consumers. "Even in the special realm of community and religious ceremonies, the ubiquity of market-based transactions continually challenges Lakotas to define and to redefine their values and practices within new contexts of commodities and cash sales" (Pickering 2000b: 61). In the sections that follow, we will examine mainstream exoticization of bison meat and explore the incorporation of Lakota culture into tourism commodity chains.

Second Coming, and Going, of the Buffalo?

Until the buffalo were nearly destroyed in the late 1800s, the Lakota relied on them for food, clothing, and shelter and integrated them into Lakota cosmology and social structure (Pickering 2000b: 4). "The great buffalo herds, which once numbered as high as seventy million animals, were almost killed to extinction by Euro-American settlers for hides, tongues, sport, and for control of the Native nations that depended upon them" (Village Earth 2012). Subsequent adoption of foods from global commodity chains led to abandonment of traditional Lakota practices and the emergence of a health crisis. In 2010, more than half of Pine Ridge households had at least one member with diabetes, and nearly 18 percent had at least one member with cancer. The ill health of one individual can be devastating for semiproletarian Lakota households. When ill health eliminates one contributor from the household resource pool, other family members or informal provisioning chains must be engaged to offset this loss. Such extended self-exploitation of household members generates high levels of fatigue, stress, and anxiety that can trigger health problems for additional household members (Pickering and Mizushima 2008).

Traditionally, Lakota people view their lives and households as being interdependent with nature, and those beliefs are embedded in their use of ecological resources. In a seven-year longitudinal study of three hundred Pine Ridge households, more than 80 percent of respondents maintained that their spiritual beliefs are connected to the way they view nature. Although 73 percent of Lakota households use natural resources for trade and subsistence, they situate those activities within their ecological ideology that humans, animals, and plants survive through interdependence on one another (Pickering and Jewell 2008:153). It is in this context that past and present buffalo-revitalization efforts have occurred. Interest in buffalo-restoration efforts were first initiated in the late nineteenth century after the great herds were nearly extinguished from the native prairie grasslands. In the 1880s, the Ghost Dance movement emerged as an indigenous effort to remove the growing populations of white settlers and to restore buffalo to lands confiscated by whites (Sherman 2004). Contemporary Lakota households have been quietly returning buffalo to the reservation landscape, either as a transition from cattle ranching or as a new microenterprise. In addition to a tribally owned herd, there are several dozen individual Lakota bison farmers. Although bison are popularly viewed as wild game, 95 percent of the approximately five hundred thousand bison in North America are privately owned (Van Lanen 2007: 130). The Lakota Caretakers Buffalo Cooperative is a group of small-family buffalo caretakers who are "committed to the restoration of the northern plains ecology and self-sufficiency and to strengthening the sovereignty and self-determination of the Ogala Lakota Nation and all indigenous peoples" (Village Earth 2012). When asked about their motivations for raising buffalo, 68 percent of Lakota buffalo farmers expressed nonmarket rationales, including reviving the traditional Lakota diet and restoring the spiritual importance of buffalo. Moreover, 75 percent of the buffalo caretakers used their surplus animals for nonmarket purposes, including family consumption and ceremonial applications (Sherman 2004).

The role and status of women are intertwined with the buffalo in Lakota cultural history. White Buffalo Calf Woman appeared with a sacred pipe that she instructed the Lakota to smoke as a commitment to internal peace and cooperation. She demonstrated the seriousness of respecting women by disintegrating a man who had lascivious thoughts about her when she first appeared in human form. She also instructed the people to respect their elders and to take care of their relatives, forming the foundation for the *tiyospaye* as the hallmark of social organization of informal provisioning chains. Coupled with the notion of *mitakuyeoyasin'* (all my relatives), Lakota spiritual dedication to respect and care is extended beyond blood relatives to encompass all human beings, all living things, and all elements of the universe, including rocks, stars, and seasons (i.e., the philosophy underlying informal provisioning chains). Lakota society models itself after the Buffalo Nation, which positions strong women to provide leadership for families and households (Pickering 2000b: 3, 6, 30). Consequently, women feature prominently in the households of contemporary buffalo farmers. As a home-based operation, buffalo caretaking depends on women fiscal managers who orchestrate the pooling and distribution of resources in ways that integrate the buffalo into Lakota economic, social, and spiritual livelihoods. When buffalo operations experience economic shortfalls, women assume expanded responsibility for filling the gaps in household resource pools by working for wages or producing home-based items for informal-sector marketing. One male buffalo caretaker summed up the centrality of women when he reported that "help" from wives makes buffalo revitalization "possible." In addition to their unpaid support roles, women are leading the community toward healthier diets that reintegrate buffalo and other traditional foods and toward healthier lifestyles that involve getting back to activities tied to the land and to the ecosystem (Sherman 2004).

Rising rates of obesity and diabetes in the United States are tied to high levels of consumption of processed and unhealthy foods generated by global agroindustrial food commodity chains. As a result, a national search for healthier foods is drawing a large range of new commodities into the global marketplace. As exotic-food commodity chains reach into peripheral rural areas once ignored by global capitalists, elements of the diets of Global South peasants (Raynolds 1994; Grosfoguel 1995) and of indigenous peoples (e.g., Chalfin 2004) are being exported from peripheral communities and integrated into the global agroindustrial food system (Friedmann 1993). In the United States, public policies are pushing citizens to lower consumption of high-fat meats, and health NGOs have fetishized alternative protein sources, triggering contemporary fads in consumption of substitutes, like soy and buffalo. The American Heart Association includes buffalo in its dietary guidelines, and several commercial weight-loss programs recommend buffalo. Compared with beef, bison meat is lower in fat, calories, and cholesterol but higher in iron and vitamin B-12 (Van Lanen 2007).

Lakota buffalo are exported as part of external buyer-driven commodity chains that shift bison cultivation from an indigenous cultural process to production of a national and global meat that is regulated by state and transnational policies. In the United States, public guidelines require supervised slaughter in a USDA-inspected meatpacking facility. According to the Lakota Buffalo Caretakers Cooperative, the indigenous alternative to this universal USDA standard "is raising buffalo their entire lives on open pastures and respectfully ending their lives in the field. In fact, some families have made this into a sort of rite of passage for young men, [and they] prepare them in ceremonies to take the lives of the buffalo in a respectful manner. It is said that . . . the animals within those particular families are much calmer during the harvests" (Village Earth 2012).

However, such indigenous cultural considerations are "not rational" and "not efficient" (A. Pratt 2008: 97) in contrast to competing agribusiness commodity chains that are organized to maximize profits. On the one hand, the special arrangements that must be made for a USDA inspector to witness field harvesting of buffalo place significant time constraints and considerable logistical burdens on the Lakota operators. In addition, traditional field processing is costlier and more unpredictable because "it requires the use of a mobile-processing truck to drive out to the pasture, so the animals can be gutted and cleaned within 45 minutes of the kill. . . . The families could be saving approximately $180 per animal by trucking live animals directly to a slaughter facility. . . . [And] scheduling the truck is very unpredictable [because] it is not able to drive onto their pastures if they are wet or covered in snow" (Village Earth 2012).

Despite the state constraints and the added costs, most Lakota bison producers choose to continue traditional harvesting methods. In other parts of the world, a majority of small producers have abandoned traditional methods of producing export-food commodities in order to acquire higher profits or to meet the constraints of buyers (Grosgofuel 1995; Chalfin 2004). The Lakota Buffalo Caretakers Cooperative worries that future Pine Ridge bison producers might make similar decisions (Village Earth 2012).

The future survival of Lakota buffalo is threatened by a second negative impact of the bison-export commodity chain. Although the rising price of bison meat might appear to be a success story, the integration of Lakota bison into global commodity chains is placing buffalo survival at risk once again. The demand for bison meat is so great that the harvesting rates are exceeding the natural capacity for the buffalo to reproduce. As part of an external buyer-driven commodity chain, animals are sought from small producers to meet market demands without any concern for sustainable buffalo reproduction. Unless Lakota caretakers prevent unsustainable yields, short-term profits may once again bring about the second demise of the Buffalo Nation.[4] White Buffalo Calf Woman warned the Lakota that when the buffalo are gone, the sacred hoop of the Lakota will end (Village Earth 2012).

Commodity Chains to Market Indigenous Heritage

Internationally, the World Bank and the World Trade Organization (WTO) advocate global tourism as a growth industry for poor, non-Western communities. One of the high-demand commodities is experiential access to indigenous cultures and lifestyles (Blundell 1994; Pickering 2004; Pilcher 2008; Turner 2008). However, indigenous communities are undercompensated when their unique cultural attributes are integrated into external buyer-driven commodity chains (Clancy 1998). Corporations are protected by international trademark and copyright laws, but most indigenous cultural attributes are not shielded by WTO intellectual property rights and are traded as part of the "free" public domain (Riley 2004). As a result, indigenous communities absorb consumer demand and generate external capital accumulation while they subsidize corporate transportation, lodging, and travel services that provide little or no compensation for their cultural production. Hospitality services are integral to the tourist experience but are largely uncompensated in communities that lack tourism infrastructure that is integrated into nodes of travel capitalism commodity chains. Although tourism has increased access of some Lakota business owners to the cash economy, the gains have been marginal because they cannot compete with regional suppliers who are positioned within international tourism commodity chains. Pine Ridge has one motel and a handful of small bed-and-breakfasts, so the vast majority of tourists fly into Rapid City, where they spend funds on motels, rental cars, and restaurants. Subsequently, visitors drive to Pine Ridge, expecting Lakota people to share their history and culture without charge. When Lakota people are reluctant to do so, the community is condemned as hostile and inhospitable. Disproportionately, Lakota women are the ones who provide the time and energy to feed and inform the American, European, and Asian tourists who are seeking exotic tepees, buffalo, and spiritual titillation. Because most tourists have no conception of the Lakota semiproletarian household, they stereotype their cultural liaisons as females who have nothing better to do because they are unemployed. Even though most Lakota express positive attitudes about the benefits of tourism, there is widespread concern about the danger that Lakota spirituality will be commodified (M. Graham 2009).

Lakota artists produce the handicrafts and artworks that are marketed as tourist souvenirs, but most of the profits from sales accumulate at other nodes of the commodity chain. Regional and national retail outlets demand high prices for indigenous cultural artifacts but pay minimal prices to indigenous producers. At present, 61 percent of Lakota artists have an annual household income of less than $10,000, and 30 percent of them acquire more than half their household income from their art production. In contrast, artists connected to regional markets and direct retail outlets garner four times more per marketed item (Pourier, Sherman, and Dorion 2012). In addition to this on-the-books capital accumulation from indigenous cultural items, regional markets and retail outlets are subsidized by invisible, unpaid female labor. Fifty-eight percent of Lakota artists are women who produce traditional crafts as one element of their diversified semiproletarian household survival portfolio. Moreover, 83 percent of Pine Ridge households produce traditional arts because females can multitask this commodity production alongside unpaid household labor. Because of frequent need for quick cash to meet emergencies and household shortfalls, women can be easily exploited to sell their items for less than the market value of labor time and inputs involved in production of those commodities (Pickering 2000b: 44, 47).

In addition to exploitation of household producers of cultural commodities, Lakota artisans are threatened by the imported goods that are being absorbed into tourism commodity chains.[5] Although the Indian Arts and Crafts Act of 1990 claims to protect Indian artists and craftspeople from competition from inauthentic items fraudulently marketed as "Indian made," enforcement hinges on consumers reporting sales to the Indian Arts and Crafts Board and the local U.S. attorney (Indian Arts and Crafts Board 2012; U.S. Public Law 111.211 2010). Despite this legal prohibition, the global trade in reproductions of indigenous American artifacts is widespread. Cheaper machine-made Asian imports compete with higher-priced handmade Lakota items in National Park Service gift shops, upscale Indian jewelry retail outlets, and vendor tables at regional and national powwows. At a recent powwow, a vendor with tables of imported beadwork items perverted the tradition of *mitakuyeoyasin'* when he defended his commodities by claiming they were produced by "all my relatives."[6] The unequal power relations involved in the efforts of indigenous communities to protect their cultural heritage is exemplified in the recent efforts of the Navajo Nation to sue Urban Outfitters for selling nonauthentic products as "Navajo" artifacts. Urban Outfitters indicates that it will not alter its marketing strategies because "the Native American–inspired trend, and, specifically, the term 'Navajo' have been cycling through fashion, fine art and design for the last few years" (Quinn 2012).

• • •

We have explored three facets of indigenous integration into contemporary commodity chains. First, we explicated the conceptual and economic complexities of semiproletarianized Lakota households that ground their survival primarily in resources acquired from nonwaged activities and sources. Second, we investigated how indigenous underdevelopment and poverty have been integrated into NGO-controlled commodity chains that appropriate knowledge, labor power, and decision-making authority from Lakota people. Third, we examined how Lakota households are currently experiencing the effects of two types of buyer-driven commodity chains (Gereffi and Korzeniewicz 1994: 7; Bair 2009: 19–21). Immanuel Wallerstein (1995b: 4–5) argues that

> those who operate within the framework of a capitalist system seek to commodify ever more operations. And since it is also true that the spread and routinization of commodified activities tends to diminish their profitability, it is logical as well that monopolizing capitalists repeatedly encourage the search for new niches to commodify. The results we know: over time there has been a thrust towards the commodification of everything.

As a result of this historical process, Lakota household survival and women are being threatened by commodity chains that fetishize their traditional culture and livelihood strategies into exotic commodities for consumption by distant, wealthier households. In response to the bison meat industry, the buffalo, an animal of cultural significance to the Lakota, has been transformed into a global commodity. Bison farming was initially represented as an opportunity to increase economic development on the reservation, but excessive consumer demand now threatens a second extinction of the buffalo. Lakota people are also inundated by global consumption of "native experiences," so indigenous arts and culture are increasingly exploited and endangered by their integration into global tourist commodity chains.

CHAPTER NINE

Commodity-Chained Fishing Households

PEASANT SUBSIDIZATION OF EXPORTS IN A PHILIPPINE SEAFOOD-EXTRACTIVE ENCLAVE

Maria Cecilia Ferolin

In 1994, the World Bank congratulated the Philippines for being one of the "most deregulated" economies in Asia and predicted that the country was right on track for full economic recovery by 2000 (*Asia Money Magazine*, March 1996 Supplement). In sharp contrast to that optimistic rhetoric, the Philippines has declined from the most dynamic economy in Asia during the 1950s to a nation facing fiscal crisis and economic stagnation. Before neoliberalism, the Philippine economy was growing at rates of 6 to 10 percent annually, fueled by its import substitution industrialization program. In spite of several rounds of structural adjustment polices mandated by the International Monetary Fund (IMF) that began in the late 1970s, the Philippines is now less industrialized than it was in 1980. After decades of market-oriented economic reforms, the Philippine export structure is now less diversified than it was before the era of neoliberal globalization (Lim and Montes 2002). At present, the Philippines has the lowest rate of economic growth in Southeast Asia, and its foreign direct investment decreased by 83 percent in the early years of the twenty-first century (Escobar 2004).

In reaction to nine IMF-imposed structural adjustment programs, the Philippine government designed fishery-modernization and development goals that prioritized rapid exploitation of ecological resources and deeper integration of the country into the global agroindustrial food system (Republic of the Philippines 1975, 1992, 1998, 2000). Within less than two decades, the country's productive systems were transformed into food-extractive enclaves producing cheap consumer commodities for Japan, western Europe, China, and the United States. To meet its export goals since 1980, the Republic of the Philippines (1975, 1992, 1995, 1998, 2000) set the following development goals:

1. To stimulate and subsidize rapid destruction of a majority of its mangroves
2. To reallocate ecological resources to larger agribusinesses

3. To widen its dependence on genetically modified species and the imported inputs needed to produce them
4. To promote and subsidize large farms and fishing enterprises
5. To prioritize food production for export over outputs for local consumption

As a result, the country has severely damaged its farmlands and waterways, and narrowed its ecological biodiversity significantly (*Philippines Environmental Monitor* 2000).

TARGET AREA AND METHODS OF INQUIRY

This case study is situated in the troubled region of Mindanao, the largest Philippine island. To fuel its export-growth agenda since 1980, the Philippines has been exploiting the rich ecological resources and farmlands of Mindanao. This island is pivotal to national economic-growth goals because it produces 42 percent of the country's seafood, 40 percent of the country's farm crops, and 70 percent of the country's output of seaweed. In its Medium-Term Development Plan (Republic of the Philippines 2000), the government targeted Mindanao as the country's primary agrofishery export zone. Because the target study area, Panguil Bay, is one of Mindanao's richest ecosystems, it has been transformed into a food-exporting enclave that is dependent on imported green/blue/gene-revolution science and technology. Consequently, this fishery has been driven to the point of severe crisis over the past thirty years as its ecological resources and its peasants have been integrated into global commodity chains. The bay region was quickly degraded by export agendas, has undergone more than a decade of failed ecological rehabilitation (MSU Naawan Foundation 2006), and has experienced intensified resource extraction since 2000 (Republic of the Philippines 2000). Between 1982 and 1991, small-scale, family-owned fishponds aimed at domestic markets were displaced by export-oriented aquaculture (JEP-ATRE 2004). In the same period, commercial capture fishing expanded finfish exports dramatically (Bureau of Fisheries and Aquatic Resources [BFAR] 1983–92). In addition, Panguil Bay is ringed by farms and food-processing industries (MSU Naawan Foundation 2006). However, the livelihoods of a majority of the households along Panguil Bay have been threatened and marginalized by these export agendas.

In order to capture the global, national, regional, and local community vantage points for this investigation, I combined ethnographic field research (including focus-group sessions and interviews); analysis of electronic statistical databases (especially those of the Bureau of Agricultural Statistics [BAS], the BFAR, and Quickstat, the country's census databases); and information collected from government, NGO, and newspaper archives.

SEAFOOD COMMODITY CHAINS IN A
FOOD-EXTRACTIVE ENCLAVE

Since 1980, the Philippines has transformed its production systems into globalized food-extractive enclaves that have shifted away from production for local consumption. The country's export agendas are grounded in state promotion of commodities with higher value in global markets. Consequently, the state promotes and subsidizes a narrow range of selected agricultural crops, farmed seaweed, and captured or farmed species of fish, shellfish, crustaceans, and exotic seafoods (Republic of the Philippines 2000). By 2009, less than one-quarter of Panguil Bay farmlands were being used to cultivate crops that were primarily consumed locally, and a majority of fishery production was being exported to Manila and to foreign markets.[1] Even though Panguil Bay encompasses only 0.6 percent of the country's coastal water and 1.2 percent of the country's population, this region produces a disproportionate share of the country's captured and farmed fish (BFAR 1978–2009). Two-thirds of the fish production in this region is derived from capture fishing, the other third from aquaculture. Nearly 70 percent of capture fishers are poor peasants who rely on small, wooden, nonmotorized boats and simple netting systems to generate daily per capita incomes of less than US$2 (MSU Naawan Foundation 2006).

Transformation of the Panguil Bay Fishery

In 1978, peasant fishers accounted for two-thirds of the region's production, and most of their catch was consumed locally. However, capture fishing has transformed dramatically since the 1970s. Change came abruptly to Panguil Bay in the 1980s when the national government began to prioritize the integration of its resources into the global agroindustrial food system. As fishing has been transformed for greater exporting from the region, smaller fishing operations have steadily declined, and peasant fishers have been increasingly marginalized. By 2007, 136 commercial operators generated nearly 42 percent of total output, while more than 15,000 peasant fishers captured only 21 percent of the total fishery production. In 2007, small and midsize boats in municipal waters averaged about 4 kilograms of catch daily, while commercial vessels averaged 333 kilograms. Today, a peasant fisher feels lucky to catch a kilogram of fish after a day's work. The average daily catch is only about 16 percent of the average daily catch in 1978 (BFAR 1978–2009).

In addition to the reorientation of capture fishing to meet national export goals, this region has moved its fish farming away from local consumption. By 1995, fishpond development had expanded to 28,250 hectares, fourteen times the 1951 level. At that point, nearly 13 percent of the country's fishponds were operating in this region. Despite its small coastal water area, Panguil Bay ranked twenty-eighth in the country in aquaculture outputs during the 1990s. Regional fish-farming outputs began to rise sharply in the late 1990s, and export aquaculture has continued unabated into the twenty-first century. As regional export outputs rose, aquaculture and capture-fishing outputs for domestic consumption steadily dropped (BFAR 1978–2008).

In order for communities and their ecosystems to be transformed into extractive enclaves that export foods, subsistence sectors must be minimized or displaced to make way for the creation of new economic activities. Since the 1970s, the Panguil Bay region has undergone massive change to restructure its relations of food production around export activity. Panguil Bay's resources and fishers have been integrated at two levels. First, Panguil Bay is a production regime whose fishery production is planned and choreographed in response to the country's international market agendas. It is an extractive food enclave that transfers commodities to Manila for reexport to foreign and national markets. Second, it exports raw materials (fish bait, livestock and aquaculture feed, hatchery inputs) to support productive systems in other regions of the country. Panguil Bay communities have been fundamentally changed because they are embedded in export chains that move food commodities to the National Capital Region. Panguil Bay's external trade linkages have been restructured to move a majority of fishery commodities to Manila, where the country's largest agribusinesses, food processors, and exporters are concentrated. This city acts as an entrepôt to process raw materials into value-added commodities for reexport to foreign markets and for redistribution inside the country.

Panguil Bay Export Commodity Chains

Like the rest of the country, Panguil Bay communities have been integrated into the global agroindustrial food system (McMichael 1994) through a multilevel market structure in which absentee foreign and national investors and a regional comprador bourgeoisie (Amin 1976) monopolize natural resources and control the flow of food commodities. A small interlocking network of resident petty capitalists and regional brokers and commission merchants controls the commodity chains that transfer regional foods to national wholesalers and processors. Spatially, the villages, towns, and cities of the Philippines are hierarchically structured into interlocking zones of production, distribution, and consumption. Nationwide, layers of markets are connected among small villages, regional trading hubs, and city bulking centers, commodity-importing cities, and trade entrepôts. In the Panguil Bay region, the largest cities (e.g., Ozamiz City, Tangub City) are hubs of commercial interaction with other regional communities and with distant territories. Export commodities are centralized in those towns where wholesalers, larger traders, merchants, and manufacturers are located. Capitalist trading triggers a network of commodity chains in which larger trading hubs subsume nearby smaller villages. In this way, the fragile local economies of the region's small fishing villages are integrated into the spatial organization of the global agroindustrial food system. Small villages move commodities to towns that have better access to transportation or are more commercialized. From these regional cities, trade goods move to Manila and a few other national trading hubs that provide export linkages for the distant transport of bulky or perishable produce and import linkages for the wholesale distribution of foreign commodities.

In addition to their structured linkages to Manila, these regional commodity chains exhibit five striking features. First, only lower-quality seafoods are targeted for local markets. In the local markets, small fish vendors sell only those seafoods that have such low global value that wholesalers will not purchase them. Smaller regional wholesalers and consignment traders sell bulk supplies that have little commercial value, including substandard tilapia and milkfish, to local retailers. Second, the commodity chains are polarized between those agents who market the most profitable seafoods that will leave the country in fresh or frozen form and those who handle finfish. Because shrimp, prawns, and crabs have the highest market values nationally and globally, the trade chains for these commodities are much more vertically integrated than the trade in finfish. The handling of the most expensive commodities is more rationalized among fewer layers of agents to ensure expeditious transport to Manila or foreign markets. Third, a majority of fishers and small fishpond operators are financed by, and must market their outputs through, wholesalers who have the capacity to manage long-distance transport, the technology to prevent spoilage, and the linkages required to market the commodities at the national or international levels. Indeed, there are numerous points in the commodity chains at which the lower-level producer or trader is financed by the next higher level. Fourth, these are noncompetitive trading chains in which a few wholesalers or brokers dictate terms and conditions to many producers and to lower-level traders. Finally, the largest producers are assured of greater advantages. Because wholesalers are in a position to compare prices competitively, they extend pricing advantages to large producers.

Consequently, the financed small operator is at a market handicap at two levels. Indebted fishers and fishpond operators must market their outputs noncompetitively to their financiers and cannot seek out or take advantage of higher prices. Because smaller operators are already controlled through credit terms, wholesalers do not view them as preferred clients to whom they need to extend special favors to sustain supply flow. To complicate matters, there are numerous points at which producers can be cheated or have their output quantities diminished in favor of the trader or wholesaler. On the one hand, peasant fishers or small fishpond operators never know the prices at which their commodities are sold. On the other hand, producers are never paid for the full quantity of their outputs because wholesalers shift to producers the risk of spoilage losses by discounting the weight 9 percent or more (fisher interviews). In the sections that follow, I will explore the impacts of integration into global food commodity chains from the vantage point of fishing communities by examining the mechanisms through which export commodity chains (1) externalize production costs to peasant households and (2) extract hidden household subsidies from them.

EXTERNALIZED PRODUCTION COSTS IN EXPORT COMMODITY CHAINS

To maximize profits, capitalists must exploit as many "costless" social and natural conditions as possible. Thus capitalists shift to society, to the culture, to the ecosystem, and to human laborers most of the real costs of commodity production (Chapter 3). If households and nature did not absorb so many externalities from commodity chains, the global production process could not endlessly accumulate the capital that is essential to economic growth (Wallerstein 1999). In reality, seafood commodity chains externalize to peasant households and to nature most of the costs of production. As the resources of Panguil Bay have been integrated into global food commodity chains, seafood exporting has externalized five costs to peasant households.

Loss of Access to Ecological Resources

Loss of access to ecological resources is the first cost that export commodity chains externalize to local households. Commercial aquaculture expansion requires elimination of common property rights and the reallocation of mangroves to monopolistic use by pond operators. Mangroves are deforested for the development of privatized monocultures that benefit a select few (Nickerson 1999). The national government issues long-term leases that assign fishpond operators control over mangroves and waterways. This land redistribution closes off access of subsistence households to these forests and transforms fisher households into unwelcome squatters around fishponds. In addition, the country's seafood-export agenda eliminates natural resources that have provided the bases for peasant household survival. Industrial fish farming and commercial capture fishing cause massive deforestation, loss of biodiversity, salinization of farm lands and drinking water, and destruction of coral reefs (*Philippines Environmental Monitor* 2000).

Every acre of an industrial fish farm destroys two hundred acres of productive ecosystem. Aquaculture ponds degrade the ecosystem so extensively that fish catches are lowered too much to sustain peasant fisher livelihoods. To make matters worse, the Philippine government does not provide safe public water systems in most rural areas, so aquaculture pollutants threaten household drinking water (Primavera 1997).

These ecological changes have affected Filipino fishing women more negatively than men. Female resource gatherers who have traditionally relied on mangroves, coastal waters, and rivers face several externalized costs associated with the elimination of community property rights. In addition to losing significant food resources and craft materials, women must work harder to secure fuelwood or charcoal for household cooking. Now that fish farming has appropriated most of the waterways and mangroves, women have been marginalized from fishing and out of many of their traditional artisan crafts into marginal activities, such as shell gathering or craft piece-work on a putting-out basis. Although males work in boats, women are more directly exposed to diseases, pollutants, and parasites because they wade into water on a consistent daily basis to gather resources. In addition, environmental threats to water safety require females to assume increased caregiving responsibility for sickened family members. Because public water sources are often contaminated, diarrhea is a major cause of death around Panguil Bay. Forced to rely on rivers and canals for bathing and laundry, a large proportion of bay residents are infected with incurable, life-threatening schistosomiasis (health clinic interviews).

Deterioration of Local Livelihoods

Deterioration of livelihoods is the second cost that is externalized to local households. Capture fishing and aquaculture are grounded in short-term economic motives. Capture fishing of natural reserves of fish, crustaceans, and shellfish rapidly depletes those ecological resources. Moreover, commercial capture-fishing firms generate a majority of the export production and marginalize peasant fishers who do not own exploitative fishing gear to compete with their outputs. After a productive lifespan of only five to ten years, fish farms leave massive ecological damage and dead resources that can no longer be used for agriculture or resource gathering (Naylor 2003). For those reasons, the highest incidence of poverty occurs in those Philippine regions where capture fishing and aquaculture have expanded most rapidly (Jacinto 2004). Export fish farms require few waged workers. Indeed, export aquaculture is a "rape and run industry" that decimates fifteen jobs for each it creates, and it destroys US$5 to US$10 of ecological and economic capital for every dollar earned through exports (Shiva 2000).

Most peasant fisher households derive no income from aquaculture, and the vast majority cannot afford to start a small fish farm (Irz 2004). Export fishery agendas provide little income to local people, but they eliminate the ecological access that is required to support the fishing, agriculture, livestock raising, and handicrafts through which peasant households generate livelihoods.

Debt Bondage

Debt bondage is the third externalized cost. When their livelihoods were threatened, Panguil Bay peasants were left with few options that did not absorb them into export commodity chains that trapped them in debt bondage. Panguil Bay peasant fishers have been integrated into a putting-out system that has reshaped traditional livelihoods into export activities and has stimulated debt bondage. In the face of declining catches and a lack of alternative income sources, peasant fishers adopted more exploitative fishing technologies that require financing. In a spiraling fashion, impoverished fishers are driven by the need to meet debt obligations, and their only option is to increase seafood outputs for market disposal. Relentlessly, Panguil Bay peasant fishers have been locked into commodity chains that use debt bondage to anchor primary producers in marketing networks. In this context, financiers and traders expropriate a much larger share of the surplus (both overt and concealed) because they acquire commodities at below-market prices. Moreover, they guarantee future commodities to export because they capture low-paid, nonwaged workers (and their households) for long periods.

By the mid-1970s, credit was "the essence" of the economic relationship between fishers and traders, and debt bondage was common among middle-sector peasant fishers (W. Davis 1973: 72). By 1980, large traders and wholesalers who had more capital and access to transport held "monopsonistic control over external marketing" of local fish. About half of peasant fishers were now tied to traders through debt bondage (M. Hopkins and McCoy 1976: 83). By the mid-1980s, when national development strategies initially targeted Panguil Bay for increased export outputs, the linkage between fisher debt and marketing was in place at all trading levels. It was common practice for middle-sector traders to act as moneylenders in order to acquire the outputs of fishers and fish farmers (Russell 1987). It was through local traders that a majority of peasant fishers were integrated into export commodity chains. By 1990, a majority of local traders offered credit and capital advances to peasant fishers, but new conditions made the debt bondage more pernicious. Traders now devalued fish for local consumption and specified the kinds, sizes, prices, and marketability standards of species that were "valuable"; those preferences were a careful reflection of export species being demanded by larger traders and wholesalers.

By the early 1990s, a majority of traders were extending loans to fishers and fish farmers through contract fish farming, contract seaweed production, sharecropping arrangements, and financing of harvest technologies. In all these contexts, fishers are tied by debt bondage to traders or wholesalers who advance capital for fishing gear or household needs, and their future outputs are committed to those lenders until all debts are paid (Ushijima and Zayas 1994). Many large traders operate a sharecropping system in which the broker advances a boat, a household hut, and credit to a fisher household. Brokers purchase the catch at about half the market price and deduct accumulated debts. The shift to more productive technologies generated another treadmill of mounting debts. In the early twenty-first century, Panguil Bay fishers have been integrated into monopsonistic commodity chains that link indebtedness to production in order to allow the exporter to obtain commodities at below-market prices, externalize more risks and costs to producers, and extract more hidden surpluses from producer households. At all levels, the traders seek to establish a degree of monopolistic control over the commodity supply while externalizing costs of production to primary producers. Long-term trade and credit linkages to lower-level traders and producers ensure greater national and international corporate control over fish supply, price setting, and profit margins.

Loss of Food Security

Food insecurity is the fourth externalized cost. Peripheral countries that specialize in export-oriented capture fishing and aquaculture have grown less and less food self-sufficient over the past two decades. Since 1993, Philippine seafood output has not kept pace with combined export goals and national food needs, so there has been an annual consumption shortfall of six hundred thousand metric tons (BFAR 1993–2009; Quickstat). Panguil Bay peasant households must compete in five ways for dwindling sources of affordable protein. First, massive outputs of seafoods are exported, and prices have risen too high for a majority of peasants to afford fish, shellfish, and crustaceans. Per capita finfish consumption has steadily declined since 1980, and Filipinos now eat minuscule amounts of shrimp, shellfish, and crustaceans (BFAR 1980–2009). Second, two-thirds of the species swimming in rich-nation aquariums derive from the Philippines and Indonesia, and many of these endangered species once constituted part of the local food chain of fishing households. Third, massive levels of food fish and shellfish are required to feed the export species grown in aquaculture ponds. Indeed, fish farming results in a net loss of protein because five to ten kilograms of wild fish or shellfish are required to produce one kilogram of farmed fish (Naylor 2003). While farmed fish and shrimp are fattened for export through their consumption of natural protein, one-third or more of Philippine households suffer malnutrition, and the highest incidence is among peasant fisher families (Food and Nutrition Institute 2005). As one Philippine fisher puts it, "The shrimp live better than we do. They have electricity, but we don't. The shrimp have clean water, but we don't. The shrimp have lots of food, but we are hungry" (Environmental Justice Foundation 2003: 1). Fourth, aquaculture facilities destroy or waste massive levels of food fish. Every time a fishpond applies chemicals or opens its gates for seawater exchange or to flush out wastes, it destroys fish and shellfish that could be consumed in local food chains (Primavera 1997). As a result of all these factors, the quantity and quality of protein resources in Panguil Bay waters have declined dramatically (MSU Naawan Foundation 2006), and malnutrition is widespread among the region's households. Since the mid-1980s, the diet of Panguil Bay fishing households has been limited to a few vegetables, small amounts of fish, and cornmeal or rice (when it can be afforded), and protein is missing from many meals and on many days (Food and Nutrition Institute 2005). For instance, one fisher wife observed, "We rarely have fish, and we eat even less meat. In the morning, our children open all our pots and usually find them empty."

Fifth, export agriculture and aquaculture threaten food security through loss of rice lands to export crops and pond expansion (Primavera 1997). Although the Philippines exports high levels of fruits, vegetables, nuts, and fishery outputs, it has become so dependent on grain imports that the country's agricultural sector now registers an annual trade deficit.[2] Export-oriented agriculture and aquaculture have absorbed former rice lands, diminishing the country's rice production and causing consumer prices to rise steadily over the past two decades. With far fewer fish to sell, many peasant households can no longer afford rice and are substituting cornmeal, which can be purchased at about 60 percent of the cost of rice. Income from small fish sales cannot cover the cost of imported rice and salt, which have been heavily centralized under the control of a few wholesalers and retailers (household interviews).

In fact, workers in food-extractive enclaves like Panguil Bay are the hungriest, most malnourished people in the world. At the turn of the twenty-first century, the richest fifth of the world consumes nearly half of all meat and fish, the poorest fifth only 5 percent (Spieldoch 2007). Protein-energy malnutrition, iron deficiency anemia, iodine deficiency, and vitamin A deficiencies are typical of countries that export high levels of seafoods (World Health Organization 2001). At least one-third of the Filipino population is now chronically malnourished. In a country that produces iron-rich fish for export, per capita food consumption has declined dramatically. Deficiencies of iron, iodine, calcium, and vitamin A are common because most Filipino diets lack adequate levels of fruits, green vegetables, fats, oils, cereals, poultry, fish, and meats (Food and Nutrition Institute 2005). In 2003, nearly one-third of the families in northern Mindanao lacked sufficient income to provide food for their households, and nutritional deficiencies are a major cause of death in this area (National Statistical Coordination Board 2003). More than one-third of northern Mindanao children are underweight and underheight. Two of every five northern Mindanao children are stunted, and another 8 percent suffer from *miasma* (wasting). Iron deficiency anemia occurs in 20 percent of northern Mindanao children and about one-third of pregnant and lactating women. Because they are iodine deficient, one-third of northern Mindanao residents are at risk of goiter or impaired cognitive and motor development. Iodine is a crucial nutrient during pregnancy because deficiencies can cause brain damage in the fetus, low birth weight, premature labor, and increased perinatal or infant mortality. Two-fifths of northern Mindanao children and one-quarter of the pregnant women are vitamin A deficient and at risk of blindness.

Alteration of Gendered Work Roles

Alteration of gendered work roles is the fifth externalized cost. The frequency with which interviewees focused on the topic suggests that women's increased workload represents the most dramatic transformation. The widening and deepening of capitalism results in dramatic shifts in productive systems and in transformations of laborer households. Crises and shortages generate revised definitions of the appropriate responsibilities of women within and outside the household.

> These changes, however, do not mean that old forms of the asymmetric sexual division of labor are abolished or replaced by egalitarian ones. They are only redefined according to the requirements of the new production system. . . . Because of the preservation of the asymmetric division of labor between the sexes in the ongoing processes, these changes do not lead to greater equality between women and men of the pauperized classes, but, rather, to a polarization between them. The social definition of women as housewives plays a vital role in this polarization. (Mies 1982: 5)

The wife's burden of unpaid household labor remains unchanged, but her income-earning and resource-pooling activities outside the household must increase to overcome shortages.

Panguil Bay women describe increased commingling of household-based labor and market labor. For these women, who often produce marketable commodities or services in their homes, there is no line of demarcation between household and market-related labor. In short, fisher wives are both semidomesticated and semiproletarianized (Mies 1982) because of their widening portfolio of diverse forms of household and extrahousehold labor and of unpaid and income-earning pursuits. Females spend hours every day gathering food and fuel resources from the mangroves and from coastal waters, processing those resources into edible meals or marketable goods, and cooking without electricity. Traditionally, wives have played several key roles in supporting the fishing work of husbands and older sons, including preparation of provisions for fishing trips, marketing fish, net repairs, securing credit and paying debts related to fishing, and help with boat repairs. A majority of wives assist males directly with fishing, but a high proportion of women have broadened their incursion into "men's" fishing labor and are now using boats and nets to harvest fish (household interviews).

In addition to these forms of unpaid labor, women have expanded their income-earning and income-substituting activities. Globally, the Philippines is unique in the degree to which males dominate the informal sector. Even though they are not as deeply embedded in the informal sector as males, women are still far more likely to earn income from informal-sector activities and putting-out systems than from waged jobs (United Nations 2003). Women produce and sell crafts, livestock, dried oysters, and fish and operate small stores. Panguil Bay women routinely engage in casualized labor through cottage industries and putting-out systems. Traders and regional agents provide inputs from which women produce marketable commodities on a piecework basis, like roof shingles thatched from nipa trees or wooden jewelry and baskets. Fishing women have double or triple work burdens that combine unpaid household labor with waged labor, informal-sector vending, home-based industries, illegal activities, and services (e.g., laundry, herbalist, midwife). Because wives are now engaged in new forms of income-earning labor, fewer of them are marketing male fish catches and making daily household purchases. Thus husbands now exert greater decision-making control over daily expenditures. This transformation represents a dramatic shift in power relations within households in which wives have traditionally managed family budgets (household interviews).

Some Western feminists (e.g., Atkinson and Errington 1990: 96) celebrate "the relative economic equality" of men and women in the Philippines, but Panguil Bay fishing wives do not agree. Philippine society culturally constrains women to prioritize child rearing and household maintenance while simultaneously limiting economically and ecologically their capacities and opportunities to fulfill that role. "If you just count on the earnings of your husband," one fisher wife observed, "it is not enough" (Eder 1999: 114). Despite wives' diverse labor portfolio inside and outside households, their income-earning pursuits remain marginalized, low-paid, and sometimes stigmatized. Moreover, a woman faces contradictory pressures to remain a "respectable housewife" and to undertake whatever income-earning work will sustain her household. When interviewees described themselves as housewives, they reconstructed traditional social expectations to encompass with that term whatever efforts they undertook for the benefit of their households. Most women in fishing households must do some form of income-generating or income-substituting labor while managing child care and household maintenance without male assistance.

Thus fisher wives are caught in contradictory demands to meet household needs and to stay within rigid social conventions about appropriate "housewife" roles. To overcome this cultural conflict, fisher wives appeal to the Filipino cultural ideal of "sacrificial motherhood." As Afshar and Agarwal (1989: 1) have observed:

> Under the banner of this idealised, heroic nurturance a truly womanly
> woman is enjoined to do anything, to make any sacrifice, for the sake
> of household welfare, for the sake of her husband, and especially for
> the sake of her children. . . . However much the ideal is invoked to justify
> female passivity and subordination, it can also be invoked to justify
> activity, particularly to justify the potentially deviant and compromising
> behaviour involved in working outside the home. Taking up employment
> is frequently defined, both by working women and their families, as a
> form of female sacrifice for family well-being.

In the face of this feminization of responsibility, fisher wives take on additional income-earning tasks to cover unexpected costs related to children's schooling or health care. As a result of their broadening portfolio of forms of labor, women estimated that they are now working three to four hours more per day (about a 20 percent increase since 1980). Panguil Bay fisher wives report that they juggle the contradictory pressures of unpaid household labor and market-related work by reducing personal sleep and leisure.

HOUSEHOLD SUBSIDIZATION OF EXPORT COMMODITY CHAINS

In addition to the five types of costs that commodity chains externalize, export capitalists maximize profits by extracting hidden surpluses from peasant households. Integration of subsistence fishers into export commodity chains has not pulled their households out of poverty. Instead, members of that small group who are drawn into the waged labor force are "located in household structures in which the work on this new 'export-oriented activity' form[s] only a small part of the lifetime revenues. . . . In this case, other household activities which bring in revenues in multiple forms can 'subsidize' the remuneration for the 'export-oriented activity,' thereby keeping the labor costs very low" (T. Hopkins and Wallerstein 1987: 777). At every point in a commodity chain, households subsidize capitalists' low wages in order to sustain the laborers who produce the commodity. Those waged laborers who make contributions to export sectors do not earn a living wage that is sufficient for the reproduction of the household unit. Her husband's fishpond wages were "never enough," one fisher housewife explained. "I have to work in order for the family to survive. I bear the hardship because we could not depend solely on a monthly salary which is actually less than what we need to purchase household essentials." In fact, the hidden inputs of households are preconditions for the productivity of household members who engage in external waged labor required to produce the goods that are traded in the world-economy. In reality, nonwaged labor generates the bulk of household resources and subsidizes the accumulation of profits within the commodity chain (Chapter 3).

Peasant households subsidize commodity chains through low-paid, non-waged direct inputs into the production process, for example, harvesting wild resources for use in fishponds. Such household-based labor generates market commodities or informal-sector inputs into the export-production process, but this labor—especially that of women—has typically remained socially invisible and has received below-market prices (Mies 1982). Women and households subsidize seafood commodity chains through four forms of invisible nonwaged labor. First, the biological reality of women's lives is sexual and reproductive; thus mothers make their first subsidy to capitalism through the bearing and raising of successive generations of laborers. Despite its dependency on this natural female contribution, however, capitalism has externalized laborer reproduction outside the realm of the economic. Second, the household is the site in which women undertake unpaid labor for those members who are waged laborers. By keeping production costs lower, women's hidden inputs subsidize the production process throughout the commodity chain and thereby keep consumer prices lower and profits higher. Third, fisher wives subsidize commodity chains through informal-sector activities. When they produce low-priced crafts (like baskets) or provide nonwaged services (such as packing, transport, or trading) that support the export process, they are integrated directly into the commodity chain. However, their contributions remain poorly remunerated and socially invisible. The fourth way in which women subsidize the commodity chains in which their households are situated is more deeply hidden. The inputs of Panguil Bay households subsidize distant consumers. The low wages, malnutrition, and degraded ecosystems of fishing households subsidize production costs and permit the distant buyer to eat those externalities at cheap prices. While the Panguil Bay fisher wife and her children lack essential protein and iron, the Japanese middle-class housewife and her offspring eat an abundance of their hidden sacrifices and neither pay for nor acknowledge them.

CONCEPTUAL REPRISE

In Asian countries, access to seafoods and rice delimits the food security of a majority of the population. Even though malnutrition and food prices are rising in countries like the Philippines, the national governments of these countries are still engaging in export agendas that threaten the availability of essential nutrients to most of the population. In line with world-systems analysts (Dunaway 2012), neo-Marxist feminists (Mies 1982), and ecofeminists (Mies and Shiva 2001), this study views the household as the basic unit of the material and nonmaterial forms of labor that are essential to reproduce and maintain the workforce that is essential to the persistence of the capitalist world-economy. Because its members are underpaid in that capitalist system, the household is the unit that makes laborer survival possible through inequitable resource pooling and distribution (Chapter 3). Because full proletarianization into waged workers would increase the cost of production and lower profits, the capitalist world-system has structured a controlling mechanism by which the demands of workers for increased compensation can be restrained. That mechanism is the semiproletarianized household, which is now the dominant mode worldwide. In such households, the income accrued from capitalist activities (either as wages or income) falls below the survival level, and the household is forced to locate most of its basic needs through nonwaged, informal-sector, and subsistence activities (Wallerstein 1995b: 5–6). For that reason, export prices do not reflect the true costs of producing fishery commodities because externalities are concealed in the value chain. Because social and environmental costs are externalized from the costs of production, that which is expensive and wasteful is rendered fictitiously cheap in the marketplace.

Consequently, it is not through waged labor that global commodity chains exploit a majority of the world's women, especially peasants. Instead, these chains maximize profits by externalizing costs of production to, and extracting hidden surpluses from, semiproletarianized households that acquire most of their survival needs outside formal waged sectors (Chapter 4). To provide household basic needs, women juggle an ever-widening work portfolio in order to have a security net that provides a "hedge against failures in any one component of their survival package" (Illo and Polo 1990: 109–10). As fishing households become integrated into global food chains both as exporters and importers, self-exploitation and self-deprivation become their survival strategies. As one fisher observed, "It is solely your body that earns a living. . . . If you rest, you will have nothing to eat" (Ledesma 1982: 171). In the face of the loss of ecological resources that once supported their livelihoods, peasant fisher households have developed an uneasy and inequitable array of coping strategies that includes debt bondage, intensified self-exploitation through working longer hours, and increased self-deprivation through eating less, purchasing fewer survival needs, and removing children from school. One Philippine fisher described the constant state of crisis this way.

> A bird wakes up at dawn and immediately flies about looking for
> food. . . . The bird spends his days doing this. The next day is the same.
> Me, too. I wake up and scurry around looking for food and work
> wherever I can find it . . . becoming dizzy trying to keep my family alive.
> By evening, I'm tired and weak. At dawn, I have to be up again doing the
> same, like the birds. (Ledesma 1982: 51)

PART V TRANSNATIONAL LABORERS AS COMMODITIES IN GLOBAL CHAINS

CHAPTER TEN

Global Care Chains

BRINGING IN TRANSNATIONAL REPRODUCTIVE
LABORER HOUSEHOLDS

Nicola Yeates

Thanh-Dam Truong (1996: 47) cogently encapsulated much of what was missing from burgeoning globalization literatures when she argued that "no production system operates without a reproduction system." It should not be surprising, she contended, "that the globalization of production is accompanied by its intimate 'Other,' i.e. reproduction." Supporting Truong's assertion is the considerable presence of migrant women who work in the expanding domestic- and sexual-service sectors in Europe, North America, and Asia. Indeed, marketing of reproductive labor is becoming increasingly significant as a source of household livelihood, global economic profits, and government revenue. Moreover, it is evident that there is an international division of reproductive labor in which migrant women from peripheral countries supply the reproductive labor previously provided by females in richer countries. This essay is organized around three themes. In the first section, I explore the intellectual progression from commodity chain analysis to care chain analysis. In the second section, I provide an overview of the global care chain perspective in which I examine the weaknesses of its initial conceptualization and show its intellectual development beyond that starting point. In the third section, I employ global care chain analysis to explore the transnationalization of nursing labor and elucidate the wider social significance of cross-border circuits of capital and labor revolving around social reproduction.

FROM GLOBAL COMMODITY CHAIN TO GLOBAL CARE CHAIN

Even though the three approaches to commodity and value chain analysis (Bair 2010) have paid inadequate attention to labor, households, social reproduction, and international services, there are valuable conceptual parallels that have encouraged an intellectual progression from "commodity" chain to an expanded global care chain analytic framework.[1] Key ideas from the world-systems perspective have been particularly useful in shaping thinking about global care chains. First, world-systems scholars contend that laborers are drawn into low-paying waged work for globalized export-production systems that expropriate local subsistence resources, degrade local ecologies, and externalize social costs to communities. They emphasize that peripheral laborers are drawn into export-oriented agriculture and industry through superexploitation, a process in which capitalist wages are insufficient to maintain social reproduction (Wallerstein 1995a). Second, transnational migration occupies a significant place within world-systems approaches to commodity chains. Movement into such production is spatialized, involving national migration (often from rural areas) to globalizing cities and international migration to wealthier countries that offer higher wages than are available locally (Grosfoguel and Cervantes-Rodriguez 2002). Migrant remittances become critical to the survival of those remaining in the source locality because they supplement other household livelihood strategies (Wallerstein and Smith 1992).

In addition, foundational thinkers and feminist scholars of the world-systems perspective emphasize the gendered basis of labor relations within capitalist production systems. Wallerstein and Smith (1992) demonstrate the extent to which "modern" industrialization processes have benefited from state and local patriarchal structures and informal systems of labor relations. Foundational thinkers of the world-systems perspective urged scholars to conceptualize households "neither as isolates nor as small units of social organization related to national economies, but instead as basic units of an emerging world-system" (Wallerstein 1984: 18). As crucial elements of global commodity chains, households were conceptualized as units of productive and reproductive, paid and unpaid, nonwaged and waged labor (Wallerstein and Smith 1992; Wallerstein 1995a). Feminist scholars stress that global industrialization superexploits female labor in two ways. Female waged laborers receive lower compensation than their male counterparts, and women continue to make a range of nonwaged resource inputs into labor reproduction through their bodies, general household provisioning, and caregiving for household members (Dunaway 2012). In their thinking, any account of the social relations of capitalist production and the generation and distribution of surpluses must necessarily attend to gendered labor systems (Wallerstein and Smith 1992; Wallerstein 1995a; Dunaway 2001). On the one hand, women are the most exploited laborers in the commodity chains situated in peripheral countries. On the other hand, the generation and distribution of surpluses are predicated on capitalist production that externalizes the full costs of labor reproduction within and among nodes across a commodity chain. Long before the expropriations underpinning the inequitable division of surpluses among the core, the semiperiphery, and the periphery can occur, "the commodity chain structures the maximal exploitation of underpaid and unpaid labor" flowing from the subsistence, informal, and illegal economies. This unequal exchange is "embedded in the gendered relations of households" (Dunaway 2001: 10).

These conceptual emphases provide vitally important perspectives that inform the development of the initial global care chain notion into an expanded analytic framework. The common theoretical lineage is evident in (1) the expanded definition of labor and labor inputs as both productive and reproductive, (2) recognition of nonmaterial and material inputs into commodity chains, (3) explication of gendered labor relations, and (4) the conceptualization of households as sites of both production and reproduction.

My global care chain framework derives four important themes from the commodity chain approach developed by the world-systems perspective. First, both types of chains depict geographically dispersed but coordinated families linked together by the provision and consumption of waged and nonwaged care work. For example, global nanny chains create transnational family linkages as a result of household outsourcing and migration strategies. Outsourcing mobilizes care-labor supply through kinship and nonkinship networks and through market mechanisms. Household transnationalization in sending countries takes the form of female emigration for employment in distant care work. In destination countries, household transnationalization takes the form of recruitment of imported laborers (Yeates 2005a).

Second, both types of chains express territoriality mainly in terms of the length of the chains. Like commodity chains, global care chains vary in the number of links, the sociogeographic spread of the links, and the intensity of their connective strength. Chains may have one transnational link or several. Many care chains start in poor countries and end in richer ones, sometimes via one or more intermediate countries that may be located in different regions. In global care chains, there are varied regional and subregional divisions of reproductive labor tethered to global hierarchies. For example, young women from poorer Asian countries travel to richer countries of southeastern or western Asia, the Middle East, western Europe, and the United States to work in various branches of the international careservices economy. Those from Latin America travel to the United States, while others from central and eastern Europe migrate to western Europe and the United States (Yeates 2009a).

Third, both approaches analyze global chains as networks that structure relations of social inequality among the participants. In global care chains, labor inequality is acutely dichotomized in that households in richer destination countries are served by female adults from peripheral countries. Moreover, employment relations are constructed around the conceptualization of these forms of labor as servitude. Furthermore, global care chains structure inequalities through the disparate economic values ascribed to care labor. This value decreases down the chain and often becomes unpaid at the end of it (e.g., an older daughter who substitutes for her migrant mother in providing informal care for her younger siblings). Conversely, motherly care labor is commodified in the consuming countries of the chain, and its economic value is increased. For instance, the same motherly labor that was provided in the Philippines as unpaid household labor is now provided in the United States on a waged basis. In this sense, the international nanny trade constitutes a global circuit organized around the commodification of motherly care labor. The economic value of that labor reflects the differential position of households within global and national hierarchies.

Fourth, global care chains distribute costs and benefits inequitably. For instance, three obvious benefits derive from the international division of reproductive labor. Labor-exporting countries receive valuable revenue from migrant remittances sent home by commodified motherly care laborers. Transnational labor migration enables recruiting states to avoid enactment of labor measures that ensure a living wage and to ignore development of public child care strategies. Employer parents are relieved from gender conflicts over the division of domestic labor and are enabled to take up waged work, and their children are the recipients of "surplus love" (Hochschild 2000: 136). However, the costs associated with the international division of reproductive labor disproportionately affect peripheral countries and households. While richer countries and peripheral governments accrue most of the benefits, most of the costs of the global care chain are externalized to transnational migrant workers and their families. Moreover, costs are predominantly borne by migrant mothers and their children, who experience intense loss and deprivation from long-term separation. This systematic extraction of peripheral labor constitutes a care drain in which source countries are depleted of vital resources in ways that are no less exploitative and no less economically significant than the extraction of and trade in natural resources (Hochschild 2000; Yeates 2004b, 2005b). Finally, care migration deprives source countries of female laborers who could sustain social solidarities and the "emotional commons" (Isaksen, Devi, and Hochschild 2008: 411).

THE GLOBAL CARE CHAIN PERSPECTIVE

The migration-care nexus has generated a vibrant multidisciplinary research agenda, and global care chain analysis occupies a pivotal place within this project.[2] The global care chain concept was groundbreaking because it applied the tenets of global commodity chain analysis to an area that had not previously been analyzed in this way. Indeed, the care chain concept originated as a way of framing in global terms the struggle for gender equality at home and in the workplace. The originator of this concept, Arlie Hochschild (2000), called attention to the trend toward the provision of child care by migrant female laborers. She depicted the global care chain as being driven by a woman living in a rich country who faces the labor contradictions of dependent children and full-time employment. In order to free herself from a second shift of unpaid household work, she hires a poorer female to provide it on her behalf. Because the migrant laborer cannot fulfill her own domestic duties in her home country, she either hires another female or exploits a family member (typically a female) to provide that reproductive labor. Thus Hochschild envisions a global care chain as consisting of a series of "personal links between people across the globe based on the paid or unpaid work of caring" (Hochschild 2000: 131).

Hochschild's (2000) initial conceptualization of the global care chain concept drew attention to the significance of care-labor migration and its relation to commodified and noncommodified structures of reproduction. However, it did not fully specify the nature of the cross-border circuits that mobilize and sustain organized migration. In addition, the initial care chain conceptualization overlooked two questions:

1. What are the channels, agencies, and socioinstitutional arrangements involved in (a) connecting reproductive labor to waged work and (b) mobilizing the supply of and demand for migrant care labor across the network?
2. How are relations of unequal exchange structured among different actors involved in the network?

Second, the original conceptualization of care flows was criticized for its oversimplification of the global flows and of the relations linking transnational laborers and households. Hochschild (2000) presented these flows as one-way traffic that involved the transfer of care labor away from the migrant mother's own children toward the employer's offspring. But studies have emphasized that migrant women's mothering of their own children does not necessarily cease or rupture upon emigration. Recent studies have explored the ways in which household reproductive labor is transformed to continue in transnational modes. Indeed, emigrant mothers tend to remain responsible for the economic and emotional security of their own children at the same time at which they are caring for the children of their distant employers (Parrenas 2001, 2005).

Third, the original conceptualization portrayed the migrant flows as being driven by labor-market participation of women in destination countries, but this is not true of all global care chains. Non-labor-market factors are important in the recruitment of migrant caregivers (Parrenas 2001). In the United States, migrant domestic workers are not always recruited to relieve women of having to work a double shift. Middle Eastern countries were among the first major targets for care-labor migration in the second half of the twentieth century, even though Middle Eastern women do not have high labor-market participation rates. Moreover, care chain scholars have argued that the analysis needs to be more complex because social status operates on both ends of the chain. At the recruiting end, the capacity to employ domestic servants is often associated with higher social status. Increased social status also helps explain why women leave professional employment to participate as laborers in domestic care-labor streams (Yeates 2005a). Through higher wages earned from domestic work abroad, Philippine women seek to secure middle-class status in their home country, provide college educations for children, and fund status-enhancing social activities, such as festivals (Parrenas 2001; Yeates 2009a).

Fourth, the original care chain concept overlooked historical precedents for contemporary transnational outsourcing practices. Studies have documented past practices of exporting care labor and reliance on foreign laborers to perform household tasks across contexts as diverse as Britain, Latin America, the Caribbean, the United States, Australia, and South Africa. The historical presence of transnational laborers is also evident outside the household sphere. For example, nursing and religious care labor have been deeply intertwined with global migrations and colonialism dating back several centuries (Yeates 2009a). Similarly, transnational families have been significant to slave, colonial, and settler societies since the Middle Ages (Bryceson and Vuorela 2002; Johnson et al. 2011).

Fifth, subsequent scholars have moved beyond the narrow focus on waged domestic labor emphasized by Hochschild (2000). The choice of occupation (domestic work or child care) and work setting (individualized households) played well to the traditional theoretical concerns of Marxist feminism, but those conceptual directions were too narrow to capture the complexities of the contemporary international division of reproductive labor. Indeed, the initial conceptualization did not go far enough in delineating the organizational features and distributive properties of global systems of production and trade in care workers, nor did it adequately recognize the multidirectional dynamics of care-labor flows or the extent to which they are conditioned by sociocultural and historical contexts. Moreover, the focus on the U.S. nanny trade underestimated the significance of migrant labor in care-labor forces worldwide and the extent to which care-labor migration has become a commodified, profitable segment of the world-economy (Yeates 2009a).

A brief examination of international marriage migration provides a sense of the scale of the global trade in domestic labor beyond child care. With annual profits estimated at between US$7 billion and US$12 billion, the international mail-order-bride business is thought to be the third most profitable illegal trade after drugs and arms smuggling (UNFPA 2006). There are more than 800,000 Internet sites that appeal to a mass market. For instance, the Mail Order Bride Warehouse and Planetlove receive 22 million visits annually. Scholarly concerns center on the practices of match-making agencies and the power inequalities of the "imported" bride that render her "vulnerable to domestic slavery, violence and abuse" (Gaburro 2004: 10–11). As in the case of paid domestic work, the supply of female "marital" labor is conditioned by uneven development worldwide. "Some countries become acquirers of brides and others supply them, roughly re-flecting their relative positioning in the international political economy" (Pellerin 1996: 181).

Sixth, the initial conceptualization was preoccupied with household-based care labor. Subsequent scholars have explored a wide variety of care services that are provided in institutional and commercial settings, such as residential and nursing-care homes, hospitals, hospices, clinics, and child-care centers. Moreover, migrant labor is present in many care occupations other than child care, sex work, and domestic work. These labor sites and occupations encompass diverse capital-labor input intensity, working conditions, and levels of remuneration, organization, and regulation. For instance, the sex trade is unregulated, labor intensive, unskilled, and atom-ized. In contrast, the professional nursing trade involves capital-intensive corporate operations, skilled labor, and public regulation (Yeates 2004b, 2009a). The differentiated organizational features of different parts of the care sector have implications for labor migration in the areas of recruit-ment, regulation, the conditions under which care work is carried out, and the nature of laborer social rights. These features are consequential for relations between participants in the global care chain and for the distribu-tion of risks, costs, and benefits of migration among all actors within the network.

Initially focused on the nanny trade and cross-border transfers of moth-erly care in the U.S.-Philippine context, the theoretical and methodological tenets of global care chain analysis have been substantively broadened to encompass a wide range of occupations, sectors of the care-services econ-omy, and regions of the world. The next section of this chapter develops this discussion by considering global care chains as they operate in relation to a quite different sector of the reproductive economy than that which has pre-occupied much feminist scholarship on care-labor migration: nursing labor.

GLOBAL NURSING-CARE CHAINS

Labor migration is particularly significant to health care, which employs one of every three transnational migrants.[3] Of the 60 million migrant health workers, the vast majority are frontline health-service providers, such as doctors, nurses, midwives, and associated health professionals (e.g., physiotherapists, speech and language therapists, and occupational therapists). In addition to migrant laborers, global nursing-care chains (GNCCs) consist of several public and private, for-profit and not-for-profit actors. Organizational linkages within the labor network can include households, informal social networks, not-for-profit organizations, and commercial entities that arrange recruitment, travel, training, and settlement in the destination countries. Migratory-labor dynamics are shaped by a matrix of conflicting interests. GNCCs are highly regulated by international agreements, state immigration services, licensing authorities, and accreditation or examination-management authorities. Nonstate actors, such as professional organizations, trade unions, and NGOs, exert influence on GNCCs. Informal networks of families, friends, and colleagues finance entry into nursing, shape the decision to emigrate, and influence the choice of destination country and migration trajectory. Finally, it is important to emphasize that GNCCs are the outcomes of strategic decisions and actions that involve several state and nonstate actors that affect migration policy, training, education, recruitment, and human resource management, as well as labor organization, mobilization, and settlement. In the sections that follow, I will explore seven significant elements of the structure and governance of GNCCs.

Directions and Determinants of Nursing Labor Flows

Nurse-migration flows reflect global inequalities in power and wealth. Labor forces in richer countries in the chain are supplied by those positioned in the periphery of the world-system. Although the general flow is from peripheral to core and semiperipheral countries, there are also regional divisions of labor, with flows from more economically stagnant countries to economically stronger countries. Labor forces can move between richer countries that must, in turn, make up losses through recruitment from poorer countries. For example, the United States recruits nurses from Canada, Canada attracts workers from the United Kingdom to make up for its losses to the United States, the United Kingdom imports from South Africa to fill its vacancies, and South Africa draws from Swaziland. Several countries predominate as nurse exporters (e.g., the Philippines, India) or as importers (the Middle East). However, other countries simultaneously import and export nursing labor. For example, Ireland and the United Kingom acquire nursing staff from both peripheral and core countries and export nurses to the United States and Australia. Similarly, South Africa imports nurses from poorer neighboring countries and exports nurses to core economies. The problem for countries at the bottom of the nursing chain is that there are no poorer countries from which to recruit workers to overcome the losses of their own nurses. These countries tend to become dependent on charitable labor, and that labor is often provided by the same countries that recruit their nurses (Yeates 2010).

Determinants of nurse-migration flows are, in the first place, economic. Salary differentials between exporting and importing countries in a GNCC (e.g., between the United States and the Philippines or India) widen further when we take into account the value of nonwage benefits, such as tax allowances, subsidized housing, and transportation. However, not all migration is premised on economic benefits. Wider professional experience, better and more specialized training, and more labor autonomy are significant factors in decisions to migrate, as are desires for travel, adventure, a better climate, and personal safety. Emigration may be structured into the selection of nursing as a career, and often this decision is a family matter. Families finance the nurse training of a daughter or wife in the expectation that their investment will return future remittances to their households. In parts of India, enrollment in nurse training can permit a reduction in the dowry requested by future in-laws.

Roles of States in Exporting and Importing Nurses

State strategies to develop a labor-export industry constitute a major input into the formation of GNCCs. Several Asian states, including Indonesia, the Philippines, Korea, China, and Vietnam, have adopted export-oriented nurse-production policies. Although the Asian nurse-export industry is at a variety of different stages of development, states have been critical in managing its expansion and in ensuring international market compatibility. Because recent Asian market entrants are disadvantaged by lack of English and their countries do not offer nurse-education programs that are accredited by Western importing countries, they tend to be confined to lower-value regional labor markets. Export-oriented nurse labor-production systems are also developing in the Caribbean, where a regionally coordinated program of managed health-labor migration is emerging. The region is being encouraged to use trade and multilateral agreements to regulate nurse migration and to adopt export-oriented nurse-training models as a route to development (Yeates 2010).

Recruiting-country policies are also decisive in the formation of GNCCs. Nurse vacancies are produced by fiscal austerity policies that seek to reduce the public costs of social reproduction, but such staffing cuts lead to increased workload, mandatory overtime, and wage stagnation. For those reasons, fewer women choose nursing as a career, and significant numbers exit the profession because of low pay, long and stressful working hours, unfavorable employer policies, and reduced time for patient care. Transnational nurse-recruitment strategies have aimed to compensate for the failure to recruit and retain homegrown nurses. Such strategies include fast-track visa systems, such as that introduced by Ireland in 2000. Governments may also intervene to validate the qualifications of incoming nurses, as in the United States.

Governance and Credentialing

Transnational recognition, licensing, and accreditation agreements have been of decisive importance in shaping global nurse labor mobility. One issue is whether the educational qualifications and nursing experience in the exporting country are recognized by destination countries. The devaluation of nursing qualifications by the West is one of the main reasons that some Asian nurses are restricted to regional and local labor markets. By the same token, mutual recognition agreements explain why Ghanaian nurses tend to migrate to the United Kingdom, where they do not need to sit for an exam, as they would have to do in the United States. Accreditation processes and exams effectively function as part of the nurse-migration regime, and credentialing can present barriers to successful entry into another country's nursing labor force. Both the United States and Canada have stringent market entry requirements that lead to high rates of failure by foreign nurse applicants. Similar barriers to the incorporation of skilled migrant care workers exist in Southeast Asia.

Since the late 1990s, the number of transnational nursing mutual recognition agreements has expanded slightly, especially in the European Union, central, eastern and southern Africa, the Caribbean, and North America. The Trilateral Initiative for North American Nursing (TINAN) illustrates the complex institutional framework for, and the glacial progression of, such agreements. Set up in 1994 as a collaborative venture among nursing groups in Canada, Mexico, and the United States, TINAN completed its first phase only in 2003. During that decade, only thirty-five nursing, governmental, and other organizations drew up recommendations for mutually acceptable criteria for licensing and certification. Although efforts are under way to move toward regimes of cooperation and synchronization in relation to qualifications, there is no such move toward global standards to govern the licensing of nurses. Each country or locale sets its own requirements for nurses to practice, and this credentialing process is further complicated by the disparate levels of nurse proficiency.

Impacts of Immigration Regimes

Mutual recognition, accreditation, and licensing agreements shape entry into the profession, but state regulations determine the conditions of immigration into a country and the labor rights of imported workers. These immigration regimes involve a wide variety of gatekeepers, including state policy makers in both exporting and receiving countries, government immigration personnel, professional accreditation bodies, and educational institutions. Economic needs increasingly frame the discourse on immigration policy. In practice, however, migration policies are influenced by a wide range of political and economic interests and imperatives. For instance, most Asian countries are highly selective about the migrant nationalities and ethnicities they will admit, and some states maintain isolationist migration regimes even when there is a dire need for foreign labor.

When emigrants are making their decisions about destination and length of stay, they compare different migratory and social reproduction regimes. For example, many nurses prefer Western countries, where it is possible to settle, buy a house, raise a family, and obtain citizenship. None of these possibilities exist in Middle Eastern states, where migrants are confined to narrow economic roles and are excluded from social and political involvement. Legal rights of migrant families are another crucial element of nursing labor regimes. In this regard, Canada and Australia are particularly attractive because they allow the offspring of migrant nurses the same access to education and social services as the children of citizens (Yeates 2011).

Labor Recruitment and Brokerage

As public immigration regimes have increased in complexity, so has the layer of private-sector mediators, brokers, and agents. Recruitment involves a broad spectrum of public employment services, private firms, and informal networks. Formal recruitment agencies are key organizational links in these chains because they coordinate training, testing, certification, immigration, and transportation. Their business is thriving as they position themselves to help states realize savings through the lower costs of recruiting foreign-trained nurses, as compared with training homegrown health-care providers. In the United Kingdom, for example, the cost of recruiting a foreign nurse is less than 10 percent of the Department of Health's estimated cost of £40,000 for producing a homegrown nurse. In response to increased demand abroad and anticipated profit margins, recruitment agencies and training organizations have expanded dramatically in exporting countries. In India, this growth has been characterized by considerable investment from both transnational and domestic health-care staffing corporations. The state and capital have allied in nurse production and recruitment because the government subsidizes health-care facilities that are oriented to serving local and foreign elites. Given the profit margins involved, the emergence of these kinds of public-private partnerships is not surprising. Some states emulate the commercial practice of taking a share of the salary earned by the nurse. The Chinese state charges Chinese nurses working in Singapore and Saudi Arabia 10 to 15 percent of their annual salaries as "handling fees." Because state interests are closely tied to brokering nurse-recruitment contracts and receiving a share of nurse salaries, it is doubtful that exporting states are likely to advocate on behalf of migrant laborers when contracts and work agreements are breached.

State regulation of recruitment brokers encompasses registration and licensing systems, the setting of industry standards, and the development of enforcement systems. These measures provide some protection to migrants, but abuses are frequent. Even though the Philippine state strongly controls the export of labor, many exploitative practices of this migration industry remain unmonitored. Migrant nurses frequently complain that recruitment agencies misrepresent pay and working conditions. In some cases, the position of nurses resembles that of bonded labor and is much like the lower social status of domestic or sex workers. Moreover, migrants can be pressured into signing supplementary contracts with recruitment agents that require them to pay additional fees. When such problems occur abroad, the nurses are outside the jurisdiction of the exporting state. Thus migrant nurses are left with few options to address grievances because they can pursue resolution with recruitment agencies only in their home countries.

Labor Integration and Management

Working conditions differ widely between public and private health-care institutions and between unionized and nonunionized environments. The worst recorded abuses have occurred in the private sector and in nonunionized settings. Migrant workers in unionized public hospital systems are more likely to receive the same pay and working conditions as their nonmigrant colleagues, and they have some protection against discriminatory pay and exploitative conduct. Such protections are not available to workers in nonunionized systems. Moreover, migrant care laborers in household settings are more isolated and powerless because they have no organized support in negotiating or enforcing terms of employment. Overall, the involvement of trade unions shifts the balance of power between migrant care workers and their employers.

The organization of migrant labor forces has been of growing importance to trade unions in industrialized Organisation for Economic Co-operation and

Development countries. In some countries, unions have expanded through efforts to organize sectors in which migrant labor predominates. One feature of this is the recognition that migrant workers have particular needs, so some unions organize their migrant members separately. In Ireland, the Services, Industrial, and Professional Trade Union (the largest Irish union) has established a separate section to address the needs of migrant workers. This form of union organization can bring benefits to nurses that extend beyond collective bargaining over pay and conditions to issues such as family migration rights, spousal employment, and children's educational and health benefits. For example, the Irish Nurses Organization and unions warned that Philippine workers, on whom the delivery of patient care depended, would leave for countries that offer broader family rights. To forestall this health crisis, Ireland legalized employment for nurse spouses and extended constitutional protection to their children.

Distributive Spatialities of Global Nursing-Care Chains

Gains and losses from nurse migration are unevenly distributed among states, labor, and capital across GNCCs, with severe consequences for social reproduction at the periphery of the chain. Destination countries bear minimal costs and enjoy most of the economic benefits from recruitment of migrant nurses. Savings to health-labor budgets are considerable. Between 2003 and 2004, the recruitment of 1,021 Ghanaian nurses saved the United Kingdom £35 million in training costs. In contrast, the emigration of each enrolled nurse-midwife from Malawi represents a loss to that country of about $72,000. With the import of cheaper labor from poorer states comes the export of core-nation staffing and training problems to exporting countries. Furthermore, gains to the individual laborer from migration, though relatively substantial, are mediated by social structures and practices of exploitation. Labor brokers and other industry actors extract surplus value from migrant nurse labor, and benefits accruing to migrants are tempered by the effects of deskilling. When their nursing credentials are not recognized by the destination countries, many qualified migrants are employed in low-paying residential care homes. Others are channeled into low-skilled, low-paid menial and noncareer grades in unpopular specialties and positions that do not match their training and experience. Indeed, it is not uncommon for qualified nurses with specialist skills to work in residential nursing-care homes or in the hospital laundry service. Even when their nursing credentials are recognized, their foreign experience may not be, so they are placed at the bottom of their grades. Recognition of foreign nursing experience is a factor that attracts Indian and Filipino nurses to migrate to Ireland rather than the United Kingdom.

Economic gains to the individual nurse are also tempered by intersecting racial and gender labor hierarchies. In the United States, Filipino nurses tend to be general nurses, while European nurses are more specialized. In Saudi Arabia, European nurses receive higher wages than Asian nurses even when they are less qualified. Nearly 20 percent of ethnic-minority nurses in the United Kingdom's National Health Service (NHS) attribute their reduced access to training and promotion to discrimination. More than half of South Asian nurses report racial harassment from NHS co-workers and patients. Gender inequality compounds such divisions of labor. Although the NHS is female dominated and has a high proportion of staff from ethnic-minority groups, males and whites enjoy significant advantages over female, black, and Asian nurses in promotion. The lifetime earnings loss of this inequality for black and Asian nurses is estimated at £26,000 to £35,000 for females and £30,000 to £38,000 for males.

For exporting states, transnational remittances are the principal benefit from nurse migration. However, these benefits can be limited. Unless the state taxes migrant remittances, they are private transfers that do not enrich public coffers or translate into funding for local health-system improvements. Benefits to exporting states are outweighed by the loss of long-term investment in the education and training of migrant nurses. Remittance advantages are further offset by the costs of a depleted health labor force to the citizenry of the sending country. Indeed, nurse emigration has been described as a "fatal flow" because of its adverse impacts on health outcomes. In Malawi, for example, 64 percent of nursing posts are unfilled, and the lack of trained midwives and nurses has led to high maternal mortality and the incapacity to expand AIDS therapies.

Consequently, the nurse-migration trade is regressively redistributive because it entails a net flow of benefits from poor to rich countries. Furthermore, the economic value of nurse migration from poorer to richer countries far exceeds the volume of international medical aid to developing countries. Various recruiting countries and international organizations have adopted codes of conduct in response to concerns about the development impacts of the export of health labor by peripheral countries. Given the shortcomings of private corporate codes of social responsibility in other labor domains (see, e.g., Chapter 7), such weak nursing codes are not likely to be effective.

• • •

I have argued that the globalizations of reproduction and production are inextricably linked. Transformations in systems, institutions, and practices of social reproduction are not simply a consequence of the restructuring of systems of economic production. Rather, they mutually constitute one another and unfold in concert. Transnational circuits of labor and capital are significant features of diverse segments of the care economy. Although these circuits are not historically new, global care chains since 1960 have (1) commodified to become a major site of wealth accumulation and profit generation, (2) proliferated and drawn into them increasing numbers of households and laborers, (3) corporatized in the sense of being colonized by organized commercial interests that have a global reach, (4) extended in geographic scale, and (5) institutionalized through the development of public- and private-sector infrastructures and governance mechanisms. However, global care chains are distinguishable from global commodity chains in two ways. Unlike global commodity chains, which move material consumer goods around the world, global care chains commodify social reproduction, involve the massive export of human beings, and link systems of public health and welfare across political borders. Second, global care chains target peripheral female laborers to an even greater extent than do global commodity chains.

It would be premature to speak of a single, integrated global reproductive economy marked by a unified division of reproductive labor. However, globalized chains of care laborers are evidenced by the intensification of outsourcing and internationalization processes that have driven labor-export strategies of states, corporations, and households. One of the most pronounced manifestations of the globalization of care and reproductive services is the proliferation of care-labor-migration industrial complexes. These public-private partnerships between states and corporations structure transnational labor chains in order to profit from the systematization of care-labor production for export.

These characteristics are apparent in a wide range of care sectors, but especially the context of global nursing-care chains. The underlying dynamics of GNCCs are structured within health-care migration-industrial complexes that consist of international institutional infrastructure linkages, public health-care systems, nursing labor forces, families, and patients across geographically dispersed zones of the world-economy. GNCCs also extract surplus value from poorer countries and transfer it to richer countries. For those countries that export nurses into these global labor chains, the trade constitutes a form of superexploitation because of its deleterious effects on public health and social reproduction.

The International Division of Reproductive Labor and Sex-Trafficking Commodity Chains

Nadia Shapkina

Although there is a growing body of literature on the global sex trade in the sociology of gender and sexualities, scholars have paid little attention to development of theoretical and methodological tools to analyze its transnational production and consumption. In this essay, I demonstrate that world-systems analysis, particularly commodity chain analysis, can provide a valuable conceptual framework to explore the economic dynamics of sex-trafficking circuits. By focusing on the gendered aspects of global transformations, world-systems analysis overcomes "women's invisibility" by embedding commodity chain analysis in the total range of women's productive and reproductive labor (Wallerstein and Smith1992; Dunaway 2012). I also employ approaches to political economy, gender and sexualities, and the intersections of ethnicity and sex marketing to examine ethnographic data from trafficked survivors. Using their (her) stories, I pinpoint the factors that account for the rising entry of women from post-Soviet countries into the global sex trade. First, I investigate the transnational organization of sex trafficking by applying commodity chain analysis. Then I analyze the supply and demand factors that fuel the expansion of transnationalized sex marketing.

Throughout the essay, I recount firsthand experiences derived from interviews conducted with female survivors of sex trafficking who received rehabilitation assistance through NGOs in Ukraine and Russia between 2004 and 2006. The experiences and circumstances of the trafficked women vary significantly. However, all but one of the interviewees voluntarily migrated as a survival strategy in the face of economic, family, housing, and employment problems. Ranging in age from eighteen to thirty-six years, nineteen were unmarried when they were interviewed. Nine of the twenty had had children. Six were employed full-time, five were attending vocational training, and nine were unemployed. One had a university degree, two had some higher education, two had vocational certificates, ten had high-school diplomas, and five had not finished high school (Shapkina

2008: 4–19). I situate their experiences against the backdrop of conceptual explanations of changing socioeconomic structural conditions that lay the basis for proliferation of global sex-trafficking chains and for the recruitment of transnational reproductive workers into these risky labor contexts. Pseudonyms have been use to protect the identities of the interviewees.

COMMODITY CHAINS IN THE GLOBAL SEX TRADE

Studies that focus on sex trafficking often emphasize its criminal organization (Stoker 2002; Erokhina and Buryak 2003; Orlova 2004). However, I argue (1) that the social context of this crime needs to be considered through the lens of globalization and (2) that transnationalization of the sex trade is one of the processes of the global economy. I apply the global commodity chain approach to describe the transnationalization of production, consumption, and profit-making activities in sex-trafficking markets. The commodity chain approach was first formulated by representatives of world-systems analysis. Terence Hopkins and Immanuel Wallerstein (1986: 159) define a commodity chain as "a network of labor and production processes whose end result is a finished commodity." Their model is equally useful for the analysis of transnationalization of material commodity production (Gereffi and Korzeniewicz 1994) and of transnational services (Yeates 2009a). Commodity chain analysis renders visible the spatially dispersed stages of global production, distribution, and consumption of a product or service. Moreover, this approach allows researchers to explicate the gendered inequalities and risks to laborer households that occur at each local node of the production and delivery network (Dunaway 2001).

Hochschild (2000: 118–19) applies this approach to the analysis of the global transfer of reproductive labor. She suggests that global care chains are "a series of personal links between people across the globe based on the paid and unpaid work of caring." A large number of migrant women perform caring work or reproductive labor. Domestic services, care of children and the elderly, restaurant service, the entertainment industry, and the sex trade have experienced large increases in the employment of migrant women. The migration of women to sites with higher standards of living reflects the international transfer of reproductive labor (Tyuryukanova and Malysheva 2001). A typical example of this global care chain is the employment of an immigrant woman as a domestic worker to take on the reproductive labor of a wealthier housewife while another female assumes the immigrant's caregiving responsibilities for her distant children or elders (Parrenas 2001; Yeates 2005b).

Cuba provides an instructive case in which commodity chain analysis sheds light on how this economically isolated country has been integrated into the global sex trade. Sex tourism expanded in the context of the government's attempts to revive the economy after its collapse in the 1990s. Pressures to meet foreign debt obligations led to government promotion of tourism. The state's reliance on tourism revenues, privatization of tourism-related venues (restaurants, apartments, cabs), and the introduction of hard-currency stores facilitated the development of the country's sex tourism. "The economic crisis and its effect on women were particularly acute in Cuba during the early 1990s, and this translated into women becoming willing to sell sexual services for dollars, ultimately making Cuba a bargain basement destination for sex tourists" (Clancy 2002: 80). The organization of global sex-tourism chains in Cuba involves the branding and marketing of a tourist destination, transportation, provision of housing and entertainment, and consumption of sexual services. Cuba's sex trade is relatively free from brokers, such as pimps or bar and brothel owners. Women come into contact with customers directly and collect payments (although these are not enough to support the women and their families). Cuba differs from other tourism chains in which the sex trade is highly controlled by intermediaries between workers and consumers. Although there are occasional third-party involvements (e.g., landlords, cabdrivers), women initiate most sex-trade encounters on the streets and in clubs.

However, the global sex trade is not as organized in Havana as it is in Amsterdam, where the public policy of legalized prostitution stimulated rapid growth of the sex industry. Although the Netherlands does not rely on tourism revenues as much as other European countries, Amsterdam brings in large profits from sex tourists. The legalization of commodified sex enabled the establishment of brothels and other entertainment establishments and concretized labor rights for sex workers. In practice, however, there has been far greater emphasis on developing a good business climate for the sex industry and its consumers than on protecting sex workers' rights. NGOs like the Men/Women and Prostitution Foundation and the Association of Operators of Relaxation Businesses strive to establish legitimacy for the organized sex-trade industry. "Despite the growth of organized business interests in the sex trade, the city's economic benefit from sex tourists, and the greater legitimacy accorded sex work, current policy does not appear to be strengthening the hand of sex workers. . . . [Instead,] the focus of regulation is increasingly on improving the 'merchandising' environment for the sex industry and for consumers, and reducing disruption to local citizens" (Wonders and Michalowski 2001: 557–58).

Because of the increased influx of transnational migrants, the Amsterdam sex trade is being transformed into a "split labor market" (Bonacich 1972) that is grounded in ethnic and nationality differences. The legal market employs women with Dutch citizenship, while an illegal underground sector provides employment for undocumented migrants. Illegal immigrants working in the underground sector of the sex trade create a high degree of competition in that trade (and lower prices for sexual services) and thus split the market into several tiers with different degrees of legality. Even though the sex trade is legalized in Amsterdam, the market consists of both legal and illegal segments. Because the informal underground sex trade lies outside regulation, it has become a destination for the victims of sex trafficking (Wonders and Michalowski 2001: 557–58).

Clancy (2002) concludes that local links within global sex tourism are organized differently because they come under the influence of disparate global, national, or local factors. In Cuba, the determining factor is state policy in relation to prostitution. The government is prohibitionist toward the organized sex trade but turns a blind eye to individual women who earn a living in the sex trade. However, Wonders and Michalowski (2001) argue that global structural conditions are facilitating the growth of sex tourism. Under pressures to compete globally for economic growth or from the International Monetary Fund to repay external debts, national governments promote tourism as a strategy for economic development and stimulate expansion of the sex trade as a market to absorb workers who have been displaced by economic restructuring or crises (Beneria and Feldman 1992).

SEX TRAFFICKING AND GLOBAL COMMODITY CHAINS

There are three main components of global commodity chain analysis: the input-output structure that traces the cycle of commodity circulation, territorial dispersion of the chain, and a governance structure that describes power relations within a chain (Gereffi 1994). I will employ these analytic components to outline the main characteristics and political and economic contexts in which global sex-trafficking chains operate.

Input-Output Structure

Whereas sex tourism delivers customers to exotic destinations to consume sexual services, sex trafficking is organized as an underground source of cheap laborers for places of sexual consumption. Transnational criminal traffickers capture women's bodies and affective labor and transform them into commodities to be marketed. The final products in the input-output structure of this global commodity chain are the services that these low-paid workers offer to produce people's affective experiences. In the first stage, the recruiter can be a person or an organization (e.g., an employment agency or a dancing show) that advertises high-paying employment abroad. The most typical job offers are in domestic services, care of children and the elderly, and the entertainment industry, and recruitment often occurs through acquaintances. For example, a friend of Liza's husband recruited her to work for a German family as a governess. The recruiter worked in a tourist agency and had knowledge about tourist visa procedures. At the recruitment stage, a recruiter obtains the woman's consent to travel. The consent can be formalized as a work contract or marriage certificate, or it can include an informal agreement to find a place of employment.

Another means of recruitment is abduction. Natasha was kidnapped from her hometown in southern Ukraine. Because most trafficked victims migrate voluntarily, Natasha's case is one of the few instances of kidnapping that antitrafficking NGOs have documented. Natasha was a parentless minor who studied at a boarding school. Traffickers often recruit at orphanages and boarding schools. Natasha had just graduated from boarding school but could not find a job. The recruiters tried to persuade Natasha to travel with them but resorted to abduction after she refused. The risks for women at this stage of trafficking include law violations related to obtaining illegal passports or visas. Traffickers often rely on corrupt state officials to obtain the travel documents. If border police detain women who travel with fake documents, the women can face criminal charges (Brunovskis and Tyldum 2004).

Transportation is the second stage in sex trafficking. Women may travel to destinations alone or with traffickers or recruiters, and they may cross borders legally or illegally. Liza traveled to Germany with a legal tourist visa arranged by a recruiter. Vika traveled to Macedonia with a group of dancers who all had entertainment visas. Illegal border crossing is especially risky for the women because it makes them dependent on traffickers. Nina described her experience of illegal border crossing from Egypt to Israel as extremely dangerous. "Risk was there, I understood this when we crossed the border. The [border police] could shoot [us], literally. The [smugglers] wore helmets, night vision goggles, and bullet-proof vests, but we walked and crawled."

Upon arrival in the destination country, traffickers sell women to bars, clubs, or brothel owners or market the women's services themselves. Accompanied by a smuggler, Natasha walked across the border illegally and was sold to a local pimp to work as a call girl.

> I wanted to scream, but [the smuggler] who was walking me across the border said he would kill me if I screamed. When we arrived at Chisinau, [the smuggler] told me that if I tell anyone about how I arrived here and what I do, my brother will be killed. [The pimp] took me to the dispatcher apartment. We worked not as prostitutes, but as call girls. We did not stay in one spot. They drove us around to different places. We lived in rented apartments and were taken to work in hotels, saunas, houses.

Natasha's case demonstrates the extensive organization of the sex-trafficking chains. The criminal group involved a recruiter, a trafficker, a smuggler, a dispatcher, and a local pimp.

Nina offered more details about the transnational organization and coordination of the sex-trafficking chains. Operators in several countries

> are tightly connected. Everything begins in Russia. But, when a girl comes to Israel, her boss already knows everything about her, including how she looks. In Moscow, the owner of the transit apartment telephones to Israel with descriptions of his available girls. Sometimes [the recruiter] would get an advance order, "I need a blond girl, with such breasts, and of such height." And they would send a girl [who matched those criteria]. When we were transferred from Moscow to Egypt, [the pimps] already knew about me, and they had already designated me to go to a certain place. So, it's not like [traffickers] bring a group of girls and then find places for them. They know in advance who the owners will be.

The process of traveling to a foreign country puts women in an extremely dependent position and makes them vulnerable to the control of traffickers. The women typically do not speak local languages, their documents are taken away, and they are told that they have violated the law and are at risk of legal prosecution. In addition to their illegal status and their lack of financial resources, these women face health risks and threats to their lives.

The third stage of the input-output structure of a global sex-trafficking chain is consumption at destination sites. The main agents during this stage are the pimps who market sex services and the clients who purchase those services in bars, clubs, brothels, hotels, apartments, or homes. Nina mentioned that women trafficked from abroad are especially popular with customers because they are "fresh" commodities on the market. The trafficked women are called "tourists" because pimps often resell them to other establishments. Customers express their dissatisfaction when a woman lacks sexual experience. Natasha reported that clients in Moldova complained about her lack of experience to a pimp. "I did not know what to do," she said, "so they whisked me out of the house. Clearly, I could not know what to do. I was a little girl. I was sixteen. Actually, fifteen."

Traffickers use different means to coerce women into providing a wide range of sexual services to clients. The main agents involved in the control of women are the owners and employees of bars and clubs, guards, and pimps. Control is a central element in trafficking and is the basis of exploitation in the sex trade. Zoya pointed to the difficulties of resistance and escape. "How was I supposed to leave when [the owner] was a huge man with a shaved head? I was scared even to look at him. When he threatened

me, I was not thinking about my money, I was thinking about my survival."
Twenty-five-year-old Olga, a Russian migrant to Turkey, explained how the
language barrier serves as a control strategy in sex-trafficking chains.

> First, I did not know the language. I could not learn the language because
> they kept me alone for a long time. Because [clients] did not speak
> Russian, I needed to learn the language. [Pimps] are not interested in you
> learning the language. The less you know, the easier it is for them to
> control you. After I learned some phrases, I was able to communicate
> with a young man who helped me to escape.

Traffickers also use isolation as a control strategy. Pimps disempower
and terrorize the women by separating them, locking them up, or dispersing
them to different work sites. Isolation of the women from others of similar
cultural and linguistic backgrounds is intended to sever friendships and to
diminish opportunities for female solidarity building that might lead to es-
capes. As a result, the trafficked women have very few social contacts, and
they are permitted to telephone home only rarely. Nina indicated that isolation was the most difficult aspect of being trafficked into the sex trade. She
and other women were not allowed to go outside their workplaces, where
they had to purchase clothes and makeup at inflated prices. In addition,
they could visit a doctor only at their own expense. Other forms of control
include threats to the women's Ukrainian or Russian relatives, trafficker appropriation of women's documents and belongings, and coerced addiction
to drugs and alcohol. During her first weeks in Israel, the pimp gave Nina a
pill every evening that affected her perception and slowed her reactions. But
despite traffickers' multiple forms of control, women find ways to escape.
For example, Olga ran away after she saved some money and learned
enough Turkish phrases to communicate with a local male who was helped
her to escape.

Territorial Dispersion of the Chain

Global sex-trafficking chains include three geographic locations: sending
countries, transit countries, and countries of destination. For example, Russia is simultaneously a sending country (e.g., to western Europe and the
Middle East), a receiving country (from Ukraine and central Asian countries), and a transit country (for migrants traveling from Asia to western
Europe). Moscow is the main transit city through which migrants reach
western Europe and North America. As a sex trade entrepôt, Moscow has
numerous transit apartments to house migrants temporarily while they wait
for their documents and departure. Besides transnational sex trafficking,
there are domestic sex-trafficking chains that typically connect provincial
regions and cities. In Russia, Moscow and St. Petersburg are the global cities

where the sex trade flourishes. In Ukraine, Kiev and the Crimean Peninsula are the main destinations. Sex trafficking from the former Soviet region has multiple receiving countries, so it operates over three smuggling routes. The Baltic route goes through Lithuania and is used for transportation of migrants to Germany, Scandinavia, and the United States. The Georgian route uses open-border policies to transport migrants to Turkey, Greece, and the Mediterranean. The Chinese-Siberian route is a channel for Russian migration to China, as well as a route of Chinese migration to western Europe through Moscow (Stoker 2002).

Why do certain countries become destinations for sex trafficking? The main destinations may be global cities, military zones, tourist resorts, and other places with high purchasing power. However, we must also take into account the previously established migrant chains in the regions. For example, the most frequent destinations for sex trafficking from the former Soviet region are Israel, Germany, Turkey, and Russia. In the past, there were several waves of migration from the former Soviet republics to Israel that established family, business, and other connections between them. Many recruiters and some traffickers are former Soviet citizens or persons who hold dual citizenship. According to Gershuni (2004: 137), the "key to the 'Israel connection' may be found in the mass migration of Soviet citizens to Israel during the 1990s. This created a cultural milieu in which it was possible to 'import' women from the former Soviet Union without their appearing out of place, sometimes in the guise of legal immigrants." Similarly, Germany experienced a wave of the post-Soviet migration. Turkey and Greece have numerous connections to the former Soviet countries through tourism and through the transborder shuttle trade that Dedeoglu describes in Chapter 6. Moreover, Russia is a major destination and a travel node because of simplified migration regulations for citizens of the former Soviet republics, lack of linguistic barriers, and the existence of multiple connections with the former Soviet republics.

Organization and Governance of Chains

Finally, different national regulations affect distribution within the sex trade. On the one hand, the chains are shaped by public governance structures. Whether the sex trade takes legal or illegal forms is often determined by public policies of prohibition or legalization. On the other hand, there are relations of power that are exercised within the chain (Yeates 2005b). These include control strategies that intermediaries use to assert their power over trafficked women and sanctions that are imposed on women for violating the rules. Internal rules can be verbal (e.g., regulation of movements and activities, curfew, instructions about client services). However, some stages of sex-trafficking chains are grounded in codified rules (e.g., a contract between the club owner and the entertainment worker). Because trafficking involves an abuse of trust of the trafficked, the governance within the chains is not legitimate, and the trafficked women often resist it in multiple ways.

Gereffi (1994) distinguishes between vertical and horizontal organization of economic networks. A producer-driven chain is a vertically organized network in which large corporations control the production and distribution process. A buyer-driven chain is more decentralized and horizontally organized. In global sex-trafficking chains, there are elements of both models. In sex-trafficking chains that involve organized crime, the internal governance structure approximates vertical organization. However, sex-trafficking chains, like buyer-driven chains, also demonstrate flexibility of production and distribution.

External governance is effected through immigration legislation, sex-trade regulation, and law-enforcement institutions and procedures in countries involved in the chain. Criminalization in some countries (e.g., Sweden) deters internal distribution of sex-trafficking activities but externalizes consumption into neighboring countries. In countries where the sex trade is legalized (e.g., the Netherlands, Germany), traffickers supply women for the unregulated segment of the sex-trade market. This splits the market into a "two-tiered hierarchy of sex work" that is regulated and underground and in which women in the unregulated sector earn lower pay and experience the greatest risks (Wonders and Michalowski 2001: 568). Another aspect of external governance is the regulation of transnational migration. Although technology enables easy travel and communication between countries (and often helps the operations of trafficking chains), there are barriers to mobility of unskilled workers. When migration control prevents low-skilled workers from accessing better-paying jobs in other countries, smugglers and traffickers promise high-paying jobs. Finally, connections between traffickers and corrupt officials are another element of the governance structure. Trafficker links to state officials are forms of social capital that enable them to run the trafficking chains and to avoid law enforcement.

SUPPLY FACTORS IN SEX TRAFFICKING

Sex trafficking is an organized criminal activity that increasingly takes place in the context of transnational migration. Supply and demand sides of sex-trafficking markets are related to push and pull factors of the transnational migration of women. In order to understand the supply side of the sex-trafficking market, we need to examine the push factors that stimulate female decisions to migrate. The incorporation of the post-Soviet countries into the global economy has had numerous gendered effects, one of which is the increasing feminization of migration. The opening of the borders after the collapse of the Soviet Union made travel abroad possible. Women from the former Soviet countries represent the largest proportion of early twenty-first-century sex-trade migration to western Europe, North America, Asia, and the Middle East.

Economic Hardship

Women often explain their decisions to migrate in terms of economic hardship. When employment opportunities are scarce in their home countries, migration seems like the only viable strategy to generate income to support children or parents. When twenty-five-year-old divorcée Olena could not find employment in her home village in southern Ukraine, she decided to migrate to Israel.

> There was not much support, and I needed money. My parents are old, and I have a child. When I got divorced, we had only my mom's income, and this was not enough. I could not work because I needed to stay with my child. My husband left the village. I worked at a fish-processing plant until it closed. After graduating from school, I got certified to work in sales, but I could not find a job. There are not so many jobs in our village or around it. I [decided to go abroad] to look for something like cleaner or maid that pays at least $200—$100 for me and $100 that I could send to my mother and my child.

Domestic violence, divorce, and lack of social support were important factors in thirty-two-year-old Alexandra's decision to migrate from western Ukraine to Poland to find a job to support her nine-year-old daughter.

> I was married, but then I got divorced. He was an alcoholic, and he abused me. After I left him, I found a job, but the pay was not sufficient. I had to live with my parents. I was told [by her parents], "If you want to leave your husband, you have to find some work. We will not be helping you." This is why I decided to go abroad. I realized that I could not count on my parents.

Thirty-one-year-old divorcée Liza found herself in a similar situation in western Ukraine. Even though she had earned two college degrees, she could not find employment that would provide sufficient income for her household.

> I used to work in a school. I was a schoolteacher, a deputy principal. My salary was very small, about $50, but I had two children. I had a husband back then, but he did not support us. A friend of my husband offered me an opportunity to work as a governess in Germany. She had a job related to arranging tourist visas. In Germany I was going to take care of children and teach them English, and I was offered [a much higher salary]. I agreed to go there to work during my summer vacations.

In similar fashion, twenty-two-year-old Nina decided to seek foreign employment because she was in desperate need of money. Because her mother and stepfather were long-term alcoholics, she was the main caregiver for her younger siblings. The children earned money by picking and marketing mushrooms and berries. They had to move into one room and lock the door to stop their alcoholic parents from selling their belongings. Despite this difficult family situation, Nina successfully graduated from high school and moved to a large nearby city, where she worked as a saleswoman at a local market. Soon, Nina's sister joined her to attend vocational school. Nina's salary was not enough to support them, so she accumulated a large debt. Nina decided to post a job-seeking ad at the market where she worked. A recruiter contacted her with an offer to migrate to Israel to work as a maid for a prosperous Russian household. He promised to pay Nina's debt and to cover her transportation, passport, and visa expenses. The offer of a well-paying job in Israel seemed not only like a solution to financial problems but also a strategy for upward mobility.

Economic Crisis in Ukraine and Russia

In the 1990s, Ukraine and Russia underwent a rapid shift from state control to a neoliberal free-market economy. The transition to capitalism was accompanied by privatization of public enterprises, price and trade liberalization, and cuts in welfare spending. When the post-Soviet states transferred government property to private owners, workers often did not receive salaries for months. By the time the workers did receive their earnings, their purchasing power was much lower because of hyperinflation. At the same time, the prices of rent, gas, and electricity increased as the states sought to deregulate prices. In addition, many state employees lost their jobs because the economic restructuring led to the closure of numerous enterprises and to the decline of manufacturing and agriculture. These economic crises created powerful push factors for people to seek other employment opportunities, some of which involved migration.

Thirty-six-year-old Zoya spoke angrily about Ukrainian state policies that push people into transnational labor migration.

> I did not have a good life here. I had a good job, but no pay. Our government often did not pay any salaries for months. We could eat somehow, but we could not pay the apartment rent. And in 2000 the state required us to pay the debt. We had several thousand [hryvnas] in debt. The condition was that if you don't pay in two months, they will evict your family. How many people were evicted! Of course, women started [migrating] because they could not protect themselves socially here. There

was an order from the city administration to evict in one day. They [the bailiffs] were coming at noon or midnight, showing a court order, and throwing people out and sealing the apartment. Traffickers used this situation. They would say, "We will pay your debts; the apartment stays in your possession, if you go abroad." When people did not get paid for months, where were they supposed to get the money to pay these rents? They really had no other choice but to rely on traffickers. This is such genocide of the population!

During the socioeconomic perestroika, Russians faced sharply rising poverty, rapid reduction of living standards, extreme polarization of incomes, unemployment, and dismantling of the welfare system. When Russia underwent financial crises in 1992, 1995, and 1998, people lost their savings because of hyperinflation. The economic shock therapy of 1992 involved a series of state policies intended to bring about a market-oriented economy by liberalizing trade, removing price controls, eliminating state subsidies, and privatizing publicly owned enterprises. By 1993, public institutions were dysfunctional and social safety nets had been eliminated, but 80 percent of the population was impoverished (Rimashevskaia 2002). These problems were exacerbated because the government delayed wage payments for months. When state employees were forced to survive without their salaries, they engaged in bribery and rented out state properties (Gerber 2004).

A major result of neoliberal restructuring was a decline in state spending for social welfare. The Russian and Ukrainian governments ended or reduced many social programs and benefits for women and left families to survive without the social safety nets on which they had depended in the past. This abrupt change represented the state's divorce from women, to whom the burdens were shifted to become household breadwinners. Even though women were inequitably responsible for sustaining households when the state withdrew family subsidies, they faced greater difficulty securing jobs because employers were now expected to absorb the expense for worker benefits that the state had previously covered (Kiblitskaya 2000). Ukraine underwent a similar "transformational crisis of social reproduction" in which impoverishment, unemployment, and the collapse of welfare forced households to identify new survival mechanisms (Zhurzhenko 2001: 104). The state lowered public assistance for housing, guaranteed employment, and family assistance to minuscule levels. The disappearance of state-subsidized support required Ukrainian families to adopt new survival strategies, such as subsistence farming, greater dependence on family networks, reduced health-care spending, and increased informal-sector activities.

Gendered Impacts of Economic Crisis

The gendered effects of the troubled transition to capitalism have been extensive. Females, especially waged women, are negatively affected by structural adjustment programs, particularly in the areas of public employment, state subsidies, and benefits (Beneria and Feldman 1992). For example, delays in child-support payments have continued in Ukraine from the 1990s into the early twenty-first century.

> At the end of the 1990s, there was a growing debt with regard to social payments to families with children: in 1996, 20.1 million hryvnas; in 1999, 43.8 million. Until 1999, the calculation and payments of family allowances was a function of the enterprises and companies. Many of them were in difficult financial situations, under reorganization, or in liquidation, and they could no longer provide these social payments. Since 1999, when these functions were transferred to local offices for social protection, the situation has improved slightly. However, the local offices today still have serious problems with financing social payments. (Zhurzhenko 2004: 40)

Delays in child-support payments affect all families, but especially single mothers. For many women in the post-Soviet countries, the restructuring meant more responsibilities, lower incomes, inequality in the labor market, harsher working conditions, and diminished quality of public services (Kiblitskaya 2000; Malysheva 2001).

The Ukrainian state actively supports transnational labor migration because the government generates revenue from transnational remittances. The director of Ukraine's State Committee for Family and Youth Affairs expressed public policy this way: "People are leaving in search of work. They will continue to leave. We need to legislate this way of earning a living, but our state does not have resources to protect all socially vulnerable groups" (Dovzhenko 2002: 2). Another factor affecting women's degraded position in the former socialist countries is the advancement of "neotraditionalist" gender ideology. Post-Soviet conservatives contend that women's economic emancipation during the Soviet era is the root of contemporary family problems, so they advocate a "return" to "traditional" family and gender roles. In its advocacy of family autonomy from the state, the neotraditionalist ideology coincides with neoliberal calls for elimination of welfare and family subsidies (Zhurzhenko 2001).

In the context of widening unemployment, state officials often use the neotraditionalist argument about "women's natural function" to deny women equal employment opportunities. The gender ideology of neotraditionalism serves as a justification for the political and economic disempowerment of women. However, everyday realities in Ukraine and Russia sharply con-tradict these ideological declarations. There is a disjuncture between state intentions to "traditionalize" the nation by returning women to the family and the pressures on females to be breadwinners for their households. Such policies weaken the legitimacy of the state, which is not fiscally stable enough to afford the restoration of the traditional family (Zhurzhenko 2004).

Resexualization of Life in Post-Soviet Countries

Another aspect of the supply side of the sex-trafficking market is its reliance on social construction of gendered and sexualized bodies. "Resexualiza-tion" of life in post-Soviet countries has produced new images of feminin-ity (Attwood 1996; Lissyutkina 1993). A beautiful appearance defines the image of the "New Woman," compared with the asexual and work-oriented "Soviet Woman." The twenty-first-century ideal woman is stereotyped to be sexually liberated, tender, caring, and passionate. Inconsistently, the "New Woman" combines contradictory "Madonna" and "whore" imager-ies of domesticity and seduction. For example, overt sexualization of wom-en's bodies manifests itself in the labor market (Voronina 1994). Job adver-tisements in Russian newspapers emphasize requirements for women's appearance and age, job interviews have the hidden agenda of sexual favors, and sexual harassment at work is a frequent phenomenon (Bridger and Kay 1996). The sociocultural constructions of gendered and sexualized bodies are related to the commodification of female bodies in the sex-trafficking market. Women make decisions to travel abroad in the context of several factors, especially the necessity to provide livelihoods for households during economic downturns, lack of employment opportunities, indebted-ness, or difficulties in family relations. Economic insecurity stands out as the most significant factor that influenced migration decisions of the re-spondents in my sample. Their economic insecurity ranged from emergency situations (as in the cases of Zoya, who could have lost her house, and Nina, who had to repay borrowed money) to less urgent circumstances (such as the case of Liza, who needed short-term employment to raise extra money).

DEMAND FACTORS IN SEX TRAFFICKING

As the tourism industry and the mass media spread the culture of sexual consumerism across the world, the sex trade is globalizing its economic practices. Concentrated in global cities, tourist zones, and military bases, sex tourism has become an intrinsic part of travel capitalism and has gener-ated new forms of sexual consumption (Agathangelou and Ling 2003).

"Tourists feel free to experience the identity of 'others' by sampling cultural products, experiences, bodies, and identities" (Wonders and Michalowski 2001: 552). Women's bodies become commodities to be consumed by sex tourists, representations of "other" cultures, and objects for experiencing new "virgin" territories. The construction of demand relies on certain racialized and ethnicized images of bodies and constructions of femininity. Such images are gendered stereotypes that objectify females as exotic fetishes (Thorbek and Pattanaik 2002). These intersections of ethnicity and sexuality create "ethnosexual frontiers" (Nagel 2000: 122) where the global sex trade capitalizes on the exoticization of ethnic differences to stimulate consumption of sexual services provided by transnational migrants. In this way, diverse ethnicities become new "brands" of sexual products to be consumed. For instance, Japan and Switzerland have special visa programs that allow foreign nationals to travel to these countries as "entertainers." Although some visa recipients are not tied into the sex trade, most of the visas are issued to women who "officially" perform exotic dancing while unofficially working as hostesses and sex workers. In this way, the governments of Japan and Switzerland meet the demand for consumption of ethnosexual contacts while maintaining strict immigration policies (Nagel 2000).

In the same vein, the demand side of the sex-trafficking market constructs representations of post-Soviet women around race, culture, and gender. In terms of racialization, whiteness often defines Slavic femininity. Naming sex-trade workers from the former Soviet Union "Natasha" represents cultural "othering." In Scandinavian countries, women from the former Soviet Union are referred to as "eastern girls." Last, representations of women as possessing a mix of feminine, seductive, and patriarchal values (a Madonna/whore combination) demonstrate gendering and sexualization of women's bodies (Thorbek and Pattanaik 2002).

• • •

The rapid expansion of sex tourism is part of the global trend toward labor informalization in the twenty-first century (United Nations 2003). Portes, Castells, and Benton (1989: 12) emphasize that the informal sector is characterized by income generation through economic activities that are not legally regulated. Post-Fordist economies introduced such innovations as flexible specialization and flexible forms of labor. Key processes of this global restructuring included the deregulation of labor relations, the incorporation of cheaper foreign labor, and the weakening of the power of labor in industrialized countries. A result of the dominance of these post-Fordist economic forms is the reorganization of work, particularly the casualization of labor in which previously formalized relations are deregulated. Typically, this deregulation negatively affects the status of labor and work conditions.

The purpose of this process is to minimize the cost of labor by reducing the cost of reproduction of labor power (Chapter 12). Another process intrinsic to post-Fordism is socioeconomic polarization, which leads to formation of "alternative circuits of survival" that are located within informal sectors, "regulatory fractures," or "regulatory voids" (Sassen 2000: 510–11), like those that typify the situations from which traffickers draw their victims. In these contexts, there is a proliferation of various types of intermediaries, such as employment agencies and smugglers, who offer their services in finding transnational employment (Yeates 2005b).

Why is the informal economy of sex trafficking becoming so widespread? First, informalization is a strategy of household adjustment to global economic transformations, such as the crisis-ridden market-economy transitions that have pushed Ukrainian and Russian women into transnational sex labor migration. Unstable transitional economic conditions have forced households to identify alternative survival strategies. Decreasing opportunities for survival have also triggered a growing array of illegal strategies of profit making and the expansion of criminalized alternative global commodity chains. Second, global sex-trafficking chains merge informal-sector activities with formal-sector enterprises. Thus illicit organizations have merged their operations with legal tourism, transportation, entertainment, and media, as well as the illicit drug trade. Export of women for the sex trade has been led by transnational organizations that have high capital to establish market strategies to sell sexual services. Organized criminal circuits benefit from regulatory voids to recruit desperate female workers from unreliable informal-sector income in their unstable home countries. Traffickers elude detection and prosecution through the disjuncture between the transnational character of the global sex-trafficking chains and differences among national regulations.

Third, the sex trade capitalizes on the economic push factors that make export of reproductive services feasible and profitable. Women's bodies and their diverse burdens of paid and unpaid work have become central to these strategies (Bridger and Kay 1996). The transnationalization of production and consumption in the sex trade is grounded in transnational migration of reproductive labor (Parrenas 2001; Yeates 2005b), and these workers are increasingly integrated into global commodity chains that merge illicit and legal capitalist enterprises and intermediaries. Like other capitalists, traffickers construct their commodity chains around market segmentation and specialization, and they diversify services in reaction to consumer demands.

PART VI CONCEPTUALIZING SOCIAL REPRODUCTION AND WORKER RESISTANCE IN COMMODITY CHAINS

Decomposition of Industrial Commodity Chains, Household Semiproletarianization, and Arenas for Resistance at the Center

Dave Broad

> *It is justice, not charity, that is wanting in the world.*
> —Mary Wollstonecraft 1792: 92

> *The philosophers have only* interpreted *the world, in various ways;
> the point is to* change *it.*
> —Karl Marx 1992: 423

Most analysts focus on the waged workers who make up the formal labor force of commodity chains (Raworth and Kidder 2010). However, the vast majority of workers who service commodity chains are not fully proletarianized, and the structuring of nonwaged labor mechanisms typifies capitalism in both boom and crisis times (Broad 1991). Several scholars have emphasized capitalist structuring of casualized and subcontracted labor throughout the Global South, and a few investigators have pinpointed the linkages between export commodity chains and the informal sectors of poor countries.[1] However, there has been far less attention to the expansion of these labor strategies in rich core states.[2] For that reason, I will explore the increasing trends toward deproletarianization and semiproletarianization following decomposition of industrial commodity chains in the core. I will argue that these semiproletarianized forms of labor are "normal" for historical capitalism because they function to minimize the social reproduction costs of capital. As a result, capitalists structure contradictory junctures at which worker households can resist the mechanisms that integrate them more deeply into labor arrangements that threaten the social reproduction of their communities. In the sections that follow, I will address four questions:

1. Why does capitalism structure semiproletarianized forms of labor, such as casualization and informalization?
2. Why do these forms of semiproletarianized labor disproportionately affect women?

3. What threats to social reproduction of worker households and communities do these forms of labor generate?
4. What are worker options for resistance?

Because my goal is to offer conceptual guideposts that will be useful in future commodity chain investigations, I will pose questions for future research at the end of the chapter.

SEMIPROLETARIANIZATION OF HOUSEHOLDS

Historically in capitalist societies, production and reproduction of labor power have been based on a mix of wage labor with nonvalorized domestic, peasant, and artisan labor (Broad 1991, 2000a, 2000b). Moreover, British feminist historian Angela John (1986: 3) contends that

> many of the generalized categories used to define and describe employment—full-time/part-time, rural/urban, heavy/light, indoor/outdoor, adult/child—are inadequate, inappropriate and sometimes misleading when applied to women's experiences. Women frequently slipped in and out of such polarities, much of their work being casual and seasonal. . . . For married women in particular it might not even be perceived as employment since it did not necessarily involve going *out* to work.

This commingling of work characterized women's livelihood strategies in eighteenth- and nineteenth-century Western societies (Matthaei 1982; John 1986) and has persisted into contemporary times (Broad 2010; Huws 2011). Furthermore, this kind of "diverse labor portfolio" (Chapter 3) typifies female work throughout the contemporary Global South (Broad 2000a).

For example, some years back, my spouse and I were enrolled in a Spanish immersion program in a small town just outside San José, Costa Rica. We stayed in a three-generation household that pooled income through several labor strategies that bridged the formal and informal economies and commingled paid and unpaid labor. The matriarch and patriarch were of rural peasant background but had moved their household of four adult children, two sons and two daughters, from the countryside. Married with two children, the older son worked as a carpenter alongside his father. The second son and the older daughter earned wages in factories that were tied into global commodity chains. The matriarch organized and supervised the household of extended kin. The mother, the younger daughter, and the daughter-in-law worked in the household, hosting immersion students like us and cooking food for workmen who stopped by the house and for informal-sector marketing. During time away from paid employment, the patriarch and the adult children grew crops for household use and for marketing. The daughter-in-law cared for her children and helped the matriarch. This example is typical of the household income pooling through subsistence activities, petty commodity production, casualized or subcontracted labor, and waged work that can be found throughout the world-system (Wallerstein and Dickinson 1982). Global commodity chains typically capture only a small segment of the total livelihood complex of semiproletarianized households (Chapter 3) because household members cumulatively will spend less of their work lifetimes earning wages than they will engaging in nonwaged labor (Werlhof 1984). Thus the productive stages of commodity chains capture far more Global South labor and inputs through casualization, subcontracting, and the informal sector than from direct waged labor (Carr, Chen, and Tate 2000; Selwyn 2012).

This blending of activities has been the historical norm for households in the center states as well, but it diminished in the second half of the twentieth century (Wallerstein and Dickinson 1982). By the 1960s, a majority of households became dependent on wage labor and market consumption for household provision (Beechey and Perkins 1987). Even though working-class females had never been absent from paid economic activity (Matthaei 1982), a much higher proportion of women (re)entered the formal labor market to maintain family living standards after 1960 (Andersen 2001). Starting in the 1980s, the core deindustrialized in the face of corporate relocation to capture cheaper labor in the Global South (R. Ross and Trachte 1990). As core industrial commodity chains decomposed, workers were disconnected from the waged livelihoods in which their household provisioning had been embedded (M. Nelson and Smith 1989). Rapidly, the social reproduction of deindustrialized communities was put in jeopardy because core workers were forced to make the transition to lower-paying jobs (and often fewer jobs) in the service sectors (Brady and Denniston 2006). In the face of the global "wage race to the bottom" (R. Ross and Chan 2003: 1016) and insufficient new job growth at the core (Brady and Denniston 2006), many terminated workers were unable to locate new employment that would support their standard of living (Broad 1997; Broad and Hunter 2009). Women were hit disproportionately hard by the geographic relocation of industrial commodity chains (Andersen 2001), and a new feminization of poverty emerged among lower-middle-class households (Browne 2000). Moreover, income earning from part-time, casualized, subcontracting, and informal-sector linkages to commodity chains began to grow faster than full-time waged employment (Portes and Sassen 1987).

At the turn of the twenty-first century, many core households must merge erratic waged jobs with several forms of part-time and other casual labor to try to pool sufficient household income (Broad 2010). For instance, my wife and I know a family in which each parent has formal waged employment, but the father and the daughter work on condominium maintenance contracts. Father, mother, and daughter paint houses, and the daughter does "electronic cottage work" and acts as an informal waged caregiver for an elderly male. With the onset of state austerity programs and the post-2007 great recession (Stuckler and Basu 2013), this need for mixing income-earning endeavors has expanded in the core. Along with cuts to public welfare programs, concession bargaining has resulted in erosion of worker benefits and pensions and has externalized more of the costs of social reproduction to laborer households. In the 1960s, feminists spoke of the double day of paid work and household labor. With (re)casualization and increasing multiple jobholding in the core, however, women face at least a triple day of work (Broad 2000a, 2010).

THE PRESENT AS HISTORY: (RE)CASUALIZATION OF LABOR AT THE CORE

My home country of Canada deindustrialized faster than the United States, so by 1985 only about one-quarter of workers remained in manufacturing jobs, and more than 69 percent were concentrated in the service sector (Resnick 1989). In the same period, formal part-time work increased significantly in Canada and other Western capitalist countries (Broad 1991), and three-quarters of these part-timers were women (Beechey and Perkins 1987). Initially, scholars and practitioners claimed that employers instituted this form of semiproletarianized labor because women "preferred" to work part-time in order to prioritize family responsibilities. This explanation begged three questions.

1. What were the world-systemic trends that accounted for the increase in part-time work in many economic sectors in this period?
2. Did women "prefer" part-time work, as employers claimed, or was this a socially constructed stereotype used to justify semiproletarianization? Is part-time labor institutionalized because it is a strategy through which employers can cut social reproduction costs?
3. Do capitalist employers actually offer jobs on terms that sustain social reproduction of worker households? If so, what explains the long history of trade-union and social reform struggles in core states?

Clearly, a larger structural explanation was needed because the rise in part-time work corresponded to simultaneous expansion of temporary jobs, contract work, and self-employment (Broad 2000a). Indeed, growth in these labor strategies was part of the longer-term restructuring process that was occurring in the capitalist world-system (Broad 1991). Moreover, the preponderance of part-time work can be understood only in the contexts of women's work historically and of the intersection of the formal and

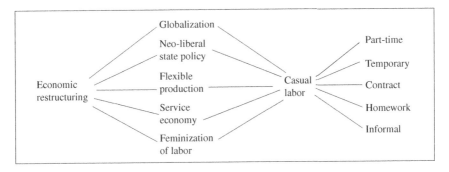

Figure 12.1. Casual labor and economic restructuring

informal economies that accompanied geographic relocation of global commodity chains in search of cheaper labor (Broad 1991, 1995a, 1995b, 1997, 2000a, 2000b, 2010). On the one hand, part-time work was not new because there had been steady growth in this form of labor over two previous decades of economic boom, which implies that this type of casualization is more than a cyclical phenomenon (Broad 1991). On the other hand, capitalist commodity chains structured (re)casualization of labor during two decades of economic crisis (see Figure 12.1). By the 1980s, the core's share in total world production was sharply declining, especially in manufactured goods (Bergesen and Sahoo 1985). Portes (1983: 171) detected an "ongoing reorganization" of nonwaged labor strategies "for the purpose of reversing the trend toward a fully contractual and regulated labor market." Thus the rise in part-time work in the 1980s was part of the worldwide "race to the bottom" (R. Ross and Chan 2003: 1016) that would set in motion deproletarianization of the core (Barkin 1985).

Semiproletarianization, Casualization, and Informalization as the Norm

In the late nineteenth century, British capitalists used casualization to cope with economic crisis, and contemporary capitalists have revitalized this strategy in the face of the post-1960s crisis (Broad 2000a). However, this trend does not represent a simple return to a bygone era. Neither capitalist globalization nor casualization is new. Even though construction of the international division of labor is part of historical capitalism, we must scrutinize it carefully within the context of neoliberal restructuring. For clarity, we need to position discussions of the persistence and resurrection of casualization within the context of the historical failure of capitalism to proletarianize labor fully. "If we now look at global empirical reality throughout the time-space of historical capitalism," Wallerstein (1995a: 27) explains, "we suddenly discover that the location of wage-workers in *semi*-proletarian households has been the statistical norm." Globally, the number of waged laborers has always been much smaller than the number of nonproletarian workers. In reality, full-time proletarian labor is not now, nor has it ever been, the norm in capitalist societies. Even if we overlook hidden unpaid workers (Chapter 3), a majority of the world's laborers earn their livelihoods in casualized and informal contexts (United Nations 2003).

The modern world-system has not exhibited the full proletarianization of labor because capital has not supported it. Although the commodification of labor may provide capital with readily accessible workers, "the proportion of the costs of reproduction borne by the 'employer' or 'market purchaser' . . . is significantly greater in the case of life-time than part-life-time proletarian households" (T. Hopkins and Wallerstein 1982: 68). Consequently, complete proletarianization of labor would be economically damaging to capital (Frobel 1982). In contrast, "one of the major forces behind proletarianization has been the world's work forces themselves" (Wallerstein 1995a: 36). Along with the commodification of everything (Wallerstein 1995a), proletarianization is one of the important secular trends of the capitalist world-economy. However, capital is unwilling to use enough of its profits to bring proletarianization to full fruition. Instead, semiproletarianized households effectively reproduce and sustain the reserve armies of labor (Marx 1990, vol. 1) that are reflected in the rapid growth of casual, part-time, temporary, subcontracted, and informal workers who have been integrated into the current global economic restructuring of commodity chains (J. Foster, McChesney, and Jonna 2011).

Is the Proletarian Dead?

More than a quarter of a century ago, Claudia von Werlhof (1984: 131) announced that "the proletarian is dead." However, it is her subtitle, "long live the housewife?" that is most intriguing. Along with the feminization of labor, the world-economy is exhibiting what Mies, Bennholdt-Thomsen, and Werlhof (1988: 29) term the "housewifization of labor." The term is used to refer to the historical process in which the workforce takes on the characteristics of housewifery that is done by both women and men. According to Fernandez-Kelly (1985: 208), "an analysis of feminization must go beyond notice of women's increasing participation in the labor markets of central and peripheral economies. We must also consider another fact: a growing number of jobs in countries like the United States are acquiring characteristics formerly associated with female employment." Increasingly, formal work is low-status, low-paid, and ostensibly low-skilled, but employers expect the creativity, sacrifices, and unrelenting output that are typical of housework. Peasants and housewives persist because they provide most of the resources for the social reproduction of workers and communities (Mies, Bennholdt-Thomsen, and Werlhof 1988: 168–81) and because they subsidize the productive costs of global commodity chains enough to keep prices cheap for distant consumers (Chapter 4). At the heart of all these processes, the work of women provisions and socially reproduces households, from which global commodity chains derive needed laborers and other productive inputs (Chapter 3).

Although global commodity chains are creative in their integration of semiproletarianized and nonwaged workers, neoliberal economic restructuring did not "free" capital from proletarianized labor for the first time (Sivanandan 1990: 4). Instead, casualization and informalization are not historically new labor mechanisms (Broad 1991, 2000a). When we take a *longue durée* view, we see that the forms may be new, but the substance of casual labor has historical precedents (Broad 2000b).[3] These forms of work can be found throughout the history of capitalism and have constituted the majority of women's paid work, even in the core (Mackenzie 1986). What is new is that geographic relocation of commodity chains is threatening the core proletariat, "to their great horror" (Werlhof 1984: 138). As continuing evidence of contradiction in the capitalist world-system, deproletarianization in the core (Barkin 1985) is being accompanied by widespread integration of semiproletarianized Global South workers (Brady and Denniston 2006). Consequently, the early twenty-first century is characterized by "proletarianization without the creation of a classical proletariat, de-industrialization and de-proletarianization, peasantization and re-peasantization" (Waterman 1988: 293).

Why Labor Is Being (Re)Casualized at the Core

Although semiproletarianization is not new in core states, rich countries are exhibiting (re)casualization of labor and renewed importance of the household economy. Through class struggles, core proletarian labor had, by the twentieth century, gained rights and higher standards of living from increased wages and welfare-state benefits. Labor's hard-won rights and benefits gave the proletariat strength as a class and thus impinged on capital's ability to dictate relations of production and to maintain high profits. To weaken labor and renew profitability, capital undertook a post-1960s program of global restructuring that is oriented toward altering labor markets and the organization of work. This restructuring is producing deeper polarization within core societies. One aspect of global restructuring, and an element of social repolarization, is the trend toward weakening full-time proletarian labor and cutting labor costs by substituting innovative forms of casual labor. Thus there has not been just a casualization of labor but a recasualization of labor at the core (Broad 2000a).

THE CENTRALITY OF INFORMAL WORK TO GLOBAL COMMODITY CHAINS

To understand the persistence and revival of the informal economy, I draw on Braudel's articulation of capitalism, the market, and everyday life. Braudel (1982) discerns that capitalist society is structured in three overlapping tiers that he likens to the floors of a house. At the top is capitalism, "the high-profit zone"; the second tier is the market economy (Braudel 1977: 113). The third, bottom tier is "everyday life," which encompasses production for household consumption, production for the market, and production for capital. It is in this tier that the informal-sector activities of households occur. The three tiers intersect to varying degrees historically, but the informal sector has grown in scope and size over time (Tabak and Crichlow 2000). The tiers tend to move together as the capitalist world-economy develops, but contradictions and tensions arise from conflicting interests among subsistence/reproduction, competition/exchange, and monopoly accumulation/superexploitation that emanate from the different tiers. The resultant structural tensions among these tiers give rise to class, gender, national, regional, and other contradictions that are embedded in the dynamics of global commodity chains.

Using monopoly power and state intervention historically (Braudel 1982), capital expanded its exploitation of the lower levels of the informal economy and everyday life (Broad 2000b). By the mid-twentieth century, proletarianization and commodification subsumed much of these lower levels in core states. To cut the social reproduction costs associated with the broad scope of waged labor, capital resorted to global economic restructuring and the creation of a "new" international division of labor (Frobel 1982). In short, capital sought to revive itself through mechanisms that trade unions and welfare-state regulations had temporarily constrained (Broad 2000a; Broad and Antony 2006). Alongside (re)casualization of labor in the core, capitalists expanded outsourcing to the Global South through construction of commodity chains that decentralized production processes (Dicken 2011: 54–56). Because "everyday life" is the backbone of both the market economy and capitalism (Braudel 1977), recent global restructuring includes superexploitation of labor through resuscitation of the informal economy and through deepening threats to household survival mechanisms. Household informal-sector activities are functional for capitalist commodity chains in three ways. First, they alleviate for capitalists the costly consequences of the proletarianization process by diminishing wage levels and worker benefits

(Wallerstein 1995a: 90–92). Second, the informal sector provides households with access to cheap goods and services, often defusing advocacy for worker rights and gender equality (Portes 1983: 162–63). Third, women's work represents the intersection par excellence of the formal and informal economies. Households and women play crucial roles in production and reproduction because these are the everyday sites where capitalists externalize costs that could limit their profit taking (Chapter 3).

The informal economy is not separate from the formal economy and is, in fact, essential to the process of global capital accumulation.[4] In reality, the global informal working class is at least 1 billion strong, "making it the fastest growing, and most unprecedented, social class on earth" (M. Davis 2006: 178). The informal economy has been a mainstay of peripheral states, but there has been an expansion of informal economic activities in the core (Portes, Castells, and Benton 1989; Tabak and Crichlow 2000). Furthermore, superexploitation of labor at the lower levels of informal economic activity supports capital accumulation at the highest nodes of a commodity chain (Portes and Sassen 1987: 37). To maximize profits, the production, supply, and marketing enterprises that constitute a commodity chain rely on informal producers, collectors, retailers, and households for productive and reproductive labor. These diverse forms of labor input are structured as backward and forward linkages that intensify the capital-accumulation process from commodity chains (Wallerstein 2000b). By examining each of the boxes or nodes of commodity chains allows, scholars can more clearly understand how different forms of labor organization can be integrated into the world-economy and how households play a crucial role in processes of production and reproduction (Dunaway 2001, 2012). Casual labor has been incorporated into the world-economy through neoliberal economic restructuring that reaches into the informal economies of core and periphery (Broad 1991, 2000a). Because (re)casualization and informalization of labor are situated within households, females are disproportionately represented among casual and informal workers (United Nations 2003).

NEOLIBERAL RETRENCHMENT OF STATE RESPONSIBILITIES FOR SOCIAL REPRODUCTION

Social reproduction consists of those "historically contingent processes" through which households, communities, and states "reproduce the conditions and relations of economic and social security" (Feldman, Geisler, and Menon 2011: 2). Two areas of state intervention directly impinge on social reproduction: (1) regulation of labor markets and (2) regulation of household reproduction. Labor-standards legislation has proved to be an area of contested terrain that can have crucial impacts on casual labor and women's work in general. Child day-care policy may be the most direct way in which state action or inaction exacerbates or lightens women's household labor. Access to day care determines whether females can pursue full-time formal work or are forced into low-paying part-time or informal labor (Broad 1997; Broad and Hagin 2004). Two routes have been used historically to improve employment and working conditions: (1) actions by workers' organizations and (2) development of public policy measures. These two routes are, of course, not mutually exclusive.

Labor-standards policies are more advanced in western European welfare states than in North American countries. This is partly due to the longer and more successful history of labor and social democratic political struggles in Europe, with the Nordic states serving as models. The United States has the most market-liberal political model and the least developed welfare state of the Western capitalist countries. Thus the labor movement in the United States has been less successful in translating its actions into state power.[5] In Canada, two provinces stand out for their progressive public policy. Quebec politics is more akin to the politics of continental Europe than politics in the English-speaking provinces. Saskatchewan had a history of social democratic politics throughout much of the twentieth century, although this has been eroded in the neoliberal era. In the early 1990s, Saskatchewan's newly elected New Democratic Party government overhauled the province's Trade Union and Labor Standards Acts. The Labor Standards Act (LSA) was seen as a vehicle for improving the conditions of casual workers by setting new minimum standards. One of the problems with part-time work is that workers are often treated as an on-call labor force. For women, who are the majority of part-timers, this has meant sitting by the phone waiting to be called for a shift. If those with young children are called, they must find child care. This is a prime example of capital relying on women and households to reduce labor costs. Part-timers also tend to be excluded from benefits, such as health care. Moreover, most part-time workers are not unionized, and it is difficult for them to organize to fight for their rights. The revisions to the LSA included provisions to address these issues and to prevent unfair termination of employment (Broad and Hagin 2004).

An important element of the revised LSA was a provision allowing part-time workers to take up extra hours of work on the basis of seniority where these became available. In effect, this provision, dubbed the "most available hours" provision, would permit part-timers to become full-time employees. Not surprisingly, this provision was controversial because employers use part-timers precisely to cut costs and to "flexibilize" worker hours (Pettinger 2002). Consequently, the province's business organizations pushed the government to set up a commission for public hearings that pitted the Saskatchewan labor movement and progressive activists against the business lobby. The government succumbed to business and removed the provision from the act. These events accord with Teeple's (2000) argument that all political parties in Western countries have adopted neoliberalism and differ only in style and degree.

In the area of child-care policy, states have also succumbed to neoliberalism since the 1990s and have implemented very little hat is new and beneficial to women and their households (L. Foster and Broad 1998, Broad and Foster 2003; Struckler and Basu 2012). Despite years of struggle and advocacy by the Canadian labor and women's movements, activists and advocates have been unable to secure a national child-care policy that would support the kind of child-care programming that exists in some Nordic countries. The post-1970s era of neoliberalism has been a difficult one in which to obtain new social welfare policy and programming. The public education and health-care policies of the Keynesian era stand in sharp contrast to the attacks on the welfare state and the dearth of new social programming of the neoliberal era. Provision of public child care challenges capital's push to externalize costs of social reproduction to households. Most women take paid employment out of economic necessity, but current limited public subsidies will not cover the cost of child care at home or in a center.[6] Currently, child-care prospects are not good because Canada and other Western nations are slashing state funding for social programming as part of the turn toward deeper austerity in the post-2007 great recession (Stuckler and Basu 2013). Neoliberal retrenching of labor standards and child-care policies make it clear that the state is a relation of production and a terrain of gendered struggle. As feminists have noted, the welfare state is not gender neutral because its policy makers assume that the appropriate paid laborer is a male, full-time proletarian and that households should be the responsibility of women (Benoit 2000).

Wallerstein (2000b) points to the role of the state in the construction and reconstruction of commodity chains. The state often plays the role of defending capitalism despite capitalists' own short-term interests, as was the case with post-1980 neoliberal attacks on Keynesian social safety nets. Keynesian forms of intervention were not just about promoting social welfare reform but about stabilizing the capitalist economic system. Conversely, the extreme deregulation of the neoliberal era has brought economic instability and has, at the very least, exacerbated the economic downturn of the post-2007 great recession (J. Foster and Magdoff 2009). During economic downturns and restructuring, "informal activities and the unpaid domestic economy expand to pick up the slack of the formal economy and that of the public sector as fiscal austerity brings about reduction in social services" (Beneria and Floro 2002: 13).

SEMIPROLETARIANIZED HOUSEHOLDS AS BREEDING GROUNDS FOR RESISTANCE

The intersection of households and formal economies is an important terrain for resistance. The history of incorporation of households into global commodity chains has included cyclical struggles by workers "to maintain or create subsistence activities, petty commodity production, and proletarian distribution networks (and in the twentieth century to increase income from the state), and to demand the restoration of wages or higher wages from capitalist production units" (Wallerstein and Dickinson 1982: 457). In recent decades, this struggle has been complicated by capital's push for the (re)casualization of labor, expansion of the informal economy, and attacks on welfare-state programs (Broad 2000a; Teeple 2000; Broad and Antony 2006; Broad and Hunter 2009). These attacks on worker households are rife with contradictions. On the one hand, capital's revival of nonproletarian labor and the informal economy reduces consumer demand through erosion of household incomes (Wallerstein and Dickinson 1982; Broad 2000a). On the other hand, social and ecological destruction of access to the means of subsistence results in semiproletarian laborers remaining tied to capital in a sort of enforced economic servitude. Globally, we have seen the growing immiseration of these semiproletarianized households, but we are not witnessing their exclusion from commodity chains (Cockcroft 1986; J. Foster, McChesney, and Jonna 2011).

Adequate conceptualization is necessary to support effective political action that will benefit women and worker households. Scholars need to consider the importance of class and other social struggles in their examinations of socioeconomic trends, but they also need to envision conceptualization itself as a revolutionary process.[7] Exploring the conceptual weaknesses of three threads of policy recommendations about the informal sector will provide an example of the need for clear, change-oriented conceptualization. One school of thought envisions the informal economy as a dynamic seedbed for growth of the capitalist entrepreneurial spirit (Soto 1989), a position that fails to analyze capitalism as a fundamentally exploitative and oppressive socioeconomic system. Second is the position that we can solve the problems of informal work by formalizing it (Bacchetta, Ernst, and Bustamente 2009). For example, the International Labour Organization (ILO) seeks to improve the working and living conditions of superexploited informal workers, a majority of whom are women (www.ilo.org). However, the ILO position fails to recognize the structural intent of capitalists to reproduce the informal economy in order to maximize exploitation of these vulnerable workers. A third argument is that the informal economy can be cultivated as a "progressive alternative" to capitalism. Proponents like Jeremy Rifkin (2002) are shortsighted when they argue that informal activities can be used to create a "social economy" that alleviates the shortcomings of the capitalist market economy. Indeed, they fail to see that capitalism has historically been able to shape, bend, and absorb informal activities into its global commodity chains and create new spaces for capitalists to external-ize costs to households and women and to deepen poverty and misery.

It is crucial that scholars conceptualize the structurally contradictory nature of semiproletarianization, including informal-sector workers, in a more revolutionary fashion.[8] Because growth of informal activities is part of the systemic crisis of the capitalist world-system (T. Hopkins and Wallerstein 1996; Broad and Antony 2006), the informal economy can be a breeding ground for reactionary politics (M. Davis 2006). Informal activi-ties both support and undermine capital accumulation, and there is a dialec-tic of mutual destruction of formal and informal economies through coales-cence and opposition. Henry (1988: 49–53) observes that "the domestic economy facilitates capitalism" but may be "a prime candidate for under-mining the wider matrix of capitalism." Furthermore, one "illustration of the generation of contempt for capitalist institutions is the growth of self-help groups" in the informal economy. Informal economies develop social networks that contain "communal, social, and intimate strains" that are "founded in part on a network of altruistic and balanced reciprocity." Infor-mal activities further the exchange of goods and services, but they also pres-ent a counterforce to the individualistic and commodity-fetishized relations of capital accumulation. Thus informal economies "might best be described as semi-autonomous parts of the capitalist whole."[9]

There are two contradictory elements in the historical struggle to incor-porate households into the commodity chains of the world-economy. One element is capital's push to create a core proletariat despite household resis-tance to this integration. The second element is capital's drive to externalize costs of social reproduction, set against worker struggles to secure better wages and benefits for their households. Incorporation of noncapitalist households into capitalist commodity chains required transformation of gender relations within households, with increasing "male control over val-ues that were purchased on the market" (Wallerstein and Dickinson 1982: 447). This historical process has involved numerous struggles structured around divisions of class, nation, and gender. Because of the contradictory nature of capitalism, options for resistance are opened to the workers and households that are linked to the system's commodity chains. However, ad-vocates for change need to operate from an adequate conceptualization of the historical workings of the world-system if they are to develop viable al-ternatives. Much has been written about the need for antisystemic move-ments to engage in sound analysis in developing their actions to build a better world (Amin 2008, 2011; Wallerstein 2011). Articulation of economic exploitation and forms of oppression obfuscates the nature of the system to divide and conquer working people globally. Consequently, we need to explicate the differences between what might be possible to achieve through short-term social reforms and what requires longer-term actions to transform the socioeconomic system. An important starting point is recognition that gender-based and other forms of oppression are essential to capital accumulation and to reproduction of capitalism (Werlhof 1984). For that reason, communal informal activities (Henry 1988) and the paid and unpaid work of women should take on greater significance in resistance campaigns for change.[10] Only in this way, can activists counter Margaret Thatcher's claim that "there is no alternative" (TINA) to capitalism.

For the future, we need to conceive a socioeconomic system that is not structured around global commodity production but prioritizes empowered workers who recognize the importance of social justice, equality, and diversity (Guevara 1965; Gil 1992). This means getting off the economic-growth treadmill and promoting environmental preservation (Broad 2011). Indeed, any fundamental struggle to improve the working and welfare conditions of casual workers has to be an anticapitalist struggle. For women and households, this means recognizing the fallacy of the "family values" ideology that has emerged as part of the social conservatism tied to neoliberal politics. True family values embrace communal, social, and intimate strains that derive from the altruistic and balanced reciprocity that characterizes much of the paid and unpaid work of women.[11] To realize this potential, we need to build a socialist society as the basis for liberating women and households from both capitalist commodity chains and oppressive notions of family. This is the work of women and men through a vision of people's shared humanity and the need to build genuine community.

• • •

As guideposts for future research, I would like to propose three directions for investigations that will move scholars outside the closed box of commodity chain analysis that Collins criticizes in Chapter 1. First, most commodity chain analyses fail to recognize that global production networks are not proletarianizing Global South labor forces. Even when they are integrated into export chains through waged labor, a majority of these households still accumulate most of their household livelihoods through nonwaged labor strategies. In an era when the numbers of global commodity chains have exploded, the informal sector, casualized work, and subcontracting have accounted for most of the new job growth throughout the Global South (United Nations 2003). In reality, there is no global commodity chain that produces a finished product by using only waged workers, so analysis captures only a small part of the picture if there is no investigation of the complex diversity of labor strategies that are employed. Researchers should assume that waged and nonwaged labor strategies exist side by side and should seek to reveal the mechanisms through which commodity chains embed (but hide) the nonwaged labor forms. They need to recognize that capitalists intentionally conceal their low-paid nonwaged labor arrangements and their attempts to externalize as much of the cost of social reproduction as possible to households. Public attention to such cost-cutting measures counteracts good publicity about "corporate social responsibility." As Clelland observes in Chapter 4, extraction of the "dark value" hidden in nonwaged labor provides the capitalist a degree of monopoly over factors of production that result in cheap consumer prices. What is easily visible to researchers is often not what is of greatest significance for the everyday lives of workers and their households, so one needs to dig deeper than company records and public accounting and follow workers into their households.

Second, analysts investigate the construction of global commodity chains, but my analysis directly explores the decomposition of commodity chains. Inherent in the current neoliberal restructuring of the world-economy is a tendency for capitalists to pursue the cheapest and least protected labor and ecological resources. When workers and local communities are successful at resistance that results in increased wages, improved supports for households and women, or environmental protection, capitalists close productive sites and move to geographic space where they can still obtain lower production costs. In this essay, I have addressed the impacts on workers, households, and communities of the decomposition of industrial commodity chains at the core. However, capitalists are now industrializing and deindustrializing Global South communities after short stays. For example, the Mexican industrial maquiladoras created after passage of the North American Free Trade Agreement are now downsizing or closing as firms relocate or outsource production to China. Such examples will probably multiply in coming decades. Consequently, twenty-first-century research will increasingly need to address the question: what happens to women, worker households, communities, and states when global commodity chains decompose?

Third, I have focused on semiproletarianization as a contradictory labor strategy that supports maintenance of the capitalist system while generating arenas for the emergence of resistance. Dialectically, worker households are sites of reproduction of, and resistance to, larger world-systems structures, including global commodity chains. However, most of the research on worker resistance has not been linked to the labor mechanisms that are embedded in commodity chains. Advocates for change need clearer and more revolutionary conceptualizations as they organize twenty-first-century resistance that will lead toward a better world. To help guide that process, future research needs to examine resistance against the backdrop of both the structuring and decomposition of commodity chains. On the one hand, the exploitation and surplus extraction that occur within a commodity chain are quite often triggers for resistance. On the other hand, workers and households are even more vulnerable when commodity chains decompose and leave behind sudden unemployment, ecological degradation, and threats to economic survival of communities. Consequently, future research needs to move beyond preoccupation with commodity chains as production, marketing, and industrial processes and view them as contradictory arenas that stimulate resistance against capitalism.

CHAPTER THIRTEEN

Bringing Resistance to the Conceptual Center

THREATS TO SOCIAL REPRODUCTION AND FEMINIST ACTIVISM IN NICARAGUAN COMMODITY CHAINS

Marina Prieto-Carrón

Employment Yes, but with Dignity.
—MEC advocacy campaign.

Social reproduction is "a dynamic process of change linked with the perpetuation of social systems. It includes social as well as physical reproduction, and its meaning therefore goes beyond that of reproduction of human beings" (Beneria 1979: 205).[1] However, capitalist commodity chains structure a cleavage between the production of market goods and the production of human life and labor (see Kabeer 1994 and the Introduction to this book). Consequently, women's work is inequitably exploited in both market and reproductive arenas, and this causes feminists to point to these "two poles of a continuum of capitalist conditions of work relations and of production" (Werlhof 1984: 140). Indeed, "the parasitic relationship" between global commodity production and social reproduction constitutes "the basis of all capitalist relations of production" (Bennholdt-Thomsen 1984: 266). By placing social reproduction outside the "productive economy," capitalists construct "double exploitation" of household and female labor, and it is this false duality that makes possible greater levels of capital accumulation (Mies 1981: 492).

Since the 1970s, women's waged labor has become increasingly indispensable in export-oriented commodity chains in the Global South, and each successive industrial or agricultural strategy has been dependent on low-paid female workers (Pearson 2004: 606). At the same time, global commodity chains have unhinged worker household survival from those new forms of production. As a result, "the arena of social reproduction is where much of the toll of globalized capitalist production can be witnessed" because public services have been stricken from national budgets to prioritize economic growth through free-market and structural adjustment strategies (Katz 2001: 710, 717). "Women's incorporation into export industries has always been premised on the assumption of competition via . . . low wages, together with high productivity. . . . The very conditions offered to foreign investors by developing country governments ensured that these major employers of women workers were absolved of virtually all responsibility for the welfare of the workforce" (Pearson 2004: 607–8). Consequently, this deepening exploitation of women's labor has been accompanied by neoliberal elimination of public services, alongside massive threats to the ecological resources and foods that are central to household survival (United Nations 1999).

Despite these harsh crises that face Global South females, too much of recent feminism has taken what Nancy Fraser (1997) terms "a cultural turn" in which

> feminist fronts of struggle have been less concerned with the material conditions of women's lives and the politics of re-distribution, and more focused on issues of recognition for social groups, and assertions of difference and representation, which have emanated from the de-universalizing imperative of post-structuralist and postmodern analysis. . . . Much of this analysis in itself represents another form of representation rather than a material analysis of the multiple and complex dynamics of the ways in which the gendered nature of the global economy is constituted and represented. (Pearson 2004: 604)[2]

To complicate matters, feminist theoretical debates about women in globalization have "not extended further into the arena of social reproduction."

METHODS OF INQUIRY AND RESEARCH DIRECTIONS

To move beyond forms of feminist analysis that ignore Global South social reproduction, I have for fifteen years engaged with the complexities of women's everyday lives in Nicaragua through the cooperation of the María Elena Cuadra Working and Unemployed Women's Movement (MEC), a Nicaraguan women's organization that has worked with women in export-processing zones (EPZs) and other sectors since the mid-1990s. This essay derives from my alliances with Central American and British women's organizations. Through my involvement with the Central American Women's Network (CAWN), I have collaborated with the MEC since 1998 to carry out extensive research that focuses on women's organizations, gender, and labor rights (Prieto and Quinteros 2004; Prieto 2008). My research aims to encourage social change in the "good company of those who have committed their daily life to social change" (G. Pratt 2004: 9; Wright 2009). Following such inspiration, I began during my doctoral work to employ a feminist activist research approach (Prieto 2002) in which the investigator is also an activist with a strong commitment to social justice. This essay draws on women worker testimonies that were offered during focus groups and in-depth interviews with leaders of the MEC.[3] To protect identities of women workers, I have substituted pseudonyms and eliminated personal descriptive details.

I strongly agree with Ruth Pearson (2004: 605) that "a more informed and differentiated analysis is necessary if feminist economic analysis is to be translated into effective political action." Consequently, I join Pearson's call for directions that break with some of today's most popular feminist paradigms. I will develop four themes in this essay. Against the backdrop of the lives of women workers in a Nicaraguan EPZ, I will first examine the ways in which productive and reproductive forms of labor overlap, and I will emphasize that workplace and household form an unbroken continuum in the lives of women. Second, I will explore the conditions that threaten social reproduction for these women and their communities. Third, I will reconceptualize the intersections of social reproduction and labor rights. In the final section, I will focus on the MEC, a Nicaraguan women's movement that operates under an innovative and holistic feminist approach that merges gendered labor rights with methodologies intended to alleviate threats to social reproduction.

THE FALSE DIVIDE BETWEEN ECONOMICALLY VALUABLE AND REPRODUCTIVE

Social reproduction is simultaneously personal, public, and political (Bakker and Gill 2003; Peterson 2003; Hoskyns and Rai 2007). As Cindy Katz (2001:710) puts it, social reproduction is "the fleshy, messy and indeterminate stuff of everyday life." The term encompasses biological reproduction and child care, household maintenance, and several forms of nonwaged labor that sustain the household and the community, including unpaid voluntary participation in organizations and community work (Moser 1993; see the Introduction to this book). Feminists call attention to the intertwined levels at which women's work is more deeply exploited than men's work. Women's unpaid social reproductive work is essential to the long-term maintenance of the modern world-system (Elson 1995b). However, capitalism and economic growth are grounded in a "false analytical divide between production and reproduction" (Pearson 2004: 617).

I argue that women's workplace lives are inextricably linked to their lives as mothers and household managers and that social reproduction cannot be separated from social and cultural gender norms or from national and global economies (cf. F. Robinson 2006). Globally, women have always borne the main burden of social reproduction, that is, the primarily unpaid work carried out in the home and community that helps sustain the formal economic system of production. With the increasing feminization of labor (Standing 1999) over the past few decades, women's work burden has become intensified as they have assumed additional roles in the productive as well as the reproductive sphere. Global South women have assumed breadwinner roles in the restructuring of the global economy in ways that alter traditional gender roles in small ways while reinforcing and exacerbating gender inequalities (Marchand and Runyan 2000; Peterson 2003; Chapters 6 and 9). Women's lives as workers cannot be viewed in isolation from their social reproductive roles because females bear a triple burden of paid work, unpaid care work, and voluntary work (Moser 1993).

Since the 1980s, neoliberal policies forced on most developing nations by the World Bank and the International Monetary Fund have mandated public spending cuts in areas such as health, food subsidies, and education. This assault on social reproduction has placed greater income-earning burdens on women (Elson 1995b; Whitehead 2003), especially heads of household. While their survival strategies expand outside their households, women face increased caring work but diminished public provision of care (F. Robinson 2006: 338). In line with global neoliberal strategies to dismantle the welfare state (Folbre 1994), national governments have shifted responsibility to households and have externalized the cost of current and generational labor-force development to women (Pearson 2004). Therefore, Ruth Pearson (2004: 618) contends that scholars need conceptually to "link international inequalities with the specific contributions of women to international trade while emphasizing how the sexual division of labour still gives women overwhelming responsibility for reproductive tasks at all levels of society."

NICARAGUAN CONDITIONS THAT THREATEN SOCIAL REPRODUCTION

With a population of over 5 million people, Nicaragua is the second-poorest country in Latin America, and 46 percent of its population lives below the poverty line. In 2007, the United Nations Human Development Index ranked Nicaragua 124th out of 175 countries (UNDP 2007: 5). This represents a drop from a rank of 60 in 1990, at the end of the first Sandinista government. Neoliberal economic restructuring occurred during a sweeping political transition from the 1979 revolutionary state (the Sandinista Front for National Liberation) to right-centrist governments led by Violeta Chamorro, Arnoldo Alemán, and Enrique Bolaños after 1990. Despite rhetoric to the contrary, the regimes led by former revolutionary activists have implemented neoliberal democratic policies. Their dismantling of social safety nets has had significant negative impacts on women (Babb 2001). Family relations are patriarchal and unequal and are often characterized by informal polygamy, irresponsible paternity, and domestic violence. To make matters worse, 34 percent of Nicaraguan households are headed by females (ECLAC 2004), and the majority of women live in poverty (Montenegro 2000).

Gendered Inequalities in Social Reproduction

Women's testimonies attest to the double bind of workplace and household responsibilities. Beatriz emphasized the links between production and reproduction this way.

> Women not only work excessively long hours in the [EPZ job], they also work heavily in the [household]. They have an extra burden when, for example, basic services such as water and electricity are limited, and when they are obliged to take on additional income-generating activities, such as domestic service [or] casual selling.

Anna explained that women often have sole responsibility for household reproduction.

> At home, I am the only one who does anything. I am both father and mother to my children, and only I work. I spend all day in the [EP] Zone. I go to work at 6 in the morning and get out at 6 in the evening. That does not leave any time for anything else. But, when I get home, I have to start cooking and cleaning. I have no choice.

On average, Nicaraguan women allocate twice as much time to reproductive tasks as men. This inequality exacerbates household poverty because it limits female participation in income-earning pursuits (Espinosa 2005). In the focus groups, women stressed that most females live in poverty, have little free time and inadequate sleep, engage in paid work in both formal and informal contexts (often simultaneously), and account for most of the unpaid work at home and in the community. Although other family members may contribute income to households, females provide a majority of the unpaid household work. Only a small minority of younger women without children and adult females who are accessing education have a lower social reproductive burden.

Two gender inequalities come into play with respect to education of females. First, women are disproportionately responsible for children's educational expenses. Olga explained, "We have parties, raffles to collect money for the electricity, water and so on. We give money to the teachers so they can buy things like paper and pens. We have to be supportive in other ways too." Second, females are less likely to attend school because of their household responsibilities. A common experience mentioned in focus groups was the shifting of child care to other females in the household, such as older siblings or grandmothers, who are expected to take over this role from the mother when she assumes the role of breadwinner. Older offspring, usually girls, are often expected to assume the maternal role, so they drop out of school and are thus more prone to future poverty. Gender inequalities occur when households cannot afford to send all children to school. As María explained, "The more children we have, the more we have to spend. The salary we get is not enough for all of us. We send some of the kids to school, but not others. We usually give priority to the boys. The rest remain illiterate. These are the ideas we inherited, the idea that girls will get married and be supported by a husband, so there's no point in sending them to school." Anna added, "We want to have the same rights as men enjoy to study; we also want to have a degree and not to be always washing and ironing."

Gender Inequalities in EPZ Labor Practices

The International Labour Organization (2007) estimates that 65 million people are employed in 3,500 Economic Processing Zones (EPZ) around the world, 5 million of them in Central America and Mexico, where a majority of the EPZ labor force is female. In search of cheaper, more "docile" workers, transnational corporations located production in the Global South to target young females. These women workers often face long work days, are paid wages that do not cover the cost of basic household necessities, and suffer human and labor rights violations (Pearson 1998). In Mexico and Central America, EPZ industries are identified with the feminine terms "maquilas" or "maquiladoras" to reflect heavy dependence on women workers (Mendes 2011). The situation of women workers in the maquila industries of Nicaragua's one EPZ (Las Mercedes) is alarming because of limited economic opportunities and extensive labor rights violations (MEC 2008). Wages well below basic subsistence needs are prevalent in the EPZs. For that reason, women work overtime or engage in some income-earning activity other than EPZ jobs. Waged females who complete a second shift of reproductive labor often engage in a third shift of informal-sector activities, and some have a fourth shift of voluntary work in community organizations.

In MEC focus groups, women argued that wages, job security, discrimination, maternity benefits, leave time, and health and safety are all gendered and cannot be separated from the social reproductive lives of women and their households. Moreover, females experience gender discrimination in promotion opportunities. In the words of Maribel, "There is an injustice. Men always get preference when it comes to promotion. They get the best positions, better salaries and incentives." Age discrimination complicates gender inequalities. Employers prefer to hire younger women with fewer household responsibilities, and older women with more children are more likely to lose jobs. Job insecurity is prevalent, and women are overrepresented among those who are downsized when companies relocate. More than 17,000 jobs were cut in the EPZs in less than two years. Between June 2006 and December 2007, 2,715 jobs were cut after six companies went into bankruptcy.[4] In 2008, the largest Taiwanese consortium, Nieng Hsing, announced its departure from Nicaragua to transfer more than 14,000 jobs to Vietnam to acquire cheaper labor. Some of the companies leave without paying wages and benefits to the workers, a phenomenon called *capitales golondrinas* (swallow capital).

Women often do not receive the maternity benefits to which they are entitled. In 2007, MEC lawyers processed maternity benefit claims for nearly one hundred pregnant women. Besides benefit rights, these cases involved health and safety, the right to time off for postnatal check-ups, and medical appointments when babies were ill. According to Filo, "When the babies get sick, it's a huge problem. We don't get leave in order to take them to the clinic as [the supervisors] say someone else from home should take them. But, it's the mother who should go with them because we know better than anyone what the baby is going through." Employers routinely dock a day's pay when women take children to medical appointments or stay home to care for them. In some cases, caring for a sick child means losing one's job. Consequently, fear of losing employment is tightly connected to social reproduction. Lack of child care is a major problem facing women workers because of the twelve-hour workday and additional overtime. There are cases in which "the women work every day and they leave their children alone," Cecilia explained. Working mothers recognize that they have to trade off adequate child care for income to feed and educate children. Although there is one child-care facility in the Managua EPZ, Susana explained that "most of the women workers do not have access to it." Ramona stressed that she "would like the government to have child-care centers for our children so we can go to work and not be worried." Despite these widespread problems, many women are reluctant to complain for fear of losing their jobs. In general, women's gendered responsibilities for care of the family contribute to their marginalization and their vulnerabilities as EPZ workers. Women spoke of how they often have to prioritize nutrition, health care, and education of their children over their struggle for their rights in the workplace. As Maribel succinctly put it, "We just get on with our work because we have kids at home who need to be fed."

Gendered Violence

Many women workers face harassment in the workplace, domestic violence in the household, and violence from gangs of disfranchised young people in their communities (Prieto-Carrón, Thomson, and Macdonald 2007). Many women are left vulnerable to violence because their shifts end late in the evening, when there is no safe transport home. Especially in Managua, women are forced to walk home late at night after buses have stopped running, and they cannot afford to pay for taxis. Even when public transport is available, the conditions are unsafe. According to Elena, "The buses are always packed. We are abused by the drivers and helpers. They are rude to us and force too many people to get on the bus. When there are transport strikes, we have to walk miles to get to work. When the bus arrives, the men practically beat us in order to make sure they get on the bus before we do." Even walking from the bus stop to the house is problematic. Raquel indicated that "some women workers have to walk through dangerous areas [where] there have been rapes and assaults." Women are trapped in a vicious no-win cycle in which they try to juggle the contradictions between paid labor and social reproduction. If they work excessive overtime because wages are too low, they face the risks of street violence, and their children may be left unattended. When young people are unsupervised and out of school, they are more likely to join gangs that, in turn, increase the problem of gendered violence in their communities. In line with other CAWN researchers (especially Cabrera 2010), I contend that feminist scholarship and activism must comprehend gendered violence as a phenomenon that operates along the continuum of community, household, and workplace.

INTERSECTIONS BETWEEN SOCIAL REPRODUCTION AND LABOR RIGHTS

Because of the structural contradictions between waged labor and social reproduction, Latin American women's groups call for moving beyond "traditional" labor rights to include emphasis on issues of child care, children's education, and gendered violence. Workplace abuses of women mirror and reinforce the inequitable treatment that females encounter in households and communities and in public policies. Male-preference labor rights are shaped by gender-based societal norms about social reproductive roles. In the focus groups, women workers pinpointed that many problems they face with regard to the conflicts between their productive and reproductive pressures are absent from the delineation of labor rights. Their experiences and frustrations make it clear that the labor policies of the state and of employers provide a narrow range of protections and benefits that favor the conditions of men's lives in the workplace. As I have previously noted, labor rights do not adequately safeguard women in the workplace, and these standards ignore the ways in which waged workforce participation endangers social reproduction. Clearly, feminists and labor advocacy organizations need to move beyond traditional labor rights to encompass social reproduction (F. Robinson 2006). Moreover, commodity chain scholars need to integrate both labor rights and social reproduction to a much greater degree than they have in the past. Commodity chain analysis offers a critical inquiry strategy through which NGOs and activist movements can draw attention to the inequalities and exploitation embedded in the labor strategies of global production networks (Bair 2005). Before such a goal can effectively inform politics, however, activists must all better understand the contradictory intersections between labor rights and social reproduction. On the one hand, those labor standards are grounded in gender discrimination. On the other hand, labor rights have assumed an unstated gender-biased compartmentalization that separates workplace protection of workers from the social reproductive rights of workers. In my years of listening to Nicaraguan women, they have emphasized that labor "rights" have protected men to the exclusion of women. Moreover, workplace-related rights do not integrate methodologies that prevent or eliminate threats to social reproduction, such as gendered violence inside and outside the workplace or lack of attention to women's caregiving responsibilities within households that conflict with their workplace productivity.

Through the 1998 Declaration on Fundamental Principles and Rights at Work, the International Labour Organization (ILO) established four core labor standards to define the rights of formal-sector workers around the world, including collective bargaining, elimination of child labor, elimination of forced labor, and freedom from all forms of discrimination.[5] Feminists have criticized the gender biases of these standards because they are based on the duality of "a 'male breadwinner,' typically a wage-earner, pursuing employment in the public sphere and a 'female caregiver' confined to the private sphere, subject to protective measures, and only gaining access to the social wage indirectly" (Vosko 2004: 2). Such assumptions about labor rights are widespread because labor movements typically emulate the ILO standards in their delineation of workers' rights (F. Robinson 2006: 333). Most labor movements have failed to recognize the contradictory and heterogeneous subjectivities that are produced in the processes of global capitalism. To develop a more inclusive transformative vision that recognizes the daily realities of women's lives, movements must take into consideration gendered, racial, and class-based constraints on women's lives. In the sections that follow, I will unpack the gender biases of labor rights in practice.

Although there have been some gendered advances in Central America, such as women rising to leadership positions in banana trade unions (D. Frank 2005), the male-dominated regional trade-union movement lacks commitment to blending attention to reproductive contradictions with its advocacy for labor rights (Bickham-Mendez 2005; Prieto, Hadjipateras, and Turner 2002; Prieto and Quinteros 2004). Nicaraguan unions limit their organizational efforts to formal wage earners and exclude informal-sector workers. Although they offer worker training about trade and the economy, they typically ignore the inequitable impacts on women and extra workplace risks to community and household social reproduction. As Coronado and Staudt (2004: 143) observe, gendered activism is required to move the rights debate "beyond a narrow focus on labor in terms of paid work and attend to unpaid or informal work, along with violence in the home and on the streets." Indeed, efforts to organize and empower women workers must adopt an approach that addresses the gendered differences and inequalities that cut across a broad continuum of women's labor that includes reproduction, subsistence, unpaid contributions to commodity production, informal sector activities, home-based contracts to produce export commodities, and formal-sector waged jobs (Pyle and Ward 2003). Because of the unwillingness of trade unions to integrate gender inequalities into their advocacy, autonomous women's organizations have carved out female spaces to address the intersections of social reproduction and labor rights (Bickham-Mendez 2005). Since the 1990s, Central American movements of EPZ women workers have mobilized to advocate for improvements in working conditions and to combat a variety of injustices (Alvarez, Gagnino, and Escobar 1998). One such organization is the MEC, with which I have worked since 1998.

THE MEC APPROACH: A NICARAGUAN EXEMPLAR

The MEC emerged in 1997 in the political vacuum left by unions that ignore gender inequalities and social reproduction. Many of its founders had previously been trade unionists in the Sandinista Trade Union. By 2007, the MEC had offices in eight regions of the country and a membership of 70,000 women, nearly one-third of them working in EPZs (Gamboa, D'Angelo, and Kries 2007: 87). Membership encompasses women who work in the maquilas, agriculture, and mining, in addition to domestic servants and the unemployed. One of the greatest strengths of the MEC is its diverse membership, which represents the complex rainbow of all the unpaid, waged, and nonwaged forms of Nicaraguan women's work. Dickinson and Schaeffer (2001: 179–81) point to the importance of "social reproduction movements" that acknowledge "labor's total workload."

> An increasingly important stage for women-centered movements is not the factory floor in isolation from the home but the factory in relationship to the home. . . . The movements that address both wage and nonwage work issues and attempt to subvert the gender and age divisions that separate working class households into fragmented components are extremely important. . . . These organizing social identities have split

households and limited their ability to organize against formal institutions. Social movements that undermine the gender divide offer new opportunities to unite workers. Movements that address wage and nonwage work also provide ways to fight ethnic divides . . . [because racial/ethnic minorities represent] the vast majority of the world's population that needs to rely heavily on nonwage income.

Such organizations challenge advocacy for traditional "labor rights" that prioritize waged workplaces to the exclusion of the settings in which a majority of workers are concentrated. For that reason, the MEC draws activists from the continuum of forms of women's labor to develop resistance strategies that reach across waged/nonwaged, racial/ethnic, class, and age intersections with gender.

Goals and Strategies of the MEC

The MEC networks with regional and transnational feminist organizations, such as the Central American Women's Network (CAWN) the Central American Network of Women in Solidarity with Maquila Workers (REDCAM) and the Association for Women's Rights in Development (AWID). The MEC is funded by international development resources from Britain, the Netherlands, Canada, and a few other countries. The main foci of the MEC are improvement of working conditions and promotion of labor rights through leadership training, as well as public campaigns and political lobbying. A large proportion of MEC resources is devoted to a wide range of training activities. It has also undertaken an economic literacy training project (CAWN 2008), microcredit projects, counseling, legal aid, and a new leadership-training academy. The MEC's training uses a holistic approach that integrates social reproduction alongside pursuit of political and economic rights for women. Although the MEC uses a grassroots approach (*organización de base*) in its work, it does not isolate workers' rights from social reproduction because many of the problems faced by women workers are linked to poverty and gendered violence. On the one hand, the MEC trains women in global political economy (e.g., free-trade agreements), citizenship rights, labor rights, and health and safety. On the other hand, the organization emphasizes gendered problems, such as self-esteem, domestic violence, and sexual and reproductive rights. In the words of one MEC regional leader, "It is through the training on many issues . . . that MEC has helped women to be empowered and to develop an identity as citizens with rights: the right to make demands, to be listened to and to expect answers to their demands." The MEC helps women campaign for better wages and working conditions, but it also offers them microcredit loans for household expenses. In workshops and educational programs for maquila workers, organizers examine violence against women within a broad framework of gender and power, drawing connections among violence in the home, male violence on the shop floor, and street violence (Bandy and Bickham-Mendez 2003). Maquila workers specifically asked the MEC to provide self-defense training to help them be less vulnerable to different forms of violence.

The MEC sharply focuses on the intersections of class and gender issues. Whereas the trade-union approach primarily focuses on class issues, the MEC attaches equal importance to addressing gender issues. Sandra Ramos, director of the organization, comments that "the trade-union movement is only privileging the class struggle, and they forget that there is a gender struggle inside." In all its efforts, the MEC follows an empowerment approach. Through awareness-raising and training, the MEC seeks to build women's skills and confidence so they will be empowered to fight for better working conditions in the maquilas and, at the same time, demand greater equality in their households and communities. MEC training incorporates information about reproductive health while also building awareness of strategies for coping with workplace discrimination. The MEC provides counseling for victims of domestic violence and helps mothers secure financial aid when the fathers of their children abandon them.

Furthermore, the MEC has played an active part in lobbying for changes aimed at improving the conditions of grassroots women workers. In 1998, the MEC promoted an ethical code that was officially adopted by the Labor Ministry and by employers in the Free Trade Zone (Prieto, Hadjipateras, and Turner 2002). Designed around the slogan "Employment— Yes, but with Dignity," this advocacy campaign was widely publicized through television and radio spots and other public methods. It has been important for the organization to be part of the tripartite commission with the employers, the government, and the trade unions. The MEC director reports that it was the employers who pressed for the inclusion of the MEC because of the large membership base of the organization. Indeed, the active and committed involvement of grassroots women accounts for the successful outcomes of such campaigns. One MEC activist explained that "the potential is to learn about our rights, to be organized at work and in communities and to be part of consultations [on new laws] so we have our own voice and our demands are listened to." To enable that process, the MEC organizes annual colloquiums that convene more than one thousand Nicaraguan women and receive considerable national press coverage.

This holistic and gender-focused way of working with women has given rise to what I call "gendered knowledge in action." In the process of acquiring a gendered understanding of political economy and social reproduction, women have been able to put this knowledge into action and thereby to transform many aspects of their lives, both at home and in the workplace.

According to Ramona, "MEC taught us how to defend our labor rights in the factories, not to allow ourselves to be beaten and exploited and how to stop our husbands abusing us in the home." Similarly, Elizabeth said, "Through the MEC workshops, I have learned a huge amount. I have learned how to defend myself, how to value myself as a person and to claim my rights." Through the MEC, individual understanding transposes into collective organizing, multiplying the benefits of its work. In a voice saturated with emotion, Flor, a longtime MEC member, exclaimed, "I have attended every single workshop and training provided by MEC since it was founded in 1994. With the knowledge and experience I have gained, I now help to organize women in the factory and have become a leader in my community."

MEC's Future Challenges and Contradictions

In this final section, I will explore future challenges that face organizations like the MEC as they confront twenty-first-century structural contradictions of the world-economy and its economic crises. The MEC has been successful in reinventing new organizational strategies and enjoys widespread recognition in the EPZs, nationally and internationally. Despite its successes, the MEC will be increasingly challenged by the globalization of production processes, especially the local instabilities caused when companies relocate from Nicaragua. In the future, women will be more likely to lose waged jobs than men. The more EPZ organizations succeed in their struggles to improve wages and working conditions, the more corporate profits will decline. In this context, more companies will engage in capital flight and leave behind high levels of unemployment for both men and women. Moreover, there is an observable trend, not only in Nicaragua but also in countries in the region and beyond, toward an increasing proportion of male employment in EPZs.[6] Prieto and Quinteros (2004) explore the question whether MEC should try to operate as a trade union empowered to negotiate collective agreements, as organizations have done in El Salvador, South Africa, and South Korea. Indeed, the MEC represents 25.6 percent of the workers in the Managua EPZs of Sebaco, Estelí, León, and Chinandega, but only 3.8 percent of workers in the these zones are affiliated with trade unions (Gamboa, D'Angelo, and Kries 2007: 85–87). Despite that significant difference in activism, we concluded that the MEC should not follow the path of unionization because it would encounter resistance from Nicaraguan unions that would exacerbate tensions in communities and households and further endanger social reproduction.

Two MEC procedures contradict its mission to prioritize social reproduction. First, its organizational work is conducted during women's scarce "leisure" time and thereby adds to the strains of their workloads and constrains time spent with children. The MEC also lacks child care for participating women and has not been able to overcome funding constraints to provide such assistance. By broadening its scope into masculinities, MEC might eventually be able to trigger longer-term change in which males assume greater caring responsibility while women attend workshops. These gendered problems will lead the organization into internal debate about how it weighs short-term and longer-term goals. Although the MEC does not exclude men, it admits only those (few) men who are able to prove their commitment to the struggle against women's discrimination. By focusing solely on women and their social reproductive roles, the MEC runs the risk of reinforcing gender-biased notions of women. Thus it is realistic to question whether the MEC should challenge men to take on a fairer share so as to relieve the inequitable burden on women (Chant and Gutmann 2002). The MEC will need to encourage intense debates on the question: Should the MEC collaborate with men's groups (e.g., Centro de Información y Servicios de Asesoría en Salud and Association of Men against Violence) to challenge conventional "masculinities"? Is this a more effective strategy to transform and improve the lives of both men and women (Sternberg 2000; Welsh 2007)? However, the MEC will need to weigh such longer-term coalition building against the backdrop of the needs of its growing female constituency that are already overloading its limited economic and human resources.

• • •

If scholars and activists are to effect positive changes in worker household maintenance and gendered inequalities, they must bring their conceptual and political spotlights back to social reproduction. Using the case of Nicaraguan *maquila* industries, I have argued that capitalist commodity chains, especially in the current era of neoliberalism, are grounded in a false divide between economically valuable and reproductive labor (see the Introduction). Consequently, I have called for close analytic assessment of the intersections between struggles for labor rights and advocacy for social reproduction. Although ILO conventions are a good starting point, these standards are gendered and do not prioritize social reproduction. We need to move beyond traditional labor rights to include issues that are very important to women, such as insufficient wage levels to meet household survival, child care, children's education, and gendered violence. These issues need to be put in the context of the reproductive lives of women workers and their households, and we need to analyze the links among them by taking our analysis beyond the workplace to the household and the community, as the MEC is doing.

Introduction

1. For analysis of women's unpaid work in twenty-first-century global production, see Hoskyns and Rai (2007). For women's casualized and informal labor in industrial production, see Carr, Chen, and Tate (2000); Beneria (2001); Pyle and Ward (2003); Bacchetta, Ernst, and Bustamente (2009); Broad and Hunter (2009); and Huws (2011). For feminization of agriculture and fishing, see Dolan and Sorby (2003); Deere (2005); Frank (2005); Dunaway and Macabuac (2007); Spieldoch (2007); and Ramamurthy (2010, 2011). For women's waged work in industry, see Freeman (2000); Seguino (2000); Wills and Hale (2005); Wright (2006); and Caraway (2007).

2. In the 1970s and 1980s, world-systems thinkers conceptualized households in capitalism. See *Review of the Fernand Braudel Center* 5 (3), 7 (2), 8 (3), and 10 (1), special issues available through JSTOR.

3. See Bair (2009: 7–14) for a discussion of the differences among these approaches.

4. This book's bibliography includes one hundred analyses of women's labor in global production that were published between 1980 and 2012, but these represent only a small portion of the entire scholarship.

5. On 31 December 2012, a search of the massive publication database of the Global Value Chain website (www.globalvaluechains.org) yielded only eight studies by five authors that use the keywords "gender," "household," or "women."

6. In preparation for this project, I spent two years researching the three threads of commodity chain research to identify scholars who have integrated gender, women, or households into commodity or value chain analysis (even at minimal levels). I found only a small number of authors who gendered commodity and value chain analyses between 1980 and 2012; these are included in the Bibliography.

7. Bair (2009) provides empirical evidence that the vast majority of GCC/GVC analysts ignore gender, women, and households. She defined her goal to be that of assessing the state of the field, so she did not "see" gender, women, or households evidenced strongly in the cumulative research agendas of the field. In her overview of the state of the field, Bair neither identifies gender or women as an area of GCC/GVC research nor pinpoints any GCC/GVC analysts who routinely integrate gender. All the references to women in the index of her edited book refer to one

chapter that provides brief empirical information about female workers but does not offer a gendered analysis.

8. See *Feminist Economics*, no. 3 (1996), a special issue about the links between production and reproduction.

9. Feminist economists have pushed especially hard to draw attention to the economic value of unpaid household labor, women's provisioning, and women's informal-sector work (e.g., Gardiner 1997; Adam 2002). Since the 1970s, feminist scholars have measured the time inequalities in the allocation of unpaid household labor (Antonopoulos and Hirway 2010) and have proposed approaches for integrating the value of unpaid household labor into national GDP (e.g., Waring 1989; Beneria 1992; Seguino 2000; Perrons 2000; Himmelwitt 2002; Luitzel 2005).

10. The term "off the books" is not meant to imply that all these workers are fully undocumented or that it is extremely difficult for researchers to locate and to observe their labor as part of commodity chains. Several of the essays in this book suggest methodologies for researching off-the-books laborers.

11. For conceptual discussion of the overlap among informal, formal, unpaid, and public-sector labor, see Beneria and Floro (2002).

12. *Global Networks* 4 (3) (2004) and 5 (4) (2005) focus on the transnational family. Parrenas (2005) estimates that more than one-quarter of Philippine children are separated from migrant parents.

Chapter 1

1. Personal communication with Immanuel Wallerstein, 12 August 2011.

2. Bair and Werner (2011: 988) also claim that anthropologists have come late to the study of commodity chains, whereas including this work as part of the tradition would have put them there from the beginning.

3. Personal communication with Jeffrey Paige, 12 August 2011.

4. Global Value Chains website, www.globalvaluechains.org.

Chapter 2

1. A *poonam* is a sari made of imported polyester rather than the traditional cotton.

2. For more detailed accounts, see Ramamurthy (2000, 2003, 2004, 2010, 2011).

3. For reviews of world-systems theorizations of commodity chains, see the Introduction to this book and Bair (2005).

4. For description of lead firms, see Chapter 7.

5. On the feminization of labor-intensive, export-oriented industrial production, see the Introduction.

6. On the feminization of agriculture, see Collins (1995), Da Corta and Venkateshwarlu (1999), Dolan and Sorby (2003), Deere (2005), Lastarria-Cornheil (2006), and Ramamurthy (2010).

7. Bt cotton is a genetically modified seed that was introduced in India by the Monsanto Corporation. This seed has become predominant throughout areas of the country where cotton is grown. While it has somewhat lowered pesticide use, it has had numerous negative impacts on small farmers, workers and women (Sharma 2010).

8. Similarly, in their study of the apparel commodity chain, Bonacich and Appelbaum (2000) prioritize class over gender.

9. For critiques of these essentialist forms of global feminism, see Kaplan (1995) and Grewal (1999).

Chapter 3

1. For assessments of household economy literature, see Wilk (1987) and Bryson (1996).

2. For an overview of the weaknesses of separate-spheres thinking, see Dunaway (2008: 5–10).

3. This unusual study was funded and conducted by the U.S. National Bureau of Economic Research with the goal of conceptualizing these externalized costs and estimating their market value if capitalists had to embed them into their prices. Since the 1920s, many mainstream U.S. economists have argued for inclusion of unpaid household labor in measures of economic growth, including Nobel laureate Simon Kuznets (1941: 1:10). For a survey of economists who have taken this position, see Perelman (2011: 200–212).

4. Folbre (1982: 323) argues that not all expropriations of value are economic or material. "Inequality of rates of exploitation in the family may reflect purely voluntary material sacrifices [as well as] sacrifices related, perhaps, to the intangible and emotional aspects of family life."

5. Folbre (1982: 321) reminds us that household behavior is motivated by both survival and market imperatives and that household objectives vary across classes and change over time.

6. Chekhov wrote "The happy man only feels at ease because the unhappy bear their burdens in silence, and without silence happiness would be impossible." See *Goodreads*, www.goodreads.com/author/quotes/5031025.Anton_Chekhov.

Chapter 4

1. Baran and Sweezy's definition of surplus is not the same as Marx's (1990: vol. 3) "surplus value," that is, the value added to commodities by labor power that is greater than the costs of reproducing that labor through the commodified provision of survival necessities.

2. I employ "surplus drain" and "surplus transfer" as synonyms. Alternative terms that appear in the literature include "economic drain," "surplus extraction," and "capital drain" or "capital transfer." "Unequal exchange" is often used as a synonym, but the originator of that term (Emmanuel 1972) and most subsequent analysts (Amin 1974; Raffer 1987; Kohler and Tausch 2002) intend more narrow usages.

3. For classical Marxist treatments, see Hobson (1902), Luxemberg (1951), Lenin (1960), Bukharin (1972), and Hilferding (1981).

4. I present an ideal-type model and recognize the existence of many variants in the real world. For example, my model assumes that commodities originate in the periphery and are consumed in the core. Many commodity chains are restricted to the core or to the periphery, and some flow between semiperipheries or between periphery and semiperiphery. I am convinced that my abstract model can be applied to most of these alternative chains.

5. In reality, many nodes of a commodity chain can be internalized within a single firm. As Williamson (1981) explains, this is done to avoid paying a "transaction cost," that is, paying the cost of an external firm's profits. In the externalized commodity chain, the outsourcer receives what I term a "transaction benefit."

6. It was Marx's (1990: vol. 3) genius to see that the production of social surplus, economic growth, profits, and the accumulation of capital are all based on a hidden process. However, the components of this process are documented on the books of the capitalist firm as labor costs and profit. Because these components of production and trade appear in the standard accounting system, I regard them as parts of the system of the collection of "bright value." The theory of these visible forms of exploitation is the essence of Marxism. For an assessment of visible "bright-value" drains, see Clelland (2012).

7. This is a play on the wording of Derrida's (1974: 163) claim that "there is nothing outside the text."

8. Since the 1970s, scholars have been measuring time inequalities in the allocation of unpaid household labor (Budlender 2007; Antonopoulos and Hirway 2010). In addition, the United Nations and the World Bank have funded national time-use surveys to quantify unpaid household labor (Clermont and Aligisakis 1995; African Centre for Women 2002).

9. See Philippine Overseas Employment Administration, www.poea.gov.ph. The female occupations are captured in transnational care chains (Yeates 2009a).

10. This generalized version of the coffee commodity chain was chosen because of its relative simplicity and the availability of data. The works of Talbot (1997, 2004) were helpful in distinguishing the nodes of the commodity chains and the points at which surpluses were retained.

11. Although my approach draws on the insightful and groundbreaking information offered by Talbot (1997, 2004), we approach analysis of the coffee commodity chain quite differently. Even though Talbot describes how the surplus is distributed and documents the small proportion retained by small producers, he does not examine the gendered work exploitation that I emphasize, nor does he address the degree to which worker households subsidize coffee production through hidden surplus extractions. Indeed, Talbot focuses solely on what I term "bright value" that is visible and publicly accounted for (see Clelland 2012) and misses the hidden subsidy to coffee consumer prices that I term "dark value." Because Talbot does not investigate from the standpoint of small producers and workers, he also ignores the contributions of women and households to the surplus produced within the commodity chain.

12. A full analysis of dark value would include underpaid costs of all factors of production, including those based on subsidies and the unpaid costs of environmental and human health externalities (see Clelland 2012). For simplicity, I have not included estimates of those elements of dark value.

13. This is an expansion of the thesis of "the aristocracy of labor" of Engels and Lenin (cf. Strauss 2004) that is found in Amin (1974) and Wallerstein (1976). This position does not deny the centrality of productivity in advancing the wage level of the core working class.

Chapter 5

1. The term "masters of the universe" was applied to finance capital in the fiction of Tom Wolfe (1987: 9), but it need not be restricted to that sector.

2. Much of the historical and conceptual information in this essay is drawn from my previous research, especially R. Ross and Trachte (1990) and R. Ross (2004, 2006, 2011).

3. The extent to which social movements have succeeded in penetrating that veil of protection is another matter that is beyond the scope of this discussion.

4. Interview with a Bangladeshi female trade-union activist. Also see Clean Clothes Campaign (2013).

5. Lured to the United States from Thailand, seventy-two workers were discovered in a slave factory in El Monte, California, in 1995. The list of retailers for which the clothing was bound was a who's who of mainstream (and upscale) retailing in California, including Neiman Marcus and the Mays chain.

6. "Value added" is an economic concept that denotes the estimated value that is added to a product or material at each stage of its manufacture or distribution. It is unclear why Waldinger and Lapp would not hypothesize that such a gap would indicate lower wages in relation to retail price.

7. Information from the Wages and Hours Division of the U.S. Department of Labor and from the New York Labor Department.

Chapter 6

1. The author gratefully acknowledges financial support from the Scientific and Technological Research Council of Turkey, grant 106K258, and from the International Labor Organization, Ankara office.

2. After 2007, the automotive industry began to lose its strength as the leading export sector.

3. Men are also constrained within the circle of kinship relations and networks. In Turkish society, these networks provide access to employment opportunities. However, the major gender difference is that women's labor is not easily released into the labor market in the absence of these relations and networks.

4. Hsiung (1996: 145–67) observed similar work roles of owners' wives, indicating that these patriarchal patterns have not disappeared.

5. These twenty-first-century women directly parallel the home-based Indian lace makers described by Mies (1981) three decades earlier. In both cases, the women "combine 'reproductive work—meaning housework—with 'productive work' for an external, even global, market" (Mies 2010: 165–66).

Chapter 7

1. For a discussion of the conceptual differences between "global commodity chains" and "global value chains," see Bair (2005).

2. I conducted fifty-two in-depth interviews with actors involved in the Chilean fruit export sector and the GLOBALGAP certification program, including growers, exporters, industry representatives, auditors, government officials, and retailers. Interviews were also conducted with actors who may affect and who are affected by GLOBALGAP standards, including workers, labor advocates, and government officials from the Ministries of Agriculture, Labor, Health, and Women. Within Chile, these interviews were conducted in the capital, Santiago, as well as in the towns and surrounding areas of Melipilla, Vicuna, and Talca, which lie in the key fruit-growing regions of Metropolitan, Coquimbo, and Maúle. These interviews took place between August and December 2005. In March 2006, I conducted telephone interviews with representatives of two major European retailers. I also conducted participant observation of work sites and content analysis of historical studies and technical literature related to GLOBALGAP and the Chilean fruit export sector.

3. Interviews with staff of the Centro de Estudios para el Desarrollo de la Mujer.

4. For more information about Chilean peasant women's activism, see Cosgrove (2010) and Estrada (2007).

Chapter 8

1. This study was made possible through the financial support of the National Research Initiative of the Cooperative State Research, Education, and Extension Service, USDA, Grant no. 0190121, Annie E. Casey Foundation Grant no. 201.1855, National Science Foundation Career Award no. 0092527, and a Monfort Family Foundation's Colorado State University Monfort Professorship.

2. This part of our research was partially funded by the National Science Foundation.

3. Staff Interview, Pine Ridge Area Chamber of Commerce, Kyle, SD, 11 October 2010.

4. Staff Interview, Lakota Buffalo Caretakers Cooperative, Kyle, SD, 27 September 2011.

5. In this essay, we have not addressed the lucrative commodity chains that trade legally and illegally in indigenous artifacts that are collected and traded by wealthy consumers. There is a trend toward global production chains of indigenous artifact reproductions that are manufactured in China for the Western tourism industries. The same replications are marketed as "authentic" representations of many different indigenous groups.

6. Vendor, NCIPA powwow, 19 August, 2011, Fort Collins, CO.

Chapter 9

1. Analysis of land, crop-production, and export statistics, BAS databases.

2. Analysis of land, crop-production, and export statistics, BAS databases. Fishery outputs are reported as part of agricultural statistics.

Chapter 10

1. See Bair (2009) for a comparison of the three approaches: world-systems analysis, global commodity chain analysis and value chain analysis. Except for early world-systems conceptualization (Dunaway 2012) and limited treatment of these units as consumers and recyclers of final commodities (Gereffi and Korzeniewicz 1994: 12), households have been noticeably absent from the accumulated research of all three approaches (see the Introduction). Several world-systems analysts have integrated labor into their investigations of commodity chains, as a search of *Review of the Fernand Braudel Center* (available at JSTOR) and the *Journal of World-Systems Research* will demonstrate. However, the other two approaches have sorely neglected labor as a factor of production (Yeates 2004b; Raworth and Kidder 2009; Barrientos 2011). Commodity and value chain analysts also ignore a majority of the world's service sectors that do not directly provide financial, insurance, transport, or advertising services to nodes of chains. Although Bair (2011: 180) notes that "the absence of GVC research on service value chains is particularly problematic,"), Bair (2010) fails to acknowledge the central role of laborers and households in global value chains or the accumulated body of scholarship on laborcentric global valuechain analyses of services.

2. For a review and bibliography of this literature, see Yeates (2005a, 2009a).

3. This section is summarized from my accumulated research. See Yeates (2004a, 2009a, 2009b, 2010, 2011) for more information and for evidentiary sources.

Chapter 12

1. For scholars who have analyzed Global South women as casualized, temporary or subcontracted laborers, see Elson and Pearson (1981); Beneria and Roldan (1987); Wolf (1992); Hsiung (1996); Pearson (1998); Prugl (1999); Carr, Chen, and Tate (2000); Collins (2000, 2003); Kabeer (2000); Pearson and Razavi (2004); Chalfin (2007); Dedeoglu (2008); Bain (2010a); Barrientos (2011); and Selwyn (2012). See Beneria (2001); Dunaway (2010, 2012); and Clelland (2012) for linkages between informal sectors and commodity chains.

2. In addition to my own work, Beechey and Perkins (1987), Portes and Sassen (1987), and M. Nelson and Smith (1989) are among the few scholars who have examined these semiproletarianized forms of labor in rich core countries.

3. For instance, the casual labor markets in contemporary New York City and nineteenth-century London show marked parallels (Jones 1984).

4. For discussion of the broad range of activities that are encompassed within the informal sector, see the special issue of *Social Justice* 15, no. 3 (1988).

5. There is, of course, great variety, with some U.S. states being more progressive and others being extremely antilabor. In the neoliberal era, there has been a vicious attack on social welfare and labor rights throughout the United States, most recently in Wisconsin and neighboring states.

6. Instead of state-sponsored day-care centers, Canada's current neoliberal government offers families CAN$100 per month per child to purchase child care or to raise children at home. This subsidy is an insult to child-care advocates and the women's movement because it is part of the right-wing "family values" ideology that defines "motherhood" and "housewife" as the only appropriate roles for women.

7. My conceptualization of the (re)casualization of labor and women's work runs counter to notions of proletarianization and the development of capitalism that have been advocated by both left-wing and right-wing writers. I also needed to envision an alternate conceptualization of the history of capitalism to the one often presented on the left.

8. Even mainstream advocate Hernando de Soto (1989: 27, 118) conceived of the informal sector as both an arena of "capitalist entrepreneurial spirit" and a potential "seedbed of terrorism."

9. For example, I witnessed examples of this aspect of the informal economy while I was visiting Nicaragua in the early 1990s, after the devastating U.S.-sponsored Contra War against the Sandinista government and the return of the right wing to office. In this bleak period, Nicaraguans created informal services, like child day-care centers and soup kitchens, that prioritized the human needs that the state and capitalists were ignoring.

10. For instance, Chandler (1994) argued that female unpaid household work could be valued at 63.3 percent of the 1980s Canadian GDP.

11. "Let me say, with the risk of appearing ridiculous," Che Guevara (1965: 19–20) observed, "that the true revolutionary is guided by strong feelings of love."

Chapter 13

1. I am grateful to Angela Hadjipateras, codirector of the Central American Women's Network (CAWN), for her encouragement and support. I dedicate this essay to the women workers who participated in the focus-group exercises and to their struggles for better lives at work, at home, and in their communities. CAWN is a London-based organization that supports, publicizes, and learns from the struggles of women in Central America. For more information, see www.cawn.org.

2. Pearson (2004: 603–8) offers a fuller critique of recent feminist approaches.

3. In 2007, seven focus groups averaging ten women workers were conducted in Nicaragua. Funded by the United Kingdom Department of International Development, the focus groups were part of a CAWN project on economic literacy. CAWN staffers Rebecca Eileen Zúñiga Hamlin, Tessa Mackenzie, and Helen Dixon helped with facilitation of the focus groups. In-depth interviews were conducted in London in 2007–8 with the director of the MEC, Sandra Ramos, and three MEC women leaders.

4. Interviews with the director of the MEC, Sandra Ramos, and the International Union of Food, Agricultural, Hotel, Restaurant, Catering, Tobacco and Allied Workers' Association. See also Trucchi (2009).

5. See www.ilo.org/declaration/lang--en/index.htm. The discrimination clause is open to various interpretations, and the clause on collective bargaining does not automatically bring gender equality in the workplace (Prieto 2008).

6. The proportion of women in the maquila workforce in Mexico dropped from 71 percent in 1990 to 54 percent in 1997 (F. Brown and Dominguez 1997: 2).

Adam, Barbara. 2002. "The Gendered Time Politics of Globalization: Of Shadowlands and Elusive Justice." *Feminist Review* 20:3–39.

Adorno, Theodor. 1991. *The Culture Industry: Selected Essays on Mass Culture*. London: Routledge.

African Centre for Women. 2002. "A Conceptual and Analytical Framework for Gender Mainstreaming in National Accounts and National Budget." Addis Ababa, Ethiopia: UN Economic Commission for Africa, Working Paper, www1.uneca.org/Portals/ngm/CrossArticle/1/Documents/Conceptual-Analyti calFramework2003.pdf.

Afshar, Haleh, and Bina Agarwal, eds. 1989. *Women, Poverty and Ideology in Asia: Contradictory Pressures, Uneasy Resolutions*. London: Macmillan.

Agarwal, Bina. 1986. *Cold Hearths and Barren Slopes: The Woodfuel Crisis in the Third World*. London: Zed Books.

Agathangelou, Anna, and L. H. Ling. 2003. "Desire Industries: Sex Trafficking, UN Peacekeeping, and the Neoliberal World Order." *Brown Journal of World Affairs* 10 (1): 133–48.

Akers, Andrea. 2011. "Lakota Women: The Anti-systemic Link in the Capitalist World-System." B.A. honors thesis, Colorado State University

Alexander, Jacqui, and Chandra T. Mohanty, eds. 1997. *Feminist Genealogies, Colonial Legacies, Democratic Futures*. London: Routledge.

Altieri, Miguel, and Alejandro Rojas. 1999. "Ecological Impacts of Chile's Neoliberal Policies, with Special Emphasis on Agroecosystems." *Environment, Development and Sustainability* 1:55–72.

Alvarez, Sonia, Evelina Dagnino, and Arturo Escobar, eds. 1998. *Culture of Politics/Politics of Cultures: Re-visioning Latin American Social Movements*. Boulder, CO: Westview Press.

American Apparel and Footwear Association. 2008. "TRENDS: An Annual Statistical Analysis of the U.S. Apparel and Footwear Industries." https://www .wewear.org/assets/1/7/Trends2008.pdf.

Amin, Samir. 1974. *Accumulation on a World Scale: A Critique of the Theory of Underdevelopment*. New York: Monthly Review Press.

———. 1976. "Social Characteristics of Peripheral Formations: An Outline for Historical Sociology." *Berkeley Journal of Sociology* 21 (1): 27–43.

———. 2008. *The World We Wish to See: Revolutionary Objectives in the Twenty-First Century*. New York: Monthly Review Press.

————. 2011. "Historical Capitalism in Decline: The Tricontinental Mission of Marxism." *Monthly Review* 62 (9): 1–18.

Andersen, Margaret. 2001. "Restructuring for Whom? Race, Class, Gender, and the Ideology of Invisibility." *Sociological Forum* 16 (2): 181–201.

Ansal, Hacer. 1995. *Teknolojik gelişmelerin sanayide kadın istihdamına etkileri: Türk dokuma ve elektronik sanayilerinde teknolojik değişim ve kadın istihdamı araştırması* [Effects of technological improvement on female employment in industry: Women's work in Turkish textile and electronic industries]. Ankara: Kadın ve Aile Bakanlığı.

Antonopoulos, Rania, and Indira Hirway, eds. 2010. *Unpaid Work and the Economy: Gender, Time-Use, and Poverty in Developing Countries.* New York: Palgrave Macmillan.

Appadurai, Arjun, ed. 1986. *The Social Life of Things: Commodities in Cultural Perspective.* Cambridge: Cambridge University Press.

Arrighi, Giovanni, and John Saul. 1968. "Socialism and Economic Development in Tropical Africa." *Journal of Modern African Studies* 2 (1): 141–69.

Atkinson, Jane, and Shelly Errington, eds. 1990. *Power and Difference: Gender in Island Southeast Asia.* Stanford, CA: Stanford University Press.

Attwood, L. 1996. "Young People, Sex and Sexual Identity." In *Gender, Generation and Identity in Contemporary Russia*, ed. Hilary Pilkington, 95–120. London: Routledge.

Ayata, S. 1990. *The Labour Market in the Small Industry Town.* Istanbul: Friedrich Ebert Vakfı.

Babb, Florence. 2001. *After Revolution: Mapping Gender and Cultural Politics in Neoliberal Nicaragua.* Austin: University of Texas Press.

Bacchetta, Marc, Ekkehart Ernst, and Wanna P. Bustamente. 2009. *Globalization and Informal Jobs in Developing Countries.* Geneva: International Labour Organization.

Bain, Carmen. 2010a. "Governing the Global Value Chain: GLOBALGAP and the Chilean Fresh Fruit Industry." *International Journal of Sociology of Agriculture and Food* 17 (1): 1–23.

————. 2010b. "Structuring the Flexible and Feminized Labor Market: GLOBAL-GAP Standards for Agricultural Labor in Chile." *Signs* 35 (2): 343–70.

Bair, Jennifer. 2005. "Global Capitalism and Commodity Chains: Looking Back, Going Forward." *Competition and Change* 9(1): 153–80.

————, ed. 2009. *Frontiers of Commodity Chain Research.* Stanford, CA: Stanford University Press.

————. 2010. "On Difference and Capital: Gender and the Globalization of Production." *Signs* 36 (1): 203–26.

————. 2011. "Constructing Scarcity, Creating Value: Marketing the *Mundo Maya*." In *The Cultural Wealth of Nations*, ed. Nina Brandelj and Frederick Winery, 177–96. Stanford: Stanford University Press.

Bair, Jennifer, and Marion Werner. 2011. "Commodity Chains and the Uneven Geographies of Global Capitalism: A Disarticulations Perspective." *Environment and Planning A* 43: 988–97.

Baker, Jonathan. 1995. "Survival and Accumulation Strategies at the Rural-Urban Interface in Northwest Tanzania." *Environment and Urbanization* 7 (1): 117–32.

Bakker, Isabella, and Stephen Gill, eds. 2004. *Power, Production, and Social Reproduction, Human In/security in the Global Political Economy.* London: Palgrave Macmillan.

Bandy, Joe, and Jennifer Bickham-Mendez. 2003. "A Place of Their Own? Women Organizers Negotiating National and Transnational Civil Society in the Maquilas of Nicaragua and Mexico." *Mobilization* 8 (2): 173–88.

Baran, Paul. 1957. *The Political Economy of Growth.* New York: Monthly Review Press.

Baran, Paul, and Paul Sweezy. 1966. *Monopoly Capital: An Essay on the American Economic and Social Order.* New York: Monthly Review Press.

Barkin, David. 1985. "Global Proletarianization." In *The Americas in the New International Division of Labor,* ed. Steven Sanderson, 26–45. New York: Holmes and Meier.

Barndt, Deborah. 2002. *Tangled Routes: Women, Work and Globalization on the Tomato Trail.* Lanham, MD: Rowman and Littlefield.

Barrientos, Stephanie. 2011. "Labour Chains: Analysing the Role of Labour Contractors in Global Production Networks." Brooks World Poverty Institute, Working Paper 153. www.manchester.ac.uk/bwpi.

Barrientos, Stephanie, and Catherine Dolan, eds. 2006. *Ethical Sourcing in the Global Food System.* London: Earthscan

Barrientos, Stephanie, Catherine Dolan, and Anne Tallontire. 2003. "A Gendered Value Chain Approach to Codes of Conduct in African Horticulture." *World Development* 31 (9): 1511–26.

Barrientos, Stephanie, Naila Kabeer, and Naomi Hossain. 2004. "The Gender Dimension of the Globalization of Production." Working Paper 17. Geneva: International Labour Organization.

Baudrillard, Jean. 1998. *The Consumer Society: Myths and Structures.* Thusand Oaks, CA: Sage.

Bedford, Kate, and Shirin Rai. 2010. "Feminists Theorize International Political Economy." *Signs* 36 (1): 1–10.

Beechey, Veronica, and Tessa Perkins. 1987. *A Matter of Hours: Women, Part-Time Work, and the Labour Market.* Cambridge, UK: Polity Press.

Beneria, Lourdes. 1979. "Reproduction, Production and the Sexual Division of Labour." *Cambridge Journal of Economics* 3: 203–25.

———. 1992. "Accounting for Women's Work: The Progress of Two Decades." *World Development* 20 (11): 1547–60.

———. 1999. "The Enduring Debate over Unpaid Labor." *International Labour Review* 138: 287–309.

———. 2001. "Shifting the Risk: New Employment Patterns, Informalization and Women's Work." *International Journal of Politics, Culture and Society* 15 (1): 27–53.

Beneria, Lourdes, and Shelley Feldman. 1992. *Unequal Burden: Economic Crisis, Persistent Poverty, and Women's Work.* Boulder, CO: Westview Press.

Beneria, Lourdes, and Maria Floro. 2002. "Distribution, Gender and Labor Market Informalization: A Conceptual Framework with a Focus on Homeworkers." In *Informalization: Poverty, Precarious Jobs and Social Protection,* ed. Neema Kudva and Lourdes, Beneria, 9–27. Ithaca, NY: Cornell University Open Access Repository.

Beneria, Lourdes, and Martha Roldan. 1987. *The Crossroads of Class and Gender: Industrial Homework, Subcontracting, and Household Dynamics in Mexico City*. Chicago: University of Chicago Press.

Bennholdt-Thomsen, Veronika. 1984. "Towards a Theory of the Sexual Division of Labour." In *Households and the World-Economy*, ed. Joan Smith, Immanuel Wallerstein and Hans Evers, 252–71. Beverly Hills: Sage.

Benoit, Cecilia M. 2000. *Women, Work and Social Rights: Canada in Historical and Comparative Perspective*. Toronto: Prentice Hall.

Berger, John. 1974. *The Look of Things*. New York: Viking.

Bergeron, Suzanne. 2011. "Economics, Performativity and Social Reproduction in Global Development." *Globalizations* 8 (2): 151–61.

Bergesen, Albert, and Chintamani. Sahoo. 1985. "Evidence of the Decline of American Hegemony in World Production." *Review of the Fernand Braudel Center* 8 (4): 595–611.

Bettio, Francesca, and Alina Verashchagina, eds. 2008. *Frontiers in the Economics of Gender*. London: Routledge.

Bickham-Mendez, Jennifer. 2005. *From the Revolution to the Maquiladoras: Gender, Labor, and Globalization in Nicaragua*. Durham, NC: Duke University Press.

Biel, Robert. 2006. "The Interplay between Social and Environmental Degradation in the Development of the International Political Economy." *Journal of World-Systems Research* 12 (1): 109–47.

Bingen, Jim, and Andile. Siyengo. 2002. "Standards and Corporate Restructuring in the Michigan Dry Bean Industry." *Agriculture and Human Values* 19 (4): 311–23.

Blowfield, Mick. 1999. "Ethical Trade: A Review of Developments and Issues." *Third World Quarterly* 20 (4): 753–70.

Blumberg, Rae. 1979. "Rural Women in Development: Veil of Invisibility, World of Work." *International Journal of Intercultural Relations* 3 (4): 447–72.

Blundell, Valda. 1994. "Take Home Canada: Representatioons of Aboriginal Peoples as Tourist Souvenirs." In *The Socialness of Things: Essays on the Socio-semiotics of Objects*, ed. Stephen Riggins, 251–84. London: Walter de Gruyter.

Bodley, John. 2008. *Victims of Progress*. Lanham, MD: Altamira Press.

Bonacich, Edna. 1972. "A Theory of Ethnic Antagonism: The Split Labor Market." *American Journal of Sociology* 37 (5): 547–59.

Bonacich, Edna, and Richard Appelbaum. 2000. *Behind the Label: Inequality in the Los Angeles Apparel Industry*. Berkeley: University of California Press.

Bowker, G., and S. Star. 1999. *Sorting Things Out: Classification and Its Consequences*. Cambridge, MA: MIT Press.

Boydston, Jeanne. 1986. "To Earn Her Daily Bread: Housework and Antebellum Working-Class Subsistence." *Radical History Review* 35 (1): 7–25.

Bradby, Barbara. 1984. "The Remystification of Value." *Capital and Class* 17: 114–33.

Brady, David, and Ryan Denniston. 2006. "Economic Globalization, Industrialization and Deindustrialization in Affluent Democracies." *Social Forces* 85 (1): 297–329.

Brass, Tom. 1999. *Towards a Comparative Political Economy of Unfree Labour: Case Studies and Debates*. London: Frank Cass.

Braudel, Fernand. 1977. *Afterthoughts on Material Civilization and Capitalism.* Baltimore: Johns Hopkins University Press.

———. 1979. *Afterthoughts on Material Civilization and Capitalism.* Translated by Patricia Ranum. Baltimore: Johns Hopkins University Press.

———. 1982. *Civilization and Capitalism, 15th–18th Century,* Vol. 1, *The Structures of Everyday Life.* New York: Harper and Row.

———. 2012. "History and the Social Sciences: The *Longue Durée.*" Trans. Immanuel Wallerstein. In *The* Longue Durée *and World-Systems Analysis,* ed. Richard Lee, 241–76. Albany: State University of New York Press.

Bridger, Sue, and Rebecca Kay, 1996. "Gender and Generation in the New Labor Market." In *Gender, Generation and Identity in Contemporary Russia,* ed. Hilary Pilkington, 21–38. London: Routledge.

Broad, Dave. 1991. "Global Economic Restructuring and the (Re)Casualization of Work in the Centre: With Canadian Illustrations." *Review of the Fernand Braudel Center* 14 (4): 555–94.

———. 1995a. "Globalization and the Casual Labour Problem: History and Prospects." *Social Justice* 22 (3): 67–91.

———. 1995b. "Globalization versus Labour." *Canadian Review of Social Policy* 36: 75–85.

———. 1997. "The Casualization of the Labour Force." In *Good Jobs, Bad Jobs, No Jobs: The Transformation of Work in the 21st Century,* ed. Ann Duffy, Daniel Glenday, and Norene Pupo, 53–73. Toronto: Harcourt Brace and Company.

———. 2000a. *Hollow Work, Hollow Society? Globalization and the Casual Labour Problem.* Halifax: Fernwood Publishing.

———. 2000b. "The Periodic Casualization of Work: The Informal Economy, Casual Labour and the *Longue Dureé.*" In *Informalization: Process and Structure,* ed. F. Tabak and M. Crichlow, 23–68. Baltimore: Johns Hopkins University Press.

———. 2010. "Peripheralization of the Centre: W(h)ither Canada? (Revisited)." *Alternate Routes* 22: 123–32.

———. 2011. "The Productivity Mantra: The Profit Motive versus the Public Good." *Socialist Studies* 7 (1): 65–94.

Broad, Dave, and Wayne Antony, eds. 1999. *Citizens or Consumers? Social Policy in a Market Society.* Halifax: Fernwood Publishing.

———. 2006. *Capitalism Rebooted? Work, Welfare and the New Economy.* Halifax: Fernwood Publishing.

Broad, Dave, and Lori Foster. 1992. *The New World Order and the Third World.* Montreal: Black Rose Books.

———. 2003. "The Child Care Policy That Wasn't." *Canadian Review of Social Policy* 51: 103–13.

Broad, Dave, and Fern Hagin. 2004. "Women, Part-Time Work and Labour Standards: The Case of Saskatchewan." *Prairie Forum* 29 (1): 61–84.

Broad, Dave, and Garson Hunter. 2009. "Work Welfare and the New Economy: The Commodification of Everything." In *Interrogating the New Economy: Restructuring Work in the 21st Century,* ed. Norene Pupo and Mark Thomas, 21–42. Toronto: University of Toronto Press.

Brown, Flor, and Lilia Dominguez. 1997. "Determinants of Wage Differentials in the Maquila Industry in Mexico: A Gender Perspective." University of Utah,

International Working Group on Gender, Macroeconomics and International Economics. www.econ.utah.edu/genmac/WP/07-6.pdf.

Brown, Sandy, and Christy Getz. 2008. "Privatizing Farm Worker Justice: Regulating Labor through Voluntary Certification and Labeling." *Geoforum* 39: 1184–96.

Browne, Irene. 2000. "Opportunities Lost? Race, Industrial Restructuring, and Employment among Young Women Heading Households." *Social Forces* 78 (3): 907–29.

Brunovskis, Anette, and Guri Tyldum. 2004. *Crossing Borders: An Empirical Study of Transnational Prostitution and Trafficking in Human Beings*. London: Interface Media.

Bryceson, Deborah, Cristobal Kay, and Jos Mooij. 2000. *Disappearing Peasantries? Rural Labour in Latin America, Asia and Africa*. London: Practical Action.

Bryceson, Deborah, and Ulla Vuorela, eds. 2002. *The Transnational Family: New European Frontiers and Global Networks*. Oxford: Berg.

Bryson, Lois. 1996. "Revaluing the Household Economy." *Women's Studies International Forum* 19 (3): 207–19.

Budlender, Debbie. 2007. "A Critical Review of Selected Time Use Surveys." Geneva: UNRISD, www.unrisd.org.

Bukharin, Nicolai. 1972. *Imperialism and the Accumulation of Capital*. London: Allen Lane.

Bureau of Agricultural Statistics (BAS). 1980–2010. Manila: Philippines Department of Agriculture. www.bas.gov.ph and http://countrystat.bas.gov.ph.

Bureau of Fisheries and Aquatic Resources (BFAR). 1978–2009. "Philippines Annual Fisheries Profile." Manila: Philippines Department of Agriculture. www.bfar.da.gov.ph.

Burns, Peter. 1999. *An Introduction to Tourism and Anthropology*. London: Routledge.

Busch, Lawrence. 2000. "The Moral Economy of Grades and Standards." *Journal of Rural Studies* 16: 273–83.

Busch, Lawrence, and Carmen Bain. 2004. "New! Improved? The Transformation of the Global Agrifood System." *Rural Sociology* 69 (3): 321–46.

Butler, Judith. 1990. *Gender Trouble: Feminism and the Subversion of Identity*. London: Routledge.

———. 1993. *Bodies That Matter: On the Discursive Limits of "Sex."* London: Routledge.

Cabrera, Patricia. 2010. "Intersecting Violences: A Review of Feminist Theories and Debates on Violence against Women and Poverty in Latin America." London: Central American Women's Network. www.cawn.org.

Cagatay, Nilufer, and Sule Ozler. 1995. "Feminization of the Labor Force: The Effects of Long-Term Development and Structural Adjustment." *World Development* 23 (11): 1883–94.

Caraway, Teri. 2007. *Assembling Women: The Feminization of Global Manufacturing*. Ithaca, NY: Cornell University Press.

Carlson, Jon. 2002. "The 'Otter-Man' Empires: The Pacific Fur Trade, Incorporation and the Zone of Ignorance." *Journal of World-Systems Research* 8 (3): 390–442.

Carney, Judith, and Michael Watts. 1991. "Disciplining Women? Rice, Mechanization and the Evolution of Mandika Gender Relations in the Senegambia." *Signs* 16 (4): 651–81.

Carr, Marilyn, Martha Chen, and Jane Tate. 2000. "Globalization and Home-Based Workers." *Feminist Economics* 6 (3): 123–42.

Central American Women's Network (CAWN). 2008. "Economic Literacy: A Tool for Women's Empowerment in Nicaragua." Briefing paper, October.

Chalfin, Brenda. 2007. *Shea Butter Republic: State Power, Global Markets and the Making of an Indigenous Commodity*. London: Routledge.

Chandler, W. 1994. *The Value of Household Work in Canada*. Ottawa: National Income and Expenditure Accounts.

Chant, Sylvia, and Mathew Gutmann. 2002. "Men-Streaming Gender? Questions for Gender and Development Policy in the Twenty-First Century." *Progress in Development Studies* 2 (4): 269–82.

Chapkis, Wendy, and Cynthia Enloe. 1983. *Of Common Cloth: Women in the Global Textile Industry*. Amsterdam: Transnational Institute.

Chilcote, Ronald, ed. 1982. *Dependency and Marxism: Toward a Resolution of the Debate*. Boulder, CO: Westview Press.

Chow, Gon Ling. 1992. "Garment Sweatshops in the Ethnic Enclave: Alterations Needed." B.A. thesis, Harvard College.

Clancy, Michael. 1998. "Commodity Chains, Services and Development: Theory and Preliminary Evidence from the Tourism Industry." *Review of International Political Economy* 5 (1): 122–48.

———. 2002. "The Globalization of Sex Tourism and Cuba: A Commodity Chains Approach." *Studies in Contemporary International Development* 36 (4): 63–88.

Clapp, Jennifer, and Doris Fuchs, eds. 2009. *Corporate Power in Global Agrifood Governance*. Cambridge, MA: MIT Press.

Clean Clothes Campaign. 2010. "Action for Safe Factories in Bangladesh on the Fifth Anniversary of Spectrum Disaster." www.cleanclothes.org/news/2010/04 /11/action-for-safe-factories-in-bangladesh-on-5th-anniversary-of-spectrum -disaster.

Clean Clothes Campaign. 2013. "Fatal Fashion: Analysis of Recent Factory Fires in Pakistan and Bangladesh." www.cleanclothes.org/resources/publications/fatal -fashion.pdf/view.

Clelland, Donald A. 2012. "Surplus Drain and Dark Value in the Modern World-System." In *Routledge Handbook of World-Systems Analysis*, ed. Salvatore Babones and Christopher Chase-Dunn, 197–205. London: Routledge.

Clelland, Donald A., and Wilma Dunaway. 1995. "Book Review: Commodity Chains and Global Capitalism." *Journal of World-Systems Research* 1 (1): 101–3.

Clermont, Luisella, and E. P. Aligisakis. 1995. "Measures of Unrecorded Economic Activities in Fourteen Countries." UNDP Occasional Paper 20.

Clough, Patricia, and Jean Halley, eds. 2007. *The Affective Turn: Theorizing the Social*. Durham, NC: Duke University Press.

Cockcroft, James D. 1986. "Immiseration, Not Marginalization: The Case of Mexico." In *Modern Mexico: State, Economy and Social Conflict*, ed. N. Hamilton and T. Harding, 233–59. Beverly Hills, CA: Sage.

Collins, Jane. 1995. "Gender and Cheap Labor in Agriculture." In *Food and Agrarian Orders in the World-Economy*, ed. P. McMichael, 217–32. Westport, CT: Greenwood Press.

———. 2000. "Tracing Social Relations through Commodity Chains: The Case of Brazilian Grapes." In *Commodities and Globalization: Anthropological*

Perspectives, ed. A. Haugerud, P. Little, and P. Stone, 97–112. New York: Rowman and Littlefield.

———. 2003. *Threads: Gender, Labor, and Power in the Global Apparel Industry.* Chicago: University of Chicago Press.

———. 2005. "New Directions in Commodity Chain Analysis of Global Development Processes." *Research in Rural Sociology and Development* 11: 1–15.

Comaroff, Jean, and John Comaroff. 2000. "Millenial Capitalism: First Thoughts on a Second Coming." *Public Culture* 12 (2): 291–334.

Communist Working Group. 1986. *Unequal Exchange and the Prospects of Socialism.* Copenhagen: Manifest Press.

Coronado, Irasema, and Kathleen Staudt. 2004. "Resistance and *Compromiso* in the Global Frontlines: Gender Wars at the US-Mexico Border." In *Critical Theories, International Relations and "the Anti-globalisation Movement": The Politics of Global Resistance,* ed. Catherine Eschle and Bice Maiguasscha, 139–53. London: Routledge.

Cosgrove, Serena. 2010. *Leadership from the Margins: Women and Civil Society Organizations in Argentina, Chile, and El Salvador.* New Brunswick, NJ: Rutgers University Press.

Cravey, Altha. 1998. *Women and Work in Mexico's Maquiladoras.* Lanham, MD: Rowman and Littlefield.

da Corta, Lucia, and D. Venkateshwarlu. 1999. "Unfree Relations and the Feminization of Agricultural Labor in Andhra Pradesh, 1970–1995." In *Rural Labour Relations in India,* ed. T. J. Byres, Karin Kapadia, and Jens Lerche, 71–139. London: Frank Cass.

Dalla Costa, Mariosa, and Giovanna Dalla Costa. 1999. *Women, Development and Labor of Reproduction.* Trenton, NJ: Africa World Press.

Dalla Costa, M., and S. James. 1970. *The Power of Women and the Subversion of the Community.* Bristol, UK: Falling Wall Press.

Dalvie, Mohamed, et al. 2011. "Urinary Dialkyl Phosphate Levels before and after First Season Chlorpyrifos Spraying amongst Farm Workers in the Western Cape, South Africa." *Journal of Environmental Science and Health Part B* 46: 163–72.

Dangler, Jamie F. 2000. "The Periodic Resurgence of Non-Factory-Based Production: The Case of Waged Homework." In *Informalization: Process and Structure,* ed. F. Tabak and M.A. Crichlow, 47–68. Baltimore: Johns Hopkins University Press.

Davis, Angela. 1981. *Women, Race, and Class.* New York: Random House.

Davis, Mike. 2006. *A Planet of Slums.* London: Verso Books.

Davis, William. 1973. *Social Relations in a Philippine Market: Self-Interest and Subjectivity.* Berkeley: University of California Press.

Dedeoglu, Saniye. 2008. *Women Workers in Turkey: Global Industrial Production in Istanbul.* London: I B Tauris.

Deere, Carmen. 1990. *Household and Class Relations: Peasants and Landlords in Northern Peru.* Berkeley: University of California Press.

———. 2005. "The Feminization of Agriculture? Economic Restructuring in Rural Latin America." Occasional Paper 1. Geneva: UNRISD.

Delphy, Christina 1976. *The Main Enemy.* London: Women's Research and Resource Center.

Denning, Steve. 2011. "Scalable Collaboration in Lessons from China: Li and Fung." *Forbes* (8 October), www.forbes.com/sites/stevedenning/2011/10/08 /scalable-collaboration-lessons-from-china-li-fung.

Derrida, Jacques. 1974. *Of Grammatology*. Baltimore: Johns Hopkins University Press.

Dicken, Peter. 2011. *Global Shift: Mapping the Changing Contours of the World Economy*. New York: Guilford Press.

Dickinson, James, and Bob Russell. 1986. *Family, Economy and State: The Social Reproduction Process under Capitalism*. London: Croom-Helm.

Dickinson, Torry. 1995. *Common Wealth: Self-Sufficiency in American Communities, 1830 to 1993*. New York: University Press of America.

Dickinson, Torry, and Robert Schaeffer. 2001. *Fast Forward: Work, Gender and Protest in a Changing World*. Boulder, CO: Rowman and Littlefield.

Dixon, Jane. 2002. *The Changing Chicken: Chooks, Cooks and Culinary Culture*. Sydney: University of New South Wales Press.

Dolan, Catherine, and John Humphrey. 2004. "Changing Governance Patterns in the Trade in Fresh Vegetables between Africa and the United Kingdom." *Environment and Planning A* 36: 491–509.

Dolan, Catherine, and Maggie Opondo. 2005. "Seeking Common Ground: Multistakeholder Initiatives in Kenya's Cut Flower Industry." *Journal of Corporate Citizenship* 18: 87–98.

Dolan, Catherine, and Kristina Sorby. 2003. "Gender and Employment in High-Value Agriculture Industries." Agriculture and Rural Development Working Paper 7. Washington, DC: World Bank.

Dovzhenko, Valentyna. 2002. "Statement for Ukraine's State Committee for Family and Youth Affairs." Plenary Meeting of the Special Session on Children. New York: United Nations (9 May). www.un.int/ukraine/Ukr-UN/SecCoun/debate /2002/vyst-ss-children-e.htm.

Dunaway, Wilma A. 1994. "The Southern Fur Trade and the Incorporation of Southern Appalachia into the World-Economy, 1690–1763." *Review of the Fernand Braudel Center* 17: 215–41.

———. 1995. "'The Disremembered' of the Antebellum South: A New Look at the Invisible Labor of Poor Women." *Critical Sociology* 21 (3): 89–106.

———. 1996. *The First American Frontier: Transition to Capitalism in Southern Appalachia, 1700–1860*. Chapel Hill: University of North Carolina Press.

———. 2000. "Women at Risk: Capitalist Incorporation and Community Transformation on the Cherokee Frontier." In *A World-Systems Reader*, ed. Thomas Hall, 195–210. Lanham, MD: Rowman and Littlefield.

———. 2001. "The Double Register of History: Situating the Forgotten Woman and Her Household in Capitalist Commodity Chains." *Journal of World-Systems Research* 7 (1): 2–29.

———. 2003a. *The African-American Family in Slavery and Emancipation*. Cambridge: Cambridge University Press.

———. 2003b. "Women's Labor and Nature: The 21st Century World-System from a Radical Ecofeminist Perspective." In *New Theoretical Directions for the 21st Century World-System*, ed. W. Dunaway, 182–202. Westport, CT : Praeger.

———. 2003c. *Slavery in the American Mountain South*. Cambridge: Cambridge University Press.

————. 2008. *Women, Work and Family in the Antebellum Mountain South.* Cambridge: Cambridge University Press.

————. 2010. "Nonwaged Peasants in the Modern World-System: African Households as Dialectical Units of Capitalist Exploitation and Indigenous Resistance, 1890–1930." *Journal of Philosophical Economics* 4 (1): 19–57.

————. 2012. "The Semiproletarian Household over the *Longue Durée* of the Modern World-System." In *The* Longue Durée *and World-Systems Analysis,* ed. Richard Lee, 97–136. Albany: State University of New York Press.

Dunaway, Wilma A., and M. Cecilia Macabuac. 2007. "'The Shrimp Eat Better Than We Do': Philippine Subsistence Fishing Households Sacrificed for the Global Food Chain." *Review of the Fernand Braudel Center* 30 (4): 313–36.

Dupuis, Melanie. 2002. *Nature's Perfect Food.* New York: New York University Press.

Dwyer, Daisy, and Judith Bruce, eds. 1988. *A Home Divided: Women and Income in the Third World.* Stanford, CA: Stanford University Press.

Economic Commission for Latin America and the Caribbean. (ECLAC). 2004. "Social Panorama of Latin America and the Caribbean, 2002–2003." Santiago, www.eclac.org.

Eder, James. 1999. *A Generation Later: Household Strategies and Economic Change in the Rural Philippines.* Honolulu: University of Hawaii Press.

Ehrenreich, Barbara, and Arlie Hochschild, eds. 2002. *Global Woman: Nannies, Maids, and Sex Workers in the New Economy.* New York: Metropolitan Books.

Eisenstein, Zillah 1990. "Constructing a Theory of Capitalist Patriarchy." In *Women, Class and the Feminist Imagination: A Socialist-Feminist Reader, ed.* K. Hansen and I. Philipson, 128–47. Philadelphia: Temple University Press.

Elson, Diane. 1995a. "Gender Awareness in Modeling Structural Adjustment." *World Development* 23 (11): 1851–68.

————, ed. 1995b. *Male Bias in the Development Process.* Manchester, UK: Manchester University Press, 2nd ed.

————. 1999. "Labor Markets as Gendered Institutions: Equality, Efficiency and Empowerment Issues." *World Development* 27 (3): 611–27.

Elson, Diane, and Ruth Pearson. 1981. "Nimble Fingers Make Cheap Workers: An Analysis of Women's Employment in Third World Export Manufacturing." *Feminist Review* 7 (1): 87–107.

Emmanuel, Arghiri. 1972. *Unequal Exchange: A Study of the Imperialism of Trade.* London: New Left Books.

Engels, Friedrich. 1972. *The Origin of the Family, Private Property, and the State.* New York: International Publishers.

Enloe, Cynthia. 1990. *Bananas, Beaches, and Bases: Making Feminist Sense of International Politics.* Berkeley: University of California Press.

Environmental Justice Foundation. 2003. *Smash and Grab: Conflict, Corruption and Human Rights Abuses in the Shrimp Farming Industry.* London: Environmental Justice Foundation.

Eraydin, Ayda, and Asuman Erendil. 1999. "The Role of Female Labour in Industrial Restructuring: New Production Processes and Labour Market Relations in the Istanbul Clothing Industry." *Gender, Place and Culture* 6(3): 259–72.

Erokhina, Lyudmila, and Maria Buryak. 2003. *Torgovlia zhenshinami I det'mi v tseliakh seksual'noi ekspluatatsii v sotsial'noi I kriminologicheskoi perspective.*

[*Trade in women and children for the purposes of sexual exploitation in social and criminological perspective*]. Moscow: Profobrazovanie.

Escobar, Pepe. 2004. "The Philippines: Disgraceful State; A Five-Part Series." *Asia Times.* www.atimes.com.

Eskenazi, Brenda, et al. 2007. "Organophosphate Pesticide Exposure and Neuro-development in Young Mexican-American Children." *Environmental Health Perspectives* 115 (5): 792–98.

Espinosa, Isolda. 2005. *Las metas del milenio y la igualdad de género: El caso de Nicaragua* [*The Millenium Development Goals and gender equality: the case of Nicaragua*]. Santiago: ECLACMujer y Desarollo Serial No. 68.

Estrada, Daniela. 2007. "Chile Indigenous Women Make Their Voices Heard." *IPS News*, 3 March. www.ipsnews.net.

EUREPGAP. 2004. "EUREPGAP Control Points and Compliance Criteria: Fruit and Vegetables, Version 2.1." www.eurepgap.org/documents/webdocs /EUREPGAP_CPCC_FP_V2-1_Oct04_update_01July05.pdf.

Feenberg, Andrew, and Alistair Hannay, eds. 1995. *Technology and the Politics of Knowledge.* Bloomington: Indiana University Press.

Feldman, Shelley, Charles Geisler, and Gayatri Menon. 2011. *Accumulating Insecurity: Violence and Dispossession in the Making of Everyday Life.* Athens: University of Georgia Press.

Fenelon, James. 1998. *Culturicide, Resistance, and Survival of the Lakota.* New York: Garland.

Ferguson, James 1990. *The Anti-politics Machine: "Development," Depoliticization, and Bureaucratic Power in Lesotho.* Cambridge: Cambridge University Press.

Fernandez-Kelly, Patricia. 1983. *For We Are Sold, I and My People: Women and Industry in Mexico's Frontier.* Albany: State University of New York Press.

———. 1985. "Contemporary Production and the New International Division of Labor." In *The Americas in the New International Division of Labor,* ed. Steven Sanderson, 201–222. New York: Holmes and Meier.

Fieldhouse, David. 1961. "Imperialism: An Historical Review." *Economic History Review* 14 (2): 187–209.

Folbre, Nancy. 1982. "Exploitation Comes Home: A Critique of the Marxian Theory of Family Labour." *Cambridge Journal of Economics* 6: 317–29.

———. 1991. "The Unproductive Housewife: Her Evolution in Nineteenth-Century Economic Thought." *Signs* 16 (3): 463–84.

———. 1994. *Who Pays for the Kids?* London: Routledge.

Foley, Duncan. 1983. "Commodity." In *A Dictionary of Marxist Thought,* ed. Tom Bottomore, 86–87. Cambridge, MA: Harvard University Press.

Food and Nutrition Institute. 2005. "Statistics." Manila: Republic of Philippines. www.fnri.dost.gov.ph.

Foster, John, and Fred Magdoff. 2009. *The Great Financial Crisis: Causes and Consequences.* New York: Monthly Review Press.

Foster, John, Robert McChesney, and Jamil Jonna. 2011. "The Global Reserve Army of Labor and the New Imperialism." *Monthly Review* 63 (6): 1–31.

Foster, Lori, and Dave Broad. 1998. *Flexible Child Care for Flexible Workers.* Regina: University of Regina Social Policy Research Unit.

Fox, Bonnie. 1980. *Hidden in the Household: Women's Domestic Labour under Capitalism.* Toronto: Women's Press.

Fox-Piven, Frances, and Richard Cloward. 1971. *Regulating the Poor: The Functions of Public Welfare.* New York: Pantheon Books.

Frank, Andre Gunder. 1969. *Latin America: Underdevelopment or Revolution?* New York: Monthly Review Press.

———. 1979. *Dependent Accumulation and Underdevelopment.* London: Macmillan Press.

———. 1981. *Crisis in the Third World.* New York: Holmes and Meier.

Frank, Dana. 2005. *Bananeras: Women Transforming the Banana Unions of Latin America?* Cambridge, MA: South End Press.

Fraser, Nancy. 1989. *Unruly Practices: Power, Discourse, and Gender in Contemporary Social Theory.* Minneapolis: University of Minnesota Press.

Freeman, Carla. 2000. *High Tech and High Heels in the Global Economy: Women, Work, and Pink-Collar Identities in the Caribbean.* Durham, NC: Duke University Press.

Freire, Paulo. 1970. *Pedagogy of the Oppressed.* New York: Continuum International.

Friedman, Milton. 1977. *There's No Such Thing as a Free Lunch.* New York: Open Court.

Friedmann, Harriet. 1978. "World Market, State, and Family Farm: Social Basis of Family Production in an Era of Wage Labour." *Comparative Studies in Society and History* 20: 545–86.

Friedmann, Harriet. 1988. "Family Wheat farms and Third World Diets: A Paradoxical Relationship between Unwaged and Waged Labor." In *Work without Wages: Domestic Labor and Self-Employment within Capitalism,* ed. Jane Collins and Martha Gimenez, 181–204. Albany: State University of New York Press.

———. 1993. "The Political Economy of Food: A Global Crisis." *New Left Review* 197: 29–58.

Frobel, Folker. 1982. "The Current Development of the World-Economy: Reproduction of Labor and Accumulation of Capital on a World Scale." *Review of the Fernand Braudel Center* 5 (4): 507–55.

Gaburro, G. 2004. *Domestic Slavery: Servitude, Au Pairs and Mail Order Brides.* Council of Europe. http://assembly.coe.int.

Gamboa, Maribel, Almachiara D'Angelo, and Sara Kries. 2007. "Flexibilización del mercado laboural en Nicaragua: Un aporte al debate sobre sus implicaciones de género." UNIFEM. www.unifemca.org.

Gardiner, Jean. 1997. *Gender, Care and Economics.* New York: Macmillan.

Gerber, Theodore. 2004. "When Public Institutions Fail: Coping with Dysfunctional Governments in Post-Soviet Russia." *Contexts* 3 (1): 20–28.

Gereffi, Gary. 1994. "The Organization of Buyer-Driven Global Commodity Chans: How U.S. Retailers Shape Overseas Production Networks." In *Commodity Chains and Global Capitalism,* ed. Gary Gereffi and Miguel Korzeniewicz, 95–122. Westport, CT: Greenwood Press.

Gereffi, Gary. 2001. "Shifting Governance Structures in Global Commodity Chains, with Special Reference to the Internet." *American Behavioral Scientist* 44 (10): 1616–37.

Gereffi, Gary, John Humphrey, and Timothy Sturgeon. 2005. "The Governance of Global Value Chains." *Review of International Political Economy* 12 (1):78–104.

Gereffi, Gary, John Humphrey, Raphael Kaplinsky, and Timothy Sturgeon. 2001. "Globalisation, Value Chains and Development." *IDS Bulletin* 32 (3), www.ids .ac.uk/files/dmfile/gereffietal323.pdf.

Gereffi, Gary and Raphael Kaplinsky. 2001. "The Value of Value Chains." Institute for Development Studies, www.ids.ac.uk/idspublication/value-of-value-chains.

Gereffi, Gary, and Miguel Korzeniewicz, eds. 1994. *Commodity Chains and Global Capitalism*. Westport, CT: Greenwood Press.

Gershuni, Rochelle. 2004. "Trafficking in Persons for the Purpose of Prostitution: The Israeli Experience." *Mediterranean Quarterly* 15 (4): 133–46.

Gibson, Chris and John Connell. 2004. "Cultural Industry Production in Remote Places: Indigenous Popular Music in Australia." In *Cultural Industries and the Production of Culture*, ed. Dominic Power and Allen Scott, 243–67. New York: Psychology Press.

Gil, David. 1992. *Unravelling Social Policy: Theory, Analysis, and Political Action towards Social Equality*. Rochester, VT: Schenkman Books, 5th ed.

Global Labour Rights. 2010. "21 Workers Die and 31 Injured Sewing Sweaters in Bangladesh." Pittsburgh, www.globallabourrights.org/reports?id=0002.

GLOBALGAP. 2007. "The Grasp Project Report: Towards Good Social Practices in Agriculture." http://www.globalgap.org/cms/upload/Resources/Publications /GRASP-Report-Part-I.pdf.

Gonzalez de la Rocha, Mercedes. 2001. "From the Resources of Poverty to the Poverty of Resources?" *Latin American Perspectives* 28 (4): 72–100.

Gouveia, Lourdes. 1997. "Reopening Totalities: Venezuela's Restructuring and the Globalisation Debate." In *Globalising Food: Agrarian Questions and Global Restructuring*, ed. David Goodman and Michael Watts, 305–23. New York: Routledge.

Graham, Julie, and Katherine Gibson. 1996. *The End of Capitalism (as We Knew It): A Feminist Critique of Political Economy*. London: Blackwell.

Graham, Melanie. 2009. "From Souvenir to Sundance: Perceptions and Participation Of Residents in Cultural Tourism on the Pine Ridge Indian Reservation." M.A. thesis, Colorado State University.

Grewal, Inderpal. 1999. "Travelling Barbie: Indian Transnationality and New Consumer Subjects." *Positions* 7 (3): 799–826.

Grewal, Inderpal, and Caren Kaplan, eds. 1994. *Scattered Hegemonies: Postmodernity and Transnational Feminist Practices*. Minneapolis: University of Minnesota Press.

Grosfoguel, Ramon. 1995. "Depeasantization and Agrarian Decline in the Caribbean." In *Food and Agrarian Orders in the World-Economy*, ed. Philip McMichael, 233–54. Westport, CT: Greenwood Press.

Grosfoguel, Ramon, and Ana Cervantes-Rodriguez, eds. 2002. *The Modern/Colonial Capitalist World-System in the Twentieth Century*. Westport, CT: Praeger.

Grossman, R. 1979. "Women's Place in the Integrated Circuit." *South East Asian Chronicle* 66 (1): 2–17.

Guevara, Ernesto Che. 1965. *Socialism and Man in Cuba*. Havana: Campamento 5 de Mayo.

Guthman, Julie. 2009. "Unveiling the Unveiling: Commodity Chains, Commodity Fetishism, and the 'Value' of Voluntary, Ethical Food Labels." In *Frontiers of Commodity Chain Research*, ed. Jennifer Bair, 190–206. Stanford, CA: Stanford University Press.

Haddad, L., and R. Kanbur. 1990. "How Serious Is the Neglect of Intra-household Inequality?" *Economic Journal* 100 (4): 866–81.

Hall, Thomas, and James Fenelon. 2004. "The Futures of Indigenous Peoples: 9-11 and the Trajectory of Indigenous Survival and Resistance." *Journal of World-Systems Research.* 10 (1): 153–97.

———. 2009. *Indigenous Peoples and Globalization: Resistance and Revitalization.* Boulder, CO: Paradigm.

Harrison, Jill. 2004. "Invisible People, Invisible Places: Connecting Air Pollution and Pesticide Drift in California." In *Smoke and Mirrors,* ed. E. Melanie DuPuis, 288–304. New York: New York University Press.

Harrison, Jill. 2008. "Abandoned Bodies and Spaces of Sacrifice: Pesticide Drift Activism and the Contestation of Neoliberal Environmental Politics in California." *Geoforum* 39: 1197–1214.

Harriss-White, Barbara. 2003. *India Working: Essays on Society and Economy.* Cambridge: Cambridge University Press.

Hart, Gillian. 1992. "Household Production Reconsidered: Gender, Labor Conflict and Technological Change in Malaysia's Muda Region." *World Development* 20 (6): 809–23.

Harvey, David. 1989. *The Condition of Postmodernity: An Enquiry into the Origins of Cultural Change.* London: Blackwell.

———. 2003. *The New Imperialism.* New York: Oxford University Press.

Henry, Stuart. 1988. "Can the Hidden Economy Be Revolutionary? Toward a Dialectical Analysis of the Relations between Formal and Informal Economies." *Social Justice* 15 (3/4): 29–60.

Henson, Spencer, and Thomas Reardon. 2005. "Private Agri-food Standards: Implications for Food Policy and the Agri-food System." *Food Policy* 30 (3): 241–53.

Heyzer, Noeleen. 1986. *Working Women in South-East Asia: Development, Subordination, and Emancipation.* Milton Keynes, UK: Open University Press.

Higgins, Vaughan, and Wendy Larner. 2010. "Standards and Standardization as a Social Scientific Problem." In *Calculating the Social: Standards and the Re-configuration of Governing,* ed. Vaughan Higgins, and Wendy Larner, 1–17. London: Routledge.

Hilferding, Rudolf. 1981. *Finance Capital: A Study of the Latest Phase of Capitalist Development.* Trans. M. Watnick and S. Gordon. London: Routledge.

Himmelwitt, Susan. 2002. "Making Visible the Hidden Economy: The Case for Gender-Impact Analysis of Economic Policy." *Feminist Economics* 8 (1): 49–70.

Hirschman, Albert. 1977. "A Generalized Linkage Approach to Development with Special Reference to Staples." *Economic Development and Cultural Change* 25 (Supplement): 67–98.

———. 1986. *Rival Views of Market Society, and Other Essays.* New York: Viking.

Hobson, John. 1902. *Imperialism: A Study.* London: Allen and Unwin.

Hochschild, Arlie. 2000. "Global Care Chains and Emotional Surplus Value." In *On the Edge: Living with Global Capitalism,* ed. Will Hutton and Anthony Giddens, 122–40. London: Jonathan Cape.

Hondagneu-Sotelo, Pierette, and Ernestine Avila. 1997. "'I'm Here, but I'm There': The Meanings of Latina Transnational Motherhood." *Gender and Society* 11 (5): 548–70.

Hoodfar, Homa. 1984. "I'm Hungry, Mum: The Politics of Domestic Budgeting." In *Of Marriage and the Market: Women's Subordination in International Perspective*, ed. Kate Young, Carol Wolkowitz, and Roslyn McCullagh, 88–112. London: Routledge.

hooks, bell. 1984. *Feminist Theory: From Margin to Center*. Boston: South End Press.

hooks, bell. 1992. *Black Looks: Race and Representation*. Boston: South End Press.

Hopkins, M., and E. W. McCoy. 1976. "Marketing of Fisheries Products by Municipal Fishermen in Panguil Bay, Philippines." Publication no. 11. Auburn University, International Center for Aquaculture.

Hopkins, Terence, and Immanuel Wallerstein. 1977. "Patterns of Development of the Modern World-System." *Review of the Fernand Braudel Center* 1 (2): 11–145.

———. 1982. *World-Systems Analysis: Theory and Methodology*. Beverly Hills, CA: Sage Publications.

———. 1986. "Commodity Chains in the World Economy prior to 1800." *Review of the Fernand Braudel Center* 10 (1): 157–70.

———. 1987. "Capitalism and the Incorporation of New Zones into the World Economy." *Review of the Fernand Braudel Center* 10 (3/4): 763–80.

———. 1994. "Conclusions about Commodity Chains." In *Commodity Chains and Global Capitalism*, ed. Gary Gereffi and Miguel Korzeniewicz, 48–50. Westport, CT: Greenwood Press.

———, eds. 1996. *The Age of Transition: Trajectory of the World-System, 1945–2025*. London: Zed Books.

Hoskyns, Catherine, and Shirin Rai. 2007. "Recasting the Global Political Economy: Counting Women's Unpaid Work." *New Political Economy* 12 (3): 297–317.

Hsiung, Ping-Chun. 1996. *Living Rooms as Factories: Class, Gender, and the Satellite Factory System in Taiwan*. Philadelphia: Temple University Press.

Huws, Ursula. 2011. "Passing the Buck: Corporate Restructuring and the Casualization of Employment." *Work Organization, Labour and Globalization* 5 (1): 1–9.

Illo, Jeanne, and Jaime Polo. 1990. *Fishers, Traders, Farmers, Wives: The Life Stories of Ten Women in a Fishing Village*. Quezon City: Ateneo de Manila University.

Indian Arts and Crafts Board. 2012. "The Indian Arts and Crafts Act of 1990."Washington, DC: Department of Interior. http://www.iacb.doi.gov/act .html.

"Industry Report: Roasted Coffee." 2011. Roasted Coffee Market Reports. http://business.highbeam.com/industry-reports/food/roasted-coffee.

Innis, Harold. 1930. *The Fur Trade in Canada: An Introduction to Canadian Economic History*. Toronto: University of Toronto Press.

———. 1940. *The Cod Fisheries: The History of American International Economy*. New Haven, CT: Yale University Press.

International Labour Organization (ILO). 2007. "Export Processing Zones." www .ilo.org.

Irz, X. 2004. "Aquaculture and Poverty: A Case Study of Five Coastal Communities in the Philippines." Working Paper 4. University of Reading, Department of International Development.

Isaksen, Lise, Uma Devi, and Arlie Hochschild. 2008. "Global Care Crisis: A Problem of Capital, Care Chain, or Commons?" *American Behavioral Scientist* 52 (3): 405–25.

Jacinto, Ernesto. 2004. "Research Framework on Value Chain Analysis in Small Fisheries." Unpublished working paper, Tambuyog Development Center.

Jarvis, Lowell, and Esperanza Vera-Toscano. 2004. "The Impact of Chilean Fruit Sector Development on Female Employment and Household Income." Policy Research Working Paper no. 3263. Washington, DC: World Bank.

JEP-ATRE. 2004. "Panguil Bay: Forestry Resource Management Program: Inception Report for the Philippine Bureau of Fisheries and Aquatic Resources, Region 10, tss.

Jewell, Benjamin. 2008. "The Food That Senators Don't Eat: Politics and Power in the Pine Ridge Food Economy." M.A. thesis, Colorado State University.

Joekes, Susan. 1985. "Working for a Lipstick? Male and Female Labour in the Clothing in Morroco." In *Women, Work and Ideology in the Third World*, ed. Haleh Afshar, 183–213. London: Tavistock.

———. 1987. *Women in the World Economy.* Oxford: Oxford University Press.

John, Angela, ed. 1986. *Unequal Opportunities: Women's Employment in England, 1800–1918.* Oxford: Basil Blackwell.

Johnson, Christopher, David Sabean, Simon Teuscher, and Francesca Trivellato, eds. 2011. *Transregional and Transnational Families in Europe and Beyond: Experiences since the Middle Ages.* Oxford: Berghahn.

Jones, Gareth. 1984. *Outcaste London.* London: Penguin Books.

Joseph, Miranda. 1998. "The Performance of Production and Consumption." *Social Text* 54 (1): 25–61.

Kabeer, Naila. 1994. *Reversed Realities: Gender Hierarchies in Development Thought.* London: Verso.

———. 2000. *The Power to Choose: Bangladeshi Women and Labour Market Decisions in London and Dhaka.* London: Verso.

Kalecki, Michel. 1954. *Theory of Economic Dynamics: An Essay on Cyclical and Long-Run Changes in the Capitalist Economy.* London: Allen and Unwin.

Kaplan, Caren. 1995. "'A World without Boundaries': The Body Shop's Trans/National Geographics." *Social Text* 43: 45–66.

Kapsen, Suzanne. 2009. "The Unstoppable Fung Brothers." *CNN Money* (9 December), http://money.cnn.com/2009/12/07/news/international/li_fung.fortune/index.htm?section=magazines_fortuneintl/.

Kardulias, Nick. 2007. "Negotiation and Incorporation on the Margins of World-Systems: Examples from Cyprus and North America." *Journal of World-Systems Research* 13 (1): 55–82.

Karmakar, Asim. 2001. "Dadabhai Naoroji, Drain Theory and Poverty: Towards a Discourse in Political Economy." In *Economic Thoughts of Dadabhai Naoroji*, ed. P. D. Hajela, 65–77. New Delhi: Deep and Deep.

Katz, Cindi. 2001."Vagabond Capitalism and the Necessity of Social Reproduction." *Antipode* 33 (4): 708–27.

Kernaghan, Charles. 2011. "Sexual Predators and Serial Rapists Run Wild at Wal-Mart Supplier in Jordan." Institute for Global Labour and Human Rights. www.globallabourrights.org/admin/reports/files/Content-Classic-0607-final.pdf.

Kiblitskaya, Marina. 2000. "Russia's Female Breadwinners. The Changing Subjective Experience." In *Gender, State and Society in Soviet and Post-Soviet Russia*, ed. Sarah Ashwin, 55–70. London: Routledge.

Knack, Martha. 2001. *Boundaries Between: The Southern Paiute, 1775–1995*. Lincoln: University of Nebraska Press.

Kohler, Gernot, and Arno Tausch. 2002. *Global Keynesianism: Unequal Exchange and Global Exploitation*. New York: Nova Science.

Konefal, Jason, and Maki Hatanaka. 2011. "Enacting Third-Party Certification: A Case Study of Science and Politics in Organic Shrimp Certification." *Journal of Rural Studies* 27: 125–33.

Korten, David. 2001. *When Corporations Rule the World*. Bloomfield, CT: Kumarian Press.

Korzeniewicz, Roberto, and William Smith, eds. 1996. *Latin America in the World-Economy*. Westport, CT: Greenwood Press.

Kunt, V., and H. Zobu. 2011. "Harnessing Sustainable Linkages for SEMs in Turkey's Textile Sector." Geneva: United Nations. www.mdgfund.org/program/harnessingsustainablelinkagessmesturkey%E2%80%99stextilesector.

Kuznets, Simon. 1941. *National Income and Its Composition, 1919–1935*. 2 vols. Washington, DC: National Bureau of Economic Research.

Laffont, J. 2008. "Externalities." In *New Palgrave Dictionary of Economics*, 263–65. London: Macmillan-Palgrave.

Lastarria-Corheil, Susana. 2006. "Feminization of Agriculture: Trends and Driving Forces." World Bank Background Paper. http://siteresources.worldbank.org/INTWDR2008/Resources/2795087-1191427986785/.

Ledesma, Antonio. 1982. *Landless Workers and Rice Farmers: Peasant Subclasses under Agrarian Reform in Two Philippine Villages*. Laguna, Philippines: International Rice Research Institute.

Lee, Ching. 1998. *Gender and the South China Miracle: Two Worlds of Factory Women*. Berkeley: University of California Press.

Levine, Philippa, ed. 2004. *Gender and Empire*. London: Oxford University Press

Lewis, Jane. 2001. "Decline of the Male Breadwinner Model: Implications for Work and Care." *Social Politics* 8 (2): 151–69.

Lim, Linda. 1990. "Women's Work in Export Factories: The Politics of a Cause." In *Persistent Inequalities: Women and World Development*, ed. Irene Tinker, 101–19. New York: Oxford University Press.

Lim, J., and M. Montes. 2002. "Structural Adjustment Program after Structural Adjustment Program, but Why Still No Development in the Philippines?" *Asian Economic Papers* 1 (3): 90–119.

Lindholm, Charles. 2008. *Culture and Authenticity*. Malden, MA: Blackwell Publishing.

Lissyutkina, L. 1993. "Soviet Women at the Crossroads of Perestroika." In *Gender Politics and Post-communism. Reflections from Eastern Europe and the Former Soviet Union*, ed. Nanette Funk and Magda Mueller, 272–86. London: Routledge.

Littlefield, Alice, and Larry T. Reynolds. 1990. "The Putting Out System: Transitional Form or Recurrent Feature of Capitalist Production?" *Social Science Journal* 27 (4): 359–72.

Longino, Helene. 1996. "Cognitive and Non-cognitive Values in Science: Rethinking the Dichotomy." In *Feminism, Science, and the Philosophy of Science*, ed.

Lynn Nelson and Jack Nelson, 29–48. Dordrecht: Kluwer Academic Publishers.

Love, Joseph. 1980. "Raul Prebisch and the Origins of the Doctrine of Unequal Exchange." *Latin American Research Review* 15 (3): 45–72.

Luitzel, Heinrich. 2005. "Household Production and National Accounts." Paper submitted to the Second ECE/INSTRAW Joint Meeting. Geneva: UNRISD, www.unrisd.org.

Luxemburg, Rosa. 1951. *The Accumulation of Capital*. London: Routledge.

Malysheva, Marina. 2001. *Sovremennyi patriarkhat. Sotsial'no-ekonomicheskoe esse*. [*Contemporary patriarchy. a socio-economic essay*]. Moscow: Academia Press.

Marchand, Marianne, and Anne Runyan, eds. 2000. *Gender and Global Restructuring: Sightings, Sites, and Resistances*. London: Routledge.

María Elena Cuadra Working and Unemployed Women's Movement (MEC). 2008. "Informe anual, avances y retrocesos: Derechos de las mujeres en las maquilas de Nicaragua." Unpublished manuscript.

Martin, William. 1994. "The World-System Perspective in Perspective: Assessing the Attempt to Move beyond Nineteenth-Century Eurocentric Conceptions." *Review of the Fernand Braudel Center* 17 (2): 145–86.

Marx, Karl. 1992. *Early Writings*. London: Penguin Books.

———. 1990. *Capital: A Critique of Political Economy*. 3 vols. London: Penguin Books.

Matthaei, Julie. 1982. *An Economic History of Women in America: Women's Work, the Sexual Division of Labor, and the Development of Capitalism*. New York: Schocken Books.

Matthei, Linda, and David Smith. 1996. "Women, Households, and Transnational Migration Networks: The Garifuna and Global Economic Restructuring." In *Latin America in the World-Economy*, ed. Roberto Korzeniewicz and William Smith, 133–50. Westport, CT: Greenwood Press.

McArthur, Jacqueline. 2011. "The Cost of Coffee Cultivation." *Global Coffee Review*, August. www.globalcoffeereview.com/economies/view/the-cost-of -coffee-cultivation.

McCall, Leslie. 2005. "The Complexity of Intersectionality." *Signs* 30 (3): 771–800.

McGuire, Randall, Joan Smith, and William Martin. 1986. "Patterns of Household Structures and the World-Economy." *Review of the Fernand Braudel Center* 10 (1): 75–97.

Mackenzie, Suzanne. 1986. "Women's Responses to Economic Restructuring: Changing Gender, Changing Space." In *The Politics of Diversity*, ed. Roberta Hamilton and Michele Barrett, 81–100. Montreal: Book Center.

McMichael, Philip. 1994. "Agro-Food Restructuring: Unity in Diversity." In *The Global Restructuring of Agro-food Systems, ed*. Philip McMichael, 1–20. Ithaca, NY: Cornell University Press.

Mendez, Pedro. 2011. "Nicaraguan Progress and Obstacles in the Maquilas." International Trade Union Confederation, www.ituc-csi.org/nicaragua -progress-and-obstacles?lang=en.

Meyers, Albert. 1983. "Household, Labor Relations, and Reproductive Strategies among Small Cane Farmers in Jamaica." *Review of the Fernand Braudel Center* 7 (2): 181–214.

Mies, Maria. 1981. "Dynamics of Sexual Division of Labour and Capital Accumulation: Women Lace Workers of Narsapur." *Economic and Political Weekly* 16
(4): 487–500.

———. 1982. "Into the World Market." In *Women and Development: The Sexual
Division of Labor in Rural Societies*, ed. Lourdes Beneria, 1–26. Westport,
CT: Praeger.

———. 1986. *Patriarchy and Accumulation on a World Scale: Women in the
International Division of Labor.* London: Zed Books.

———. 2010. *The Village and the World.* Trans. Madeline Ferretti-Thelig.
Melbourne: Spinifex Press.

Mies, Maria, Veronika Bennholdt-Thomsen, and Claudia von Werlhof. 1988.
Women: The Last Colony. London: Zed Books.

Mies, Maria, and Vandana Shiva. 2001. *Ecofeminism.* London: Zed Books.

Miller, Peter, and Ted O'Leary. 1987. "Accounting and the Construction of the
Governable Person." *Accounting, Organizations and Society* 12:235–65.

Mintz, Sidney. 1986. *Sweetness and Power: The Place of Sugar in Modern History.*
New York: Penguin.

Modern Girl Research Group. 2008. *The Modern Girl around the World: Consumption, Modernity, and Globalization.* Durham, NC: Duke University Press.

Mohanty, Chandra, Ann Russo, and Lourdes Torres, eds. 1991. *Third World
Women and the Politics of Feminism.* Bloomington: Indiana University Press.

Montenegro, Sofia. 2000. "La Cultura Sexual en Nicaragua." Managua: CINCO.
www.cinco.org.ni/publicaciones/6.

Moser, Caroline. 1993. *Gender Planning and Development: Theory and Practice.*
London: Routledge.

———. 1996. *Confronting Crisis: A Comparative Study of Household Responses
to Poverty and Vulnerability in Four Poor Urban Communities.* Washington,
DC: World Bank.

MSU Naawan Foundation. 2006. "Resource and Socio-economic Assessment
Monitoring of Panguil Bay: Final Report." Miasmis Oriental, Philippines:
Mindanao State University at Naawan.

Nagel, Joane. 2000. "Ethnicity and Sexuality." *Annual Review of Sociology* 26:
107–33.

Naidoo, Saloshni, Leslie London, Alex Burdorf, Rajen Naidoo, and Hans Krom-
hout. 2011. "Spontaneous Miscarriages and Infant Deaths among Female
Farmers in Rural South Africa." *Scandinavian Journal of Work and Environmental Health* 37 (3): 227–36.

Nakano-Glenn, Evelyn. 1992. "From Servitude to Service Work: Historical
Continuities in the Racial Division of Paid Reproductive Labor." *Signs* 18 (1):
1–43.

Nash, June, and Patricia Fernandez-Kelly, eds. 1983. *Women, Men and the
International Division of Labour.* Albany: State University of New York Press.

National Statistical Coordination Board. 2003. "Poverty Statistics." Manila:
Republic of Philippines. www.nscb.gov.ph.

Naylor, Rosamond. 2003. "Nature's Subsidies to Shrimp and Salmon Farming."
Science Magazine 282 (5390): 883–88.

Nelson, Julie. 1998. "Labour, Gender and the Economic/Social Divide." *International Labour Review* 137 (1): 33–46.

Nelson, Margaret, and Joan Smith. 1989. *Working Hard and Making Do: Surviving in Small Town America*. Berkeley: University of California Press.

Nickerson, Donna. 1999. "Trade-offs of Mangrove Area Development in the Philippines." *Ecological Economics* 28(2): 279–98.

ODEPA. 2005. *Agricultura Chilena, 2014: Una perspectiva de mediano plazo*. Santiago: Government of Chile.

Ong, Aihwa. 1987. *Spirits of Resistance and Capitalist Discipline: Factory Women in Malaysia*. Albany: State University of New York Press.

Online Clothing Study. 2012. "Actual Garment Production Cost: The Way Factory Calculates It." www.onlineclothingstudy.com/2012/06/actual-garment -production-cost-way.html.

Online Clothing Study. 2013. "How to Calculate Raw Material Cost for Garments." www.onlineclothingstudy.com/2012/06/how-to-calculate-raw-material -cost-for.html.

Orlova, Alexandra. 2004. "From Social Dislocation to Human Trafficking: The Russian Case." *Problems of Post-Communism* 51 (6): 14–22.

O'Rourke, Dara. 2006. "Multi-stakeholder Regulation: Privatizing or Socializing Global Labor Standards?" *World Development* 34 (5): 899–918.

Paige, Jeffery. 1978. *Agrarian Revolution*. New York: Free Press.

———. 1998. *Coffee and Power: Revolution and the Rise of Democracy in Central America*. Cambridge, MA: Harvard University Press.

Pareake, Mead. 1996. "Genealogy, Sacredness and the Commodities Market." *Cultural Survival* 20 (2), www.culturalsurvival.org/ourpublications/csq/article /genealogy-sacredness-and-commodities-market.

Parrenas, Rhacel. 2000. "Migrant Filipina Domestic Workers and the International Division of Reproductive Labor." *Gender and Society* 14 (4): 560–80.

———. 2001. *Servants of Globalization: Women, Migration, and Domestic Work*. Stanford, CA: Stanford University Press.

———. 2005. *Children of Global Migration: Transnational Families and Gendered Woes*. Stanford, CA: Stanford University Press.

Patnaik, Prabhat. 2008. "The Accumulation Process in the Period of Globalisation." *Economic and Political Weekly*, 28 June, 108–13.

Pearce, Fred. 2012. *The Land Grabbers: The New Fight over Who Owns the Earth*. Boston: Beacon Press.

Pearson, Ruth. 1998. "Nimble Fingers Revisited." In *Feminist Visions of Development: Gender, Analysis, and Policy*, ed. Cecile Jackson and Ruth Pearson, 171–88. London: Routledge.

———. 2000. "All Change? Men, Women and Reproductive Work in the Global Economy." *European Journal of Development Research* 12 (2): 219–37.

———. 2004. "The Social Is Political: Towards the Re-politicization of Feminist Analysis of the Global Economy." *International Feminist Journal of Politics* 6 (4): 603–22.

———. 2007. "Beyond Women Workers: Gendering CSR." *Third World Quarterly* 28 (4): 731–49.

Pearson, Ruth, and Susan Razavi, eds. 2004. *Globalization, Export-Oriented Employment, and Social Policy: Gendered Connections*. London: Palgrave.

Pellerin, Helene. 1996. "The Politics of Migration Regulation." In *Globalization: Theory and Practice*, ed. Eleonore Kofman and Gillian Youngs, 177–92. London: Pinter.

Pellow, David, and Lisa Park. 2002. *Silicon Valley of Dreams: Immigrant Labor, Environmental Injustice, Immigrant Workers, and the High-Tech Global Economy.* New York: New York University Press.

Peluso, N. 1996. "Fruit Trees and Family Trees in an Anthropogenic Rainforest: Property Rights, Ethics of Access, and Environmental Change in Indonesia." *Comparative Studies in Society and History* 38 (3): 510–48.

Perelman, Michael. 2011. *The Invisible Handcuffs of Capitalism: How Market Tyranny Stifles the Economy by Stunting Workers.* New York: Monthly Review Press.

Perrons, Diane. 2000. "Care, Paid Work, and Leisure: Rounding the Triangle." *Feminist Economics* 6 (1): 105–14.

Peterson, V. Spike. 2003. *A Critical Rewriting of Global Political Economy: Integrating Reproductive, Productive, and Virtual Economies.* London: Routledge.

Petit, Claire, et al. 2010. "Impact on Fetal Growth of Prenatal Exposure to Pesticides Due to Agricultural Activities: A Prospective Cohort Study in Brittany, France." *Environmental Health* 9 (71): 1–12.

Petras, James. 1999. "NGOs: In the Service of Imperialism." *Journal of Contemporary Asia* 29 (4): 429–40.

Pettinger, Richard. 2002. *Managing the Flexible Workforce.* Oxford: Capstone Publishing.

Philippines Environmental Monitor. 2000. Manila: World Bank Group.

Pickering, Kathleen. 1995. "Articulation of the Lakota Mode of Production and the Euro-American Fur Trade." In *Proceedings of the Sixth North American Fur Trade Conference*, 57–69. East Lansing: Michigan State University Press.

———. 2000a. "Alternative Economic Strategies in Low-Income Rural Communities: TANF, Urban Relocation and the Case of the Pine Ridge Indian Reservation." *Rural Sociology* 65(1): 148–67.

———. 2000b. *Lakota Culture, World Economy.* Lincoln: University of Nebraska Press.

———. 2001. "Legislating Development through Welfare Reform: Indiscernible Jobs, Insurmountable Barriers, and Invisible Agendas on the Pine Ridge and Rosebud Indian Reservations." *Political and Legal Anthropology Review* 24 (1): 38–52.

———. 2003. "The Dynamics of Everyday Incorporation and Antisystemic Resistance: Lakota Culture in the 21st Century." In *Crises and Resistance in the 21st Century World-System*, ed. Wilma Dunaway, 201–17. Westport, CT: Greenwood Press.

———. 2004. "Decolonizing Time Regimes: Lakota Conceptions of Work, Economy and Society." *American Anthropologist* 106 (1): 85–97.

Pickering, Kathleen, Mark Harvey, Gene Summers, and David Mushinski. 2006. *Welfare Reform in Persistent Rural Poverty: Dreams, Disenchantments, and Diversity.* University Park: Pennsylvania State University Press.

Pickering, Kathleen, and Benjamin Jewell. 2008. "Nature Is Relative: Religious Affiliation, Environmental Attitudes, and Political Constraints on the Pine Ridge Indian Reservation." *Journal for the Study of Religion, Nature, and Culture* 2 (1): 135–58.

Pickering, Kathleen, and Beth Mizushima. 2008. "Lakota Health Care Access and the Perpetuation of Poverty on Pine Ridge." *Research in Economic Anthropology* 26: 11–33.

Pilcher, Jeffrey. 2008. "The Globalization of Mexican Cuisine." *History Compass* 6 (1): 529–51.

Piper, Nicola, and Mina Roces, eds. 2003. *Wife or Worker? Asian Women and Migration*. Lanham, MD: Rowman and Littlefield.

Porter, Michael. 1980. *Competitive Strategy*. New York: Free Press.

Portes, Alejandro. 1983. "The Informal Sector: Definition, Controversy, and Relation to National Development." *Review of the Fernand Braudel Center* 7 (1): 151–74.

Portes, Alejandro, Manuel Castells, and Lauren Benton, eds. 1989. *The Informal Economy: Studies in Advanced and Less Developed Countries*. Baltimore: Johns Hopkins University Press.

Portes, Alejandro, and Saskia Sassen. 1987. "Making It Underground: Comparative Material on the Informal Sector in Western Market Economies." *American Journal of Sociology* 93 (1): 30–61.

Pourier, Lori, Kathleen Sherman, and Patrick Dorion. 2012. *Artists of the Northern Plains*. Minneapolis, MN: Northwest Area Foundation.

Pratt, Andy. 2008. "Cultural Commodity Chains, Cultural Clusters, or Cultural Production Chains?" *Growth and Change* 39 (1): 95–103.

Pratt, Geraldine. 2004. *Working Feminism*. London: Edinburgh University Press.

Prebisch, Raul. 1984. "Five Stages in My Thinking on Development." In *Pioneers in World Development*, ed. Gerald Meier and Dudley Seers, 175–204. New York: Oxford University Press.

Prieto, Marina. 2002. "Thoughts on Feminist Action Research." Working paper, New Academy of Business.

———. 2008. "Gender, Labour Rights and the Ethical Trading Initiative." www .cawn.org.

———. 2009. "Women Workers, Industrialisation, Global Supply Chains and Corporate Codes of Conduct." *Journal of Business Ethics* 83 (1): 5–17.

Prieto, Marina, Angela Hadjipateras, and Jane Turner. 2002. "The Potential of Codes as Part of Women's Organizations' Strategies for Promoting the Rights of Women Workers: A Central America Perspective." In *Corporate Responsibility and Labour Rights: Codes of Conduct in the Global Economy*, ed. Rhys Jenkins, Ruth Pearson, and Gill Seyfang, 146–59. London: Earthscan.

Prieto, Marina, and Carolina Quinteros. 2004. "Never the Twain Shall Meet? Women's Organizations and Trade Unions in the Maquila Industry in Central America." *Development in Practice* 14 (1): 149–57.

Prieto-Carrón, Marina, Marilyn Thomson, and Mandy Macdonald. 2007. "No More Killings! Women Respond to Femicides in Central America." *Gender and Development* 15 (1): 25–40.

Prigogine, Ilya. 1996. *The End of Certainty: Time Chaos, and the Laws of Nature*. New York: Free Press.

Primavera, J. 1997. "Socio-economic Impacts of Shrimp Culture." *Aquaculture Research* 28: 815–27.

Prugl, E. 1999. *The Global Construction of Gender: Home-Based Work in the Political Economy of the 20th Century*. New York: Columbia University Press.

Pyle, Jean, and Kathryn Ward. 2003. "Recasting Our Understanding of Gender and Work during Global Restructuring." *International Sociology* 18:461–89.

Quickstat Databases. Manila: Philippine Census Bureau. www.census.gov.ph.

Quinn, Rob. 2012. "Navajo Suing Urban Outfitters: Tribe Says Its Trademark Is Being Violated." *Newser*, 1 March.

Raffer, Kunibert. 1987. *Unequal Exchange and the Evolution of the World System.* New York: St. Martin's Press.

Ramamurthy, Priti. 2000. "The Cotton Commodity Chain, Women, Work, and Agency in India and Japan: The Case for Feminist Agro-food Systems Research." *World Development* 28 (3): 551–78.

———. 2003. "Material Consumers, Fabricating Subjects: Perplexity, Global Discourses, and Transnational Feminist Research Practices." *Cultural Anthropology* 18 (4): 524–50.

———. 2004. "Why Is Buying a 'Madras' Cotton Shirt a Political Act? A Feminist Commodity Chain Analysis." *Feminist Studies* 30 (3): 734–69.

———. 2010. "Why Are Men Doing Floral Sex Work? Gender, Cultural Reproduction, and the Feminization of Agriculture." *Signs* 35 (2): 387–424.

———. 2011. " "Rearticulating Caste: The Global Cottonseed Commodity Chain and the Paradox of Smallholder Capitalism in South India." *Environment and Planning A* 43:1035–56.

Raworth, Kate. 2004. *Trading Away Our Rights: Women Working in Global Supply Chains*. Oxford: Oxfam.

Raworth, Kate, and Thalia Kidder. 2009. "Mimicking 'Lean' in Global Value Chains: It's the Workers Who Get Leaned On." In *Frontiers of Commodity Chain Research*, ed. Jennifer Bair, 165–89. Stanford, CA: Stanford University Press.

Raynolds, Laura. 1994. "The Restructuring of Third World Agro-Exports: Changing Production Relations in the Dominican Republic." In *The Global Restructuring of Agro-food Systems*, ed Philip McMichael. Ithaca, NY: Cornell University Press, 214–37.

———. 2001. "New Plantations, New Workers: Gender and Production Politics in the Dominican Republic." *Gender and Society* 14 (1): 7–28.

———. 2004. "The Globalization of Organic Agro-food Networks." *World Development* 32 (5): 725–43.

Rees, Tobias. 2008. "Introduction." In *Designs for an Anthropology of the Contemporary*, ed. Paul Rabinow, George Marcus, James Faubion, and Tobias Rees, 1–12. Durham, NC: Duke University Press.

Republic of Philippines. 1975. "Fisheries Modernization Act." Manila. www.gov.ph.

———. 1992. "Medium-Term Development Plan, 1993–98." Manila. www.gov.ph.

———. 1995. "Act No. 6657: Comprehensive Agrarian Reform Program, Modified." Manila. www.gov.ph.

———. 1998. "Fisheries Modernization Act, Modified." Manila. www.gov.ph.

———. 2000. "Medium-Term Development Plan for 2004–2010." Manila. www.neda.gov.ph.

Resnick, Philip. 1989. "From Semiperiphery to Perimeter of the Core: Canada's Place in the Capitalist World-Economy." *Review of the Fernand Braudel Center* 12 (2): 263–98.

Rifkin, Jeremy. 2002. *The End of Work: The Decline of the Global Labor Force and the Dawn of the Post-market Era*. New York: Putnam Books.

Riley, Mary. 2004. *Indigenous Intellectual Property Rights: Legal Obstacles and Innovative Solutions*. Lanham, MD: Rowman Altamira.

Rimashevskaia, Natalia. 2002. *Economy and Social Policy: Gendered Dimensions.* Moscow: Academia Press.

Robinson, Cyril. 1988. "Exploring the Informal Economy." *Social Justice* 15 (3/4): 3–16.

Robinson, Fiona. 2006. "Beyond Labour Rights." *International Feminist Journal of Politics* 8 (3): 321–42.

Robinson, William. 2004. *A Theory of Global Capitalism: Production, Class, and State in a Transnational World.* Baltimore: Johns Hopkins University Press.

Rodney, Walter. 1982. *How Europe Undeveloped Africa.* Washington, DC: Howard University Press.

Rosas, Rocio. 2002. "Women and Survival Strategies in Poor Urban Contexts: A Case Study from Guadalajara, Mexico." *Journal of Development Studies* 18 (1): 81–103.

Roseberry, William. 1984. *Coffee and Capitalism in the Venezuelan Andes.* Austin: University of Texas Press.

Ross, Anne, Kathleen Sherman, Henry Delcore, Jeffrey Snodgrass, and Richard Sherman. 2011. *Indigenous Peoples and the Collaborative Stewardship of Nature: Knowledge Binds and Institutional Conflicts.* Walnut Creek, CA: Left Coast Press.

Ross, Robert J. S. 2004. *Slaves to Fashion: Poverty and Abuse in the New Sweatshops.* Ann Arbor: University of Michigan Press.

———. 2006. "A Tale of Two Factories: Successful Resistance to Sweatshops and the Limits of Firefighting." *Labor Studies Journal* 30 (4): 1–21.

———. 2011. "The Rag Trade as the Canary in the Coalmine: The Global Sweatshop, 1980–2010." *New Labor Forum* 20 (1): 42–49.

Ross, Robert J. S., and Anita Chan. 2003. "Racing to the Bottom: International Trade without a Social Clause." *Third World Quarterly* 24 (6): 1011–28.

Ross, Robert J. S., and Kent Trachte. 1990. *Global Capitalism: The New Leviathan.* Albany: State University of New York Press.

Russell, Susan. 1987. "Middlemen and Moneylending: Relations of Exchange in a Highland Philippine Economy." *Journal of Anthropological Research* 43:139–61.

Safa, Helen. 1981. "Runaway Shops and Female Employment: The Search for Cheap Labor." *Signs* 7 (2): 418–33.

———. 1995. *The Myth of the Male Breadwinner: Women and Industrialization in the Caribbean.* Boulder, CO: Westview Press.

Safri, Maliha, and Julie Graham. 2010. "The Global Household: Toward a Feminist Postcapitalist International Political Economy." *Signs* 36 (1): 99–125.

Salaff, J. W. 1981. *Working Daughters of Hong Kong: Filial Piety and Intrafamilial Power.* Cambridge: Cambridge University Press.

Salzinger, Leslie. 2003. *Genders in Production: Making Workers in Mexico's Global Factories.* Berkeley: University of California Press.

Sarris, A., and D. Hallam, eds. 2006. *Agriculture Commodity Markets and Trade: Approaches to Analyzing Market Structure and Instability.* London: Edward Elgar.

Sassen, Saskia. 1996. "Service Employment Regimes and the New Inequality." In *Urban Poverty and the Underclass,* ed. Enzo Mingione, 64–82. New York: John Wiley and Sons.

————. 2000. "Women's Burden: Counter-geographies of Globalization and the Feminization of Survival." *Journal of International Affairs* 53 (2): 503–25.

Scheper-Hughes, Nancy. 1991. *Death without Weeping: The Violence of Everyday Life in Brazil*. Berkeley: University of California Press.

Schlemmer, Bernard. 2000. *The Exploited Child*. London: Zed Books.

Schutz, David. 2012. "Integrating Participatory Methods and Livelihoods Approaches into Development Practice: A Case Study of an NGO-Run High School in the Ecuadorian Amazon." M.A. thesis, Colorado State University.

Scott, Joan. 1986. "Gender: A Useful Category of Historical Analysis." *American Historical Review* 91 (5): 1053–75.

Sea-Ling, Cheng. 2000. "Assuming Manhood: Prostitution and Patriotic Passions in Korea." *East Asia: An International Quarterly* 18 (4): 40–79.

Seguino, S. 2000 "Accounting for Asian Economic Growth: Adding Gender to the Equation." *Feminist Economics* 6 (3): 27–58.

Sehgal, Rakhi. 2005. "Social Reproduction of Third World Labour in the Era of Globalisation." *Economic and Political Weekly* 40 (22): 2286–88.

Selwyn, Ben. 2012. *Workers, State, and Development in Brazil: Powers of Labour, Chains of Value*. Manchester: Manchester University Press.

Senses, Fikret. 1994. "Labor Market Responses to Structural Adjustment and Institutional Pressures: The Turkish Case." *METU Studies in Development* 21 (3): 405–48.

Shapkina, Nadia. 2008. "Operation Help: Counteracting Sex Trafficking of Women from Russia and Ukraine." Ph.D. diss., Georgia State University.

Sharma, Dinesh. 2010. "Bt Cotton Has Failed Admits Monsanto." *India Today* (3 March), http://indiatoday.intoday.in/story/Bt+cotton+has+failed+admits+Monsanto/1/86939.html.

Sherman, Richard. 1988. *A Study of Traditional and Informal Sector Microenterprise Activity and Its Impact on the Pine Ridge Indian Reservation Economy*. Washington DC: Aspen Institute for Humanistic Studies.

————. 2004. "Northern Plains Buffalo Caretaker Survey Results and Recommendations." Unpublished manuscript, Honor the Earth, White Earth, MN.

Shiva, Vandana. 1988. *Staying Alive: Women, Ecology and Development*. New York: St. Martin's Press.

————. 1992. *The Violence of the Green Revolution: Third World Agriculture, Ecology and Politics*. London: Zed Books.

————. 2000. *Stolen Harvest: The Hijacking of the Global Food Supply*. Cambridge, MA: South End Press.

Simoniello, M., et al. 2008. "DNA Damage in Workers Occupationally Exposed to Pesticide Mixtures." *Journal of Applied Toxicology* 28: 957–965.

Sinclair, Upton. 1934. *I, Governor of California and How I Ended Poverty*. Los Angeles: By Author.

Sivanandan, A. 1990. "All That Melts into Air Is Solid: The Hokum of New Times." *Race and Class* 31 (3): 1–30.

Sklair, Leslie. 1993. *Assembling for Development: The Maquila Industry in Mexico and the United States*. San Diego: Center for US-Mexican Studies.

Smith, Joan. 1984. "Non-wage Labor and Subsistence." In *Households and the World Economy*, ed. Joan Smith, Immanuel Wallerstein and Hans Evers, 64–89. Beverly Hills: Sage.

Smith, Joan. 1988. "All Crises Are Not the Same: Households in the United States during Two Crises." In *Work without Wages: Domestic Labor and Self-Employment within Capitalism*, ed. Jane Collins and Martha Gimenez, 128–41. Albany: State University of New York Press.

Smith, Joan. 1994. "The Creation of the World We Know: The World-Economy and the Re-creation of Gendered Identities." In *Identity Politics and Women*, ed. Valentine Moghadam, 27–41. Boulder, CO: Westview Press.

Soto, Hernando de. 1989. *The Other Path: The Informal Revolution*. New York: Harper and Row.

Spieldoch, Alexandra. 2007. *A Row to Hoe: The Gender Impact of Trade Liberalization on Our Food System, Agricultural Markets, and Women's Human Rights*. London: Institute for Agriculture and Trade Policy.

Spivak, Gayatri. 1987. *In Other Worlds*. New York: Methuen.

Standing, Guy. 1989. "Global Feminization through Flexible Labor." *World Development* 17 (7): 1077–95.

———. 1999. "Global Feminization through Flexible Labor: A Theme Revisited." *World Development* 27 (3): 538–602.

Stauth, Georg. 1983. "Capitalist Farming and Small Peasant Households in Egypt." *Review of the Fernand Braudel Center* 7 (2): 181–214.

Steans, Jill, and Dainela Tepe. 2010. "Social Reproduction in International Political Economy: Theoretical Insights and International, Transnational and Local Sitings." *Review of International Political Economy* 17 (5): 807–15.

Sternberg, Peter. 2000. "Challenging Machismo: Promoting Sexual and Reproductive Health with Nicaraguan Men." *Gender and Development* 8 (1): 89–101.

Steward, Julian. 1956. "Introduction." In *The People of Puerto Rico: A Study in Social Anthropology*, ed. Julian Steward et. al., 1–33. Urbana: University of Illinois Press.

Stewart, Francis. 2001. "Externalities." In *Encyclopedia of Political Economy*, 513–14. London: Routledge.

Stiglitz, Joseph, Amartya Sen, and Jean-Paul Fitoussi. 2010. "The Measurement of Economic Performance and Social Progress." http://www.stiglitz-sen-fitoussi.fr/en/index.htm.

Stoker, Sally. 2002. "Human Trafficking as a Form of Organized Crime." In *Human Trafficking. Socio-criminological Analysis*, ed. Elena Tyuryukanova and LyudmilaErokhina, 10–34. Moscow: Academia Press.

Strauss, Jonathan. 2004. "Engels and the Theory of the Labour Aristocracy." *Links: International Journal for Socialist Renewal* 25 (Jan.–June): http://links.org.au/node/45.

Striffler, Steve, and David Moberg. 2004. *Banana Wars: Power, Production, and History in the Americas*. Durham, NC: Duke University Press.

Stuckler, David and Sanjay Basu. 2013. *The Body Economic: Why Austerity Kills: Recessions, Budget Battles, and the Politics of Life and Death*. New York: Perseus Books.

Su, Julie. 1997. "El Monte Thai Garment Workers: Slave Sweatshops." In *No Sweat: Fashion, Free Trade and the Rights of Garment Workers*, ed. Andrew Ross, 143–49. London: Verso.

Tabak, Faruk, and M. Crichlow, eds. 2000. *Informalization: Process and Structure*. Baltimore: Johns Hopkins University Press.

Talbot, John. 1997. "Where Does the Coffee Dollar Go? The Division of Income and Surplus along the Coffee Commodity Chain." *Studies in Comparative International Development* 32 (1): 56–91.

———. 2004. *Grounds for Agreement: The Political Economy of the Coffee Commodity Chain.* Boulder, CO: Rowman and Littlefield.

Tallontire, Anne. 2007. "CSR and Regulation: Towards a Framework for Understanding Private Standards Initiatives in the Agrifood Chain." *Third World Quarterly* 28: 775–91.

Tallontire, Anne, Catherine Dolan, Sally Smith, and Stephanie Barrientos. 2005. "Reaching the Marginalised? Gender Value Chains and Ethical Trade in African Horticulture." *Development in Practice* 15 (3–4): 559–71.

Tallontire, Anne, Maggie Opondo, Valerie Nelson, and Adrienne Martin. 2011. "Beyond the Vertical? Using Value Chains and Governance as a Framework to Analyse Private Standards Initiatives in Agri-food Chains." *Agriculture and Human Values* 28: 427–41.

Tavernise, Sabrina. 2011. "Soaring Poverty Casts Spotlight on Lost Decade." *New York Times* (9 September), www.nytimes.com/2011/09/14/us/14census.html ?ref=censusbureau.

Teeple, Gary. 2000. *Globalization and the Decline of Social Reform: Into the Twenty-First Century.* Toronto: Garamond Press.

Terleckyj, Nestor. 1975. *Household Production and Consumption.* New York: National Bureau of Economic Research.

Thomas, D. 1990. "Intra-household Resource Allocation." *Journal of Human Resources* 25 (4): 635–63.

Thompson, Lanny. 1991. "The Structures and Vicissitudes of Reproduction: Households in Mexico, 1876–1970." *Review of the Fernand Braudel Center* 14 (3): 403–36.

Thorbek, Susanne, and B. Pattanaik, eds. 2002. *Transnational Prostitution: Changing Patterns in a Global Context.* London: Zed Books.

Tiano, Susan. 1994. *Patriarchy On the Line: Labor, Gender, and Ideology in the Mexican Maquila Industry.* Philadelphia: Temple University Press.

Trottman, Melanie. 2011. "Boeing, NLRB Clash over Non-union Plant." *Wall Street Journal*, 15 June.

Trucchi, Giorgio. 2009. "La crisis anunciada de los capitales golondrinas." www.rel -uita.org/sindicatos/maquilas/crisis_anunciada.htm.

Truong, Thanh-Dam. 1996. "Gender, International Migration and Social Reproduction: Implications for Theory, Policy, Research and Networking." *Asian and Pacific Migration Journal* 5 (1): 27–52.

Tsing, Anna. 2004. *Friction: An Ethnography of Global Connection.* Princeton, NJ: Princeton University Press.

———. 2009. "Supply Chains and the Human Condition." *Rethinking Marxism* 21 (2): 148–76.

Turner, Sarah. 2008. "Trading Old Textiles: The Selective Diversification of Highland Livelihoods in Northern Vietnam." *Human Organization* 66 (4): 389–404.

Tyuryukanova, Elena, and Marina Malysheva. 2001. *Zhentshina. Migratsia. Gosudarstvo.* [*Woman, migration, the state*]. Moscow: Academia Press.

Ulshofer, Petra. 1983. "Household and Enterprise: Towards a New Model of the Plantation." *Review of the Fernand Braudel Center* 7 (2): 181–214.

UNICEF. 2007. *Women and Children: The Double Dividend of Gender Equality.* New York: UNICEF.

United Nations. 1999. *Human Development Report.* New York: Oxford University Press.

———. 2003. *The World's Women, 2000: Trends and Statistics.* New York: Oxford University Press.

———. 2004. *Human Development Report.* New York: Oxford University Press.

United Nations Development Program (UNDP). 2007. "Evaluación de los resultados de desarrollo: Evaluación de la contribución del PNUD." www.undp.org /evaluation/documents/ADR/ADR_Reports/Nicaragua/ADR_Nicaragua.pdf.

United Nations Population Fund (UNFPA). 2006. *State of World Population: A Passage to Hope; Women and International Migration.* www.unfpa.org/swp /2006/.

United Nations Statistics Division. 2011. *Guidebook on Integrating Unpaid Work into National Policies.* www.unescap.org/stat/meet/wipuw/unpaid_guide.asp.

United Nations Research Institute for Social Development (UNRISD). 2005. *Gender Equality: Striving for Justice in an Unequal World.* Geneva: United Nations.

U.S. Bureau of Labor Statistics. 2009. "International Comparisons of Hourly Compensation in Manufacturing, 2007." www.bls.gov/news.release/pdf/ichcc.pdf.

U.S. Census Bureau. 2011. "Income, Poverty and Health Insurance Coverage: 2010." Washington, DC: //www.census.gov/newsroom/releases/pdf/2010 _Report.pdf.

U.S. Department of Labor. 1997. "U.S. Department of Labor Compliance Survey Finds More than Half of New York City Garment Shops in Violation of Labor Laws." www.dol.gov/opa/media/press/opa/archive/opa97369.htm.

U.S. Department of Labor. 2012. "The History of Labor Day." http://www.dol.gov /opa/aboutdol/laborday.htm.

U.S. Government Accounting Office. 1994. "Tax Administration: Data on the Tax Compliance of Sweatshops." www.gao.gov/products/GGD-94-210FS.

U.S. Public Law 111.211. 2010. "Indian Arts and Crafts Amendment." http://www .doi.gov/iacb/pdf/IACB-Act-2010-Final.pdf.

Ushijima, Iwao, and Cynthia Zayas. 1994. *Fishers of the Visayas.* Quezon City: University of Philippines Press.

Vallebuona-Stagno, Clelia. 2003. "Intoxicaciones agudas por plaguicidas." *El Vigía: Boletín de Vigilancia en Salud Pública de Chile* 7 (19): 45–49.

———. 2005. "Intoxicaciones agudas por plaguicidas." *El Vigía: Boletín de Vigilancia en Salud Pública de Chile* 8 (22): 50–55.

Van Lanen, James. 2007. "Economic Formations and Buffalo: Lakota Interactions and Implications for Ecological Restoration on the Northern Great Plains." *Furthering Perspectives* 1: 129–59.

Village Earth. 2012. "Lakota Buffalo Caretakers Cooperative." http://villageearth .org/global-affiliates/lakota-buffalo-caretakers-association.

Voronina, Olga. 1994. "Virgina Mary or Mary Magdalene? The Construction and reconstruction of Sex during the Perestroika Period." In *Women in Russia: A New Era in Russian Feminism,* ed. Anastasia Posadskaya, 135–145. London: Verso.

Vosko, Leah. 2004. "Confronting the Norm: Gender and the International Regulation of Precarious Work." Law Commission of Canada. http://dsp-psd .pwgsc.gc.ca/Collection/JL2-27-2004E.pdf.

Wadley, Susan. 1993. "Family Composition Strategies in Rural North India." *Social Science and Medicine* 37 (11): 1367–76.

Waldinger, Roger, and Michael Lapp. 1993. "Back to the Sweatshop and Ahead to the Informal Sector? *International Journal of Urban and Regional Research* 17 (1): 16–29.

Wallerstein, Immanuel. 1974. *The Modern World-System*. Vol. 1, *Capitalist Agriculture and the Origins of the European World-Economy in the Sixteenth Century*. New York: Academic Press.

———. 1976. "Semiperipheral Countries and the Contemporary World Crisis." *Theory and Society* 3 (4): 461–83.

———. 1979. *The Capitalist World-Economy*. Cambridge: Cambridge University Press.

———. 1980. *The Modern World System*. Vol. 2, *Mercantilism and the Consolidation of the European World-Economy, 1600–1750*. New York: Academic Press.

———. 1982. "Household Structures and Production Processes: Preliminary Theses and Findings." *Review of the Fernand Braudel Center* 5 (3): 437–58.

———. 1984. "Household Structures and Labor-Force Formation in the Capitalist World Economy. In *Households and the World-Economy*, ed. Joan Smith, Immanuel Wallerstein and Hans Evers, 17–22. Beverly Hills: Sage.

———. 1995a. *Historical Capitalism with Capitalist Civilization*. London: Verso Books.

———. 1995b. "The Modern World System and Evolution." *Journal of World-Systems Research* 1: 1–17.

———. 1999. "Ecology and Capitalist Costs of Production." In *Ecology and the World_System*, ed. Walter Goldfrank, David Goodman and Andrew Szasz, 3–12. Westport, CT: Greenwood.

———. 2000a. "Cultures in Conflict? Who Are We? Who Are the Others?" Y. K. Pao Distinguished Chair Lecture, Center for Cultural Studies, Hong Kong University of Science and Technology. http://fbc.bingham.edu/iw-hk-pao.htm.

———. 2000b. "Introduction." *Review of the Fernand Braudel Center* 23 (1): 1–13.

———. 2001. *Unthinking Social Science: The Limits of Nineteeth-Century Paradigms*. Philadelphia: Temple University Press.

———. 2004. *World-Systems Analysis: An Introduction*. Durham, NC: Duke University Press.

———. 2011. "Structural Crisis in the World-System: Where Do We Go from Here?" *Monthly Review* 62 (10): 31–39.

Wallerstein, Immanuel, and Torry Dickinson. 1982. "Household Structures and Production Processes: Preliminary Theses and Findings." *Review of the Fernand Braudel Center* 5 (3): 437–58.

Wallerstein, Immanuel, and William Martin. 1979. "Peripheralization of Southern Africa II: Changes in Household Structure and Labor-Force Formation." *Review of the Fernand Braudel Center* 3 (2): 193–207.

Wallerstein, Immanuel and Joan Smith. 1992. "Households as an Institution of the World-Economy." In *Creating and Transforming Households: The Constraints of the World-Economy*, ed. Joan Smith and Immanuel Wallerstein, 3–26. Cambridge: Cambridge University Press.

Waring, Marilyn. 1989. *If Women Counted: A New Feminist Economics*. London: McMillan.

Waterman, Peter. 1988. "The New Internationalisms: A More Real Thing than Big, Big Coke?" *Review of the Fernand Braudel Center* 11 (3): 289–328.

Welsh, Patrick. 2007. "Changing Masculinities in Nicaragua: A Community-Based Approach." Paper presented to the Symposium on Rethinking Aids, Gender and Development, Dakar, Senegal, www.bridge.ids.ac.uk/go/home&id=54422 &type=Document&langID=1.

Werlhof, Claudia von. 1983. "Production Relations without Wage Labor and Labor Division by Sex." *Review of the Fernand Braudel Center* 7 (2): 315–59.

———. 1984. "The Proletarian Is Dead; Long Live the Housewife?" In *Households and the World-Economy*, ed. Joan Smith, Immanuel Wallerstein and Hans Evers, 131–47. Beverly Hills, CA: Sage.

———. 2007. "No Critique of Capitalism without a Critique of Patriarchy! Why the Left Is No Alternative." *Capitalism Nature Socialism* 18 (1): 13–27.

White, Jenny. 1994. *Money Makes Us Relatives: Women's Labor in Urban Turkey.* Austin: University of Texas Press.

Whitehead, Anne. 2003. *Failing Women, Sustaining Poverty: Gender in Poverty Reduction Strategy Papers.* London: Christian Aid.

Wilk, Richard. 1987. *The Household Economy: Reconsidering the Domestic Mode of Production.* Boulder, CO: Westview Press.

Williamson, Oliver. 1981. "The Economics of Organization: The Transaction Cost Approach." *American Journal of Sociology* 87: 548–77.

Willis, Susan. 1991. *A Primer for Everyday Life.* New York: Routledge.

Wills, Susan, and Angela Hale, eds. 2005. *Threads of Labour: Garment Industry Supply Chains from the Workers' Perspective.* London: Blackwell.

Wolf, Diane. 1992. *Factory Daughters: Gender, Household Dynamics, and Rural Industrialization in Java.* Berkeley: University of California Press.

Wolfe, Tom. 1987. *Bonfire of the Vanities.* New York: Farrar, Straus and Giroux.

Wollstonecraft, Mary. 1792. *A Vindication of the Rights of Woman with Strictures on Political and Moral Subjects.* London: Joseph Johnson.

Wonders, Nancy, and Raymond Michalowski. 2001. "Bodies, Borders, and Sex Tourism in a Globalized World: A Tale of Two Cities (Amsterdam and Havana)." *Social Problems* 48 (4): 545–71.

World Health Organization. 2001. "Nutrition in South-East Asia." www.who.int.

World Trade Organization. 2008. "Merchandise Trade by Product." In *International Trade Statistics.* www.wto.org.

Wright, Melissa. 2006. *Disposable Women and Other Myths of Global Capitalism.* New York: Routledge.

———. 2009. "Gender and Geography: Knowledge and Activism across the Intimately Global." *Progress in Human Geography* 33 (3): 379–86.

Yardley, Jim. 2013. "Report on Deadly Factory Collapse in Bangladesh Finds Widespread Blame." *New York Times,* 22 May, pp. 1, 3.

Yeates, Nicola. 2004a. "Broadening the Scope of Global Care Chain Analysis: Nurse Migration in the Irish Context." *Feminist Review* 77 (1): 79–95.

———. 2004b. "Global Care Chains: Critical Reflections and Lines of Enquiry." *International Feminist Journal of Politics* 6 (3): 369–91.

———. 2005a. *Global Care Chains: A Critical Introduction.* Geneva: Global Commission on International Migration.

———. 2005b. "A Global Political Economy of Care." *Social Policy and Society* 4 (2): 227–34.

———. 2006. "Changing Places: Ireland in the International Division of Reproductive Labor." *Translocations* 1 (1): 5–21.

———. 2009a. *Globalizing Care Economies and Migrant Workers: Explorations in Global Care Chains.* London: Palgrave.

———. 2009b. "Migration and Nursing in Ireland: A Global History." *Translocations* 5 (1): 1–20.

———. 2010. "The Globalization of Nurse Migration: Policy Issues and Responses." *International Labour Review* 149 (4): 423–40.

———. 2011. " 'Ireland's contributions to the global health care crisis." In *Globalisation, Migration and Social Transformation: Ireland in Europe and the World,* ed. Bryan Fanning and Ronaldo Munck, 35–50. Farnham, UK: Ashgate.

Young, Gay, and H. Alderman. 1997. "The Organization of Labor Resources in Juarez Families." *International Journal of Sociology and Social Policy* 17 (11/12): 97–115.

Zhang, X., et al. 2010. "Work-Related Pesticide Poisoning among Farmers in Two Villages of Southern China: A Cross-sectional Survey." *BMC Public Health* 11 (429): 1–8.

Zhou, Min. 1992. *Chinatown: The Socioeconomic Potential of an Urban Enclave.* Philadelphia: Temple University Press.

Zhurzenko, Tatyana. 2001. *Sotsial'noe vosproizvodstvo i gendernaia politika v Ukraine* [*Social reproduction and gender politics in Ukraine*]. Kharkov: Folio Press.

Zhurzhenko, Tatyana. 2004. "Strong Women, Weak State: Family Politics and Nation Building in Post-Soviet Ukraine." In *Post-Soviet Women Encountering Transition. Nation-Building, Economic Survival, and Civic Activism,* ed. Kathleen Kuehnast and Carol Nechemias, 23–43. Baltimore: Johns Hopkins University Press.